THE EU CHARTER OF FUNDAMENTAL RIGHTS

IUS GENTIUM
Comparative Perspectives on Law and Justice

VOLUME 8

THE EU CHARTER OF FUNDAMENTAL RIGHTS

FROM DECLARATION TO BINDING INSTRUMENT

Edited by

GIACOMO DI FEDERICO

Springer

Editor
Giacomo Di Federico
Interdepartmental Research Centre
on European Law (CIRDE)
University of Bologna
Viale Filopanti 9
40100 Bologna
Italy
gdifederico@cirdce.unibo.it

ISBN 978-94-007-0155-7 e-ISBN 978-94-007-0156-4
DOI 10.1007/978-94-007-0156-4
Springer Dordrecht Heidelberg London New York

Library of Congress Control Number: applied for PCN

Printed on acid-free paper

Springer is part of Springer Science+Business Media (www.springer.com)

Preface

The fact that fundamental rights are an essential component of the European Union is today a consolidated state of affairs. In this sense, the EU seems to have undergone a true genetic transformation, evolving from a sui generis international organisation, mainly focused on market integration, to an autonomous legal order protecting and promoting the rule of law within and outside its boundaries.

It is well known that the failure of the ambitious constitutional project did not stop the reform process undertaken with the 2001 Declaration on the Future of Europe. The reflection period which followed the French and Dutch referenda on the Treaty Establishing a Constitution for Europe ended with the Berlin Summit in March 2007. The resulting Intergovernmental Conference promptly returned a Treaty purged of all constitutional elements, but deeply rooted in the work of the Giscard d'Estaing Convention.

The final text, signed in Lisbon on 13 December 2007, provides that the European Union shall replace and succeed to the European Community. The former will be founded on the Treaty on European Union and on the Treaty on the Functioning of the European Union, with the same legal value. The repeal of the Pillar architecture, a profoundly modified institutional framework designed to ensure effectiveness and coherence, the enhanced judicial protection bestowed to individuals, the primary law status assigned to the Charter and the envisaged accession to the European Convention on Human Rights are all decisive elements in the affirmation of the European Union as a legal order based on the rule of law, and a credible actor on the international scene.

Although the specificities preserved in the Common Foreign and Security Policy (including the Common Defence Policy) still betray strong national resistances in relation to further integration in this area – sometimes linked to well consolidated constitutional traditions – the new provisions enhance the overall capacity of the EU to effectively respond to external threats while concomitantly promoting and defending its internal values outside its borders.

Despite the lack of a specific competence on fundamental rights, the EU has increasingly been involved in their protection, mainly to uphold the legitimacy of the system, and most notably to ensure the effectiveness of pivotal principles for European integration, such as direct effect and supremacy, vis à vis national (constitutional) prerogatives and international obligations. Since the implementation of EC/EU law was (and still is) to a large extent left to the Member States, adherence to the standard of protection ensured under the European Convention on Human Rights increasingly became an unfailing necessity for the deepening of European integration. Until the Lisbon Treaty this was achieved mainly through a "wise" judicial control over EC/EU law, as well as domestic legislation and practice falling within the scope of application of the treaties, and by virtue of a certain self-restraint on the part of the EU institutions.

On the other hand, being invariably connected to the legal traditions of the Member States and to the development of a higher international standard of protection, the respect of fundamental rights has become a priority in itself, a way to affirm the autonomous nature of the EU legal order. The elaboration of a document codifying the rights and principles guaranteed under Union law and its solemn proclamation by the three main institutions is an outstanding illustration of this resolution. Making it binding and legally enforceable means providing the Union with a true *Bill of Rights* and thus contributes to the creation of "an ever closer Union among the peoples of Europe".

For EU countries, this assimilating role has until now been played by the European Convention on Human Rights. It is suggested that the centralising effect once performed by the Strasbourg Court will now be played by the Court of Justice of the European Union. Indeed, if the Charter is a more than welcome *tertium genus* in the multilevel system of fundamental rights protection in Europe, accession to the ECHR should not distract national courts, especially Supreme and Constitutional Courts, from respecting EU law. Having "the same value as the Treaties", the Charter is now the main parameter of legality for the institutions and bodies of the Union as well as for the Member States when they apply, implement or derogate from EU law. Moreover, it acts as a compass for the development of important policies such as, for instance, Heath, Environmental and Consumer protection, once again underscoring the high prioritization of fundamental rights within the Union.

But the Charter does not extend the competences of the EU. National distrust led to an overabundance of provisions excluding this possibility (see Art. 51 (2) of the Charter and Art. 6 (1) TEU), including a Declaration by the Czech Republic and Protocol No 30 on the application of the Charter in the United Kingdom and Poland. Nevertheless, it could be argued that by exercising their renewed competences the institutions will increasingly bring domestic legislation and practice within the scope of application of EU law and thus indirectly extend the scope of the Charter.

With the rejection of the Constitutional Treaty, the emperor might have lost his robes but still rules, and integration will proceed in a renewed institutional framework where normative and judicial action must build upon and comply with the Charter. On the other hand, accession to the ECHR shall provide the system with more coherence allowing individuals to contest the compatibility of EU law and practice before the Strasbourg Court. As will be seen, although the reasons for accession are mostly political in nature, the practical consequences of membership could be quite significant. Indeed, this external supervision should be understood as complementary to the newly binding Charter, which sets the minimum standard of protection by and within the Union. By contrast, the protection offered under the Convention will remain the lowest applicable standard for Member States, when acting outside the scope of application of the treaties, and for the EU when operating within its competences.

This volume brings together a number of contributions by researchers working within the Interdepartmental Research Centre on European Law (CIRDE) of the University of Bologna and under the direction of Professor Lucia Serena Rossi. It is the result of a coordinated investigation which began within the EU CONSENT Network of Excellence (VI Framework Programme) "Wider Europe, Deeper Integration?" and was subsequently carried out in the context of the Jean Monnet Centre of Excellence "Rule of Law and Fundamental Rights: The EU Model". In light of the process which finally led to the adoption of the Lisbon Treaty it appeared useful to assess whether and to what extent the binding force attributed to the EU Charter of Fundamental Rights and the envisaged accession to the European Convention on Human Rights would impact the functioning of the EU legal order.

Since its first proclamation on 7 December 2000, the nature, value and scope of the Charter have been thoroughly investigated in legal literature, together with its use by the EU courts and national judges. Taking as a frame of reference the new Treaties, this book firstly addresses the consequences of a legally binding *Bill of Rights* in a broader perspective, taking into account its legal and political relevance, its contribution to the multilevel system of fundamental rights protection in Europe, the influence it has so far exercised on domestic and EU case law, as well as the possible repercussions on the role of the European Parliament, on judicial protection and on human rights conditionality in the EU's enlargement policy. The second part focuses on the consequences of a binding Charter in certain specific areas of law: from citizens' rights to internal market derogations; from judicial cooperation in civil and criminal matters to social rights and environmental policy making; from the common commercial policy to the common foreign and security policy.

A comprehensive analysis of the multiple consequences, legal and political, stemming from the Reform Treaty falls beyond the scope of the present volume. More sensibly, this volume is directed at offering a first assessment of possible future developments in what are believed to be some crucial domains of EU law, both in terms of legislative action and judicial practice.

Bologna, Italy Giacomo Di Federico
1 December 2009

Acknowledgments

I would like to thank Professor Lucia Serena Rossi for her unconditioned support and encouragement in the preparation and drafting of this book. The School she created in Bologna as Director of the Interdepartmental Research Centre on European Law (CIRDE) is strongly devoted to European Integration studies, with a particular focus on fundamental rights protection. This volume is a small tribute to her commitment as a researcher and scholar in this field.

I am very grateful to Professor Jean-Paul Jacqué, for his learned suggestions on how to tackle the topic under investigation and cover the many areas which are addressed herein; to Professor Andrea Biondi for his valuable feedback and to Professor Louann Haarman for her invaluable assistance and linguistic review.

I would also like to thank all the authors for their efforts in respecting deadlines and constantly updating their chapters in the process of completing this work. To them my gratitude for believing in a project which started more then two years before the entry into force of the Lisbon Treaty.

Contents

Contributors

Valentina Bazzocchi CIRDE (Interdepartmental Research Centre on European Law), University of Bologna, Bologna, Italy, vbazzocchi@cirdce.unibo.it

Valeria Bonavita University of Bologna, Bologna, Italy, valeria.bonavita@unibo.it

Marco Borraccetti Faculty of Political Science, Forlì Campus, University of Bologna, Bologna, Italy, marco.borraccetti@unibo.it

Federico Camporesi Free Lance, Bologna, Italy; Free Lance, Brussels, Belgium, federicocamporesi@me.com

Serena Coppola University of Bologna, Bologna, Italy, serena.coppola@studio.unibo.it

Stephen J. Curzon University of Bologna, Bologna, Italy, scurzon@cirdce.unibo.it

Giacomo Di Federico CIRDE (Interdepartmental Research Centre on European Law), University of Bologna, Bologna, Italy, gdifederico@cirdce.unibo.it

Luisa Ficchi Faculty of Political Science, Forlì Campus, University of Bologna, Bologna, Italy, luisa.ficchi@gmail.com

Federico Forni University of Bologna, Bologna, Italy, fedeforni@libero.it

Marco Lombardo CIRDE (Interdepartmental Research Centre on European Law), University of Bologna, Bologna, Italy, mlombardo@cirdce.unibo.it

Luca Paladini Robert Schuman Centre for Advanced Studies, European University Institute, Florence, Italy, luca.paladini@eui.eu

Giangiuseppe Sanna Studio Legale Sutti, London, UK, giangiuseppe.sanna@sutti.com

Ola Zetterquist Department of Law, University of Gothenburg, Gothenburg, Sweden, Ola.Zetterquist@law.gu.se

About the Contributors

Valentina Bazzocchi holds a joint PhD in EU Law from the University of Bologna and the University of Strasbourg. She is Research Fellow at the Interdepartmental Research Centre on European Law (CIRDE) of the University of Bologna and member of the Editorial Staff of the Observatory on Fundamental Rights in Europe (www.europeanrights.eu). Her main fields of interest are the Area of Freedom, Security and Justice and fundamental rights.

Valeria Bonavita holds an MA in International Relations and Diplomacy of the European Union from the College d'Europe (Bruge). She is currently a PhD candidate in EU law at the University of Bologna and teaching assistant for the course on the Common Commercial Policy at the China-EU Law School (Beijing – Changping, China). Her main fields of interest are international trade, common commercial policy and European foreign and security policy.

Marco Borraccetti holds a PhD in EU Law from the University of Bologna where he is Senior Researcher and Lecturer of European Union Law in the Faculty of Political Science "Roberto Ruffilli" – Forlì Campus. He is a member of the Interdepartmental Research Centre on European Law (CIRDE) of the University of Bologna. His main fields of interest are the Area of Freedom, Security and Justice, judicial protection and fundamental rights.

Federico Camporesi holds a joint PhD in EU Law from the University of Bologna and the University of Strasbourg. He currently acts as legal consultant for law firms and businesses on EU law and policies.

Serena Coppola is a PhD candidate in EU law at the University of Bologna. She collaborates with the Interdepartmental Research Centre on European Law (CIRDE) and carries out research in the field of fundamental rights with a particular focus on the protection of social rights in the EU legal order and within the Council of Europe.

Stephen J. Curzon holds a joint PhD in EU Law from the University of Bologna and the University of Strasbourg.

Giacomo Di Federico holds a PhD in EC Law from the University of Bologna, where he is Senior Researcher of International Law and Lecturer of European Union Law. He is a member of the Interdepartmental Research Centre on European Law (CIRDE) of the University of Bologna and Professor in charge of the course on the Internal Market at the China-EU School of Law (Beijing – Changping, China). His main fields of interest are EU administrative law, competition law and fundamental rights.

Luisa Ficchi holds a PhD in EC Law from the University of Bologna, where she is teaching assistant of European Union Law in the Faculty of Political Science "Roberto Ruffilli" – Forlì Campus. She currently works at the External Relations and General Affairs Department of the Banca d'Italia (Rome) on licensing of EU and non-EU banks and financial companies. Her main research interests are the external relations of the EU, the enlargement policy and fundamental rights.

Federico Forni is a PhD candidate in EU law at the University of Bologna. He currently collaborates with the Interdepartmental Research Centre on European Law (CIRDE) and is teaching assistant for the course on the Internal Market at the China-EU School of Law (Beijing – Changping, China). His main fields of interest are free circulation of goods and free movement of persons.

Marco Lombardo holds a joint PhD in EU Law from the University of Bologna and the University of Strasbourg. He is Research Fellow at the Interdepartmental Research Centre on European Law (CIRDE) and teaching assistant at the Faculty of Law of the University of Bologna. His main fields of interest are environmental and energy law, climate change, competition law and fundamental rights.

Luca Paladini holds a PhD in EU Law from the University of Bologna. He is associated with the University of Florence and is a Jean Monnet Fellow at the European University Institute – Robert Schuman Centre for Advanced Studies. His main fields of interest are international relations, with a particular focus on EU common foreign and security policy and defence policy, and fundamental rights protection.

Giangiuseppe Sanna holds a joint PhD in EU Law from the University of Bologna and the University of Strasbourg. He is currently teaching assistant at the Università Cattolica (Milan) and Senior Associate at the International Law Firm *Studio Legale Sutti* (Milan-London). His main fields of practice and research are international private law, litigation, ADR and arbitration.

Ola Zetterquist is an Associate Professor at the Faculty of Law of Lund University, Sweden. His main fields of teaching and research are European Union Law, Human Rights law and questions of legal philosophy connected to constitutional theory.

Abbreviations

AFSJ	Area of Freedom Security and Justice
AG	Advocate General
CCP	Common Commercial Policy
CFI	Court of First Instance
CFR	EU Charter of Fundamental Rights
CFSP	Common Foreign and Security Policy
EC	European Community
ECHR	European Convention on Human Rights
ECJ	European Court of Justice
ECR	European Court Reports
ECSC	European Coal and Steel Community
ECtHR	European Court of Human Rights
EHRR	European Human Rights Reports
EP	European Parliament
EPI	Environmental Policy Integration
EU	European Union
EUCJ	Court of Justice of the European Union
GC	General Court of the European Union
ILO	International Labour Organisation
OJ	Official Journal
OMC	Open Method of Coordination
TEC	Treaty establishing the European Community
TEU	Treaty on European Union
TFEU	Treaty on the Functioning of the European Union
WTO	World Trade Organisation

Part I
The Charter of Fundamental Rights in a Broader Perspective

The Charter of Fundamental Rights and the European *Res Publica*

Ola Zetterquist

1 Preliminary Remarks

This contribution aims at assessing the importance of the European Charter of Fundamental Rights (hereinafter, CFR or the Charter) for the constitutional legitimacy of the European Union (hereinafter, EU). In doing so, we will proceed from the assumption that the EU is in fact a constitutional legal order of the kind alleged by the European Court of Justice (hereinafter, ECJ or EUCJ). The point of departure is the classical idea of the *res publica*, a republican understanding of the constitution of the EU.

2 The Charter: A Brief Presentation of Its Anatomy and Treaty Location

It is well known that the Charter is the first Bill of Rights developed explicitly for the European Union. It comprises a broad range of civil, political and social rights. The Charter therefore contains both what may be called 'negative' rights (i.e. rights that call for state abstention from acting in certain areas like, for example, freedom of expression) and 'positive' rights (i.e. rights that call for state action in a given field like, for example, social security). By virtue of Art. 6 (1)1 of the Treaty on the European Union (hereinafter, TEU) as amended by the Lisbon Treaty, the Charter is part of the primary law of the EU. It will thus also be subject to the jurisdiction of what is today the Court of Justice of the European Union (hereinafter, EUCJ). Art. 6 (1) is part of Title I (Common provisions) but the Charter is not in itself reproduced in the TEU, its inclusion being by point of reference.

O. Zetterquist (✉)
Department of Law, University of Gothenburg, Gothenburg, Sweden
e-mail: Ola.Zetterquist@law.gu.se

G. Di Federico, *The EU Charter of Fundamental Rights*, Ius Gentium: Comparative Perspectives on Law and Justice 8, DOI 10.1007/978-94-007-0156-4_1,

The Charter contains 54 Articles distributed on 6 substantive Chapters structured as follows: Human Dignity (Arts. 1–5), Freedoms (Arts. 6–19), Equality (Arts. 20–26), Solidarity (Arts. 27–38) and Citizenship rights (Arts. 39–50). A final chapter (Arts. 51–54) concerns general rules on its interpretation and scope, the most important ones being that it applies to the European institutions and the Member States only when they are applying EU law and not otherwise (Art. 51), and that the Charter in no way confers new competencies on the EU (Art. 52). However it should be recalled that two Member States, Poland and the UK, have been granted exception from parts of the Charter and that a specific protocol annexed to the Lisbon Treaty provides that Title IV (Solidarity) does not apply to them.

The Charter is also closely related to the older (1950) and well-established European Convention on Human Rights (ECHR), to which all Member States are signatories, covering mainly civil and political rights. The rights laid down in the Charter are, to the extent that they are the same, supposed to have the same meaning in the Charter as in the ECHR (Art. 52(3)) and the Charter is never supposed to curtail rights conferred by the ECHR (Art. 53) therefore establishing the ECHR as the minimum standard the EU must respect. A further sign of the importance of the ECHR is the fact that the EU shall, according to Art. 6(2) TEU, accede formally to the ECHR as a contracting party and consequently be subject to the jurisdiction of the European Court of Human Rights.

3 The Background to the Charter

The protection of fundamental rights holds a very prominent place in the contemporary debate on the EU. In particular, the attention for the subject-matter was prompted in 1998 by the 50th anniversary of the United Nations Universal Declaration of Human Rights, originally adopted in 1948. And yet, the issue of rights protection in the EU is far from being a recent phenomenon. Ever since the EC started to exercise state power in accordance with the competencies accorded to it in the treaties there has been concern that this exercise by the EC institutions, and the Member States when implementing EC law, might come into conflict with the rights of the individual. Hence, the inclusion in the treaties of a court with jurisdiction to review the legality of the cases where the institutions were capable of addressing decisions directly to individuals. These concerns were strengthened once the ECJ had stated, in a string of cases during the 1960s and 1970s, that EC law had *direct effect*[1] (i.e. that the effects of EC law within

[1] Case 26/62 *van Gend en Loos* [1963] ECR 1.

a Member State is determined by EC law and not by national law and that individuals may rely on it in national courts), *supremacy* over national law (however framed)[2] and that EC-law *pre-empts*[3] *national law* (both retroactively and prospectively). With these three principles the ECJ effectively transformed the operative system of the EC from public international law to constitutional law and confirmed the EC as "a new legal order" embracing both states and individuals alike. As a consequence, fundamental rights protection had to be handled on the European level if the coherence of the EC as a legal order common *within* the Member States and not only *between* them, was to be preserved.

Indeed, both the German[4] and Italian[5] constitutional courts reacted promptly to the ECJ's case law indicating that the absence of a functioning fundamental rights protection was of such significance that there could be no question of 'real' supremacy of EC law over national constitutional provisions of fundamental rights. In other words these courts claimed that they retained an ultimate say on whether EC-law would be supreme or not in a specific case, the answer depending to no small degree on the level of rights protection afforded by the Community.

The ECJ rose to the challenge. After some initial cautiousness[6] the issue of the protection of fundamental rights has been addressed by the ECJ as a question of general principles of law[7] and thus enjoyed a de facto protection in the case law of the court. The idea was clearly formulated by the Advocate General Dutheillet De Lamothe in the *Internationale Handelsgesellschaft* case in the following terms:

> [The fundamental principles of national legal systems] contribute to forming that philosophical, political and legal substratum common to the Member States from which through the case-law an unwritten Community law emerges, one of the essential aims of which is precisely to ensure the respect for the fundamental rights of the individual.[8]

To paraphrase Voltaire's famous remark on the Deity, one could say that if constitutional rights protection did not exist in EC law before, one would

---

[2]Case 6/64 *F. Costa v. ENEL* [1964] ECR 585.

[3]Case 106/77 *Simmenthal* [1978] ECR 629.

[4]Cf. *Solange I* [1974] 2 CMLR 540.

[5]Cf. *Frontini* [1974] 2 CMLR 372.

[6]Cf. Case 1/58 *F. Stork & Cie v. High Authority of ECSC* [1959] ECR 17, where the ECJ rejected the claim that the Community would be bound by fundamental rights as these were guaranteed by national constitutions.

[7]Cf. Case 29/69 *Stauder* [1969] ECR 419.

[8]Case 11/70 *Internationale Handelsgesellschaft* [1970] ECR 1125.

have to invent it. With the Treaty of Maastricht it was (in Art. 6 TEU) officially recognised that the EU is a Union built on the respect for fundamental rights which are common to the legal traditions of the Member States and defined in the ECHR.

Still, there was widespread belief that the EU should have its proper Bill of Rights and not be dependent on the one elaborated within the Council of Europe, as defined by Member States constitutional law or as elaborated in the case law of the ECJ. The need was not perceived as stemming from insufficient levels of protection in legal practice (de facto protection). It was rather on the political level that the desire for codification was strongest. As L. Gunvén observed, it was about infusing the EU with "a soul".[9] Consequently in 1999, by appointment of the European Council, a convention under the chairmanship of the former German president Roman Herzog was convened to deal with the issue of such Bill of Rights for Europe. On 2 October 2000 the Convention completed its task.

The CFR was solemnly declared by the European institutions (the Commission, the European Parliament and the Council) at the IGC in Nice in December 2000.[10] The Charter was explicitly mentioned in the so called Laeken declaration by the European Council of 15 December 2001. The declaration contained 60 questions on the future of the Union revolving around four main themes: the division and definition of powers, the simplification of the treaties, the institutional set-up and moving towards a Constitution for European citizens. To that end, the Laeken declaration also set up a Convention (composed of representatives of the national governments and parliaments, the European Parliament and the Commission) to tackle the above mentioned issues.

The result of the Convention was a draft Constitutional Treaty which included, in Part II, the full text of the Charter. This draft version was subsequently adopted as the Treaty Establishing a Constitution for Europe (the Constitutional Treaty). Following its rejection in the 2005 French and Dutch referenda, the idea of a Constitutional Treaty was abandoned in favor of a more traditional reform treaty amending the existing treaties. After a period of reflection, called for in June 2005 by a declaration by the European Council,[11] the EU proceeded to amend the existing treaties including in Art. 6 of the new TEU a reference to the Charter attributing to the latter (which is annexed to the Lisbon Treaty[12]) full binding force.

---

[9] L. Gunvén, 'EU:s stadga om de grundläggande rättigheterna – arbetet med att ge EU en "själ"', (2001) *Europarättslig tidskrift* 13.

[10] [2000] OJ C364/1.

[11] The declaration is available at http://www.consilium.europa.eu/ueDocs/cms_Data/docs/pressData/fr/ec/85322.pdf

[12] Protocol relating to Article 6(2) of the Treaty on European Union on the accession of the Union to the European Convention on the Protection of Human Rights and Fundamental Freedoms.

4 The Charter – a Piece in the Larger Constitutional Picture

The Charter certainly was meant to answer the long standing problem of the uncertain status of fundamental rights protection in the EU but it was also intended to lay the foundations for a more proper constitutional legal order with respect to the one provided for by the original treaties. The 1950-ies treaties contained no Bill of rights precisely because they were not intended to enjoy a constitutional status vis à vis the Member states law. The funding treaties and the institutional design set therein are more consistent with the traditional international law instruments being devoid of any constitutional ambition. The development of both statutory and case law since then has however left it beyond doubt that it is no longer correct to characterize neither the treaties nor the European institutions as exclusively international in nature.[13]

In the Laeken declaration, the European Council recognised that this situation was no longer satisfactory and that there was a need for a "Constitution for European citizens" in the shape of a basic constitutional treaty that included the Charter. The idea was that a constitution is hardly complete without a Bill of rights. All Member States that have a written constitution (i.e. all with the exception of the UK) have a catalogue of rights in their constitution and the EU could hardly settle for less than its Member States in this regard.

The Constitutional Treaty did not only comprise a Bill of rights but also sought to resemble as much as possible to a constitution in structure, with a first part of general principles for the EU as a political entity followed by the Charter and then the more substantive provisions that are more functional than constitutional in character. Moreover, the Constitutional Treaty differed from the previous (and posterior) strategy of amending the existing treaties uniting all the treaties in one single text.

The very process (the convention) by which the Constitutional Treaty was elaborated also sought to replicate the making of a constitution rather than the adoption of a classic international law treaty. Whereas previous treaties were the result of scarcely transparent intergovernmental conferences, the Constitutional Treaty was elaborated by representatives of national parliaments and governments through a process that aimed at promoting public awareness.

The Constitutional Treaty strengthened the position of the European Parliament and also involved, for the first time, the national parliaments in the decision making process. These measures were taken in order to

[13] Cf. Case C-50/00 P *Unión de Pequeños Agricultores v. Council* [2002] ECR I-6677, AG Jacobs, para 78.

strengthen the democratic element of the EU and thus to alleviate the so called "democratic deficit". The measures were largely confirmed by the IGC that led to the adoption of the Lisbon Treaty.

5 The Charter as a Part of the *Res publica* of the EU

5.1 Rights Protection and Democracy

The Charter may at first glance seem not to fit into a strategy of democratization of the EU. After all, bills of rights are meant to constrain the scope of action of the democratically elected bodies. A bill of rights typically places a power of judicial review in the 'undemocratic' (i.e. non elected) bodies such as the courts. Nevertheless, it has long been argued that a bill of rights was a way to reinforce the *democratic* legitimacy of the EU. The central idea is that a democracy is not complete without a sufficiently constitutionalized system of protection of fundamental rights.[14] In addition it should be recalled that constitutions are themselves choices of the people and as such hardly 'undemocratic'.

To put it differently, democracy is not only about formulating and enforcing the will of whatever majority happens to exist at the moment being.[15] Democracy and rights protection are in this sense mutually reinforcing. This of course applies to those rights that are instrumental to the democratic process itself, like the freedom of expression. But rights also serve to underline the condition of political *equality* of the individuals that form the political community in question and the pre-condition of democracy. The constitution seeks to combine the right of the majority to shape the development of society with the right of individuals and minorities to be treated fairly and equally. Decisions taken by the majority should thus not be exclusively in their interest, at the expense of the minority, but should be compatible with the *common* good of majority and minority alike.

By preserving the equality of the members of the community it addresses, the constitution can be seen as a process of public reasoning that goes on in both political bodies and courts alike and which results in a legal order expressing a civic bond between the individuals that form part

[14] As argued by F. Mancini and D. Keeling, 'Democracy and the European Court of Justice', (1994) *The Modern Law Review* 175 and by the President of the European Court of Justice Vassilios Skouris (quoted in the House of Lords Research Paper 04/85, *The Treaty Establishing a Constitution for Europe: Part II – The Charter of Fundamental Rights* 11).

[15] For an in-depth analysis see S. Holmes *Passions & constraint – On the theory of liberal democracy* (Chicago University Press, 1995), particularly Chapter 5 (*Precommitment and the paradox of democracy*) 134.

of it. This legal order, in which common values are purported, constitutes the *res publica* of the political community in question.

The notion of *res publica*, from which the noun "republic" is derived, may need some further clarification. It is often translated as "the common good" but more properly it is what citizens hold in common and above the specific interest they share. *Res publica* departs from the conception of the legal order as a sort of moral dialogue (concerning the fundamental values of the community) based on reason thereby appealing to the rational assent of its members. Viewed as an ongoing moral dialogue striving for coherence and rationality in the law, *res publica* is better understood as a dynamic concept than as a fixed and unalterable set of values.

The connection between the law and the *res publica* is particularly prominent in theories that stress law as a reflection of public reason rather than as an expression of command and will (whether by a single ruler or an assembly). The ultimate objective is to achieve freedom understood as *non domination* of the individuals making up the legal order thereby confirming them as political equals. Non domination means that no one should be the subject of arbitrary will and command, to be freely exploited in pursuance of somebody else's benefit. It follows that the Law must be in accordance with reason (*ratio*),[16] i.e. the legal order construe a coherent structure that treats all of its subjects as political equals. Law therefore reflects the civic (moral) bond between the individuals belonging to the legal order. Locke famously argued that law expresses a civic morality among the citizens in their horizontal relation:

> [...]'tis in their *Legislative*, that the Members of a Commonwealth are united, and combined together into one coherent living Body. This *is the Soul that gives Form, Life and Unity* to the Commonwealth: From hence the several Members have their mutual Influence, Sympathy and Connexion.[17]

According to this view, which flowed into practically all modern democratic theories, the deliberative function of the parliamentary body holds a position of paramount importance for the legitimacy of the legal order. It corresponds in the first instance to the parliament to identify and elaborate, i.e. to reason upon, the fundamental values that unite the members of the political community because it is the body that represents more opinions and interests than any other institution. Such diversity in the reasoning is particularly pertinent in relation to rights regulation. Most rights are by nature more akin to principles than to rules in the sense that a right often needs to be balanced against other rights like, for example, the right of freedom to expression needs to be weighed against the right to privacy. It is

---

[16] As previously argued by Cicero in 'The Republic', in *The Republic and The Laws* (Oxford University Press, 1998) 68.

[17] J. Locke, *Two treatises of government* [1689] (Cambridge University Press, 1988) 407.

possible to come to different conclusions regarding the scope of the respective right and still respect them both as valid principles whereas rules are either followed or not. For these reasons it may seem more appropriate for a legislative body to elaborate on the more precise scope of rights and for a court of law to apply rules.

On the other hand, there are limits to what the elected assembly can decide and the power held by a democratic assembly can never be thought to be arbitrary, i.e. unreasonable, in kind.[18] A republican understanding of the nature of power and law as the instrument for securing freedom obviously calls for a check even on the democratically elected legislative. Checks on the latter are in modern constitutional law most often entrusted to the judicial power, i.e. to a court of one kind or another. However, a court will not often, apart from rather extreme cases where the most basic rights are at stake, be in a position to represent a morally superior body with respect to the elected legislator. A court that bluntly insists on imposing its own values over those of the democratically elected bodies will in the end most likely be either isolated or abolished.

Still, a judicial remedy remains essential for securing non-domination since blind trust in majority rule is not empirically sound. The approach taken in the US and Canadian supreme courts is instructive regarding the striking of balance between judicial review and majority decision-making in political bodies. According to this view it corresponds to the political bodies to identify the material values and policies to be pursued by the public authorities while the courts are charged with the duty to ensure that these values are 'universal' and applied equally to all without any (conscious or unconscious) bias with respect to minorities.[19] The underlying idea is to secure *integrity* in the law meaning that a proposition of law is true if it figures in or follows from the principles of justice, fairness and procedural due process that provide the best constructive interpretation of the legal practice of the legal order in question, i.e. that the proposition follows not only from (narrow) single statutory provisions and cases but rather from the broad scheme of principles necessary to justify it.[20]

5.2 *Is There a Need for the Charter?*

As has been pointed out, the constitutional character, and, with it, the constitutional problems of the EU stem largely from the case law of the ECJ. The latter has, through its constitutional case law, no doubt contributed in

[18] Ibid. 357.

[19] This theory is developed in J. Hart Ely, *Democracy and distrust – A theory of judicial review* (Harvard University Press, 1980).

[20] R. Dworkin, *Law's empire* (Harvard University Press, 1986) 225 ff.

laying the foundations for a European *res publica*. By virtue of the doctrine of direct effect,[21] the effects of EC law follow directly from the treaties (and secondary law adopted in accordance with the treaties) rather than mediated through the national constitution, meaning that EC law is a common law *within* the Member States and not only between them (as is the case with ordinary treaties under public international law). In this sense, the EU functions as an important source of genuine rights for European individuals, thereby making them equals under EU law. It is indeed striking that all the constitutionalising cases concerned the effective protection of the rights of individual citizens under EC law.

Transforming the treaties from public international law into constitutional law is in itself arguably both a democratic and revolution in the field of rights protection: as Federico Mancini – former judge at the Court of Luxembourg – observed, it took EC law out of the hands of governments and bureaucrats and placed it in the hands of the European individuals.[22] It could indeed be argued that this constitutionalisation process (together with the de facto protection afforded by the ECJ) is sufficient as far as the protection of rights is concerned and you should not fix something that is not broken.

In the same vein one of the American founding fathers, Alexander Hamilton, argued (in 1787) that bills of rights are not only unnecessary but even dangerous since they imply that the people hold their rights by concession from the State rather than as original proprietors thereof. He concluded this argument by stating that:

> [. . .] the Constitution is itself, in every rational sense, and to every useful purpose, A BILL OF RIGHTS.[23]

For these very reasons the U.S. Constitution originally contained no bill of rights. However, the Americans soon changed their minds and introduced a Bill of rights in 1791. By then, it was commonly accepted that there was a need for express protection against possible abuse of State power, however popularly framed. This seems to be the generally accepted view today as we witness a proliferation of international instruments for the protection of human rights (like, amongst others, the ECHR and the U.N. conventions) and appreciate the practically universal existence of bills of rights in national constitutions. It is therefore not an unreasonable suggestion that the EU is in need of bill of rights of its own if the ambition to strengthen its constitutional characteristics is to be taken seriously even though the present form of the Charter presents some problems which are presented below.

---

[21] Laid down in the seminal Case 26/62, *van Gend en Loos*, n. 1 above.

[22] F. Mancini and D. Keeling, n. 14 above, at 183.

[23] A. Hamilton, 'The Federalist no. 84', in A. Hamilton, J. Jay and J. Madison, *The Federalist* (Everymans Library, 1992) 444.

5.3 Problems Presented by the Charter

A problem of the Charter is that it provides rights that are in some sense redundant. The Charter applies only when the situation at stake falls into the field of application of EU Law. It is well known that the EU (and its institutions) operates on the principle of conferral of competences whereby the Union can only act within the limits of the competences conferred on it to achieve the objectives set out in the Treaties.[24] It may under these circumstances seem paradoxical to prescribe that the EU shall not engage in torture, slavery or capital punishment, actions which are not even allowed to the Member States themselves.

Another problem is that the Charter includes rights that are (at present) impossible for the EU to fully protect. The Charter contains, as previously mentioned, not only the 'negative' rights that courts in general and the ECJ in particular have been traditionally engaged with within the framework of judicial review and which represent the core rights of, for example, the ECHR. Bills of rights are not normally associated with legislative competence but rather, on the contrary, with legislative incompetence. However, 'positive' rights are richly represented in the Charter. Taken seriously this existence means that European individuals could go to court and claim various benefits like education, social security and employment agencies basing their claims directly on the Charter. Moreover, since EU law prevails over national law, the Member States can do little to avoid these effects should the EUCJ take them in earnest.

There may be a general understanding that these rights are not to be taken literally but, rather, they should be understood as proclamations of politically desirable objectives. It is, on the other hand, most likely these 'positive' rights that raise the concern of competence expansion of the EU through the Charter and which are the main reasons for the UK and Polish reservations to the Charter, even though it seems quite bizarre to ask for an opt-out from a bill of rights. These exceptions also risk undermining the status of the positive rights as common fundamental values of the EU.

Precisely to avoid this type of concerns, the Charter explicitly states that it is applicable only when EU law is called into question and that it does not confer any new competences to the EU. The provision illustrates that the inclusion of positive rights in the CFR is problematic. The enforcement of these rights – for example, the right to employment agencies and social security in general (including pensions) – will require a substantive competence expansion if the EU intends to ensure their full effectiveness. Indeed, in order to attain such an objective, the EU would need to be entrusted with taxation powers.

---

[24] Cf. Arts. 5.1 TEU and 5.1 and 7.1. TEC.

From a legal perspective it would be highly unsatisfactory if the inclusion of positive rights led to a 'devaluation' of the other rights contained in the Charter. In spite of these problems, however, the Charter provides a useful point of departure for the process of public reasoning that lies at the heart of the republican model. The Charter spells out, in more detail than the programmatic previous treaty provisions, the fundamental values that form the civic bond between the members of the community. The rights laid down in the Charter need to be balanced against each other. Rights are much like principles in the sense that they are not, like rules, applicable in an all-or-nothing fashion. It is possible to in some cases restrict, say, the right of freedom of expression in the interest of the right to privacy and to still say that one respects both rights. The rights are potentially in conflict with each other but must both be guaranteed to a reasonable degree. In accordance with the republican ideal it primarily corresponds to the political bodies of the EU to reason on the more precise meanings of these rights and their interrelation, thereby striking the proper balance.

Should the political bodies shun the issue of deliberation on fundamental values found in the Charter, this does not mean that the conflict between these various values goes away. It most likely means that they will instead end up in more or less willing courts for dispute resolution and the political fall-out from such a judgment can be quite severe. Judicial pro-activeness has played a decisive role in the making of the EC/EU, as the process of constitutionalisation shows, but the issues dealt with today are no longer only the shape of cucumbers, tariffs on chemicals or milk quotas. Today the competences of the EU stretch into the domain of criminal law and the core notions of public power. There is therefore a need for a politicization of the EU that matches the previous process of legalization. Once such a process has taken place the EUCJ can take one step back in its judicial law-making but will still have the paramount function of assessing whether these rights have been respected in the sense that any restriction must be able to pass the test of reference to the common good, the *res publica*, of the EU.

6 Final Remarks

The corollary of the idea of the EU as a genuine and independent source of rights is that these rights also require protection against the European institutions. It is indispensable to secure rights protection at the EU level if one is not to have recourse to protection through the national constitutions thereby breaking up the unity of the European legal order. Even though these have de facto been protected to a sufficient degree there can be no doubt that it is more proper for the EU to have a codified bill of rights rather than an unwritten one even though the fact that the Charter contains both rights that are redundant and rights that are impossible to protect is rather problematic.

A European *res publica* requires the interplay between both political and judicial institutions in order to carry out the process of public reasoning that the republic strives for. Whereas the ECJ has made crucial contributions in this regard it is time for the other institutions to catch up. In this context, the Charter serves two purposes. Firstly, it prescribes what the European institutions may and may not do in terms similar to those of the Member States and sets the framework for the process of public reasoning. Secondly, it ensures the position of the EUCJ as the overseer of the coherence of this process. In this sense the Charter will contribute to the constitutional legitimacy of the EU and even if it does not fully provide it with a soul, then at least with a kiss of life.

Fundamental Rights in the EU: Legal Pluralism and Multi-Level Protection After the Lisbon Treaty

Giacomo Di Federico

1 Preliminary Remarks

This Chapter will offer an overview of the multilevel system of fundamental rights protection in Europe. The different dimensions involved will be considered with a view to single out the many criticalities which affect the present state of affairs and, subsequently, to determine the possible added value of the Lisbon Treaty.[1]

The co-existing national, supranational and international (universal and regional) systems of fundamental rights protection and the respective systems of enforcement suffer from a lack of coordination which may affect the possibility for an individual to obtain justice. Pursuant to the Lisbon Treaty, the Charter of Fundamental Rights (hereafter CFR or the Charter) has the same status as the treaties and the Union is bound to accede to the European Convention on Human Rights (hereafter ECHR). Although the complementary nature of these two lines of action is hardly questionable, they will be examined separately: first, it will be useful to determine the true scope of a binding catalogue of fundamental rights; second, the analysis will single out the main legal implications and practical results of the future accession process.

G. Di Federico (✉)
CIRDE (Interdepartmental Research Centre on European Law), University of Bologna, Bologna, Italy
e-mail: gdifederico@cirdce.unibo.it

[1] According to Art. 1 (3) TEU, as amended by the Lisbon Treaty, the Union is founded on the Treaty on the European Union (TEU) and on the Treaty on the Functioning of the European Union (TFEU), having the same legal value. Moreover, it should be recalled that by virtue of this provision "The Union shall replace and succeed the European Community".

G. Di Federico, *The EU Charter of Fundamental Rights*, Ius Gentium: Comparative Perspectives on Law and Justice 8, DOI 10.1007/978-94-007-0156-4_2,

2 The Development and Consolidation of Human Rights Protection in Europe

2.1 The Lack of a Comprehensive Approach

In Europe human rights are protected at a national, supranational and international level. The atrocities of the World War II called for the adoption of specific and essentially intangible rules aimed at preventing the repetition of similar events in the future. A first manifestation of this resolution can be found in some of the constitutional charters which were drafted in the aftermath of the conflict.[2] Not only did these legal texts provide for basic civil and political, social and economic rights, but they also allowed for the conclusion of international agreements for their safeguard. In this regard, reference should be made, on the one side, to the United Nations and, on the other, to the Council of Europe.

In relation to the regional dimension, attention should be drawn to the following: the early signature of the ECHR,[3] accompanied by the adoption of additional Protocols; the consistent increase in the number of Member States of the Council of Europe; and, since 1998, the possibility for individuals to resort to the European Court of Human Rights (ECtHR) after exhausting domestic remedies.[4] By accepting the jurisdiction of the Court and the executive powers of the Committee of Ministers, the Member States undertake to fully comply with the agreed standards and suffer the consequences for the violations thereof.[5] This has led legal commentators to view the Strasbourg Court as "the Constitutional Court for Europe in the sense that it is the final authoritative judicial tribunal in the only pan-European

---

[2]On the establishment of fundamental rights catalogues in the Constitutions of the Member States, see A. Von Bogdandy, P. Cruz Villalón and P. M. Huber (eds.), *Handbuch ius publicum Europaeum*, Vols. I–II (Müller, 2007).

[3]A complete list of the High Contracting parties with the date of signature and ratification of the Convention (and its Protocols) can be found at www.coe.int

[4]See in general, A. Moravcsik, 'The origins of human rights regimes: democratic delegation in post war Europe', (2000) 54 *International Organization* 217; R. Blackburn and J. Polakiewicz (eds.), *Fundamental rights in Europe: The European Convention on Human Rights and its member States, 1950–2000* (Oxford University Press, 2001); D. Nichol, 'Original intent and the European Convention on Human Rights', (2005) *Public Law* 152 and S. Greer, *The European Convention on Human Rights* (Cambridge, 2006).

[5]Cf. Arts. 41 and 46 (1) ECHR. The latter provision has been interpreted by the Strasbourg Court as entailing the State's duty to "put an end to the breach and reparation for its consequences in such a way as to restore as far as possible the situation existing before the breach" (Appl. No 14556/89 *Papamichalopoulos v. Greece*, (1995) A/330B, para 34).

constitutional system there is."[6] Indeed, the Court itself has characterised the ECHR as a "constitutional instrument of European public order in the field of human rights."[7]

The European Communities Treaties are also a consequence of World War II, as social development could not be achieved without political stabilization and economic cooperation.[8] Their supranational character was promptly recognised by the European Court of Justice (hereafter ECJ or EUCJ) in *Van Gend en Loos* where the Luxembourg judges claimed the sui generis nature of the EC legal order in the international law context, "the subjects of which comprise not only member states but also their nationals."[9] Individuals could thus be the addressees of obligations, but also the beneficiaries of rights "which become part of their legal heritage." The transfer of sovereignty to common bodies with normative and implementing powers in a number of sensitive areas of law entailed on its face the risk of hindering individual rights, such as, for instance, the right to property and the pursuit of an economic activity. Nonetheless, human rights were not mentioned in the founding treaties, save for the prohibition of any discrimination on grounds of nationality[10] and, although limited to work remuneration, of sex.[11]

Fundamental rights issues may arise in the most different contexts and the relevant protection mechanisms cannot operate in splendid isolation. Inevitably, their breach by acts of the Community institutions was soon raised before the ECJ (both under the EEC and the ECSC treaties). At first, the Court showed a certain reluctance in this regard, either by refusing to consider possible violations of principles of national constitutional law,[12] or simply by relying on the (restrictive) wording of the applicable

[6] S. Greer, *The European Convention on Human Rights*, n. 4 above, at 173. See also J.F. Flauss, 'La Cour Européenne des droits de l'homme est-elle une cour constitutionnelle?' (1999) 36 *Revue française de droit international* 711 and L. Wildhaber, 'A Constitutional future for the European Court of Human Rights' (2000) 23 *Human Rights Law Journal* 161 and E.A. Alkema, 'The European Convention as a Constitution and its Court as a Constitutional Court', in P. Mahoney, F. Matscher, H. Petzold and L. Wildhaber (eds.), *Protecting human rights: the European perspective* (Carl Heymans, 2000) 41.

[7] Appl. No 15318/89, *Loizidou v. Turkey*, (1995) Series A No 25, para 239.

[8] On the political debate and process which lead to the elaboration and adoption of the ECSC, EEC and EURATOM treaties, see P. Gerbet, *La construction de l'Europe* (Impremerie Nationale, 1983); H. Von der Groeben, *The European Community. The formative years. The struggle to establish the Common Market and the Political Union* (The European Perspective Series, Commission of the EC, 1987); M.-T. Bitsch, *Histoire de la construction européenne de 1945 à nos jours* (Complexe, 1996).

[9] Case 26/62 *Van Gend & Loos* [1963] ECR 1.

[10] Former Art. 8 TEC.

[11] Former Art. 119 TEC.

[12] Case 1/58 *Stork* [1959] ECR 43.

treaty provision.[13] During this initial period of indifference, the ECJ was more concerned with the elaboration and consolidation of pivotal principles for the functioning of the EC legal order, such as primacy, direct effect and loyal cooperation. Nonetheless, as time passed, it became evident that further integration would depend on the formal endorsement of fundamental rights. In the silence of the treaties, the ECJ was forced to "outsource", making reference to the general principles common to the constitutional traditions of the Member States[14] and to the ECHR.[15] Still, the Court interpreted these "external" sources in its own "communitarian" way, transforming them into "internal" ones.

This case law, which affirmed itself in the course of the Seventies, was supported by the proliferation of non-binding documents of a political nature concerning fundamental rights.[16] Besides a short reference in the Preamble to the 1986 Single European Act, the formal commitment to observe fundamental rights as general principles of EC law is first to be found in Art. F2 (2) of the Maastricht Treaty, whose text is based upon (what had become) the standard formula used by the ECJ when dealing with fundamental rights.[17]

On the other hand, it should be stressed that in a highly anticipatory fashion, between 1979 and 1990, the Commission had presented two

---

[13]Case 40/64 *Sgarlata* [1965] ECR 279.

[14]Case 11/70 *Internationale Handelsgesellschaft* [1970] ECR 1125 and Case 4/73 *Nold* [1974] ECR 491.

[15]Case 36/75 *Rutili* [1975] ECR 1219. The Court of Justice progressively adopted the ECHR as preferential source in the field of fundamental rights protection. In this sense, legal commentators have spoken about a 'banal usage' of the ECHR on the part of the Court of Justice.

[16]Cf. the European Parliament, the Council and the Commission Joint Declaration on Human Rights (5 April 1977), [1977] OJ C 103/1; the Copenhagen Summit Declaration on European Identity of 14 December 1973; the Resolution of the European Parliament adopting the Declaration of fundamental rights and freedoms (12 April 1989), [1989] OJ C 120/51 and the Charter of the Fundamental Social Rights of Workers (9 December 1989) adopted in the form of a Declaration by the 11 Member States except the United Kingdom, which did not sign it until 1998. For an extensive overview of the developments which took place in the field of fundamental rights protection, see G.C. Rodriguez Iglesias, 'La protecion de los derechos fundamentales en la Union Europea', in *Scritti in onore di F. Mancini*, II (Giuffré, 1998) 831; A. Tizzano, 'L'azione dell'Unione Europea per la promozione e protezione dei diritti umani', (1999) 1 *Il Diritto dell'Unione europea* 149; F. Benoit-Rohmer, 'Les droits de l'homme dans l'Union européenne: de Rome a Nice', in L.S. Rossi (ed.) *Carta dei diritti fondamentali e Costituzione dell'Unione europea* (Giuffré, 2002) 19.

[17]Cf. after the *Nold* precedent, Case 136/79 *National Panasonic* [1980] ECR 2033, para 18; Case 222/84 *Johnston* [1986] ECR 1651, para 18; Case 85/87 *Dow Benelux NV* [1989] ECR 3137, para 24; Joined cases 46/87 and 227/88 *Hoechst AG* [1989] ECR 2859, para 13. It is also interesting to note that a specific reference to fundamental rights protection is to be found in Art. 3 of the Treaty instituting the European Defence Community (Paris, 27 May 1952), in Art. 2 of the Draft Treaty embodying the Statute of the European Community (10 March 1953) and in Art. 4 of the 1984 Progetto Spinelli, all of which never entered into force.

projects envisaging an accession of the Communities to the ECHR.[18] In its view it was rather awkward that Member States should be bound by the Convention and undergo close scrutiny on the part of the Strasbourg Court whilst no obligation in that respect was incumbent on the Community. Moreover, in consideration of the autonomous nature of the EC legal order, the risk of inconsistencies in the case law of the ECtHR and the ECJ was considered to be significant.[19]

These issues raised basic questions of internal legitimacy and coherence, especially since the Italian and German constitutional Courts had already started questioning the unconditioned application of the supremacy principle by invoking fundamental rights as the ultimate limit to that principle (so-called counter-limits doctrine).[20] Notwithstanding its initial qualms, the Council acknowledged that the issue deserved further attention. Consequently, it turned to the ECJ asking it to verify the possibility for the European Community to accede to the Convention. The answer, contained in the celebrated Opinion No 2/94 of 28 March 1996,[21] was in the negative as the judges deemed that the EC lacked the necessary competence to conclude an international agreement in the field of human rights.[22]

---

[18]See, respectively, 'Accession of the Communities to the Convention on Human Rights', EC Bull., Suppl. 2/79 and Commission Communication SEC (90) 2087 of 19 November 1990. See further L. Ferrari Bravo, 'Problemi tecnici dell'adesione delle Comunità europee alla Convenzione europea dei diritti dell'uomo', (1979) 4 *Rivista di diritto europeo* 347; G. Sperduti, 'Le rattachement des Communautés Européenne à la Convention de Rome sur la sauvegarde des droits de l'homme et des libertés fondamentales', (1980) 2 *Revue du Marché Commun* 170; R. Adam, 'La prospettata adesione delle Comunità alla Convenzione di Roma: si devono anche modificare i trattati comunitari?', (1980) *Rivista di diritto internazionale* 883; F. Capotorti, 'Sull'eventuale adesione della Comunità alla Convenzione europea dei diritti dell'uomo', (1980) *Rivista di diritto internazionale* 5; J.-P. Jacqué, 'Communauté Européenne et Convention européenne des droits de l'homme', in *Mélanges à Boulouis* (Dalloz 1991) 325.

[19]Press Release IP (90) 892, 31 October 1990.

[20]On the affirmation of the counter-limits doctrine and its development throughout the European integration process, see E. Cannizzaro, 'Tutela dei diritti fondamentali nell'ambito comunitario e garanzie costituzionali secondo le Corti costituzionali italiana e tedesca', (1990) *Rivista di diritto internazionale* 372; A. Oppenheimer, *The relationship between European Community law and National law: the cases* (Cambridge, 1994) 410; J. Kokott, 'German constitutional jurisprudence and European integration', (1996) 2 *European Public Law* 237; B. De Witte, 'Direct effect, supremacy, and the nature of the legal order', in P. Craig, G. De Burca (eds.), *The evolution of EU law* (Oxford University Press, 1999) 177; A. Ruggeri, 'Tradizioni cosituzionali comuni e controlimiti, tra teoria delle fonti e teoria dell'interpretazione', in P. Falzea, A. Spadaro, L. Ventura (eds.) *La Corte costituzionale e le Corti d'Europa* (Giappichelli, 2003) 505.

[21]Opinion 2/94 [1996] ECR I-1759.

[22]Ibid., para 27. The second question put forward by the Council – namely, the compatibility of the agreement with the Treaty – was declared inadmissible since the Court had not been given sufficient information as to the envisaged practical solutions submitting the Community to the jurisdiction of the ECtHR (para 21). See further, G. Gaja, 'Court of justice opinion 2/94, Accession by the Community to the European Convention

The Amsterdam and Nice Treaties did not change the situation,[23] but nonetheless injected into primary law a number of provisions regarding fundamental rights in order to enhance the legitimacy and coherence of the system as a whole. The former treaty amended Art. F2 specifying that the need to respect fundamental rights is a general principle common to the Member States.[24] Moreover, it required the Court of Justice to ensure compliance with Art. 6 (2) TEU in regard to measures adopted in the field of police and judicial cooperation in criminal matters.[25] Thirdly, it expressly provided for, inter alia, equality between men and women[26] and the protection of personal data.[27] Finally, it allowed a political control over candidate and Member States. On the one side, by codifying the existing practice,[28] Art. 49 TEU conditioned accession to the respect of fundamental rights as enshrined in the ECHR;[29] on the other, and perhaps more importantly, a serious and persistent breach by a Member State of principles mentioned in Art. 6(1) TEU could entail the suspension of certain rights deriving from the application of that Treaty, and, consequently, of the TEC.[30] The Nice Treaty broadened the scope of such monitoring and turned its function from repressive into preventive by foreseeing an *early warning system* enabling the EU Council to ascertain, and thus deter, the commission of such violations before they arose.

---

for the protection of human rights and fundamental freedoms given on 28 march 1996, not yet reported' (1996) 33 *Common Market Law Review* 973; P. Wachsmann, 'L'avis 2/94 de la Cour de la justice relatif à l'adhésion de la Communauté européenne à la Convention de sauvegarde des droit de l'homme et des libertés fondamentales', (1996) 2 *Revue trimestrielle de droit européen* 467.

[23]And this despite the requests of Austria, during the negotiations of the former treaty, and of Finland, on the occasion of the Intergovernmental conference leading to the adoption of the latter.

[24]See Art. 6 (1) TEU. This provision can be considered to be a codification of the Copenhagen Declaration on European Identity of 14 December 1973.

[25]Cf. former Art. 46 TEU.

[26]Former Arts. 2, 3, 13 TEC and Art. 119 (subsequently 141) TEC. In addition, it should be recalled that Art. 136 TEC contains an explicit reference to specific international instruments for the protection of workers (such as the European Social Charter signed at Turin on 18 October 1961 and the 1989 Community Charter of the Fundamental Social Rights of Workers).

[27]Former Art. 286 TEC.

[28]See the Conclusions of the Copenhagen European Council in 1978 and 1993 and the Conclusions of the Madrid European Council in 1995. Moreover, similar provisions had been introduced in Art. 96 ECSC and in Art. 204 EURATOM.

[29]Thereby making, de facto, EU membership conditional upon accession to the ECHR and, following the adoption of Protocol No 11, to the acceptance of the compulsory jurisdiction of the Strasbourg Court. See generally P. Alston, *The EU and Human Rights* (Oxford University Press, 1999) 689.

[30]Former Arts. 7 (2) and (3) TEU. The effects of such a decision will also affect the rights enjoyed by the interested Member State under the EC Treaty (see former Art. 309 TEC).

In the meantime, the EU Charter of Fundamental Rights had been elaborated by a multi-representative Convention,[31] solemnly proclaimed and fully accepted by the European Institutions as a parameter of legality.[32] As the 2000 Intergovernmental Conference did not incorporate it in the Nice Treaty, the Charter remained for almost a decade a non binding catalogue of fundamental rights protected within the EU legal order. Nonetheless, it was increasingly referred to in decisions by the national constitutional courts and by the community judges;[33] a *Bill of Rights*-to-be, since it was soon to become the second Part of the Treaty Establishing a Constitution for Europe.[34] The time seemed ripe to make that constitutional upgrade, that final step that the EU had to take in order to acquire the appropriate role on the international scene and, as a self contained regime, to "dress the emperor".[35] The fate of that immense effort is too well known to be dwelled upon. The reaction to the political impasse generated by the French and Dutch referenda in 2005 was ultimately overcome and the Lisbon Treaty largely endorses the results of the 2004 IGC.[36] For the purposes of the

---

[31]On the composition and working method of the Convention see, amongst the many which have commented the peculiar features of this organ, J.-P. Jacqué, 'La Charte des Droits Fondamentaux de l'Union européenne: présentation générale', in L.S. Rossi (ed), *Carta dei diritti fondamentali e Costituzione dell'Unione Europea* (Giuffré, 2002) 55.

[32]After the adoption of the Charter, a number of mechanisms were put into place to ensure the respect of the rights enshrined therein. In this sense, the commitment of the Commission, the Council and the European Parliament to obey the document despite its non binding nature was strong enough to impose a 'regulated self-restraint'. See further in this volume F. Camporesi, 'Chapter 4'.

[33]See further in this volume V. Bazzocchi, 'Chapter 3'.

[34]Treaty Establishing a Constitution for Europe, [2004] OJ C 310/41. See also K. Lenaerts, E. De Smijter, 'A Bill of Rights for the European Union', (2001) 38 *Common Market Law Review* 273.

[35]J.H.H. Weiler, *The Constitution of Europe – do the new clothes have an Emperor?* (Cambridge University Press, 1998). On the constitutional development of the European Communities, see further – F. Mancini, 'The making of a Constitution for Europe', (1989) 26 *Common Market Law Review* 595; J. Gerkrath, *L'emergence d'un droit constitutionnel pour l'Europe* (Editions de l'Université de Bruxelles, 1997); J.C. Piris, 'L'Union européenne a-t-elle une Constitution? Lui en faut-il une?' (1999) *Revue Trimestrielle de Droit Européenne* 599; L.S. Rossi, 'Costituzionalizzazione' dell'U.E. e dei diritti fondamentali', in L.S. Rossi (ed.), *Carta dei diritti fondamentali e Costituzione dell'Unione Europea* (Giuffré, 2002); J.-P. Jacqué, 'Les principes constitutionnels fondamentaux dans le projet de traité établissant la Constitution européenne', in L.S. Rossi (ed.), *Vers une nouvelle architecture de l'Union européenne* (Bruylant, 2004) 71; For a more critical approach to the phenomenon under examination see K. Lenaerts and M. Desomer, 'New models of constitution-making in Europe: the quest for legitimacy', (2002) 39 *Common Market Law Review* 1217 at 1218.

[36]See J. Ziller, *Les nouveaux traites européens: Lisbonne et après* (LGDJ, 2008); C. Craig, 'The Treaty of Lisbon: process, architecture and substance', (2008) 33 *European Law Review* 137; N. Moussis, 'Le traitè de Lisbonne: une Constitution sans en avoir le titre', (2008) *Revue du marché commun et de l'Union europèenne* 161; M. Dougan M., 'The Treaty of Lisbon 2007: winning minds, not hearts', (2008) 45

present contribution, two in particular should be mentioned: the primary law status attributed to the Charter and the commitment to accede to the ECHR, which represents "a strong political signal of the coherence between the Union and "greater Europe", reflected in the [Council of Europe] and its pan-European human rights system."[37]

2.2 A Multilevel System of Protection

Above and beyond the process which led to the current situation, and before we focus our attention on the innovations introduced by the Lisbon Treaty, what should be retained is the emergence of yet another level of protection of fundamental rights. Although, from a merely functionalist perspective, this was initially dictated by the need to 'legitimise' the attainment of specific and market-oriented objectives, the increasing number of competences transferred to the Community, and then to the Union, was matched by an increasing attention, both formal and substantial, towards individuals and their basic rights. This additional layer of protection, which avoided a dangerous legal *vacuum*, operated independently of, but not in isolation from, the other two.[38] The result was an unpalatable complication of legal avenues and a potential growing tension between the different legal orders.

The protection of human rights belongs to the State pursuant to its Constitution. Should it fail to respect the ECHR, individuals will be entitled to bring their case before the Strasbourg Court, provided they have exhausted all the available national remedies. On the other hand, whenever EU law comes into play, the competent domestic authorities must act in compliance with the latter and are thus exposed to the risk that the obligations stemming from their membership might entail liability under the

---

Common Market Law Review 617; P. Ponzano, 'Le traité de Lisbonne: l'Europe sort de sa crise institutionnelle', (2007) *Revue du droit de l'Union européenne* 569.

[37] Final Report of Working Group II, CONV 352/02.

[38] Indeed, it should not be forgotten that, concomitantly to the expansion of supranational competences, the Member States were broadening the catalogue of fundamental rights endorsed within their respective constitutional systems (e.g. in 1983 the Dutch Constitution was amended to include, inter alia the prohibition of discrimination, the freedom of expression and demonstration and a general right to privacy; in 1992, the Spanish Constitution was reformed to extend to citizens of the European Union the right to active and passive suffrage in local elections; in 2001 Greece broadened its constitutional rights with an express reference to the protection of personal data and the access to documents). On the one side, this was certainly a consequence of the developments which occurred at the supranational level; on the other, the expansion of the domestic bill of rights indirectly imposed a 'higher' standard of protection on the part of the EU. This 'cline-like-progression' determined a virtual spiral which ultimately relied on the counter-limits doctrine.

Conventional regime. On its part, the European Union is bound to respect fundamental rights as enshrined in the ECHR and is accountable for possible violations thereof resulting from an act of its institutions or of a decision by the judiciary. Moreover, it follows from the recent *Kadi* appeal judgment that the 'constitutional' duty to ensure fundamental rights protection equally applies to measures adopted in order to comply with international law obligations, most notably those stemming from the UN Charter.[39] But until accession to the ECHR occurs, the EU institutions remain "the only public authorities operating in the Council of Europe member States that are outside the jurisdiction of the European Court of Human Rights."[40]

Thus, although no jurisdiction (i.e. the national courts, the ECJ and the ECtHR) is absolved from applying fundamental human rights, the lack of a comprehensive approach to human rights favours differential standards of protection throughout Europe. Moreover, legal certainty and effectiveness have sometimes proven to be difficult to combine.[41] It is suggested that this situation does not necessarily depend on the legal pluralism which characterizes the protection of human rights in Europe,[42] but rather, on the absence of a duly coordinated system of enforcement. As noted by Shany:

> There is a special urgency to work towards improving the coherence of the international system, inter alia, through the harmonization of the work of international judicial bodies.[43]

---

[39] Joined cases C-402/ and 415/05 P *Kadi and Al Barakaat* [2008] ECR I-6351. See, inter alia, J.-P. Jacqué, 'Primauté du droit international versus protection des droits fondamentaux' (2009) *Revue trimestrielle de droit européen* 161; A. Gattini, (2009) 46 *Common Market Law Review* 213; G. Harpaz, 'Judicial review by the European Court of Justice of UN 'Smart Sanctions' against terror in the Kadi dispute', (2009) 14 *European Foreign Affairs Review* 65; C. Eckes, 'Test Case for the Resilience of the EU's Constitutional Foundations International Sanctions against Individuals: A Test Case for the Resilience of the European Union's Constitutional Foundations, (2009) 15 *European Public Law* 351.

[40] Parliamentary Assembly of the Council of Europe (PACE), Rec. 1744 (2006), para 4.

[41] The *Poirrez v. France* (Appl. No 40892/98) case provides a good example of how tortuous the road to justice may be in Europe. Here a physically challenged Ivory coast national, had been adopted as an adult by a French citizen. The competent domestic authorities refused to grant him the disability allowance he had applied for on grounds of nationality. His appeal against the decision originated a preliminary reference to the ECJ but the latter was dismissed on account of the fact that the issue at stake fell outside the scope of application of EC law. Having exhausted all the available judicial remedies, Mr. Poirrez turned to the Strasbourg Court which, 13 years after the first legal plea, recognized the discrimination condemning France for a violation of Art. 14 of the ECHR together with Art. 1 of Protocol No 1 and, ruling on an equitable basis, awarded him 20,000 euro for the damages he had suffered.

[42] See N. Kirsch, 'The open architecture of European human rights law' (2008) 71 *Modern Law Review* 183.

[43] Y. Shany, *The competing jurisdictions of international courts and tribunals* (Oxford University Press, 2003) at 118.

Although elaborated in a much broader context of analysis, this exhortation is certainly valid in the human rights sphere. The following sections are intended to clarify this assumption.

3 The Relations Between the National, Supranational and International Dimensions

3.1 The Obligation to Respect the ECHR in the Legal Orders of the EU Member States

The status of the ECHR in the legal orders of the Member States of the EU – which are all High Contracting parties of the Council of Europe[44] – varies considerably according to the hierarchical position assigned to international treaties by the respective constitutional system. In this respect, the doctrinal elements of monism and dualism play a major, yet not definitive, role in determining the rank of the Convention amongst the sources of law and whether its provisions are self-executing. This is capable of jeopardizing the effectiveness of the rights enshrined therein, especially since the ECtHR's decisions have no *erga omnes* effects and are not intended to set general and abstract maxims.

Indeed, dualism does not per se exclude primacy over subsequent statutory norms, nor does it prevent direct effect and effective judicial protection. In a comparative perspective, the ECHR may be placed above the Constitution (e.g. in the Netherlands), considered as an integral part of the latter (e.g. in Austria), placed at an intermediate level between ordinary law and the Constitution (e.g. in France, Italy and the UK) or fully assimilated to the former (e.g. in Germany).[45]

Regardless of the collocation it finds amongst the sources of law, the ECHR and the case law of the Strasbourg Court are capable of impacting forcibly on the functioning of the domestic legal systems. Independently from the monist or dualist approach which characterizes their constitutional regime, the Legislator, and most notably the Judiciary, have to adjust to the Conventional system. National courts, ordinary and/or constitutional courts depending on the specificities of the relevant legal order, are bound

---

[44] At present 47 European countries have ratified the ECHR. For a detailed list of the Member States and of the single additional protocols they have ratified, see website http://www.echr.coe.int/.

[45] For an in depth comparative analysis, see R. Blackburn and J. Polakiewicz (eds.), *Fundamental rights in Europe*, n. 4 above and H. Keller, A. Stone Sweet, *A Europe of rights, the impact of the ECHR on National legal systems* (Oxford University Press, 2008).

to interpret all legal norms in conformity with the ECHR and have progressively recognized direct effect to many of its provisions. On the other hand, domestic legislation has been amended so as to comply with the Convention, especially when the existing normative framework did not allow judicial activism to compensate for the deficiencies singled out by the ECtHR. This is particularly true for the remedies available to individuals following an adverse finding on the part of the latter court determining a progressive alignment of substantial and procedural provisions, such as those concerning the reopening of proceedings,[46] the compensation for an excessive duration of the trial[47] and the right to just and appropriate compensation for the damages suffered.[48]

3.2 The Need to Comply with the ECHR in Matters Falling Within the Field of Application of EC/EU Law

The different status of the ECHR in the various Member States does not relieve the latter from the obligation to observe its provisions, as interpreted by the Strasbourg Court. On the other hand, the primacy of EU law over conflicting national legislation, as applied by the competent (administrative and judicial) authorities, requires full compliance with the duties resulting thereof, including the respect of fundamental rights.

---

[46]See, for instance, Art. 457 of the Dutch Code of Criminal Procedure, as amended in 2002; Art. 363a of the Austrian Code of Criminal Procedure, as introduced by the 1996 reform; Arts. 626 (paras 1–7) of the French Procedural Criminal Code, as amended in 2000 and Art. 359 (6) of the German Code of Criminal Procedure, as modified in 1998. In some instances the opening of administrative and civil cases is also allowed. See, for instance, the 1985 Austrian Administrative Court Act, (*Verwaltungsgerichtshofgesetz*), the German Code of Administrative Procedure (*Verwaltungsgerichtsordnung*) as amended in 2006 and the German Code of Civil Procedure (*Zivilprozessordnung*).

[47]This is in particular the case of Italy (see Appl. Nos 7604/76, 7719/76, 7781/77 and 7913/77, *Foti v. Italy*, (1982) Series A, vol. 56; Appl. No 13023/87, *Salesi v. Italy*, (1993) Series A, vol. 257-E; Appl. No 34256/96, *Di Mauro v. Italy*, (1999) Reports 1999-V; Appl. No 31631/96, *Procaccini v. Italy*, (2000) unreported), but also of France (Appl. No 38212/97, *F.E. v. France*, (1998) Reports 1998-VIII, Appl. No 28738/02, *Le Blenchennec v. France*, (2006) unreported). With the so-called *Legge Pinto* (Law No 89 of 24 March 2001, OJ 78/2001), the Italian Legislator introduced a legal remedy which allows individuals to obtain compensation when their right to have a case heard within a reasonable time is breached. In France, compliance appears to have been achieved through judicial interpretation (See *Cour de Cassation*, 23 February 2001, *Cts Bolle Laroche c/Agent judiciaire du trésor* and *Nouhaud et a. v. France* [2002], Appl. No 33424/96) *Conseil d'Etat*, 28 June 2002, *Ministre de la Justice c/M. Magiera* and *Broca et Texier-Micault v. France* [2003], Appl. Nos. 27928//02 and 31694/02).

[48]On the liability of the State and the right to damages, see, for instance, Art. 6:162 of the Dutch Civil Code and Section 8 of the HRA.

But a breach of the ECHR by the EU cannot be reviewed by the European Court of Human Rights; even following the entry into force of the Lisbon Treaty, 'external' judicial control will operate only upon accession. This did not, however, prevent the ECtHR from assessing the admissibility of national provisions or practices originating in EC/EU law. If the Member States infringe the Convention while implementing EU law they may be held liable for what is essentially an EU action.

The repercussions on the relations between the three legal orders involved, and in particular on the dynamics which operate in cases involving the protection of human rights, are manifold and of great relevance. In the Member States of the Council of Europe *and* of the EU, the judiciary is bound to obey both systems with all the additional problems deriving from the distinct tasks respectively pursued, not to mention the lack of coordination between the two.

In order to have a better understanding of the complex relations between the national, supranational and international level it should prove useful to single out the various cases which can be brought before the different competent *fora*. As far as the Strasbourg Court jurisdiction is concerned, the two following scenarios must be considered: (1) the Court decides cases involving violations of the ECHR by Member States, with no EU law component and (2) the Court decides over actions involving EU law.

The first is the simplest and most classic situation. Here the Court is asked to decide on the compatibility of domestic legislation (e.g. a law prohibiting homosexual conduct) with the ECHR.[49] The second situation is more complicated, and requires particular attention, since the solution envisaged by the Strasbourg Court may vary according to whether the violation is the result of an act directly attributable to a Member State or, on the contrary, is imputable solely to the EU. So, in *Cantoni*[50] the Court felt free to review a French law implementing the EC medicine directive (notwithstanding the *verbatim* transposition),[51] but found no violation of the ECHR. The same *ratio* was applied in *Matthews*,[52] where the Court considered that the content of the act in question[53] was directly and solely attributable to the British government thus engaging the latter's liability under Art. 1 of the Convention for failing to secure the rights guaranteed by Art. 3 of Protocol No 1.[54]

---

[49] Appl. No 7525/76, *Dudgeon v. UK*, (1981) 4 EHRR 149.

[50] Appl. No 17862/91, *Cantoni v. France*, (1996) Reports 1996-V ECHR.

[51] Directive EEC 65/65, [1965] OJ L 369/1.

[52] Appl. No 24833/94, *Matthews v. United Kingdom*, (1999) Reports 1999-I. See further, H.G. Schemers, (1999) 36 *Common Market Law Review* 673.

[53] Annex to the 1976 Act concerning direct elections of the European Parliament whereby the UK had excluded that the direct elections would apply to Gibraltar.

[54] The international nature of the act in question was confirmed by the fact that, as primary law, it fell outside the ECJ's jurisdiction.

On the other hand, where the Member States have no discretion in deciding how to implement EU law, the Court will still claim jurisdiction over the case, but in establishing the legality of the measure in question it will apply the so-called 'equivalent protection doctrine'. In other words, since the transfer of powers to an international organization such as the EC is not incompatible with the Convention, the State will be held liable only when within that organization fundamental rights do not receive an equivalent protection.[55]

Furthermore, in *Bosphorus* the Grand Chamber clarified that it will always be possible to rebut this presumption on a case by case basis.[56] If the protection offered by the international organization appears to be 'manifestly deficient' with respect to the ECHR standard, the Court might declare the action admissible and try the case against all EU Member States, considered collectively responsible for the adoption of acts formally imputable to the EC or the EU.[57] The fact remains that to date no such action has been declared admissible, either because the Court lacked competence *ratione materiae*[58] or because the applicants were not deemed to be victims pursuant to Art. 34 ECHR.[59]

The European Court of Justice is also competent to hear cases involving breaches of human rights by Member States, but only *when implementing EU law*. In fact, unlike their colleagues in Strasbourg, EU judges have no jurisdiction over purely domestic situations concerning fundamental rights,[60] nor can they (directly) hear claims by individuals against Member States.[61] As argued by AG Poiares Maduro in *Centro Europa 7*, the ECJ is only entitled to "examine whether Member States provide the necessary level of protection in relation to fundamental rights in order to be able adequately to fulfil their other obligations as members of the Union."[62] What appears to be required here is some kind of nexus with EU law, the existence of a transnational situation capable of affecting the internal

---

[55] Appl. No 13258/87, *M & Co v. FDR*, (1990) 64 *DR* 138.

[56] Appl. No 45036/98, *Bosphorus v. Ireland*, (2005) Reports 2005-VI, para 156.

[57] Needless to say that with the entry into force of the Lisbon Treaty reference should be made to the EU solely.

[58] Appl. No 51717/99, *Guerin v. 15 Member States of the EU*, (2000) unreported.

[59] Appl. No 6422/02, *Ségi et al. v. 15 Member States*, (2002) Ser. A, 56.

[60] Case C-299/95 *Kremzow* [1997] ECR I-2629; Case C-328/04 *Vajnai* [2005] ECR I-8577 and Case C-361/07 *Polier* [2008] ECR I-6.

[61] However, individuals can indirectly contest the compatibility of national legislation with EU law through the preliminary ruling mechanism (cf. in particular Art. 234 TEC, now 267 TFEU).

[62] Opinion of 12 September 2007 in Case C-380/05 *Centro Europa 7* [2008] ECR I-349, para 20. See also, Opinion delivered on 9 December 1992 by AG Jacobs in Case C-168/91 *Konstantinidis* [1993] ECR I-1191, para 46.

market[63] or economic rights protected under the Treaty.[64] Under the former treaties, whenever the State and its articulations transposed,[65] implemented or applied,[66] or derogated from[67] EC law it was necessary to comply with fundamental rights, as general principles of Community law, guaranteed by the ECHR and resulting from their common constitutional traditions. By virtue of the *Pupino Segi*, *Pro Gestoras* and *Advocaten voor de Wereld* this rule also applied to matters falling within the former third pillar.

This 'collateral effect' of Art. 6 TEU allowed the Court to widen its jurisdiction on the respect of fundamental rights and ensure that Member States did not violate the Convention when acting within the scope of application of EU law. Although this undoubtedly favoured compliance with the ECHR, it was "neither methodologically nor dogmatically convincing".[68] Reliance on the constitutional traditions common to the Member States was essential for the purposes of deepening market integration, but as time went on the ECJ started developing an autonomous supranational standard which can hardly be traced back to the national context.

According to the circumstances this was capable of determining, *in concreto*, a variation in the degree of protection offered under the domestic (constitutional) legal order depending on whether the situation at hand fell within the scope of application of EU law. On the one hand, the improvement of the (minimum) standard of protection offered by the Union by virtue of legislative or judicial activism forced the Member States to adjust. In this sense the *Kreil*[69] and *Mangold*[70] precedents and their impact on the German legal order are most revealing. On the other hand, the *ERT*

---

[63]And yet, the case law on Art. 18 EC (now 21 TEU) demonstrates that the Court is willing to demand full compliance with EU fundamental rights above and beyond the mentioned thresholds. See further E. Spaventa, 'Seeing the woods despite the trees? On the scope of EU citizenship and its constitutional effects', (2008) 45 *Common Market Law Review* 13; A. Trifonidou, 'Reverse discrimination in purely internal situations: an incongruity in a citizens' Europe', (2008) 35 *Legal Isuues of Economic Integration* 43 and Editorial Comments, 'Two-speed European citizenship? Can the Lisbon Treaty help close the gap?' (2008) 45 *Common Market Law Review* 1. On the exclusion of the ECJ's competence to rule on strictly internal situations, cf. *a contrario*, Case C-212/06 *Government of Communauté française and Gouvernement wallon* [2008] ECR I-1683.

[64]See e.g. Case C-159/90 *Grogan* [1991] ECR I-468.

[65]See e.g. Case 222/84 *Johnston*, n. 17 above.

[66]See e.g. Case C-5/88 *Wachauf* [1989] ECR 2609 and Case 292/97 *Karlsson* [2000] ECR I-2737.

[67]See e.g. Case C-260/89 *ERT* [1991] ECR I-2925 and Case C-368/95 *Familiapress* [1997] ECR I-3689.

[68]P.M. Huber, 'The unitary effect of the Community's Fundamental rights: the ERT doctrine Needs to be revised', (2008) 14 *European Public Law* 323, at 328.

[69]Case C-285/98 *Kreil* [2000] ECR I-69.

[70]Case C-144/04 *Mangold* [2005] ECR I-9981. Cf. A. Masson, C. Micheau, 'The Werner Mangold case: an example of legal militancy', (2007) 32 *European Public Law* 587; J.H. Jans, 'The effects in national legal systems of the prohibition of discrimination on grounds of age as a general principle of Community law', (2007) 3 *Legal Issues*

doctrine required Member States to comply "with the fundamental rights the observance of which is ensured by the Court"[71] even when limiting fundamental freedoms on grounds of public policy, public morality, public security and public health, all domains which in principle fall within the latter's exclusive competence.[72] This centralisation of judicial control demonstrates the desire to guarantee compliance with fundamental rights in all situations falling within the scope of EU law, but placed a paramount responsibility on the ECJ; that of combining the national, supranational and international level of protection, while at the same time preserving the autonomy of the EU legal order and respecting the sharing of competences between the Union and the Member States.

The Court is required to keep in line with the ECHR not only in relation to national measures caught by EU law but also, and to the same extent, when appraising the action of the institutions and the lower courts. Moreover, in order to avoid the resurgence of the counter-limits doctrine, fundamental freedoms must be enforced taking into the highest consideration national constitutional specificities. Concomitantly, though, the EUCJ shall ensure the uniform application of the law. The complex balancing operations it is called to perform can be associated with those of a federal constitutional Court, a mission which the Luxembourg judges have progressively become familiar with.

On the one side, it was able to combine national constitutional sensitivities with the principles of primacy and uniform application of EC law. In *Omega*, for instance, it accepted that the principle of human dignity enshrined in Art. 1 of the *Grundgesetz*, was capable of justifying a restriction to the (economic) fundamental freedoms guaranteed under the EC Treaty.[73] Similarly, in *Dynamic Medien* it claimed that child protection, as protected under German law and guaranteed in Art. 24 (1) of the Charter, could restrict the free movement of goods.[74] Moreover, since *Pupino* the Court has focused on coherence and sensibly avoided dealing with matters falling within the former third pillar in terms of primacy. By contrast, it insisted on the necessary cooperation with national Courts, including constitutional courts, which are increasingly aware of the importance of pluralism.[75] In this sense, Maduro argued that:

---

of European Integration 53 and A. Arnull, 'Out with the old', (2006) *European Law Review* 1.

[71] Case C-260/89 *ERT*, n. 67 above, para 43.

[72] See Art. 30 TEC (now Art. 36 TFEU), Art. 46 TEC (now Art. 52 TFEU) and Art. 55 TEC (now Art. 62 TFEU).

[73] Case C-36/02 *Omega* [2004] ECR I-9609. On the balancing of fundamental rights and freedoms in the case law of the ECJ, see further in this volume S. Curzon, 'Chapter 8'.

[74] Case C-244/06 *Dynamic Medien* [2008] ECR I-505, para 41.

[75] For further considerations on the necessary (and ongoing) dialogue between national constitutional courts and the ECJ, see J.H.H. Weiler, N.J.S. Lockhart, 'Taking rights seriously: The European Court of Justice and its fundamental rights jurisprudence', (1995)

> Any legal order (national and European) must respect the identity of the other legal orders; its identity must not be affirmed in a manner that either challenges the identity of the other legal orders or the pluralist conception of the European legal order itself.[76]

The willingness on the part of the ECJ to engage in a 'constructive dialogue' with national Courts can be appreciated in *Advocaten voor de Wereld* where it claimed that the Framework-Decision on the European Arrest Warrant did not infringe the legality, equality and non-discrimination principles, and placed on the Member States the onus of guaranteeing fundamental rights protection when adopting the necessary implementing measures.[77] The same can be said with respect to the transposition of directives, and the implementation of the relevant domestic provisions, which may also presuppose "the need to strike a fair balance between the various fundamental rights protected by the Community legal order."[78]

Nonetheless, if "in judgements such as *Pupino*, *Segi*, *Advocaten voor de Wereld* the Court of Justice suggested that the EU was developing as a legal order, based on some common key principles, admittedly partly imported from the EC legal order,"[79] more recent decisions, rendered in the wake of the entry into force of the Lisbon Treaty, reinforce the idea that fundamental rights protection is to be traced amongst the "constitutional principles of the EC Treaty".[80] However it may be, the abandonment of the pillar-structure resulting from the new Treaties – albeit with notable exceptions in the Common Foreign and Security Policy – and the fact that the EU has replaced and succeeded the European Community seems to appease

32 *Common Market Law Review* 51; F.C. Mayer, 'The European Constitution and the Courts', in A. Von Bogdandy and J. Bast (eds.), *Principles of European Constitutional Law* (Hart Publishing, 2006) 281; T. Vandamme, 'Prochain Arrêt: La Belgique! Explaining Recent Preliminary References of the Belgian Constitutional Court', (2008) 4 *European Constitutional Law Review* 127; L.S. Rossi (2009) 46 *Common Market Law Review* 319; M. Bobek 'Learning to talk: preliminary rulings, the courts of the new Member States and the Court of Justice, (2008) 45 *Common Market Law Review* 1611 and A. Tizzano, 'Qualche riflessione sul contributo della Corte di Giustizia allo sviluppo del sistema comunitario' (2009) 14 *Il Diritto dell'Unione Europea* 141, at 157 ff.

[76] M. Poiares Maduro, 'Contrapunctual law: Europe's constitutional pluralism in action', in N. Walker (ed.), *Sovereignty in Transition* (Oxford University Press, 2003) at 526. For a similar take on the juxtaposition of the national and EU legal orders, Cf. L. Besselink, *A composite European Constitution* (Europa Law Publishing, 2007). But, see *contra* I. Pernice, 'Multilevel constitutionalism in the European Union', (2002) 27 *European Law Review* 511.

[77] Case C-303/05 *Advocaten voor de Wereld* [2007] ECR I-3633.

[78] Case C-275/06 *Promusicae* [2008] ECR I- 271, para 68.

[79] C. Hillion, R.A. Wessel, 'Competence distribution in EU external relations after ECOWAS: clarification or continued fuzziness?' (2009) 46 *Common Market Law Review* 551 at 556.

[80] Joined cases C-402 and 415/05 P *Kadi and Al Barakaat International Foundation* [2008] ECR I-6351, para 81.

all doctrinal concern as to the reasons behind this apparent back-step in the process of affirming the unity of the EU legal order.

On the other hand, the ECJ strived to assume the garb of a Constitutional Court of the EU in balancing fundamental rights with fundamental freedoms. Nevertheless, the two are not placed on an equal footing, the former being "relegated" to legitimate derogations to the latter. If in *Omega* human dignity prevailed over the freedom to provide services and in *Schmidberger*[81] a restriction on the free movement of goods was justified by virtue of the freedom of expression, in *Laval*[82] and *Viking*[83] the outcome was in favour of the relevant economic freedoms. With the exception of *Schmidberger*, where the Court affirmed that "the interests involved must be weighed having regard to all the circumstances of the case in order to determine whether a fair balance was struck between those interests,"[84] all the other cases were decided viewing fundamental rights as legitimate limitations to the internal market freedoms.

The *Viking* and *Laval* judgements have been criticised for impinging on the protection of social rights, treating them as 'second class' fundamental rights even though they are part of the international obligations of the Member States under the ILO Convention 87.[85] It could be argued that the more restrictive stance adopted in relation to collective bargaining with respect to other fundamental rights, such as human dignity and the freedom of expression, reveals (*rectius*, unveils) a certain deference towards the State as opposed to private action. Nevertheless, it is a matter of fact that the ECJ has consistently upgraded fundamental rights to their formal status, that of general principles of EC/EU law. As will be seen the situation is expected to change now that the Lisbon Treaty has finally become effective.

That being said, it should also be stressed that the quest for a uniform protection of fundamental rights by and throughout the Member States was not assisted by a comprehensive and effective enforcement apparatus. Leaving aside the special procedure laid down in Art. 7 TEU – strictly 'political' in nature – and the more recent creation of the Fundamental Rights Agency[86]- without any cogent instrument of enforcement – compliance

---

[81]Case C-112/00 *Schmidberger* [2003] ECR I-5659.

[82]Case C-341/05 *Laval* [2007] ECR I-11767.

[83]Case C-438/05 *Viking* [2007] ECR I-10779.

[84]Case C-112/00 *Schmidberger*, n. 81 above, para 81.

[85]See in particular, T. Van Peijpe, 'Collective labour law after Viking, Laval, Ruffert and Commission v Luxembourg', (2009) 25 *International Journal of Comparative Law* 81 at 95, and J. Malmberg and T. Sigeman, 'Industrial actions and EU economic freedoms: the autonomous collective bargaining model curtailed by the European Court of Justice (2008) 45 *Common Market Law Review* 1115 at 1130.

[86]On the role of the Agency See Weidenfeld and Wessels, 'The role of the new EU Fundamental Rights Agency: debating of the 'sex of angels' or improving Europe's human rights performance?' (2008) 33 *European Law Review* 385 and A. Von Bogdandy

with fundamental rights was mainly assessed through the preliminary reference mechanism,[87] allowing the ECJ, by interpreting the relevant Community provision, to indirectly scrutinize national legislation. This power of appraisal was nevertheless subject to the important limitations provided for in Art. 68 TEC[88] (visas, asylum, immigration and judicial cooperation in civil matters) and Art. 35 TEU (judicial cooperation in criminal matters).[89] The situation has undergone significant changes with the reform Treaty: the merging of the Pillars, in fact, has resulted in a unified system of judicial protection (with the well known exceptions applicable to the Common Foreign and Security Policy).[90]

3.3 Application of the ECHR by the European Court of Justice: Remedying Deficiencies Through Judicial Control and Interaction

As far as the EU institutions are concerned the risk of potential violations of the Convention are exacerbated by the lack of (direct) 'external' control on the part the Strasbourg Court. Under the former treaties the ECJ was called

and J. Von Bernstorff, 'The EU Fundamental Rights Agency within the European and International Human Rights Architecture: the Legal Framework and Some Unsettled Issues in a New Field of Administrative Law', (2009) 46 *Common Market Law Review* 1035. In the context of administrative supervision, its should also be recalled that the violation of general principles of law and of the Charter is considered to amount to a case of maladministration. See J. Soderman, 'The Convention, the Charter and the remedies', Speech delivered on the 25 of February 2003 at the European Policy Centre in Brussels.

[87] Art. 234 TEC (now Art. 267 TFEU).

[88] See S. Peers, 'The ECJ's jurisdiction over EC immigration and asylum law: time for a change?', in H. Toner, E. Guild and A. Baldaccini (eds.), *EU Immigration and Asylum Law and Policy* (Hart Publishing, 2007), and Editorial Comments, 'Preliminary rulings and the Area of Freedom Security and Justice (2007) 44 *Common Market Law Review* 1.

[89] Cf. S. Peers, *EU Justice and Home Affairs Law* (Oxford University Press, 2006); S. Douglas-Scott, 'Rule of Law in the EU-Putting the Security in the Area of Freedom Security and Justice, (2004) 29 *European Law Review* 219 and S. Peers, 'Salvation outside the Church: judicial protection in the third pillar after the Pupino and Segi judgments', (2007) 44 *Common Market Law Review* 883.

[90] But cf. Protocol No 36 to the Lisbon Treaty. In particular, Art. 10 reads: "As a transitional measure, and with respect to acts of the Union in the field of police cooperation and judicial cooperation in criminal matters which have been adopted before the entry into force of the Treaty of Lisbon, the powers of the institutions shall be the following at the date of entry into force of that Treaty: the powers of the Commission under Article 258 of the Treaty on the Functioning of the European Union shall not be applicable and the powers of the Court of Justice of the European Union under Title VI of the Treaty on European Union, in the version in force before the entry into force of the Treaty of Lisbon, shall remain the same, including where they have been accepted under Article 35(2) of the said Treaty on European Union". See further in this volume V. Bazzocchi, 'Chapter 10'.

upon to review the legality of acts adopted within the first and third Pillars ensuring their compatibility with the rights guaranteed by the Convention through Art. 6 TEU. By contrast, it is well known that it lacked jurisdiction over all acts of the second Pillar, a situation that has only partially been remedied by the Lisbon Treaty by allowing natural and legal persons to challenge the legality of decisions providing for restrictive measures against them.[91]

The ECJ has been presented with many cases involving infringements of the ECHR by EU institutions. In *Connolly*, for instance, the ECJ claimed that the Commission had not infringed the freedom of expression of the applicant insofar as his dismissal complied with the requirements laid down in Art. 10 (2) ECHR.[92] In *Baustahlgewebe*, instead, the ECJ found that the Court of First Instance had unreasonably protracted the proceedings thereby breaching the right to a fair trial. Consequently, it annulled part of the decision and lowered the amount of the fines it had imposed on the interested undertaking.[93] And in the recent *Kadi* decision it annulled the relevant Council Regulation insofar as the applicant had been deprived of his right – protected under Art. 1 of Protocol 1 to the ECHR – to bring his case before the competent authorities.[94]

Despite the fact that the EU is not a Member of the ECHR, the two Courts prove to be increasingly aware of each other. Besides the formal and informal contacts between them, which have increased over the last decade (the courts have held regular bilateral meetings since 1998), one can observe a progressive interest in their respective jurisprudence, especially on the part of the ECJ.[95]

This interaction is undoubtedly an example of the broader phenomenon of courts' world-wide using each other's case law, but within the European context this has specific justifications. More precisely, despite the fact that the Convention and the EC/EU treaties pursue different objectives, both judicial bodies are required to protect human rights in a common effort

---

[91] Art. 275 (2) TFEU.

[92] Case C-274/99 P *Connolly* [2001] ECR I-1611.

[93] Case C-185/95 *Baustahlgewebe* [1998], ECR I-8417. See further in this volume M. Borraccetti, 'Chapter 5'.

[94] Joined cases C-402 and 415/05 P *Kadi and Al Barakaat*, n. 80 above, paras 368–370.

[95] See F.G. Jacobs, 'The European Convention on Human Rights, the EU Charter of Fundamental Rights and the European Court of Justice. The impact of European Union accession to the European Convention on Human Rights', online at http://www.ecln.net/elements/conferences/book_berlin/jacobs.pdf.; S. Douglas-Scott, 'A tale of two Courts: Luxembourg, Strasbourg and the growing European human rights acquis', (2006) 43 *Common Market Law Review* 629; G. Ress, 'The legal relationship between the European Court of Human Rights and the Court of Justice of the European Communities according to the European Convention on Human Rights', in H-J. Blank, S. Mangiameli (eds.), *Governing Europe under a Constitution – The hard road from the European Treaties to a European Constitutional Treaty* (Springer, 2003) 279.

to promote their respect. References to decisions emanating from the other Court – and this, once again, is particularly true for the ECJ[96] – are believed to have a legitimating function.[97] Still, given the lack of any formal connection between the EU and the ECHR judiciaries, this reciprocal awareness rests on autonomy and there is little discussion of the facts that originated the precedents of the counterpart, and limited motivation as to why they should be considered relevant for the solution of the case in question.[98]

Where the Court of Human Rights has cited Luxembourg case law it has tended to do so in a sterile way, without venturing into an in-depth analysis of the relevant jurisprudence.[99] If, on the one hand, this makes it difficult to assess its attitude towards Luxembourg,[100] on the other, it reveals a fairly deferential approach to the ECJs' decisions[101] and, more in general, to the EU legal order. This can be seen, for example, in the *Hornsby* case, where finding a violation of Art. 6 ECHR the Court considered that Greece had also failed to respect EC law, as interpreted by the Court of Justice.[102] Similarly, in *Pafitis* the Strasbourg Court declared that in assessing the length of proceedings under the same provision, it would not take into account the time taken for the Luxembourg Court to respond to a preliminary reference under Art. 234 EC as this would "adversely affect the system instituted by Article 177 of the EEC treaty (now Article 234) and work against the aim pursued in substance in that Article."[103] The autonomous and independent nature of the two systems has also been stressed by rejecting applications arguing the existence under the Convention of a right to obtain a preliminary ruling by the ECJ before filing a complaint.[104]

[96]But see recently Appl. No 18603/03, *André and Others v. France*, (2008) unreported, where the ECtHR quoted Case C-305/05 *Ordre des barreaux francophone et germanophone and Others* [2007] ECR I-5305.

[97]S. Douglas-Scott, n. 95 above, at 656.

[98]J.P. Puissochet, 'La Cour européenne des droits de l'homme, la Cour de Justice des Communautées européennes et la protection des droits de l'homme', in P. Mahoney, F. Matscher, H. Petzold, L. Wildhaber (eds.), *Protection des droits de l'homme: la perspective européenne* (Heymanns, 2000) 1139; G. Harpaz, 'The European Court of Justice and its relations with the European Court of Human Rights: The quest for enhanced reliance, coherence and legitimacy', (2009) 46 *Common Market Law Review* 105 at 109.

[99]In some recent cases, however, the Strasbourg Court has carried out an extensive comparative analysis. See Appl. No 54810/00, *Jalloh v. Germany*, (2006) Reports IX.

[100]Appl. No 28957/95, *Goodwin v. UK*, (2002) 35 EHRR 447. However, it should be underlined that on this occasion the Court made reference to the European Charter of Fundamental Rights (para 100).

[101]Appl. No 28541/95, *Pellegrin v. France*, (2001) 31 EHRR 651.

[102]Appl. No 18357/91, *Hornsby v. Greece*, (1997) 24 EHRR 250.

[103]Appl. No 20323/92, *Pafitis v. Greece*, (1999) 27 ECHRR 566.

[104]See, for instance, Appl. Nos 35673/97, 35674/97, 36082/97 and 37579/97, *Schweighhofer and Others v. Austria*, (2001), unreported.

Finally, the Court duly reports the precedents of the ECJ when applying the Convention to cases which have been previously brought before it in the context of preliminary rulings[105] or enforcement actions.[106] More importantly it seems to acknowledge the evolving nature of the EU legal order and act consequently. For instance, in the recent *Cooperatieve Producentenorganisatie van de Nederlandse Kokkelvissarij v. The Netherlands* case[107] the Strasbourg Court accepted that the standard afforded under the EU legal order is equivalent to that guaranteed by the Convention under Art. 6 ECHR insofar as the Rules of Procedure provide for the reopening of the oral procedure after the opinion by the AG. This was considered to be a "realistic and not merely theoretical" possibility considering the Opinion of AG Sharpston in *Government of the French Community and Walloon Government v. Flemish Government*.[108] The *Landelijke Vereniging* precedent, on the other hand, confirms that the relevant decision is based on the merits of the case.[109]

As to the European Court of Justice, citation of the Strasbourg jurisprudence is a fairly recent phenomenon. The ECHR has been quoted by Advocates general and by the ECJ for over 30 years but the first specific reference to the Court's case law dates from 1996[110]. Since then the Luxembourg judges have increasingly been using the ECHR and the decisions by the Court as an authoritative basis in support of their positions.[111] Sometimes this helped the applicant[112] whilst on other occasions it did not.[113]

---

[105] Appl. Nos 17173/07 and 17180/07, *Sevinger and Eman v. The Netherlands*, (2007) unreported and Appl. No 13645/05, *Cooperatieve Producentenorganisatie van de Nederlandse Kokkelvissarij v. The Netherlands*, (2009) unreported.

[106] *Poirrez v. France*, n. 41 above.

[107] *Cooperatieve Producentenorganisatie v. The Netherlands*, n. 105 above. Also cf. Case C-17/98 *Emesa Sugar* [2000] ECR I-0675 and Appl. No 62023/00, *Emesa Sugar v. the Netherlands*, (2005) unreported. Although the claim was declared inadmissible *rationae materiae*, it has been submitted that in *Emesa* the ECtHR points to a right to comment on the AG's opinion under Art. 6, paragraph 1 ECHR. See further in this volume M. Borraccetti, 'Chapter 5'.

[108] Case C-212/06 *Government of the French Community and Walloon Government*, n. 63 above.

[109] Case C-127/02 *Landelijke Vereniging tot Behoud van de Waddenzee and Others* [2004] ECR I-7405.

[110] Case C-13/94 *P. v. S.* [1996] ECR I-2143.

[111] In the aftermath of the *P v S* judgment, see Case C-368/95 *Familiapress* [1997] ECR I-3689 and Case C-249/96 *Grant* [1998] ECR I-621.

[112] See Case C-60/00 *Carpenter* [2002] ECR I-6279 and C-109/01 *Akrich* [2003] ECR I-9607.

[113] See Case C-347/03 *Friuli Venezia* [2005] ECR I-378.

Recently, one can note a more knowledgeable and wiser use of the ECHR by the Community courts. In cases such as *Krombach*[114] and *Carpenter*[115], apart from a consistent human rights argumentation, the decisions, rendered in the context of preliminary references, leave little room for national courts to exercise their discretionary judgment.[116] This undoubtedly supports the idea that the Court of Justice is increasingly acting as a constitutional court. Further proof of this can be seen in the fact that the precedents by the Court of Human Rights have been carefully applied to new cases "by analogy", thus indirectly reaffirming the autonomous character of the EC legal order.[117] This also justifies the legitimate assumption of a more functionalist approach. Suffice it here to recall the *Limburse* (on the right against self-incrimination) and *Roquette Frères* (on the right to privacy of business premises) cases[118] where the ECJ, mostly concerned with the effectiveness of EC competition rules, refused to apply the more generous interpretation suggested by the Strasbourg court in similar situations.[119] In this regard, it is also revealing that in *SGL Carbon* Advocate General Geelhoed quite boldly stated that it is not possible "simply to transpose the findings of the European Court of Human Rights without more to undertakings."[120] By contrast, where the effectiveness of EC investigative powers is not at stake, the ECJ seems to adopt a more 'flexible' approach, taking in due consideration the latest jurisprudence on the applicability of Art. 8 ECHR to legal persons and acting consequently.[121] In addition, it should be recalled that in *Spain v UK*, the Court of Justice explicitly acknowledged the obligation of the latter State to comply with the *Matthews* precedent, and, insofar as the national measures adopted to that effect did not infringe EC law, dismissed the pleas brought by the applicant.[122]

---

[114]Case C-7/98 *Krombach* [2000] ECR I-1935.

[115]Case C-60/00 *Carpenter*, n. 112 above.

[116]See more recently, and in the context of an action for annulment, Case C-308/07 P *Koldo Gorostiaga Atxalandabaso* [2009] ECR I-1059.

[117]On the other hand, this technique (i.e. citing by analogy) has allowed the use of the Court of Human Rights' jurisprudence in areas covered by the third pillar (Case C-105/03 *Pupino* [2005] ECR I-5285) thereby enhancing the operative coherence of the ECJ.

[118]See, respectively, Joined cases C-305 to 307, 313 to 316, 318, 325, 328, 329, 335/94 *Limburse Vinyl Maatschappij* [1999] ECR 3283 and Case C-94/00 *Roquette Freres* [2002] ECR I-9011.

[119]See, for instance, Appl. No 43/1994/490/572, *Saunders v. United Kingdom*, (1997) 23 EHHR 313, Appl. No 37971/97, *Ste Colas Est and others v. France*, (2002) 39 EHRR 17 and, more recently, Appl. No 44647/98, *Peck v. UK*, (2003) EHRR I.

[120]Case C-301/04 P *SGL Carbon v. Commission* [2006] ECR I-5915, para 63. It should be noted that in its judgment the ECJ did not feel the need to contest this argumentation.

[121]See Case C-450/06 *Varec* [2008] ECR I-581, para. 48. In particular, the Court was called upon to balance the *audi et alteram partem* principle with the duty to respect confidentiality of the undertakings involved in a contract award procedure.

[122]Case C-145/04 *Spain v UK* [2006] ECR I- 7917, para 60.

The autonomous status of the EC/EU legal order can also be inferred by the fact that the Court of Justice is progressively willing to conduct human rights reasoning without feeling the need to quote the case law of the Strasbourg Court. In *Pergan* the Luxembourg judges assessed the Commission's power to adopt and publish its decisions in the field of competition law against the presumption of innocence principle.[123] Somewhat surprisingly, in determining the pertinence and the scope of application of the principle (including its legal consequences) the ECJ made reference to the sole Charter.[124] Perhaps this amounts to an attempt to further affirm its constitutional role; a posture which closely resembles the one adopted by the ECtHR in *Loizidou v. Turkey.*[125]

In claiming their natural role of ultimate guarantors of the fundamental rights enshrined in the respective constitutional Charters, the ECJ and ECtHR have proven willing and capable of interacting notwithstanding the lack of formal coordination between the EU legal order and the Conventional system. More recently, though, the drive towards independence seems to have taken precedence. In the *Kadi and Al Barakaat* judgment, in fact, the ECJ has relied extensively on the case law of the Strasbourg Court, but significantly characterized its role in "an autonomous legal system which is not prejudiced by an international agreement.[126] The *Hassan* appeal judgment[127] may clarify the position of the ECJ vis a vis the delisting procedure before the UN Committee of Sanctions. It is suggested that confirming the *Kadi and Al Barakaat* precedent (thereby refusing to endorse the *Solange* approach of the German Constitutional Court and supported by ECtHR in *Bosphorus* with regards to the EC/EU legal order[128]), the EUCJ would effectively 'kill two birds with one stone': firstly, it could reconcile the limited jurisdiction of the ECtHR resulting from *Behrami and Saramati*[129] with the need to respect fundamental rights and, secondly, it would prevent a resurgence of the counter-limits doctrine.

---

[123] Case C-474/04 *Pergan Hifsstoffe* [2007] ECR I-4225, paras 75 ff.

[124] See Art. 48 CFR.

[125] N. 7 above.

[126] Joined cases C-402 and 415/05 P *Kadi and Al Barakaat*, n. 80 above, para 316.

[127] Joined cases C-399/06 P and C-403/06 P *Hassan and Ayadi*, still pending.

[128] Although it cannot be excluded that future amendments to the UN listing procedure might lead the ECJ to change its stance.

[129] Appl. Nos 71412/01 and 78166/01, *Behrami and Saramati v. France*, (2007) unreported, paras 121 ff. It will be remembered that in this instance the ECtHR declined its jurisdiction in relation to a pair of cases concerning military personnel from France, Germany and Norway finding that the actions in question were directly attributable to the UN. Most notably, the Grand Chamber held that to decide otherwise would jeopardise the fulfilment of the UN's main mission, that of securing peace and security (para 149).

4 The Protection of Fundamental Rights Under the Lisbon Treaty

So far we have verified the interrelations between the various dimensions involved in the multilevel system of protection of fundamental rights. It is now possible to focus on the modifications inherent to the entry into force of the Lisbon Treaty. As previously mentioned, the latter introduces significant innovations in this regard: on the one side, the binding force of the Charter; on the other, the envisaged accession to the ECHR. These aspects will be analysed with a view to ascertain whether and how they can impact on the EU legal order.

4.1 A Binding Charter of Fundamental Rights

The rejection of the Constitutional Treaty did not affect the resolution to attribute legal force to the Charter. Through a rather peculiar legal ploy the Lisbon Treaty bestows it the status of primary law:

> The Union recognises the rights, freedoms and principles set out in the Charter of Fundamental Rights of the European Union of 7 December 2000, as adapted at Strasbourg, on 12 December 2007, which shall have the same legal value as the Treaties.[130]

It follows that the Charter becomes an integral part of the EU legal order, as opposed to an external source relied upon to affirm autonomous general principles of law. And yet, unlike the Protocols annexed to the Lisbon Treaty (including the one concerning the specific position of the UK and Poland), it has not undergone ratification by the Member States. This anomaly does not affect the binding nature of the Charter but has important legal consequences in relation to possible future amendments. In order to be effective, any modification to the text – be it through a Convention or following the speedier procedure used for its adaptation – should entail a modification of Art. 6 TEU pursuant to Art. 48 TEU.[131] The link between Art. 6 (1) TEU and the Charter is so stringent that the latter can be viewed as a normative expression of the former.[132] However, at a closer look, reference to Art. 2 TEU appears more appropriate. In fact, except for citizenship,

[130] Art. 6 (1) TEU.

[131] L. S. Rossi, 'Le rapport entre Charte des droits fondamentaux et Traité de Lisbonne, online at http://www.europeanrights.eu; L. Daniele, 'Carta dei diritti fondamentali dell'Unione europea e Trattato di Lisbona, (2008) 13 *Il Diritto dell'Unione europea* 655 at 664. For a more flexible interpretation of Art. 6 (1) cf. R. Baratta, 'Le principali innovazioni del Trattato di Lisbona', (2008) 13 *Il Diritto dell'Unione Europea* 21 at 38.

[132] See J. Ziller, *Il nuovo Trattato europeo* (Il Mulino, 2007) 53 and L. Daniele, n. 131 above, 664.

the provision reflects all the principles and rights enshrined in the Charter, specifically addressed in Art. 9 TEU.[133]

The rather peculiar accommodations which assisted the legal upgrading of the Charter include the normative qualification of the relevant interpretative standard: when applying its provisions due regard must be paid to the *Explanations* by the *Praesidium*.[134] This has generated some criticism since the circumstance is deemed to frustrate the role of the EUCJ.[135] By contrast, it is suggested that the *Explanations* may appease all concerns regarding *fuites en avant* by the Court without necessarily impinging on its power of appraisal and interpretation.[136]

In order to ascertain the impact of a binding Charter, two central issues must be addressed: firstly, the scope of the CFR; secondly, whether the existence of two binding instruments for the protection of fundamental rights is admissible and viable. According to Art. 51, the Charter is directed to the EU institutions, bodies, offices and agencies as well as to the Member States when they are "implementing Union law".[137] The provision seems to restrict the field of application of the Charter *ratione materiae* by failing to make reference to the more extensive notion of "*within the scope* of Community law" (as opposed to "when…implementing Union law") elaborated by the ECJ when processing the compatibility of national situations with fundamental rights through Art. 6 TEU.[138] Nevertheless the expression should be interpreted as including omissive internal conducts if uniformity is to prevail.[139] Indeed, the wording of the provision should not be overestimated as the Court has indeed used both formulas,

---

[133] L. S. Rossi, 'Le rapport entre Charte des droits fondamentaux et Traité de Lisbonne, n. 131 above and I. Pernice, 'The Treaty of Lisbon and Fundamental Rights', in S. Griller, J. Ziller (eds.), *The Lisbon Treaty. EU Constitutionalism without a Constitutional Treaty?* (Sprinter, 2008) 235 at 252.

[134] Art. 6 (1) 3rd indent TEU.

[135] R. Baratta, n. 131 above, at 39.

[136] L. S. Rossi, 'Le rapport entre Charte des droits fondamentaux et Traité de Lisbonne, n. 131 above. Although the situation is unprecedented, it should be recalled that when confronted with guidelines or opinions relating to the implementation of certain acts or international agreements the Court has never felt the obligation to comply with the latter. An exemplification of how the EUCJ uses interpretative tools in performing its judicial tasks is offered by Case C-281/02 *Owusu* [2005] ECR I-1383 (referring to the Jenard Report on the 1968 Brussels Convention).

[137] Cf. with the original version of the Charter, [2000] OJ C 364/1.

[138] M. Dougan, 'The Treaty of Lisbon 2007: winning minds, not hearts', n. 36 above, at 663; A. Arnull, A. Dashwood, M. Dougan, M. Ross, E. Spaventa and D. Wyatt, *Wyatt & Dashwood's European Union Law* (Sweet & Mawwell, 2006), at para 9-023; G. Braiband, 'La Charte des droits fondamentaux', (2001) 12 *Droit Social* 69, at 73.

[139] J.-P. Jacqué, 'La Charte des droits fondamentaux…', n. 31 above, at 76.

depending on whether the issue at stake arose within the first or third pillar.[140]

The unified structure of the EU resulting from the Reform Treaty justifies the lexical variation without impinging on the substance. Even after its entry into force, the Member States will remain accountable vis à vis the Union when they transpose EU law into domestic legislation or otherwise give effect to EU law and, more generally, when they derogate from the treaties. In other words – with the notable exception of CFSP related measures – non conformity with the Charter will be assessed whenever the national action (or omission) comes within the 'gravitational orbit' of Union law. It is thus possible to appreciate the scope of Art. 6 (1) and its reference to the *Explanations*. As noted by Pernice, this "may prove to be very effective and useful regarding possible divergencies of the a priori understanding and construction of any specific rights in the different legal cultures and traditions of the 27 Member States."[141]

It is well known that the Charter covers a number of guarantees which find no correspondence in the ECHR, namely social and economic rights, as well as "third generation rights". Whilst the European Social Charter has been adopted to (partially) remedy the shortcomings of the ECHR as regards the first category, the subsequent Protocols and the expansive properties of the ECtHR case law were unable to fully compensate for the lack of explicit provisions concerning new rights, such as, for instance, environmental protection.[142]

These differences reveal something more than physiological asymmetry between two texts for the protection of fundamental rights, elaborated in different times and with a distinct legal scope. To be sure, if the Convention was initially conceived to ensure compliance by the High Contracting Parties with minimum guarantees for human rights, the Charter, especially when dealing with solidarity rights and, more generally, principles[143] –

---

[140]As to the former expression, see Case C-260/89 *ERT*, n. 67 above, para 42, and Case C-159/90 *Grogan* [1991] ECR I-4685, para 31 and, more recently, Case C-246/06 *Velasco Navarro* [2008] ECR I-105, para 31. As to the use of the latter expressions, see Case C-303/05 *Advocaten voor de Wereld VZW*, n. 77 above, para 45, Case C-355/04 P *Segi* [2007] ECR I-1657, para 51; Case C-354/04 P *Gestoras Pro Amnistía* [2007] ECR I-1579, para 51. It is suggested that in these instances the words "when they implement Union Law" were the most appropriate given the lack of direct effect in this area of law.

[141]I. Pernice, 'The Treaty of Lisbon and Fundamental Rights', n. 133 above.

[142]Cf. Joint dissenting Opinion of judges Costa, Ress, Turmen, Zupancic and Steiner in *Hatton v UK* [2003], 37 EHRR 28 where Art. 37 of the Charter was used to support the incorporation of environmental rights in the ECHR. On these aspects, see further in this volume M. Lombardo, 'Chapter 12'.

[143]See Title IV of the CFR on Solidarity (Arts. 27 to 38), encompassing health care, access to services of general economic interest, environmental and consumer protection, just to mention the areas in which, following the adoption of the Charter, there has been a significant development of the European normative framework. It is also interesting to

apart from limiting the discretionary power of executive (national and supranational) organs – is also intended to act as compass for the European legislator (and the Member States), as a "constitutional tool" for the development of the EU legal order. In this regard, it is worth noting that Art. 52(5) CFR draws an important distinction between (enforceable) rights and principles, which may be successfully invoked before national courts only inasmuch as they are implemented by Union or domestic law. Pursuant to Art. 6 (1) 3rd indent TEU, the provision is intended to guide the interpretation and application of the Charter, but no straightforward criterion is offered to distinguish rights from principles.[144] However, the *Explanations* may act as a complementary, residual, legal device capable of assisting the courts in this delicate task.

Likewise, it is possible to differentiate between subjective and potential rights, the full enjoyment of the latter requiring further regulation at the EU level,[145] and between fully and partially justiciable rights, which also presuppose the existence implementing legislation, national or supranational. Social rights represent a good example of this last category as their enforceability will necessarily depend on enactment at whatever level, according to the division of competences set out in the treaties.[146] Nonetheless, if in the absence of such measures individuals may be denied 'their day in court', the Union and the Member States might still be held accountable for violations of the Charter, to the extent that the objectives and principles set out therein are considered to be sufficiently precise.[147]

As anticipated, another aspect which should addressed is the relation between the Charter and the ECHR. The coexistence of two binding instruments of human rights protection is considered admissible both under the

---

observe that pursuant to the Explanations on Art. 52(5) environmental protection falls within the category of "principles".

[144] On the legal uncertainty resulting from the mentioned distinction, see M. Dougan, 'The Treaty of Lisbon 2007', n. 138 above, at 663.

[145] See Art. 45 (2) CFR, providing that: "Freedom of movement and residence may be granted, in accordance with the Treaties, to nationals of third countries legally resident in the territory of a member State".

[146] See e.g. the wording of Arts. 9, 10 (2), 25, 26, 28, 33, 34, 36 CFR. A direct reference to this provision can be found in Case C-438/05 *Viking*, n. 83 above, para 44 and in Case C-341/05 *Laval*, n. 82 above, para 91, where the the rights in question had indeed been excercised on the basis of national provisions. By contrast, Art. 30 (protection in the event of unjustified dismissal) is an example of a directly enforceable (social) right.

[147] As noted by Jacqué, "*il existe…déjà dans les politiques communautaires des objectifs qui sont juridiquement sanctionnables par la Cour, non pas sous forme de droits subjectifs que l'on peut faire valoir par un recours individuel, mais sous la forme d'obligation d'action auxquelles ne peuvent se soustraire les institutions*". In this sense, the author distinguishes between the objective of ensuring a high level of employment (Art. 2 TEC) and the treaty provisions on environmental and consumer law protection. See J.-P. Jacqué, 'La Charte des droits fondamentaux…', n. 31 above, at 74.

Convention and under EU law. As far as the latter is concerned, their complementary nature emerges directly from Arts. 52 (3) and 53 CFR, where the meaning and scope of the rights guaranteed therein are claimed to be the same and understood to offer only a minimum standard of protection.

Art. 52 (3) CFR does not in itself preclude conflicting decisions between the Luxembourg and Strasbourg judges. It is possible to derogate from the rights contained in the Charter provided the customary principles of legality, necessity and proportionality are respected. Moreover, limitation will be tolerated inasmuch as they "meet objectives of general interest recognized by the Union or the need to protect the rights and freedoms of others". [148] Hence, the EUCJ could decide to prioritize a right over another taking into account the specificities of the EU legal order.[149] This hermeneutical operation might very well entail a violation of the Convention, as interpreted by the ECtHR. On the other hand, pursuant to Art. 53 CFR, the ECHR will remain the minimum standard from which the Union cannot depart.

Experience shows that, although improbable, the risk of the two courts offering different interpretations of the ECHR exists, even when the facts of the case at hand are essentially the same.[150] And yet divergences cannot be traced to the coexistence of the two instruments. With the entry into force of the Lisbon Treaty, above and beyond the safeguard provision laid down in Art. 53 CFR, uniformity will be ensured by the EU accession to the ECHR.[151]

That being said, it is well known that the binding nature of the Charter was feared to unduly impinge on national prerogatives. Through a specific Protocol annexed to the Treaties, the UK and Poland obtained a sort of 'opting out' on the Charter, as will the Czech Republic when the next accession take place.[152] The relevant Protocol[153] is accompanied by a number

---

[148] Art. 52 (1) CFR.

[149] See Art. 31 of the Vienna Convention. This might occur, for instance, in the field of antitrust law, where the effectiveness of the Commission's investigatory powers occasionally prevails over the rights of defence of the undertakings involved in the administrative procedure.

[150] Cf., for instance Case C-159/90 *Grogan*, n. 140 above and Appl. No 14234/88 and 14235/88, *Open Door and Dublin Well v. Ireland*, (1992) Series A No 246, and, more recently, *Ste Colas Est v. France*, n. 119 above and C-94/00 *Roquette Freres*, n. 118 above.

[151] See also, Final Report of Working Group II, CONV 352/02.

[152] See in particular European Council, Presidency Conclusions, 29–30 October 2009, para 2. It should, however, be noted that the UK government itself has expressly stated that the Protocol "does not constitute an opt out" (See House of Lords, European Union Committee, *The Lisbon Treaty: an impact assessment*, Tenth Report if Session, 2007–2008, Vol. I, p. 102).

[153] Protocol No 30 on the application of the Charter of Fundamental Rights of the European Union to Poland and to the United Kingdom. As to the reasons for this Protocol, suffice it here to recall that the United Kingdom was mainly concerned with the effect

of Declarations which, on the one side, clarify the concerns of the Polish government (namely the preservation of their conservative and religious values)[154] and, on the other, underscore the need to interpret the Charter in compliance with the constitutional traditions common to the Member States, as already apparent from the reading of Arts. 4 (2) and 6 (3) TEU.[155]

Despite the potentially disruptive nature of the Protocol, which ultimately amounts to a de-constitutionalising effort, legal commentators agree that its impact on the effectiveness of the Charter will be rather limited. Firstly, by expressly acknowledging that the Charter reaffirms existing rights it accepts to be already bound by its provisions under the acquis and the general principles it includes. Secondly, it does not call into question the duty for national authorities to follow the EUCJ's judgments:[156] if the latter ruled, in a case arising outside the UK or Poland, on a measure which applies to all Member States, the Protocol will not waive national courts and tribunals from the obligation to interpret the measure in accordance with that decision. Thirdly, EU legislation passed in areas covered by Title IV of the Charter (and adopted in conformity with the latter) will continue to be binding for both Member States. Fourthly, in cases concerning these two countries "the geographical limits to the scope of the Charter (due to the opting-outs) will probably compel the Court to keep the broader category of general principles alive, as an autonomous source of fundamental rights."[157] Indeed, it is through this 'legal device' that, on the one side, it will be possible to oppose unlikely fall-backs linked to the Protocol, and, on the other, the evolving nature of fundamental rights may be preserved.

From a national perspective, however, the Protocol might have significant side-effects, especially taking into account the different legal traditions of the interested Member States. The UK courts can rely on a solid case law concerning fundamental rights protection and possible breaches of the Charter are most likely to occur when balancing economic freedoms against social rights, a hermeneutical exercise the EUCJ itself will have to engage in the years to come. Indeed, one of the future challenges posed by the newly

---

that the social rights protected by the Charter will have on business. The Poles decided to join the British government although it is apparent from Declaration No 61 that they were mainly concerned with those provisions that risked impinging on their family law. (e.g. Art. 9 – Right to marry and right to found a family).

[154] Cf. Declarations No 61 and 62. Most notably the Poles were concerned that the Charter would prevent them from rejecting homosexual marriage and force them to modify their legislation on abortion.

[155] Declaration No 53 (Czech Republic).

[156] Cf. Art. 1 of Protocol No 30.

[157] L.S. Rossi, 'How Fundamental are fundamental principles?', in G. Ventutini, S. Bariatti (eds), Individual rights and international justice (Liber Fausto Pocar), (Giuffré, 2009) 801 at 815. See also, S. Amadeo, 'Il Protocollo n. 30 sull'applicazione della Carta a Polonia e Regno Unito e la tutela "asimmetrica" dei diritti fondamentali: molti problemi, qualche soluzione', (2009) 14 *Il Diritto dell'Unione europea* 720 at 739.

binding nature of the Charter is the need to weigh the rights it confers on individuals with the fundamental freedoms affirmed in the Treaty. The levelling of these two potentially conflicting interests demands a profound revision of the current 'rule-exception approach'. Provided it is managed soundly, this 'constitutional shift' will produce a legitimising effect and possibly frustrate what is possibly the true scope of the Protocol, that of preventing improper judicial activism from the domestic courts.

Some preoccupation remains as to the Polish judges, which operate in a rather different historical, cultural and legal context. Here the side-effects of the Protocol are undoubtedly more worrisome, although, as previously suggested, it should always be possible to contest violations of the Charter via general principles of EU law or Art. 2 TEU. Moreover, it is noteworthy that Member States, including the UK and Poland, may be subject to the procedure laid down in Art. 7 TEU for breach of minority rights and or equality between men and women.

The effective impact of the Charter should be assessed against this background, but also with respect to other Treaty provisions concerning the internal dimension – and within it the supranational and national level – as well as the external action of the EU. In regard to the former aspect, Art. 19 (1) TEU confirms that the EUCJ must guarantee compliance with the treaties and thus, through Art. 6 (1) TEU, the Charter. In doing so it will enjoy a broader competence in relation to measures allegedly in breach of fundamental rights given that, by virtue of Art. 263 (4) TFEU, individuals may challenge any "regulatory act which is of direct concern to them and does not entail implementing measures". On the other hand, it follows from Art. 67 TFEU, and the *Kadi* precedent, that the legislator, and the EUCJ, will not only have to carefully balance economic freedoms with fundamental rights (with the complications generated by the British and Polish "opting-outs"), but also weigh fundamental rights protection and international security.

As to the national level, Art. 19 (1) TFEU places on the Member States the duty to "provide remedies sufficient to ensure effective legal protection in the fields covered by Union law."[158] This provision, which codifies the consistent case law on the principle of procedural autonomy and reflects the obligation stemming from Art. 47 CFR, assigns to the national parliaments and governments the primary responsibility of guarding the respect of the Charter, but above all highlights the paramount role played by domestic courts in the multilevel system of fundamental rights protection. In this sense, Art. 267 TFEU represents an invaluable instrument in the prevention

[158] This provisions should be read jointly with Art. 291 TFEU, according to which Member States must "adopt all measures of national law necessary to implement legally binding Union acts".

of fundamental rights violations and Art. 6 (1) TEU has undoubtedly put new flesh on the bones of the *Foto-Frost* formula.[159]

Finally, it should not go unnoticed that through Arts. 3 and 21 TEU the Charter is capable of affecting the conditionality policy applied to non EU States in the framework of bilateral agreements, development aid and accession negotiations.[160] Indeed, the Union's international policy shall promote, uphold and comply with its "internal values", stated in Art. 2 TEU and further expressed in the Charter, together with the principles of the United Nations Charter and international law.

4.2 The Accession of the EU to the ECHR: Technical Arrangements, Judicial Interaction and Legal Consequences

As illustrated above, accession to the ECHR has long been on the agenda although the resolution to acquire membership did not materialize in primary law until the adoption of the Constitutional Treaty. The Lisbon Treaty confirms this intention by stating that "The Union *shall* accede to the European Convention for the Protection of Human Rights and Fundamental Freedoms."[161] Pursuant to Art. 218 TFEU,[162] the Council shall act unanimously after obtaining the consent of the European Parliament. Moreover, before it enters into force, the agreement will have to be approved by the Member States in accordance with their respective constitutional requirements. Finally, it should be noted that the EUCJ may – and most probably will – be asked to render an opinion on the compatibility of the envisaged agreement with the Treaties.[163]

The conditions to which the EU may accede are also (pre)determined: according to the specific Protocol annexed to the Lisbon Treaty the agreement shall preserve its specific characteristics and competences and leave the powers of its institutions unaltered.[164] The inclusion of a legal basis for adherence to the Conventional system is not intended to (indirectly) attribute a fundamental rights competence to the Union. In fact, Art. 6 (2) TEU clarifies that "Such accession shall not affect the Union's competences

[159] Case 314/85 *Foto-Frost* [1987] ECR I-4199. See also Case C-461/03 *Gaston Shul* [2005] ECR I-10513.

[160] See further in this volume L. Ficchi, 'Chapter 6'.

[161] Art. 6 (2) TEU (emphasis added).

[162] See in particular paras 6, lett. a, 2nd indent, and 8. Cf. also Art. III-325 of the Constitutional Treaty.

[163] Pursuant to Art. 218, para. 10 TFEU, the opinion may be sought by the Members, the Commission, the Council and the European Parliament.

[164] See Protocol No 8, relating to Art. 6 (2) of the Treaty on European Union on the accession of the Union to the European Convention on the protection of human rights and fundamental freedoms annexed to the Lisbon Treaty, Art. 3.

as defined in the Treaties", thereby guaranteeing the respect of the principle of conferral of powers.[165] As to the Member States, accession cannot modify their situation in relation to the ECHR.[166]

Within the Conventional system, Protocol No 14 – which still awaits ratification by Russia – foresees the possibility for the EU to become a member of the Convention through an amendment of Art. 59.[167] Accession will require an ad hoc agreement in the form of a treaty or an amending protocol to the ECHR.[168] Although both avenues may be pursued, the Convention responsible for drafting the Constitutional Treaty and the Steering Committee for Human Rights (CDDH) expressed preference for the former.[169] The reasons for this are twofold: on the one side, an accession treaty would allow the EU to become a Party to the Convention upon its entry into force, whilst the adoption of an amending Protocol would involve a two tier procedure. On the other side, through an accession treaty it would be possible to define comprehensively the status of the EU within the ECHR as the former organization would be bound by all the provisions contained therein, including those that do not impinge on the original version of the Convention and/or its Protocols.[170]

Be it in the form of an amending protocol or of a treaty, the accession process will need to deal with formal arrangements,[171] as well as the

---

[165]Art. 4 TFEU.

[166]Protocol No 8, n. 164 above, Art. 2.

[167]See Art. 17 of Protocol No 14. This choice followed the decision, on the part of the EU, to include a legal basis for accession in the Constitutional Treaty.

[168]This second option would require signature and ratification by all the States parties to the Convention, and accession to the amended Convention by the EU. See Steering Committee for human rights, *Working group on the legal and technical issues of possible EC/EU Accession to the European Convention on Human Rights*, Strasbourg, 17 June 2002, CDDH(2002). Alternatively, a tacit acceptance clause could be envisaged whereby after a fixed period of time and in the absence of objections, the Protocol would automatically enter into force. A tacit acceptance clause has been introduced, for instance, into the Protocol amending the European Convention on Transfrontier Television providing for its automatic entry into force after a 2 year period, in the absence of any objection (Art. 35).

[169]See, respectively, CONV 354/02, 14 and *Explanatory Report to Protocol No 14* (CETS No 194), para. 101. Nonetheless, in order to allow the future negotiators ample choice of action, Art. 17 of Protocol No 14 avoids any reference to an accession treaty.

[170]See further, P. Manin, 'L'Adhésion de l'Union Européenne à la Convention de sauvegarde des droits de l'homme et des libertés fondamentales', in L.S. Rossi (ed.), *Vers une nouvelle architecture de l'Union européenne* (Bruylant, 2004) 265. Certain supplementary provisions will need to be adopted defining the position of the EU with respect to the various additional protocols, setting out possible transitional periods and clarifying the budgetary contribution of the new member (Steering Committee for human rights, *Working group on the legal and technical issues of possible EC/EU Accession to the European Convention on Human Rights*, Strasbourg, 5 March 2002, GT-DH-EU(2002)009, accessible at http://www.coe.int.) and A. Gianelli, 'L'adesione dell'Unione europea alla CEDU secondo il trattato di Lisbona', (2009) *Dir. Un. Eur.* 678.

[171]Those ECHR provisions referring to 'State' or 'States' 'nation' and 'country' will need to be amended. See further Steering Committee for human rights,

relations between the two systems and the respective judiciaries.[172] Amongst the many, the composition of the ECtHR, its interaction with the EUCJ and the role of the EU within the Council of Ministers deserve particular attention.

As to the former aspect, the current composition of the Strasbourg Court foresees the presence of a judge by each member State so as to ensure that national specificities are duly taken into account. Likewise, the EU legal order should be represented. In this regard, a number of options have been put forward: an ad hoc judge for cases involving EU law; a full time judge with limited participation and a full time judge on equal footing with the other judges.[173] The latter solution is by and large considered to be preferable inasmuch as it would prevent any discrimination amongst the Contracting parties, and thus strengthen the authority and legitimacy of rulings against the Union,[174] but the question remains as to the modalities of the EU judge's participation in the work of the ECtHR. The issue could be settled by establishing a special Chamber with a permanent EU judge – perhaps constituted by a majority of judges elected from EU Member States[175] – or continuing to apply the existing rules, thereby making it a merely organizational matter to be decided within the Court.

The presence of a permanent EU judge in Strasbourg, whether sitting in a specialized Chamber or on equal footing with national judges, does not in itself guarantee that the application is properly addressed, and, consequently, the respect of the specificities of the EU legal order. [176]. Indeed, all problems relating to the subject responsible for a breach of the ECHR should be settled before deciding on the admissibility of the complaint, as

---

Working group on the legal and technical issues of possible EC/EU Accession to the European Convention on Human Rights, Strasbourg, 16 January 2002, GT-DH-EU(2002)006, accessible at http://www.coe.int; and E. Myjer, 'Can the EU Join the ECHR – General conditions and practical arrangements', accessible at http://www.ecln.net/elements/conferences/book_berlin/myjer.pdf.

[172]See Steering Committee for human rights, 16 January 2002, n. 171 above, and Steering Committee for human rights, 5 March 2002, n. 170 above and Reflection Paper prepared by the Secretariat, *Accession of the European Union to the European Convention on Human Rights*, Strasbourg, 8 February 2001, DG-II(2001)002, accessible at http://www.coe.int.

[173]Based on the current formulation of Art. 22 ECHR, the appointment of a full time judge appears to be the most consistent with the spirit of the ECHR. Under the first scenario – which could be implemented without modifying the Convention – for each new case involving the EU, the latter would indicate "a person of its choice who shall sit in the capacity of a judge" (Art. 27 (2) ECHR).

[174]See CONV 295/02, 6.

[175]It has been suggested that non-EU Member States could oppose this circumstance by virtue of an EU overrepresentation. Nonetheless, "à Strasbourg les juges siège à titre individuel (Art. 21, 2) et ne représentent pas la Partie contractante. La présence d'un juge siégeant au titre de l'Union à côté de juges siégeant au titre des Etats membres est donc tout à fait normale" (P. Manin, 'L'Adhésion de l'Union Européenne à la Convention de sauveguarde des droits de l'homme et des libertés fondamentales', n. 170 above, 259).

[176]Protocol No 8, n. 164 above, Art. 1, lett. b.

the latter will depend on whether the violation can be ascribed to a Member State or to the Union.[177]

On the other hand, the Union's system of allocating competences shall be preserved and the Strasbourg Court should be prevented from impinging on issues which are essentially internal to the EU legal order. Similar problems may arise, for instance, when a national Contracting Party is brought before the ECtHR following the application of a regulation or a decision by domestic authorities, or in cases concerning mixed agreements and directives with direct effect. It is true that in similar instances, the EU, intervening pursuant to Art. 36 ECHR,[178] would be entitled to participate in the proceedings, but this situation is rather different from the one where the Union would act as a co-defendant and, consequently, be entitled to the presence of an EU judge.[179] It may thus be appropriate to allow the EU to act as a co-defendant when the case has been brought against a member State, and vice-versa, perhaps after obtaining leave from the European Court.[180] This would ensure the execution of the final judgment without the Court having to decide on the sharing of competences (i.e. responsibilities) between the Union and the interested Member State.

Institutional arrangements should also cover the forms of interaction between the Strasbourg Court and the EUCJ. To a certain extent the informal contacts between the two are considered to be a viable antidote, but the underlying risks require a more sophisticated and effective response.

---

[177] This is particularly true for the requirement of the prior exhaustion of internal remedies prescribed by Art. 35 ECHR.

[178] In order to be invoked by the European Union, this provision need not be amended by changing the expression "national" into "citizen" as the former term already covers the "citizens of the Union" pursuant to Art. 9 TEU. Although the EU Member States would continue to enjoy the right to intervene on behalf of their nationals, and in that instance ask for the involvement of the EU under Art. 36 (2) ECHR, it would be preferable to add a third paragraph to the provision clarifying that the EU may intervene whenever issues of EU law are at stake.

[179] Depending on the solution adopted, this could entail the need to nominate an ad hoc judge, to request that the case be referred to a special Chamber, or to demand the presence of the EU judge. With specific reference to the special Chamber option, it has been suggested that: "a system could be envisaged whereby it would be for a panel of judges – like the one provided for under Art. 43 § 2 of the Convention – to decide, at the request of the parties and/or States concerned or of its own motion, whether in view of its serious implications for Community Law a case against a EU Member State is to be referred to the special Chamber" (*Accession of the European Union to the European Convention on Human Rights*, Strasbourg, 8 February 2001, n. 171 above). It should also be noted that in all the above mentioned scenarios referral to the Grand Chamber would always be allowed in accordance with Art. 43 (1) and (3) ECHR.

[180] See further, *Study carried out within the Council of Europe of technical and legal issues of a possible EC/EU accession to the European Convention on Human Rights*, submitted to the European Convention, Working group II 'Incorporation of the Charter / accession to the ECHR', by A. Vitorino, WD 8, 19.

Declaration No 2 annexed to the Lisbon Treaty acknowledges the existence of such dialogue, which could be reinforced when the Union accedes to that Convention. Taking into consideration the predictable increase in the number of applications before the latter court following accession, the possibility for the EUCJ to submit preliminary references to the ECtHR has received considerable attention. However conceived[181] the procedure would present major legal and political inconveniences: on the one side, it might delay the main proceedings, especially when the EUCJ itself is acting under Art. 267 TFEU;[182] on the other, it appears to contrast with the autonomy of the EU legal order, and most notably with the role and status of the Charter.

These aspects are not the only ones which will need to be tackled during the accession process. In view of the important role played by the Council of Europe in supervising the execution of judgements by the ECtHR,[183] the EU will also have to be represented therein, similarly to what happens today with all Contracting parties. The implications of this participation are twofold. Firstly, it will be a question of determining who will perform such a task. At present, only Member States are entitled to sit and vote in the Committee of Ministers,[184] and the Convention will thus have to be accommodated in order to allow the EU to intervene in the meetings of this body, especially when the latter exercises its duties under Art. 46 (2) ECHR.[185] On the side of the EU, the choice is left to the Member States and the institutions, but the specific characteristics of the Union and Union law will have to be preserved.[186] In accordance with the role it derives from Art. 17 (1) TEU, the Commission would seem to be the most suited body for the task. Its involvement in the Committee of Ministers would ensure the execution of the judgment by guaranteeing that the necessary measures are taken at the appropriate level (national or supranational). This

---

[181] See further, Steering Committee for human rights, 16 January 2002, n. 171 above and European Commission for democracy through law (Venice Commission), *Opinion on the implications of a legally binding EU Charter on Fundamental Rights on Human Rights protection in Europe*, accessible at http://www.venice.coe.int/docs/2003/CDL-AD%282003%29022-e.pdf.

[182] Although the case may never reach the ECJ by reason of an improper reliance on the *acte clair* doctrine (see Case 77/83 *Cilfit* [1984] ECR 1257).

[183] Art. 46 ECHR.

[184] Art. 14 of the Statute of the Council of Europe.

[185] It remains to be seen whether Art. 14 of the Statute of the Council of Europe should also undergo amendment. In this respect it could be argued that the new version of Art. 46 (2) ECHR could be considered a (subsequent) *lex specialis* according to Art. 30 (3) of the Vienna Convention on the Law of Treaties. Perhaps, as suggested by the Secretariat of the Council of Europe, a statutory resolution authorizing and defining the EU's participation would be enough to avoid a lengthy and hefty procedure whilst preserving legal certainty and guaranteeing the overall coherence of the new system.

[186] Protocol No 8, n. 164 above, Art. 1, lett. a.

solution would present the additional advantage of preventing infringement procedures vis à vis Member States following actions taken by the latter to comply with an ECtHR decision.

Secondly, the concrete ways of intervention must be clearly set out.[187] In this respect, the ideal solution would be "to establish a certain parallelism between the participation of the EU in the Court and in the Committee of Ministers."[188] In other words, if the EU were to be recognized the right to a full judge, a permanent seat within the Committee of Ministers should also be granted. Conversely, in the event of an ad hoc judge solution, the new member would participate only when cases concerning EU law are at stake.

Following accession, the EU bodies will be subject to external monitoring by the Strasbourg Court, tantamount to what currently happens with the public authorities of the 47 Member States of the Council of Europe. This will avoid discrepancies in the case law of the two courts, especially taking into account the newly binding nature of the Charter, but will inevitably alter the balance of powers between them. Their role in the respective legal orders, however, shall be preserved.[189] The Court of Justice will "remain the sole supreme arbiter of questions of Union law and of the validity of Union acts" and thus be assimilated, with respect to Strasbourg, to a national Constitutional or Supreme Court.[190] All actions challenging EU measures should firstly be brought before the EUCJ. The Court of Human Rights would keep on acting as an international court to which the individual can turn to plead the violation of the Convention.[191] The prior

[187] The relations between the Council of Europe and the Community currently rest on an informal arrangement. See Exchange of letters between the Secretary General of the Council of Europe and the President of the Commission of the European Communities on 5 November 1996 supplementing the "Arrangement" between the Council of Europe and the European Community concluded on 16 June 1987, accessible at https://wcd.coe.int/ and Exchange of letters agreed upon at the 575th meeting of the Minister's Deputies (14–17 October 1997). In this regard, see further Report by Jean-Claude Juncker, Prime minister of the Grand Duchy of Luxembourg 11 April 2006, Council of Europe – European Union: "A sole ambition for the European continent", 25, accessible at https://wcd.coe.int/.

[188] See Reflection Paper prepared by the Secretariat, *Accession of the European Union to the European Convention on Human Rights*, Strasbourg, 8 February 2001, n. 172 above.

[189] In particular the EUCJ must preserve its monopoly in ensuring the uniform interpretation of EU law. Cf. Opinion 1/91 [1991] ECR I-6079.

[190] CONV 354/02, accessible at http://register.consilium.eu.int/pdf/en/02/cv00/00354en2.pdf. In this regard it should also be recalled that the ECtHR considers itself incompetent to rule on the validity of national laws, interpret international treaties which are binding for the Member States and "even less to settle a dispute between the parties to the treaty as to its correct interpretation" (Appl. No 20689/08, *W. v The Netherlands*, (2009) unreported).

[191] Ibid.

exhaustion of all internal remedies should also apply to preliminary references under Art. 267 TFEU and the ECtHR could be addressed only after the EUCJ has pronounced itself on the matter.[192] On the other hand, it will be recalled that the Lisbon Treaty does not attribute the EU courts jurisdiction over individual claims against Member States for breaches of fundamental rights. Hence, the relations between the two courts should not be intended as a matter of subordination but, rather, of specialization.[193]

Joining its Member States in the ECHR, the EU will most probably cease to benefit from the relaxed conditions set out in *Bosphorus*.[194] However, albeit controversial, it cannot be excluded that this sort of "Solange II approach" will stand the test of accession. This solution has been deemed to be "legally unjustified and politically inopportune"[195] since upon accession there will be no apparent need to balance the protection of human rights with the promotion of international cooperation.[196] Moreover, as underlined by Judges Rozakis, Tulkens, Traja, Botoucharova, Zagrebelsky and Garlicki in their joint concurring opinion in *Bosphorus*:

> In spite of its relatively undefined nature, the criterion "manifestly deficient" appears to establish a relatively low threshold, which is in marked contrast to the supervision generally carried out under the ECHR. ...it seems all the more difficult to accept that Community law could be authorised, in the name of "equivalent protection", to apply standards that are less stringent than those of the European Convention on Human Rights when we consider that the latter were formally drawn on in the Charter of Fundamental Rights of the European Union, itself an integral part of the Union's Treaty establishing a Constitution for Europe.

Finally, differentiating the applicable standards would entail a discrimination between the various contracting parties, which would be particularly difficult to justify vis à vis those countries which are members of the Council of Europe but outside the EU.

Regardless of the ultimate decision concerning the form of accession, the necessary legal arrangements, the representation of the EU within the

---

[192] The situation, however, could be different if the accession agreement foresaw the possibility for the EUCJ to suspend proceedings pending before it and submit a preliminary reference to the ECtHR.

[193] C. Kruger, 'Reflections concerning accession of the European Communities to the European Convention on Human Rights' (2002–2003) 21 *Penn. Int'l Law Rev.*, at 97.

[194] As previously indicated the *Bosphorus* precedent has been recently confirmed in *Cooperatieve Producentenorganisatie v. The Netherlands*, n. 105 above.

[195] O. De Schutter, 'Written contribution for the hearing in Paris on 11 September 2007', in Committee on Legal Affairs and human rights, Accession of the European Union/European Community to the European Convention on Human Rights, accessible at http://assembly.coe.int

[196] See *Heinz v. the Contracting Parties also parties to the European Patent Convention* [1994], 76-A *Decisions and Reports* 125; Appl. No 26083/94, *Waite and Kennedy v. Germany*, (1999), Reports 1999-I, para 72, and Appl. No 28934/95, *Beer and Regan v. Germany*, (1999) unreported, para 62.

ECtHR and its role within the Committee of Ministers, the future agreement will have a notable impact on the functioning of the EU legal order placing the latter under the control of the Strasbourg Court when human rights violations arise. Taking into consideration the number of actors involved, both at an institutional level[197] and at an intergovernmental level,[198] not to mention the lengthy and burdensome procedure laid down in the EU Treaty, the risk of an unfettered procrastination is undisputedly high and negotiations should start immediately.[199]

5 Future Perspectives: Developing a Coherent System of Fundamental Rights Protection in Europe

The complex legal framework which governs the relations between the national, supranational and international dimensions have been assessed taking into account the status of the ECHR in the domestic legal order, the obligations deriving from EU membership as well as the relevant case law of the ECJ and the Strasbourg Court. In this regard, judicial interaction certainly reveals the struggle between the need to preserve the autonomous nature of the respective legal orders, but also shows the prioritization of coherence in the protection of human rights. Mutual acknowledgement, though, is not sufficient. The expansion of EU competences, combined with the binding effect of the Charter, is likely to increase the number of human rights cases brought before the EUCJ and, by consequence, the risk of divergences with respect to the jurisprudence of the ECtHR.

The Lisbon Treaty successfully addresses the need to develop a comprehensive approach to fundamental rights protection in Europe, although the process will be complete only when the Union accedes to the ECHR, and this may take some time. The complementary nature of the newly binding Charter and the ECHR, with the Strasbourg Court having the final word on cases strictly concerning "human rights violations" and the EUCJ preserving its role of Constitutional / Supreme Court will ensure that at all levels the individual is allowed the highest possible standard of protection, in a

[197]On the one side, the Council, the Commission, the European Parliament and the Court of Justice; on the other, the Council of Ministers, the Parliamentary Assembly and the Strasbourg Court.

[198]The 27 EU countries on the one hand; the 47 Member States of the Council of Europe on the other.

[199]The early start of the accession process has frequently been advocated following the adoption of the Constitutional Treaty. See, for instance, 21st Quadripartite meeting Council of Europe / European Union, CM/Inf(2005)19, 17 March 2005, accessible at https://wcd.coe.int/. Moreover, the 46 Heads of State and Government of the Council of Europe's Member States reiterated this resolution during their meeting in Warsaw in May 2005.

system where the work of the courts is harmonised and ultimately more consistent, efficient and effective.

The binding nature of the Charter, which in principle provides for a more extensive protection with respect to the ECHR, will guarantee the respect of fundamental rights *acquis* in the elaboration and implementation of EU law. In this sense, some authors have suggested that the UK and Polish Protocol on the Charter is not capable of impacting significantly on the application of the Charter in these two countries. On the other hand, it can be said that accession would lessen the risk of contrasting decisions between the two courts (curing the amnesia which on some occasions seems to affect the Court of Justice in referencing the relevant counterpart's jurisprudence[200]) and eliminate the shortcomings of the equivalent protection doctrine. Strasbourg could carry out a full and effective judicial review of EU directly applicable acts such as regulations and assess whether the EUCJ stroke the correct balance between human rights and other public and private interests, or failed to decide "within a reasonable time" pursuant to Art. 6 ECHR. The expected (and feared) increase in the workload in Strasbourg undoubtedly is cause for concern but it should not be forgotten that the entry into force of Protocol No 14 of the ECHR will allow for a less cumbersome handling of clearly inadmissible complaints and manifestly well-founded cases.[201]

However, accession should not generate dangerous misunderstandings. The new multilevel system of protection resulting from the Lisbon Treaty does not affect the relation between the national and international level, neither does it impinge on the primacy of EU law, which now comprises a binding catalogue of fundamental rights. The fact that the Charter has become effective prior to accession is believed to prevent national courts from erroneously viewing Strasbourg as the primary guarantor of fundamental rights. On the contrary, the Union will progressively become the reference point in this domain. On the one side, its impetus in the promotion of the common values enshrined in Arts. 2 and 6 TEU will hopefully be supported by a more pro-active attitude on the part of the Fundamental Rights Agency; on the other, individuals, which are increasingly aware of the administrative and judicial remedies available to them under EU law, will exploit the existence of a *Bill of rights* applicable to both the

---

[200]See Case C-50/00P *UPA* [2002] ECR I-6677; Case C-263/02 *Jégo Quéré* [2004] ECR I-3425 where the ECJ made no reference to the latest and relevant case law on Art. 6 ECHR, Appl. No 27824/95, *Posti & Rahko v. Finland*, (2002) Reports 2002-VII.

[201]See G. Cohen-Jonathan, J.-F. Flauss, *La réforme du système de contrôle contentieux de la Convention européenne des droits de l'homme* (Bruylant, 2005); S. Greer, 'Protocol 14 and the Future of th European Court of Human Rights', (2005) *Public Law* 83; B. Nascimbene, 'Le Protocole n. 14 à la Convention Européenne des droits de l'homme à la lumière de ses travaux préparatoires', (2006) 67 *Revue Trimestrielle de droits de l'homme* 531.

EU institutions and national authorities when implementing or otherwise giving effect to, or derogating from, EU law.

In conclusion, the Lisbon Treaty allows the creation of a more complete, coherent and consistent legal framework. How things will evolve in the future is of course open to speculation and a careful monitoring of the progress in this area, jurisprudential and normative, is therefore an unavoidable necessity.

The European Charter of Fundamental Rights and the Courts

Valentina Bazzocchi

1 Preliminary Remarks

This Chapter aims to highlight how the Charter of Fundamental Rights of the EU (hereinafter, CFR or the Charter) has been used by the Community Courts and national judges. This will make it possible to ascertain its legal value before the entry into force of the Lisbon Treaty. As will be seen, it is remarkable how this document has increasingly become a point of reference for the Courts.

Commentators have devoted great attention to the legal status of the Charter. After its solemn proclamation in December 2000, it was commonly accepted that, contrary to the expectations of some of the members of the Convention,[1] the CFR was formally not a legally binding instrument. However, this did not prevent the Charter from acquiring autonomous dignity being mentioned in acts adopted by the Community Institutions and quoted in the judgments delivered by the National, as well as by the European Courts.[2]

At a normative level, it can be noted that in carrying out their legislative function (i.e. submitting proposals and adopting the relevant acts) the EU Institutions seem to have taken the Charter seriously, albeit, occasionally,

V. Bazzocchi (✉)
CIRDE (Interdepartmental Research Centre on European Law), University of Bologna, Bologna, Italy
e-mail: vbazzocchi@cirdce.unibo.it

[1]On the process which led to the adoption of the Charter, see in this volume the contribution by O. Zetterquist, 'Chapter 1'.

[2]See P. Mengozzi, 'La tutela dei diritti umani nella giurisprudenza comunitaria', in L. S. Rossi, *Carta dei diritti fondamentali e Costituzione dell'Unione europea* (Giuffré, 2002) 51. The solemn declaration of the Charter marked a turning point with regards to European integration, highlighting the shift from the "Europe of the Market" to the "Europe of the Rights". See A. Manzella, 'Dopo Nizza: la Carta dei diritti "proclamata"', in L. S. Rossi, *Carta dei diritti fondamentali e Costituzione dell'Unione europea*' (Giuffré, 2002) 245.

G. Di Federico, *The EU Charter of Fundamental Rights*, Ius Gentium: Comparative Perspectives on Law and Justice 8, DOI 10.1007/978-94-007-0156-4_3,

in a rather 'formal' sense.[3] This should not come as a surprise considering the statements issued by the Presidents of the European Commission and the European Parliament at the time of its adoption, where they committed the respective institutions to comply with the rights contained in the Charter when exercising their powers.

It has correctly been stated that in this way the Charter becomes a sort of 'code of conduct' of the European Institutions which will influence the Community's legislative process,[4] with the exception of the Common Foreign and Security Policy. All acts concerning fundamental rights undergo a preliminary evaluation in order to verify their compatibility with the Charter, which is generally invoked in the Recitals. This reference should not be understood as a standard clause, but rather as a parameter of compatibility with the Charter.[5] This test is even more important after *Bosphorus*[6] where the European Court of Human Rights (hereinafter, ECtHR) found that the protection of fundamental rights by Community law can be considered to be 'equivalent' to that of the Convention.

It follows from the above that the Charter is not merely a symbolic text. So much so that references to the document can be found in the opinions of the Advocates General in the case law of the Court of First

[3] As far as the European Commission is concerned, cf. Communication of the President of the Commission, 12 March 2001, SEC (2001)380/3 and the Communication of the Commission, 27 April 2005, COM (2005) 172 final. As to the European Parliament, cf. new Art. 34 of the Internal Regulation of the European Parliament, 15 February 2005. Also see A., Iliopoulou,' Assurer le respect et la promotion des droits fondamentaux: un nouveau défi pour l'Union européenne', (2007) *Cahiers de droit européen*, 433.

[4] L.S. Rossi, '"Costituzionalizzazione" dell'UE e dei diritti fondamentali', in L.S. Rossi (ed.) *Carta dei diritti fondamentali e Costituzione dell'Unione europea* (Giuffré, 2002) 267. In the European Parliament Resolution of 15 March 2007, P6-TA-PROV(2007)0078, on compliance with the Charter of Fundamental Rights in the Commission's legislative proposals: methodology for systematic and rigorous monitoring, the European Parliament called upon the Commission to verify the compliance of legislative proposals not only with all European and international instruments regarding fundamental rights, but also with the Charter of Fundamental Rights. This resolution, that contains many pragmatic suggestions, emphasises the "self-obligation" of the European Institutions. See G. Bronzini, V. Piccone, 'Parlamento europeo, Corte di Giustizia e Corte di Strasburgo rilanciano la Carta di Nizza: un messaggio alla futura Conferenza intergovernativa?', accessible at www.europeanrights.eu. According to F. Ippolito ('Ricominciamo dalla Carta dei diritti', in G. Bisogni, G., Bronzini, V. Piccone (eds.), *I giudici e la Carta dei diritti dell'Unione europea* (Chimienti, 2006) 24) the Charter should set the legal standard to be observed by all European Institutions.

[5] In this sense, cf. the Opinion of Advocate General Colomer in case C-207/04 in which it can be read: "the Charter of Fundamental Rights of the European Union, apart from the controversy regarding its legal nature, has had a significant influence on legislation planned and approved since it was proclaimed". On the contribution Advocates General have brought to the use of the Charter, see Section 2.

[6] Appl. No 45036/98, *Bosphorus v. Ireland*, (2005) 42 EHRR. Also see Section 5.

Instance (hereinafter, CFI) and of the European Court of Justice (hereafter, ECJ or EUCJ) and has even been invoked by the ECtHR and by constitutional courts of the Member States. Still, the use made of the Charter varies considerably and deserves closer consideration.

2 The Advocates General and the First References to the Charter

The first reference to the Charter dates back to the 2001 *TRACO* case[7] where AG Colomer mentioned Art. 36 CFR ("Access to services of general economic interest") soon after Art. 16 of the EC Treaty without questioning the nature and the status of the Charter. Thereafter, Advocates General have consistently referred to the Charter,[8] although in a rather different way.

In many cases the Advocates General did not take into consideration the value of the Charter, but invoked it to confirm or to support the existence of rights resulting from the European Convention for the Protection of Human Rights and Fundamental Freedoms (hereinafter, ECHR) and/or the EC Treaty.[9] Precisely because the Charter was conceived as a document of

[7] Case C-340/99 *TNT Traco SpA v. Poste Italiane SpA* [2001] ECR I-4109, AG Alber.

[8] Suffice it to recall that in 2001, the Charter was mentioned in 17 Opinions.

[9] Case C-340/99 *TNT Traco SpA v. Poste Italiane SpA*, n. 7 above, AG Alber; Case C-126/01 *Ministère de l'Économie, des Finances et de l'Industrie v. GEMO* [2003] ECR I-13769, AG Jacobs; Case C-112/00 *E. Schmidberger and Others v. Austria* [2003] ECR I-5659, AG Jacobs; Case C-491/01 *Tobacco Investments and Imperial Tobacco* [2002] ECR I-11453, AG Geelhoed; Case C-338/00P *Volkswagen v. Commission* [2003] ECR I-9189, AG Colomer; Case C-217/00 *P Buzzi UNICEM S.p.a* [2004] ECR I-123, AG Colomer; Case C-256/01 *D. Allonby v. Accrington & Rossendale College and Others* [2004] ECR I-873, AG Geelhoed; Case C-117/01 *KB v. National Health Service Pensions Agency and Others* [2004] ECR I-541, AG Colomer; Case C-353/01 P *Mattila v. Council and Commission* [2004] ECR I-1073, AG Léger; Case C-386/02 *J. Baldinger v. Pensionsversicherungsanstalt der Arbeiter* [2004] ECR I-8411, AG Colomer; Case C-456/02 *M. Trojani v. CPAS* [2004] ECR I-07573, AG Geelhoed; Case C-36/02 *Omega Spielhallen v. Oberbürgermeisterin der Bundesstadt Bonn* [2004] ECR I-9609, AG Stix-Hackl; C-384/02 *Criminal proceedings against Knud Grøngaard and Allan Bang* [2005] ECR I-9939, AG General Poiares Maduro; Case C-457/02 *Criminal proceedings against Antonio Niselli* [2004] ECR I-10853, AG Kokott; Case C-105/03 *Criminal proceedings against M. Pupino* [2005] ECR I-5285, AG Kokott; Case C-347/03 *ERSA v. Ministero delle Politiche Agricole e Forestali* [2005] ECR I-3785, AG Jacobs (insisting on the fact that the text of the Charter was included into the European Constitution); Case C-540/03 *Parliament v. Council* [2006] ECR I-5769, AG Kokott; Case C-3/05 *G. Verdoliva v. J. M. Van der Hoeven BV and Others* [2006] ECR I-1579, AG Kokott; Case C-94/04 *Federico Cipolla* [2006] ECR I-11421, AG Poiares Maduro; Case C-354/04 P *Gestoras Pro Amnistía and Others v. Council* [2007] ECR I-1579, AG Mengozzi; Case C-428/04 *Commission v. Austria* [2006] ECR I-3325, AG Colomer; Case C-444/05 *Aikaterini Stamatelaki v. OAEE* [2007] ECR I-3185, AG Colomer; Case C-64/05

transcription and consolidation of fundamental rights protected within the EC legal order, the Advocates General considered that the Charter could not be ignored when deciding how to resolve issues regarding fundamental rights.[10]

In some cases the Charter was quoted after the ECHR to confirm a specific right contained therein. In the *Evans* case AG Alber affirmed that:

> Article 6 of the ECHR, already incorporated into Community law, and Article 47 of the Fundamental Rights Charter, which cover in large measure the same substantive ground, may serve as a guideline for this purpose.[11]

A similar solution was adopted in the *Tobacco* case where AG Geelhoed claimed that the right to an effective remedy before a tribunal laid down in Arts. 6 and 13 ECHR had been transposed into Art. 47 CFR.[12] When referring to these provisions Geelhoed insists on the distinction between the ECHR and the Charter highlighting the fact that the latter has an "internal character" and should be understood as a source of EC law.

In other cases, Advocates General used the Charter as a source of rights, emphasising that it is not in itself binding but is nonetheless of great relevance.[13] In this regard, the opinion in the *BECTU* case is noteworthy.[14] Here, AG Tizzano referred to the CFR to stress that the right to remunerated annual leaves constitutes a fundamental right. He admitted that *stricto sensu* the Charter has no legislative scope and thus no binding force. Nonetheless, this document had "the purpose of serving, where

---

P *Sweden v. Commission and Others* [2007] ECR I-11389, AG Poiares Maduro; Case C-450/06 *Varec*, accessible at http://curia.europa.eu/, AG Sharpston; Case C-267/06 *Tadao Maruko* accessible at http://curia.europa.eu/, AG Colomer; Case C-123/08 *Wolzenburg*, accessible at http://curia.europa.eu; Case 14/08 *Roda Golf & Beach Resort SL,* accessible at http://curia.europa.eu.

[10]R. Bifulco, M. Cartabia, A. Celotto, (eds.), *L'Europa dei diritti. Commento alla Carta dei diritti fondamentali dell'Unione europea* (il Mulino, 2001). See also P. Eeckhout, 'The EU Charter of fundamental rights and the federal question', (2002) *Common Market Law Review* 945.

[11]Case C-63/01 *S.S. Evans v. The Secretary of State for the Environment, Transport and the Regions* [2003] ECR I-14447, AG Alber, para 84.

[12]Case C-491/01, *British American Tobacco* [2003] ECR I-11453, AG Geelhoed, para 47.

[13]The Charter appeared as a text reaffirming rights already contained in other instruments; see Case C-270/99P, *Z v. European Parliament* [2001] ECR I-9197, AG Jacobs; C-413/99, *Baumbast and R v. Secretary of State for the Home Department* [2002] ECR I-7091, AG Geelhoed; Case C-313/99, *G. Mulligan and Others v. Minister for Agriculture and Food* [2002] ECR I-5719, AG Geelhoed; Case C-224/00, *Commission v. Italy* [2002] ECR I-2965, AG Stix-Hackl; C-50/00, *Unión de Pequeños Agricultores v. Council* [2002] ECR I-6677, AG Jacobs; Case C-111/02 P, *Parliament v. P. Reynolds* [2004] ECR I-5475, AG Geelhoed; Case C-547/03P, *AIT v. Commission* [2006] ECR I-845, AG Stix-Hackl; Case C-76/06P, *Britannia Alloys & Chemicals Ltd v. Commission* [2007] ECR I-4405, AG Bot; Case C-350/06, *Gerard Schultz-Hoff v. Deutsche Rentenversicherung Bund*, accessible at http://curia.europa.eu/, AG Trstenjak; Case C-480/08, *Maria Teixeira*, accessible at http://curia.europa.eu, AG Kokot.

[14]Case C-173/99, *BECTU* [2001] ECR I-4881, AG Tizzano.

its provisions so allow, as a substantive point of reference for all those involved – Member States, institutions, natural and legal persons – in the Community context".[15] The Advocate General concluded his analysis by explaining that in proceedings concerned with the nature and scope of a fundamental right, the relevant statements of the Charter cannot be ignored because it "provides us with the most reliable and definitive confirmation of the fact that the right to paid annual leave constitutes a fundamental right".[16] Hence, it can be argued that the inclusion of a right in the Charter confirms its status as a fundamental right.[17]

Of course, this affects the scope and value of the CFR. As AG Léger underlined in his Opinion in *Hautala*:

> the nature of the rights set down in the Charter of Fundamental Rights precludes it from being regarded as a mere list of purely moral principles without any consequences.[18]

Those principles are common to the legal traditions of the Member States, which have ultimately safeguarded their protection.[19] In *Seda Kücükdeveci,* AG Bot, referring to previous case-law concerning the prohibition of age discrimination, went so far as to state that :

> la mise en exergue d'un tel principe (de non discrimination) par la Cour correspond à l'évolution de ce droit telle qu'elle résulte, d'une part, de l'inscription de l'âge en tant que critère prohibé de discrimination à l'article 13, paragraphe 1, CE et, d'autre part, de la consécration de l'interdiction des discriminations fondées sur

---

[15] Ibid., para 28.

[16] Ibid.

[17] See also case C-350/06 *Schultz-Hoff*, n. 13 above, AG Trstenjak on the right to be paid annual leaves. The Advocate General concluded that the inclusion of this right in the Charter appears to provide the most reliable and definitive confirmation that it constitutes a fundamental right. In this case, AG Trstenjak, although recognizing that the Charter has not been attributed a genuine legislative scope, opined that it would be wrong to deny the Charter any relevance in interpreting Community law. Irrespective of the question of the definitive legal status of the Charter within the legal system of the European Union, it already constitutes a concrete expression of shared fundamental European values and it also reflects constitutional traditions common to the Member States. This premise was followed by the conclusion that it is perfectly legitimate to refer to the Charter when interpreting Community law. It is interesting to note that the same AG Trstenjak in *Martín Martín* affirmed, with regard to the provisions of the Charter, that "it should be pointed out that they fall outside the scope of the Community legal order and thus the Court has no jurisdiction over their interpretation. In their Opinions, the advocates general none the less often have recourse to them in their reasoning, and the Court itself has already mentioned the Charter in the grounds of its judgments. In this case, the provisions of the Charter can therefore be used as an aid to interpreting the provisions of Directive 85/577, but it will not be possible to rely on them in answering the question referred", Case 227/08, *Martín Martín,* at http://curia.eu.

[18] Case C-353/99 P *Hautala* [2001] ECR I-9565, AG Léger, para 80.

[19] Cf. Case C-105/04 *Grothandel op Elektrochnisch Gebied* [2006] ECR I-8725, AG Kokott, Case C-10/05 *Mattern and Cikotic* [2006] ECR I-3145, AG Kokott and Case C-555/07 *Seda Kücükdeveci,* at http://www.curia.eu, AG Bot.

l'âge comme étant un droit fondamental, ainsi qu'il résulte de l'article 21, paragraphe 1, de la charte des droits fondamentaux de l'Union européenne. Certes, le raisonnement de la Cour aurait certainement été plus convaincant s'il s'était appuyé sur ces éléments, au-delà des seuls instruments internationaux et traditions constitutionnelles communes aux États membres qui, dans leur majorité, n'identifient pas un principe spécifique d'interdiction des discriminations en raison de l'âge.[20]

It follows from the examined opinions that the provisions of the Charter have been invoked to demonstrate the increased importance of some fundamental rights within the EC legal order.

Legal commentators pointed out that the Charter could be used to clarify the content and scope of the "constitutional traditions common to the Member States", which represent a rather difficult category to define, offering a more authentic and more prominent interpretative tool with respect to the national constitutions.[21] In this sense, even before the entry into force of the Lisbon Treaty, the CFR could significantly affect the role of the ECJ, exalting its aspiration to become a Constitutional Court.[22]

In this hermeneutical effort the judges are assisted by the Presidium Explanations, which are devoid of any legal value, but are intended to shed light upon the meaning and scope of the various provisions of the Charter as they were discussed within and elaborated by the Convention.[23] Reference to the latter, for instance, can be found in the Opinion delivered by AG

[20]Case C-555/07, *Seda Kücükdeveci*, n. 19 above, para 77 (only the French version is available).

[21]L.S. Rossi, '"Costituzionalizzazione" dell'UE e dei diritti fondamentali', n. 4 above 271. The Charter has limited the discretionary power of the ECJ and CFI in appraising fundamental rights. See A. Ruggieri, 'Carta europea dei diritti e integrazione interordinamentale, dal punto di vista della giustizia e della giurisprudenza costituzionale (notazioni introduttive)', in A. Pizzorusso, R. Romboli, A. Ruggeri, A. Saitta, G. Silvestri (eds.), *Riflessi della Carta europea dei diritti sulla giustizia e la giurisprudenza costituzionale: Italia e Spagna a* confronto (Giuffré, 2003) 12 and, in the same volume, the contribution by C. Pinelli, 'La Carta europea dei diritti e il processo di "costituzionalizzazione" del diritto europeo' 70. This led many commentators to consider the Charter as a precious instrument for the protection of fundamental rights. Cf. Case C-303/05, *Advocaten voor de Wereld* [2007] ECR I-3633, AG Colomer; see also L. Diez-Picazo, 'Notes sur la nouvelle Charte des droits fondamentaux de l'Union européenne', (2002) *Revue Européenne de Droit Public* 937; C. Di Turi, 'La prassi giudiziaria relativa all'applicazione delle Carta di Nizza', (2002) *Il Diritto dell'Unione europea*, 681. See also R. Romboli, 'Carta europea dei diritti e garanzie giurisdizionali (notazioni introduttive)', in A. Pizzorusso, R. Romboli, A. Ruggeri, A. Saitta, G. Silvestri (eds.), *Riflessi della Carta europea dei diritti sulla giustizia e la giurisprudenza costituzionale: Italia e Spagna a* confronto (Giuffré, 2003) 110.

[22]M. Cartabia, 'La Carta di Nizza, i suoi giudici e l'isolamento della Corte costituzionale italiana', in A. Pizzorusso, R. Romboli, A. Ruggeri, A. Saitta, G. Silvestri (eds.), n. 21 above, 211.

[23]See also Appl. No 63235/00, *Vilho Eskelinen and Others v. Finland* (2007), accessible at www.echr.coe.int.

Misho in *D. v. Council*,[24] where they are invoked to affirm and explain the difference between marriage and homosexual unions.

There are also cases in which the Charter has been referred to in order to confirm the existence of these rights, but only in the footnotes. If, on the one hand, this demonstrates that it is not possible to ignore this text, on the other it reveals the difficulties in placing it amongst the sources of EC law.[25] On several occasions Advocates General have used the Charter as a text acknowledging existing rights with no further specification and, hence, without dwelling on its scope and value.[26] Also, the provisions contained in the CFR can clarify the meaning of the rights recognised by other texts. Indeed, in the Opinion delivered in *Bourquain*, AG Ruiz-Jarabo Colomer affirmed that:

> a clearer glimpse of this horizon is given with the independent declaration of the *ne bis in idem* principle in the Charter of the Fundamental Rights of the European Union.[27]

Some legal commentators have argued that, despite its undeniable clarifying function,[28] the Charter is capable of promoting a higher standard of protection than the one resulting from the sum of the rights contained therein. The Charter has an undeniable added value: it contributes to create

---

[24]Joined Cases C-122/99 and C-125/99 *D. v. Council* [2001] ECR I-04319, AG Mischo, para 97.

[25]Case C-49/00 *Commission v. Italy* [2001] ECR I-8575, AG Stix-Hackl; Case C-309/99 *J. C. J. Wouters and Others v. Algemene Raad van de Nederlandse Orde van Advocaten* [2002] ECR I-1577, AG Léger; Case C-60/00 *M. Carpenter v. Secretary of State for the Home Department* [2002] ECR I-6279, AG Stix-Hackl; Case C-459/99 *MRAX v. Belgium* [2002] ECR I-6591, AG Stix-Hackl; Case C-417/02 *Commission v. Greece* [2004] ECR I-7973, AG Kokott; Case C-186/04 *P Housieaux v. Délégués du conseil de la Région de Bruxelles-Capitale* [2005] ECR I-3299, AG Kokott; Case C- 503/03 *Commission v. Spain* [2006] ECR I-1097, AG Kokott; Case C-408/03 *Commission v. Belgium* [2006] ECR I-2647, AG Colomer; Case C-205/03 *FENIN v. Commission* [2006] ECR I-6295, AG Poiares Maduro; Case C-283/05 *ASML Netherlands BV v. SEMIS* [2006] ECR I-12041, AG Léger; Case C-441/05 *Roquette Frères v. Ministre de l'Agriculture, de l'Alimentation, de la Pêche et de la Ruralité* [2007] ECR I-1993, AG Kokott; Case C- 402/05P *Kadi v. Council and Commission*, accessible at http://curia.europa.eu, AG Poiares Maduro.

[26]Case C-270/99 P *Z. v. Parliament*, n. 13 above, AG Jacobs; C-413/99 *Baumbast and R v. Secretary of State for the Home Department*, n. 13 above, AG Geelhoed; Case C-313/99 *G. Mulligan and Others*, n. 13 above, AG Geelhoed; Case C-224/00 *Commission v. Italy*, n. 13 above, AG Stix-Hackl; C-50/00 *Unión de Pequeños Agricultores v. Council*, n. 13 above, AG Jacobs; Case C-111/02 P *Parliament v. P. Reynolds*, n. 13 above, AG Geelhoed; Case C-547/03P *AIT v. Commission*, n. 13 above, AG Stix-Hackl; Case C-76/06P *Britannia Alloys & Chemicals Ltd*, n. 13 above, AG Bot; Case C-317 to 320/08, *Rosalba Alassini and Others*, AG Kokot.

[27]Case C-297/07 *Bourquain* [2008], accessible at http://curia.europa.eu.

[28]The added value of the Charter can be appreciated taking into consideration the fact that many of the rights contained therein are "hidden" within the meanders of the case law.

a European identity.[29] Its elaboration falls within the EU "constitutionalisation process", codifying and reaffirming certain rights which derive from the legal traditions common to the Member States, the EU and the EC treaties, the ECHR and the case law of Luxemburg and Strasbourg courts.[30] In the Opinion delivered in *Advocaten voor Wereld*, AG Colomer affirmed that:

> the Union must respect those rights and the Court must protect them, in accordance with Articles 6 EU and 46(d) EU, whatever the legal nature and force of the instrument adopted in December 2000.[31]

This statement suggests that regardless of its legal status, substance should prevail. The Charter could be considered a privileged instrument for identifying fundamental rights. It is perceived as "an invaluable reflection of the common denominator of the legal values paramount in Member States, from which emanate, in their turn, the general principles of Community law"[32] and as "the catalogue of fundamental rights guaranteed by the Community legal order".[33]

Hence, it is not surprising that the Charter was included in the second part of European Constitutional Treaty,[34] thus becoming legally binding. It is well-known that the 2005 French and Dutch negative referenda have brought the ambitious project of a European Constitution to an end. However, it is interesting to note that during the period between the signing of the European Constitution and the decision of the European Council of Brussels of 21–22 June 2007 to proceed by adopting a new Reform

[29] L.S. Rossi, '"Costituzionalizzazione" dell'UE e dei diritti fondamentali', n. 4 above, 279 ff. See also A. Anzon, 'La Costituzione europea come problema', (2000) *Rivista di Diritto Costituzionale* 656; S. Rodotà, 'Ma l'Europa già applica la nuova Carta dei diritti?', newspaper article which appeared in *La Repubblica*, 3 January 2001.

[30] Case C-341/05 *Laval* [2007] ECR I-11767, AG Mengozzi. On the added value of the Charter, see A. Celotto, 'Giudici nazionali e Carta di Nizza: disapplicazione o interpretazione conforme?', in G. Bronzini, V. Piccone (eds.), *La Carta e le Corti.. I diritti fondamentali nella giurisprudenza europea multilivello* (Chimienti, 2007) 30. It should also be mentioned that in Case C-305/05 *Ordre des barreaux francophones et germanophone and Others* [2007] ECR I-5305, AG Poiares Maduro claimed that the Charter indicates the existence of a right (activating a sort of presumption *iuris tantum*) and offers useful indications as to its content and scope.

[31] Case C-303/05 *Advocaten voor Wereld*, n. 21 above, AG Colomer, para 77.

[32] Case C-208/00 *Überseering* [2002] ECR I-9919, AG Colomer, para 59.

[33] Case C-20/00 *Booker Aquaculture*, [2003] ECR I-7411, AG Mischo, para 126; Case C-181/03 P *Albert Nardone v. Commission* [2005] ECR I-199, AG Poiares Maduro; see also, Joined Cases C-387/02, C-391/02 and C-403/02 *Criminal proceedings against S. Berlusconi and Others* [2005] ECR I-3565, AG Kokott.

[34] The provisions of the Charter have been transposed, with some necessary adaptations, in Arts. II-61 to II-114 of the Treaty Establishing a Constitution for Europe, [2004] OJ C 310/1.

Treaty, the Advocates General have invoked the second part of the Treaty Establishing a Constitution for Europe.[35]

In relation to the future legal value of the Charter, AG Bot affirmed that the Court would inevitably be called upon to rule on cases that raise the problem of the application of Directives contributing to guarantee fundamental rights protection between individuals. This is because the fundamental rights contained in the Charter are often included in such normative instruments.[36]

At the end of this brief excursus it can be said that in most cases the Advocates General referred to the Charter considering it as a valid instrument to solve fundamental rights issues in cases pending before the ECJ.[37] As will be seen, the latter has initially failed to attribute great importance to the document although it ultimately accepted its relevance within the EU legal order.

3 The European Court of First Instance: The Forerunner in Using the Charter for Dispute Settlement

The case law of the Court of First Instance was also influenced by the adoption of the Charter. The latter was called upon to enforce this text just two months after its solemn proclamation. In *Mannersmannröhrer*[38] the appellant invoked the Charter as a source of law which needed close consideration when determining the scope of the right to maintain silence (a specific manifestation of the right of defence), protected by Art. 6 (1) ECHR. Since the contested measure was prior to the adoption of the Charter, the latter could not be used to appreciate the legitimacy of the former.[39] The solution was therefore strongly influenced by considerations attaining

[35] Case C-209/03 *D. Bidar v. London Borough of Ealing and Others* [2005] ECR I-2119, AG Geelhoed; Case C-176/03 *Commission v. Council* [2005] ECR I-7879, AG Colomer; Case C-436/04 *Criminal proceedings against L. Henri Van Esbroeck* [2006] ECR I-2333, AG Colomer; Case C-499/04 *H. Werhof v. Freeway Traffic Systems GmbH & Co. KG* [2006] ECR I-2397, AG Colomer; Case C-212/06 *Government of Communauté française and Gouvernement Wallon v. Gouvernement Flamand*, accessible at http://curia.europa.eu/, AG Sharpston; Case C-303/05 *Advocaten voor de Wereld*, n. 21 above, AG Colomer.

[36] Case 555/07 *Seda Kücükdeveci*, AG Bot n. 19 above.

[37] Case C-466/00 *Kaba* [2003] ECR I-2219, AG Colomer; Case C-317/04 *Parliament v. Council* [2006] ECR I-4721, AG Léger.

[38] Case T-112/98 *Mannersmannröhrer-Werke v. Commission* [2001] ECR II-729, para 76.

[39] For a similar position see Case C-105/04 *Grothandel*, n. 19 above, AG Kokott, where the applicability of the Charter was denied *ratione temporis*, having the latter been solemnly proclaimed after the contested decision was adopted.

to the temporal effects of the CFR.[40] Although questionable, the decision leaves open to speculation the issue of the (legal) effect of the Charter. It can be argued that if the Court wanted to deny the judicial application of a merely political document, it would have done so in this instance.

In fact, following this judgment, the CFI started to use this text as a source to confirm or to corroborate the existence of the rights already contained in the ECHR or in the EC Treaty. This is why the Charter was always referred to together with other EU/EC provisions.[41]

The first application of the Charter as an instrument comprising rights and principles set out in other sources of law can be found in the 2002 *max. mobil* judgment where the Court argued that Art. 41(1) CFR "confirms that [e]very person has the right to have his or her affairs handled impartially, fairly and within a reasonable time by the institutions and bodies of the Union".[42] Without taking a stand on its legal value, the CFI recognized the role of the Charter in codifying the general principles of law common to the constitutional traditions of the Member States and in consolidating the Community *acquis*.[43]

---

[40]See A. Barbera, 'La Carta dei diritti dell'Unione europea', (2001) *Il Diritto dell'Unione europea* 241; see also L. Azzena, 'Prospettive della Carta dei diritti e ruolo della giurisprudenza', in F. Ferrari (ed.), *I diritti fondamentali dopo la Carta di Nizza. Il costituzionalismo dei diritti* (Giuffré, 2001) 123 and L. Montanari, 'Una decisione del Tribunale di prima istanza fra CEDU e la Carta di Nizza', (2001) *Diritto Pubblico Comunitario ed Europeo* 670.

[41]Case T-474/04 *Pergan Hilfsstoffe für industrielle Prozesse GmbH* [2007] ECR II-4225; Case T-242/02 *The Sunrider Corp. v. OHIM* [2005] ECR II-2793; Case T-210/01 *General Electric Company* [2005] ECR II-5575; Case T-223/00 *Kyowa Hakko Kogyo Co. Ltd and Kyowa Hakko Europe GmbH* [2003] ECR II-2553; Case T-224/00 *ADM Company and ADM Ltd* [2003] ECR II-2597; Joined cases T-377/00, T-379/00, T-380/00, T-260/01 and T-272/01, *Philip Morris International* [2003] ECR II-1; Case T-211/02 *Tideland Signal Ltd* [2002] ECR II-3781; Case T-54/99 *max.mobil Telekommunikation Service GmbH* [2002] ECR II-313; Case T-390/08 *Bank Melli Iran v. Council*, at http://www.curia.europa.eu. In Case T-77/01 *Diputación Foral de Alava* [2002] ECR I-81 the Court ruled that "it must be pointed out that that [the principle of effective judicial protection] is a general principle of Community law which underlies the constitutional traditions common to the Member States. The principle is also laid down in Arts. 6 and 13 of the ECHR and in Art. 47 of the Charter of fundamental rights" (para 35 of the order). In Case T-193/04 *Tillack v. Commission* [2006] ECR II-3995, the CFI referred to the Charter without mentioning other sources. It affirmed that "the principle of sound administration (...) constitutes the expression of specific rights [...] for the purposes of Article 41 of the Charter of fundamental rights of the European Union, proclaimed on 7 December 2000 in Nice, which is not the case here" (para 127).

[42]Case T-54/99 *max.mobil Telekommunikation Service GmbH*, n. above 41, para 57. For an interpretation of Art. 41 CFR, also see the Order in Case T-198/01R *Technische Glaswerke Ilmenau* [2002] ECR II-2153, para 85.

[43]A. Celotto, G. Pistorio, 'L'efficacia giuridica della Carta dei diritti fondamentali dell'Unione europea' (2005) *Giurisprudenza Italiana* 434. A similar stance (i.e. not specifying the legal value of the Charter) was adopted in Case T-194/04 *The Bavarian Lager Co. Ltd* [2007] ECR II-4523; Case T-193/04 *Hans-Martin Tillack v. Commission*

In other cases, the Court of First Instance invoked the Charter specifying that this document is not legally binding. And yet, it recognized that the Charter "does show the importance of the rights it sets out in the Community legal order".[44]

Lastly, in *Jégo-Quéré*[45] the Court made reference to Art. 47 of the Charter, not as a confirmation of what was already included in the constitutional traditions of the Member States, but as a *ratio decidendi* in evaluating the admissibility of the action for annulment promoted by a legal person.[46] According to the community judges the Charter, albeit lacking binding force, represents a valid instrument capable of enhancing the protection of European citizens vis à vis the EU.[47]

Thus, it can be said that the approach adopted by the CFI goes hand in hand with the position expressed by the Advocates General in their opinions. The Charter has almost always been used to 'reaffirm'[48] and to 'confirm'[49] the rights already included in other instruments, but some commentators have interpreted these references as the definitive proof of its legally binding nature.[50] Despite this trend, in more recent cases the CFI has failed to take the Charter into account, even when so requested by the applicants.[51] This discontinuity is hard to explain and in any case will not survive the entry into force of the Lisbon Treaty.

[2006] ECR II-3995; Joined Cases T-391/03 and T-70/04 *Y. Franchet and D. Byk v. Commission* [2006] ECR II-2023; Case T-242/02 *Sunrider v. OHMI*, n. 41 above; Case T-236/01 *Tokai Carbon* [2004] ECR II-1181.

[44] Joined Cases T-377/00 etc. *Philip Morris International*, n. 41 above, para 122.

[45] Case T-177/01, *Jégo-Quéré* [2002] ECR II-2365.

[46] On this specific case and its (potential) impact on *locus standi* granted to individuals within the EC legal order, cf. in this volume the contribution by G. Sanna, 'Chapter 9'.

[47] A. Celotto, G. Pistorio, 'L'efficacia giuridica della Carta dei diritti fondamentali dell'Unione europea', n. 40 above, 437.

[48] Joined cases T-377/00 etc. *Philip Morris International*, n. 41 above, para 122; Case T-177/01, *Jégo-Quéré*, n. 45 above, para 42. Case T-390/08, *Bank Melli Iran v. Council*, at. http://curia.europa.eu, para 105.

[49] Case T-54/99, *max. mobil Telekommunikation Service*, n. 41 above, para 48.

[50] A. Spadaro, 'Verso la Costituzione europea. il problema delle garanzie giurisdizionali dei diritti', in A. Pizzorusso, R. Romboli, A. Ruggeri, A. Saitta, G. Silvestri (eds.), n. 21 above, 147.

[51] See Case T-259/02 *Raiffeisen Zentralbank v. Commission* [2006] ECR II-5961; Case T-228/02 *Organisation des Modjahedines du Peuple d'Iran v. Council* [2006] ECR I-4665; Case T-391/03 *Y. Franchet and D. Byk*, n. 43 above; Case T-439/04 *Eurohypo AG v. OHIM* [2006] ECR II-1269; Joined Cases T-22/02 and T-23/02 *Sumitomo Chemical Co. Ltd and Others Sumika Fine Chemicals Co. Ltd* [2005] ECR II-4065; Case T-71/03 *Tokai Carbon* [2005] ECR II-10; Case T-2/03 *Verein für Konsumenteninformation* [2005] ECR II-1121; Case T-67/00 *JFE Engineering Corp.* [2004] ECR II-2501; Case T-11/03 *Afari v. European Central Bank* [2004] ECR II-267.

4 The Charter and the Court of Justice

As already mentioned, the ECJ took a more cautious approach to the Charter maintaining for a long time a sort of self restraint and refusing to mention the Charter even when the latter was invoked by the Advocates General. This silence, which might be perceived as a sort of 'distrust', has recently been reconsidered in *Parliament v. Council*[52] of 2006 where the Court, operating a significant *revirement jurisprudentiel*,[53] ruled that the Charter is not a legally binding instrument, but nonetheless acknowledged its importance. Furthermore, the Court claimed that:

> the principal aim of the Charter is to reaffirm rights as they result, in particular, from the constitutional traditions and international obligations common to the Member States, the Treaty on European Union, the Community Treaties, the [ECHR], the Social Charters adopted by the Community and by the Council of Europe and the case-law of the Court and of the European Court of Human Rights.[54]

After this judgment the Charter was referred to on a few other occasions, without a specific focus on its legal value. In the *Unibet* case[55] the ECJ invoked the principle of effective judicial protection affirmed in the Charter, without calling into question other sources of EC law. An analogous solution was reached in *Advocaten voor de Wereld VZW*[56] where the Court ruled that the principle of legality and the principle of equality and non-discrimination are included in the general principles of Community law, and are also reaffirmed in Arts. 49, 20 and 21 CFR.

In the *Varec SA v. Belgium* case,[57] as well as in the recent *Kadi*[58] and *Mono Car Styling SA*[59] judgments, the Court referred to the Charter as an instrument which merely acknowledges the fundamental rights which flow from the common constitutional traditions of the Member States and are already included in the ECHR, whereas in *Dynamic Medien*[60] the Charter was mentioned amongst the various sources of law.

---

[52] Case C-540/03 *Parliament v. Council* [2006] ECR I-5769. See A. Arnull, 'Family reunification and fundamental rights', (2006) *European Law Review* 611.

[53] See A. Spadaro, 'Verso la Costituzione europea. il problema delle garanzie giurisdizionali dei diritti', in A. Pizzorusso, R. Romboli, A. Ruggeri, A. Saitta, G. Silvestri (eds.), n. 21 above, 147.

[54] Case C-540/03 *Parliament v. Council*, n. 52 above, para 38.

[55] Case C-432/05 *Unibet Ltd v. Justitiekanslern* [2007] ECR I-2271, para 37.

[56] Case C-303/05 *Advocaten voor de Wereld VZW*, n. 21 above, para 46.

[57] Case C-450/06 *Varec SA v. Belgium*, n. 9 above, para 48.

[58] Joined cases C-402/05 P and C-415/05 P, *Kadi and Al Barakaat International Foundation*, n. 25 above, para 335.

[59] Case C-12/08 *Mono Car Styling SA*, accessible at http://curia.europa.eu.

[60] Case C-244/06 *Dynamic Medien*, accessible at http://curia.europa.eu, para 41.

In the *Viking*[61] and *Laval*[62] judgments, Art. 28 ("Right of collective bargaining and action") of the Charter is listed among the instruments developed by Member States at a Community level or in the context of the European Union, together with the Community Charter of the Fundamental Social Rights of Workers.[63] The *Laval* case is particularly noteworthy since the Charter was used *a contrario* to circumscribe the scope of the right enshrined therein, namely to highlight the limits deriving from the Community and National legal order. In particular, the Court ruled that:

> although the right to take collective action must therefore be recognised as a fundamental right which forms an integral part of the general principles of Community law the observance of which the Court ensures, the exercise of that right may none the less be subject to certain restrictions. As is reaffirmed by Article 28 of the Charter of Fundamental Rights of the European Union, it is to be protected in accordance with Community law and national law and practices.[64]

Similarly to what has happened in cases pending before the CFI, the Court has sometimes failed to take the Charter into account despite the fact that it had been invoked by the applicants.[65] By contrast, in the context of preliminary rulings the ECJ has consistently answered the questions dealing with Charter related issues. In *Promusicae*,[66] for instance, the national court asked whether Directives 2000/31, 2001/29 and 2004/48, read in the light of Arts. 17 and 47 of the Charter, must be interpreted as requiring Member States to lay down, in order to ensure effective judicial protection of copyright, an obligation to communicate personal data in the context of civil proceedings. The Court of Justice, responding to this question, ruled that in order to provide the national court with a useful answer "it will have to be examined, starting from the national court's reference to the Charter, whether in a situation such as that at issue in the main proceedings other rules of Community law might require a different reading of those three directives".[67]

The Court, referring to the right to property and to the right to an effective remedy, set out in Arts. 17 and 47 of the Charter, considered that the situation called into question yet another fundamental right, namely the protection of personal data and hence of privacy. For this reason, the Court referred to Directive 2002/58, that aims at ensuring full respect of the rights

---

[61] Case C-438/05 *Viking* [2007] ECR I-10779, para 43.

[62] Case C-341/05 *Laval* [2007] ECR I-11767, paras 90 and 91.

[63] See further in this volume, S. Coppola, 'Chapter 11'.

[64] Ibid., para 91. The Court reached an analogous position in the *Viking* case, n. 61 above, para 44.

[65] Case C-76/06 P *Britannia Alloys & Chemicals Ltd*, n. 26 above; Case C-305/05 *Ordre des barreaux francophones et germanophone and Others*, n. 30 above.

[66] Case C-275/06 *Promusicae v. Telefónica de España SAU* [2008] ECR I-271, para 64.

[67] Ibid., para 46.

set out in Arts. 7 and 8 of the Charter. Focusing on these provisions, the ECJ explained that:

> Article 7 substantially reproduces Article 8 of the European Convention for the Protection of Human Rights and Fundamental Freedoms (...) and Article 8 of the Charter expressly proclaims the right to protection of personal data.[68]

The European judges concluded therefore that:

> the present reference for a preliminary ruling thus raises the question of the need to reconcile the requirements of the protection of different fundamental rights, namely the right to respect for private life on the one hand and the rights to protection of property and to an effective remedy on the other.[69]

Quite interestingly, in the case at hand the ECJ felt no need to refer to the legal value of the Charter and simply used this document as a source for fundamental rights protection.

As demonstrated, it is only in recent times that the ECJ has started to mention the Charter in its judgments and the cases in which this occurs are still limited in number. Nevertheless it should be noted that the Charter has sometimes been intended as a text merely recognizing existing rights and with no legal force, whilst on other occasions it has been referred to as a source of law that enables the judiciary to establish the scope of application of fundamental rights.

5 The Charter and the European Court of Human Rights

The delay with which the ECJ has started using the Charter is almost paradoxical[70] as it was preceded in doing so by its Strasbourg counterpart. The latter referred to the Charter in the 2002 *Goodwin v. the United Kingdom* case,[71] where it listed it amongst the international instruments in the field of human rights protection.[72] The Charter has thus not been mentioned in the factual, but in the operational part of the decision. More precisely, Art. 9 CFR was used as a counterpoint to Art. 12 ECHR in defining the scope of the right to a family.[73] The Court affirmed that the ECHR refers to men and women, whereas no such specification can be found in the Charter.

[68] Ibid., para 64.

[69] Ibid., para 65.

[70] G.F. Ferrari, L. Montanari, 'I diritti nel progetto di Costituzione europea', (2003) *Diritto Pubblico Comunitario ed Europeo* 1716.

[71] Appl. No 28957/95, *Goodwin v. The United Kingdom*, (2002) 35 EHRR.

[72] Ibid., para 58.

[73] V. Monetti, 'Sentenze della Corte di Strasburgo', in G. Bisogni, G. Bronzini, V. Piccone (eds.), *I giudici e la Carta dei diritti dell'Unione europea* (Chimienti 2006) 115. On the different wording of the rights, see *Scoppola v. Italy* (Appl. No 10249/03, accessible at www.echr.coe.int). In this judgment the Court affirmed that: "the wording of Article 49 § 1 of the Charter differs – and this can only be deliberate (see, *mutatis mutandis*, *Christine Goodwin*, cited above, § 100 *in fine*) – from that of Article 7 of

This difference became the fundamental argument to affirm that the law in force in the United Kingdom violated Art. 12 ECHR because it did not allow transsexuals to marry.

In the following *Bosphorus* case,[74] the Charter was mentioned amongst the relevant provisions concerning fundamental rights, after Art. 6 of the Amsterdam Treaty. The ECtHR affirmed that the Charter is "not fully binding", but acknowledged its incorporation into primary law as Part II of the Treaty Establishing a Constitution for Europe, signed on 29th October 2004, although the latter was still "not in force". This left the question of the binding force of the Charter open to speculation.[75] And yet, the European Court did not take into consideration the legal value of the Charter in *Sørensen v. Danemark et Rasmussen v. Danemark*[76] and more recently in *Saadi v. The United Kingdom.*[77] The Court included the Charter amongst the relevant international law documents and, more precisely, amongst the most recent European Union instruments.[78]

The *Vilho Eskelinen and others v. Finland* decision[79] should also be recalled. Here, the ECtHR affirmed that the Charter amounted to a codification of the existing case-law of the ECJ. The CFR had the important function of making more visible rights which the Court of Justice has guaranteed for the past decades. The *Vilho* case is also interesting because the European Court took into consideration the Praesidium Explanations annexed to the document[80] estimating that they constitute a "valuable tool of interpretation intended to clarify the provisions of the Charter".[81]

---

the Convention". This does not impede to conclude that there is an equivalent level of protection.

[74] *Bosphorus v. Ireland*, n. 6 above.

[75] Appl. No 73049/01, *Anheuser-Busch inc. v. Portugal*, (2007) accessible at www.echr.coe.int. In this case the Court quoted the Charter as a source of EC law.

[76] Appl. Nos 52562/99 and 52620/99, *Sørensen v. Denmark and Rasmussen v. Denmark*, (2006) accessible at www.echr.coe.int.

[77] Appl. No 13229/03, *Saadi v. The United Kingdom*, (2008) accessible at www.echr.coe.int

[78] Appl. No 55759/07, *Maresti v. Croatia*, (2009) accessible at www.echr.coe.int. See also Appl. No 34503/97, *Demir and Baykara v. Turkey*, (2008) accessible at www.echr.coe.int, para 150. In the recent *Micallef v. Malta* (Appl. No 17056/06) of 15 October 2009, the Court of Strasbourg mentioned the CFR as the main text of reference for the European Union legal order underlining the different wording of the right to a fair trial contanined in Article 47 of the CFR with respect to that of Article 6 of the European Convention of Human Rights. See Appl. No 14939/03, *Zolotukhin v. Russia*, (2009) unreported. See also Appl. No 7925/04, *Pishchalnikov v. Russia*, (2009), unreported and Appl. No 36391/02, *Salduz v. Turkey*, (2009), also unreported, in which the Court referred to Articles 48 and 52 of the CFR.

[79] *Vilho Eskelinen and Others v. Finland* (2007), accessible at www.echr.coe.int, para 30.

[80] Cf. Section 2.

[81] *Vilho Eskelinen and Others v. Finland*, n. 79 above, para 30.

Pursuant to the latter it can be argued that Art. 47 of the Charter is not confined to civil rights and obligations or to criminal matters within the meaning of Art. 6 ECHR. Hence, the Court of Strasbourg was able to conclude that, in principle, in the EU the scope of judicial control is potentially wider, the Luxembourg judges being able to rely on Art. 6 and 13 ECHR, as well as on Art. 47 CFR. For the Strasbourg Court the Charter – as well as the perspective of a future accession of the EU to the ECHR – confirms the equivalence of the standard of protection of human rights guaranteed under the Convention and within the EU legal order. Moreover, in *Demir and Baykare v. Turkey*,[82] the Court of Strasbourg expressly acknowledged that in cases such as *Goodwin, Vilho* and *Sørensen* it was guided by the CFR, despite the fact that this instrument was not binding.

Lastly, it should be noted that only seldom the Charter was referred to in a dissenting opinion[83] or in a joint concurring opinion[84] thereby confirming the willingness of the Strasbourg Court to take the Charter seriously. In this regard the separate Opinion of Judge Zagrebelsky in *Demir and Baykara v. Turkey* is indicative of this stance:

> the Court has thus expressly departed from its case-law, taking into account the perceptible evolution in such matters, in both international law and domestic legal systems. In reality, the new and recent fact that may be regarded as indicating an evolution internationally appears to be only the proclamation (in 2000) of the European Union's Charter of Fundamental Rights.[85]

6 The Charter and the Constitutional Courts of the Member States

It is particularly interesting to note that also National courts have applied the Charter. Limiting our analysis to the Constitutional Courts of the Member States,[86] the first reference to the Charter can be found in a decision by the Spanish Constitutional Court laid down on the 30th November 2000.[87] Here the Spanish judges used Art. 8 of the Charter ("Data protection") in support of their position. What is striking is that the provision was applied as if the Charter had been legally binding and in force. The Charter

[82] Appl. No 34503/97, *Demir and Baykara v. Turkey*, (2008) accessible at www.echr.coe.int, para 105.

[83] Appl. No 53924/00, *Vo. v. France*, (2004) Reports of Judgments and Decisions - VIII.

[84] Appl. No 58675/00, *Martinie v. France*, (2006) accessible at www.echr.coe.int.

[85] *Demir and Baykara v. Turkey*, n. 82 above.

[86] Basic and advanced queries on decisions by national ordinary courts referring to the EU Charter of Fundamental rights can be performed at www.europeanrights.eu.

[87] Spanish Constitutional Court, Judgment 30 November 2000, No 292.

was understood as a constitutional parameter of legality, also by virtue of its solemn proclamation by the three main institutions.

The Spanish Constitutional Court used the Charter again in 2006[88] and in 2008[89] when in affirming the fundamental right to non-discrimination founded on sexual orientation, it made reference to the case-law of the European Court of Human Rights and the ECJ and to the Charter.

The Italian Constitutional Court acknowledged the importance of the Charter in its judgment of 24 April 2002 considering it a non binding text containing the principles common to the European legal orders.[90] Some commentators have remained puzzled by this decision wondering why the Court had resorted to a document devoid of any legal force given its traditional resistance to EC law. And in fact, unlike their Spanish counterparts – who consider the international texts concerning human rights as an automatic criterion for the interpretation of the Law[91] – the Italian Constitutional judges consider the Charter a 'weak' interpretative instrument.

In a second judgment,[92] the Italian Constitutional Court referred to some international instruments, including the Charter, thereby confirming the willingness to take the latter into consideration when deciding in fundamental rights cases. This time, however, the Italian Court referred to the Charter *ad adiuvandum* without questioning its formal status.[93] It is suggested that this implies an indirect acknowledgment of the legal value of the Charter as a result of the National and supranational case-law.

In 2006, the Italian Constitutional Court adopted two other judgments,[94] in which it referred to the Charter including this text amongst the international instruments devoted to fundamental rights protection, but specifying that it is not binding. More recently, judges have questioned the constitutional legitimacy of a piece of legislation which provided for a more favourable statute of limitations and more favourable attenuating circumstances, but excluded pending first instance trials from its scope of

---

[88] Spanish Constitutional Court, Judgment 13 February 2006, No 41.

[89] Spanish Constitutional Court, Judgment 22 December 2008, No 176.

[90] Italian Constitutional Court, Judgment 24 April 2002, No 135/2002, para 2.2. A similar conclusion was reached by the Portuguese Constitutional Court in Judgment (*accordao*) No 275/02.

[91] M. Cartabia, A. Celotto, 'La giustizia costituzionale in Italia dopo la Carta di Nizza', (2002) *Giurisprudenza Costituzionale* 4485.

[92] Italian Constitutional Court, Judgment 24 October 2002, No 445/2002. See also Italian Constitutional Court, Judgment 15 December 2008, No 438/2008.

[93] The Italian Constitutional Court assumed the same position in the judgment 15 December 2008, No 438/2008. See for a similar conclusion, the Portuguese Constitutional Court, Judgment 9 July 2009, No 359/2009.

[94] Italian Constitutional Court, Judgment 23 October 2006, No 393/2006, para 6.2; Italian Constitutional Court, Judgment 8 November 2006, No 394/2006, para 6.4.

application.[95] According to the constitutional judges, these norms violate the principle of *favor rei* – which calls for the retroactive applicability of the more favourable criminal norm – enshrined in Arts. 10 and 11 of the Italian Constitution. Moreover, the latter is recognized by Art. 15 of the 1966 International Covenant on Civil and Political Rights and constitutes a "general principle of community law".[96] And yet, no reference was made to the Charter.

Finally, in a judgment of March 2009[97] the Italian Constitutional Court referred to the Charter, including this text among the sources of Community Law, pursuant to Article 11 and Article 117 of the Italian Constitution, but finally excluded that the Charter, as well as the Convention of New York on the Rights of the Child, could generate a specific obligation capable of affecting the outcome of the case at hand.

These decisions show how the Charter can be used to interpret the fundamental principles of the national Constitutions. The latter have reconsidered their normative and axiological foundations on flexible principles, open to external influences by the International Organizations they belong to.[98]

A different stance was adopted by the Belgian Constitutional Court[99] following the ECJ's judgment in *Ordre des Barreaux francophones*,[100] where Arts. 47 and 48 CFR were not mentioned despite the fact that these provisions had been invoked by the applicants and by AG Poiares Maduro. According to the Constitutional Court the Charter (quoted by the applicants in relation to the national Constitution) affirms the existence of common values of the EU which are also enshrined in the Belgian Constitution and can therefore be taken into consideration. However, because the Charter does not amount to a legally binding instrument, the Belgian Court ruled that the action was inadmissible in that it relied on the violation of the constitutional rules read jointly with the Charter.[101] In a subsequent judgment,[102] the same Court decided to follow the Charter, albeit claiming its non binding character.

The Charter, which in the meantime had been included in the Constitutional Treaty and proclaimed for the second time on 12 December 2007, was used in three other occasions by national constitutional Courts.

---

[95] *No* Law 5 December 2005, No 251.

[96] Italian Constitutional Court, Order 5 March 2007, No 93.

[97] Italian Constitutional Court, Judgment 11 March 2009, No 86.

[98] A. Ruggieri, n. 21 above, 14.

[99] Belgian Constitutional Court, Judgment 23 January 2008, No 10/2008.

[100] Case C-305/05 *Ordre des Barreaux francophones et germanophones*, n. 65 above.

[101] See also Belgian Constitutional Court, Judgment 19 March 2009, No 58/2009.

[102] Belgian Constitutional Court, Judgment 12 February 2009, No 17/2009.

On the 19 November 2004, the French *Conseil Constitutionnel* stated that the Charter was compatible with the national legal order inasmuch as the rights included therein would be interpreted in accordance with the constitutional traditions common to the Member States. The Constitutional Court concluded that neither the contents of the Charter nor its effects on the exercise of national sovereignty required a revision of the 1958 Constitution.[103] Particular importance was given to the Explanations of Charter. The reason can be found in the version of the Charter included in the Constitutional Treaty, which instructs courts to "give due regard" to the latter.

Similarly, the Spanish Constitutional Court[104] ruled that the European Constitutional Treaty was fully compatible with the national Constitution since the Charter could be considered as an interpretative instrument of the rights contained in the former.[105] This analogy can be explained by taking into consideration the fact that the Spanish legal order, as well as the French, establishes with respect to international agreements an *ex ante* system of constitutional review. In this instance, the Spanish Constitutional Court was called upon to check, pre-emptively, the legitimacy of a system of protection of fundamental rights operating on different levels (including the National Constitution, the ECHR and the Charter of Fundamental Rights, representing the second part of the European Constitutional Treaty), that could allow for diverging interpretations of the same rights.[106] The Spanish judges clarified that the domestic legal order provides for both a preventive and an ex post review of International treaties. By consequence, the compatibility with the Constitution can be effectively guaranteed since the interpretative problems posed by the multilevel system of protection will be solved on a case by case basis (and not solely in a pre-emptive and abstract way, as it would be under French law). Hence, the *Tribunal Constitucional* concluded that Arts. II-111 and II-112 of the European Constitutional Treaty (namely Arts. 51 and 52 of the Charter) were in

[103] French Constitutional Council, Decision 19 November 2004, No 2004-505 DC, para 22. See L. Azoulay, F. Ronkes Agerbeek, 'Conseil Contitutionnel, Decision No 2004-505 DC of 19 November 2004, on the Treaty establishing a Constitution for Europe', (2005) *Common Market Law Review* 871. In regard to other parts of the European Constitutional Treaty (policies and functioning of the Union and new prerogatives of National parliaments), the French Constitutional Council ruled that the permission to ratify may only be granted after the revision of the French Constitution. In France there are control mechanisms (political and judicial) which may be activated between the signature of a treaty and its ratification. The Constitutional Council is responsible for adopting the relevant decisions.

[104] Spanish Constitutional Court, Judgment 13 December 2004, DCT 1/2004.

[105] P. Caretti, 'Il Tribunal constitucional e il Conseil constitutionnel sulla Costituzione per l'Europa', (2005) *Quaderni costituzionali* 419.

[106] On the multilevel system of protection of fundamental rights in Europe, cf. the contribution in this volume by G. Di Federico, 'Chapter 2'.

line with the Spanish Constitution since they aim at ensuring only a minimum level of protection of fundamental rights within the EU. The Member States are not prevented from setting higher standards. According to the Spanish Constitutional Court, the only suitable way to avoid conflicting jurisprudence in this field is the dialogue between the Courts.[107]

After having abandoned the idea of a Constitutional Treaty governing the European Union, the French Constitutional Court was called upon to decide on the compatibility of the Lisbon Treaty with the French Constitution. In the decision of 20 December 2007, having examined the new Art. 6 of the EU Treaty (concerning the protection of human rights in the EU and granting full legal force to the CFR) the Court concluded that the Charter did not require constitutional amendments, neither as far as the content of its provisions is concerned, nor by reason of the effects it can produce.[108]

Another National Constitutional Court – traditionally sensitive to the relations between the national and European level of protection of fundamental rights – was called to rule on the matter. In its judgment of 30 June 2009, the German Constitutional Court stated that:

> according to the Treaty of Lisbon, the fundamental rights protection in the European Union is based on two foundations: the Charter of Fundamental Rights of the European Union (...) and the Union's unwritten fundamental rights, which continue to apply as general principles of the Union's law (Article 6.3 TEU Lisbon). These two foundations of European fundamental-rights protection are complemented by Article 6.2 TEU Lisbon, which authorises and obliges the European Union to accede to the European Convention for the Protection of Human Rights and Fundamental Freedoms of 4 November 1950.[109]

The German Constitutional Court further developed its case law on the level of protection of fundamental rights developed in *Solange II*[110] and *Maastricht*,[111] claiming that:

> The general provision concerning limitations under Article 52.1 of the Charter can at most restrict the human dignity guaranteed in Article 1 of the Charter, but not Article 1.1 of the Basic Law. For the European and the national levels of

---

[107] I. Gomez Fernandez, 'Una svolta nella giurisprudenza del *Tribunal Constitucional spagnolo*', (2005) *Quaderni costituzionali* 424.

[108] French Constitutional Council, Decision 20 December 2007, No 2007-560 DC, paras 11 and 12. In a similar case, the Czech Court established that the norms of the Treaty of Lisbon and of the European Union's Charter of Fundamental Rights are compatible with the principles and the Constitutional order of the State, see Judgment 26 November 2008, No 19/08.

[109] German Constitutional Court, judgment 30 June 2009, No BvR 2 BvE 2/08 2 BvE 5/08 -2 BvR 1010/08 -2 BvR 1022/08 -2 BvR 1259/08 - 2 BvR 182/09, para 35. See J. Ziller, 'Solange III (or the Bundesverfassungsgericht's, Europefriendliness). On the decision of the German Federal Constitutional Court over the ratification of the Treaty of Lisbon' (2009) *Rivista Italiana di Diritto Pubblico Comunitario,* 973.

[110] German Constitutional Court, judgment 22 October 1986, No 2 BvR 197/83.

[111] German Constitutional Court, judgment 12 October 1993, No 2 BvR 2134/92.

> fundamental rights must be distinguished. [...] Article 52.1 of the Charter might be at all relevant to the national level of fundamental rights only to the extent that due to it, a level of protection of fundamental rights on the European level that is essentially comparable to that afforded by the Basic Law within the meaning of Article 23.1 sentence 1 of the Basic Law would no longer be guaranteed. [...] It will be for future proceedings to clarify whether and to what extent a decline of the protection of fundamental rights by changes in primary law can at all be admissibly challenged on the basis of Article 1.1 of the Basic Law and what requirements as to substantiation may be placed on such a challenge.[112]

7 National and Community Courts: Role and Power of Appraisal Under the Lisbon Treaty

It follows from the above that before the Lisbon Treaty the Charter had a sui generis legal value by virtue of "spill over" and cross-fertilization effects.[113] The use of the Charter made by National and European Courts demonstrates the judicial activism in the field of fundamental rights protection, but also confirms the silence and the natural resistance of the political sphere. In fact, it can be argued that "the Courts are what make Europe", defending the rights which are part of the democratic legitimacy of the EU.[114]

The Lisbon Treaty addresses the issue by attributing full legal force to the Charter. In doing so it enhances the integration process and improves the degree of legitimacy of the EU. The EU Courts and the national judges will be bound to apply the Charter whenever EU law comes into play. While the latter will no longer be able to avoid this important source of law, the former will lose their wide discretionary power in singling out the general principles of the EU law, determining their interpretation and ultimately their implementation.[115]

---

[112] Ibid., para 189.

[113] S. Rodotà, 'La Carta come atto politico e documento giuridico', in A. Manzella, P. Melograni, E. Paciotti, S. Rodotà (eds.), *Riscrivere i diritti in Europa* (il Mulino, 2001) 73; L.S. Rossi, 'How fundamental is a fundamental principle? Primacy and fundamental rights after the Lisbon Treaty' (2008) *Yearbook of European Law*, 65. L.S. Rossi, 'Supremazie incrociate: Trattato costituzionale europeo e Costituzioni nazionali, in L. Daniele (ed.) *La dimensione internazionale ed europea del diritto nell'esperienza della Corte Costituzionale* (ESI, 2007) 399.

[114] S. Rodotà, 'Nel silenzio della politica i giudici fanno l'Europa', in G. Bronzini, V. Piccone (eds.), *La Carta e le Corti. I diritti fondamentali nella giurisprudenza europea multilivello* (Chimienti 2007) 27.

[115] Cfr. V. Skouris, 'La protezione dei diritti fondamentali nell'Unione europea nella prospettiva dell'adozione di una Costituzione europea', in L.S. Rossi, (ed.), *Il progetto di Trattato-Costituzione. Verso una nuova architettura dell'Unione europea* (Giuffré 2004) 249. On the position adopted by the United Kingdom and the Czech Republic with regard to the Charter, see G. Di Federico, n. 106 above.

The European Parliament and the EU Charter of Fundamental Rights

Federico Camporesi

1 Preliminary Remarks

This Chapter is intended to offer an overview of the role played by the European Parliament (hereafter, EP) in promoting the respect of fundamental rights within and outside the European Union. In doing so we shall investigate whether and how its activity, as it emerges from the numerous reports and resolutions it adopts on the matter, has influenced the law-making process in the internal and external fields of competence of the EU. As will be seen, the EP, apart from playing a proactive role in affirming and fostering fundamental rights protection worldwide, is called upon to ensure their observance within the EU legal order through the powers of control entrusted to it by the Treaties. It is argued that the entry into force of the Lisbon Treaty and the legal value it attributes to the Charter of Fundamental Rights enhance the position of the EP as a central actor for the protection of fundamental rights within and outside the European Union.

2 The European Parliament and Fundamental Rights

The original function of the European Parliament was to counterbalance the power assigned by the Treaties to other institutions, in particular the European Commission. And yet, the EP has always demonstrated the will to absolve other pivotal functions within the EC/EU legal order. A notable example is the desire to play an active role in the protection of fundamental rights.[1]

F. Camporesi (✉)
Free Lance, Bologna, Italy; Free Lance, Brussels, Belgium
e-mail: federicocamporesi@me.com

[1]As Harald Romer (former EP Secretary General) noted in a recent contribution on the matter: "From the outset, the European Parliament has worked to defend the values

G. Di Federico, *The EU Charter of Fundamental Rights*, Ius Gentium: Comparative Perspectives on Law and Justice 8, DOI 10.1007/978-94-007-0156-4_4,

In the early 1950s, the Common Assembly of the European Coal and Steel Community was asked to draft a treaty creating a political European Union. The Assembly proposed a document incorporating the provisions of the European Convention on Human Rights, and justified its proposal on the basis that the political Union could not be separated from human rights. Unfortunately, the project never reached the stage of ratification, and the 1957 Rome Treaties contained no provision on fundamental rights.

It was only 20 years later that, with a strong involvement of the European Parliament, the three main institutions adopted a Solemn Declaration on fundamental rights.[2] Subsequently, in 1984, the EP approved the Treaty Establishing the European Union.[3] Although it never entered into force, the latter envisaged a new framework for the European Community, with formal competencies in the field of fundamental rights. In particular, Art. 4 of the Project provided that the Union would respect fundamental rights, as guaranteed by the European Convention for the Protection of Human Rights and Fundamental Freedoms signed in Rome on 4 November 1950 and as they resulted from the constitutional traditions common to the Member States, as general principles of Community law. The norm also provided for the adoption of a Declaration on Fundamental Rights and Freedoms, which was eventually proclaimed by the European Parliament on 12 April 1989. Moreover, during the Intergovernmental Conference held in Rome in 1990, the EP insisted that the Declaration of Fundamental Rights and Freedoms be granted legal force. Its efforts were however vain. Then came the Treaty of Amsterdam and progress was made in the field of fundamentals rights by enabling the Community to take the appropriate actions to combat any kind of discrimination, to regulate delicate issues such as asylum, refugees and immigration, and to sanction Member States responsible for serious and persistent violations of human rights.

The Conclusions of the Berlin 1999 European Council marked a decisive passage as the German Presidency decided to follow the European Parliament's suggestions and entrusted to a Convention the delicate task of drafting a Charter of Fundamental Rights of the European Union (hereafter, CFR or the Charter). The EP was fully involved with the process and its members played a decisive role.

The Charter was solemnly proclaimed on 7 December 2000 by the Presidents of the three main institutions but lacked legal enforceability;

---

that underpin the European Union: freedom, democracy, respect for human rights and fundamental freedoms, and the rule of law. Starting from the principle that these values are universal, Members of the European Parliament endeavour to promote fundamental rights inside and human rights outside the European Union". See F. Benoit-Rhomer, *The European Parliament as a champion of European values* (European Parliament, Office for Official Publications of European Communities, 2008) 19.

[2] Joint Declaration of 5 April 1977 by the European Parliament, Council and Commission on the protection of fundamental rights, [1977] OJ C 103/1.

[3] This initiative is more commonly referred to as the Spinelli Project, after the well known Italian MEP.

an unfortunate circumstance the European Parliament had tried to avoid by strongly advocating its inclusion in the Nice Treaty. As is well known the Constitutional Treaty incorporated the Charter but never became operative because of the French and Dutch negative referenda in 2005. The Lisbon Treaty instead gives binding effects to the Charter by declaring, in Art. 6 TEU, that it shall have the same legal value as the Treaties.

The EP's insistence on the need to include fundamental rights in primary law is evident from the above. In addition, it has managed to expand its influence to sectors in which it enjoyed no formal competence, as is precisely the case with fundamental rights. In all its resolutions on the matter, the EP underlines that, as the representative of EU citizens, it has a particularly important responsibility in guaranteeing the principles of freedom, democracy, respect for human rights and fundamental freedoms as well as the principle of the rule of law.[4] This is mainly because of the shortcomings of the EU system in the protection of private applicants' rights, ranging from the difficulties in contesting measures with a general scope of application to the absence of a class action, from the limited jurisdiction of the Court of Justice (hereafter, ECJ or EUCJ) under the former Title IV of the EC Treaty and under former Art. 35 of the Treaty on the European Union, to the lack of competence in the field of Common Foreign and Security Policy.[5]

3 The European Parliament as a Fundamental Rights Actor

It is appropriate to begin this section with a terminological caveat. In the absence of a formal (i.e. legal) distinction between "human" and "fundamental" rights, these terms will be used according to current practice. In principle, the former expression is used when the action in question has an external dimension whilst the latter refers to the internal dimension.[6]

The EP has always played a strong role in promoting and monitoring the respect of fundamental rights both within and outside the EU. From an institutional point of view, two parliamentary committees are involved in human rights matters: (a) the Foreign Affairs committee (AFET), together with its Sub-Committee on Human Rights,[7] responsible for issues concerning human rights, for the protection of minorities and for the promotion of democratic values in third countries, and (b) the Committee on Civil

[4] Cf. Art. 6 TEU.

[5] On the protection of individual rights in the former second pillar, see in this volume L. Paladini, "Chapter 14".

[6] F. Geyer, Centre for European Policy Studies (CEPS), *A Synthesis of the former EP Resolutions in the field of Fundamental Rights*, EP publication, 2007, Directorate-General Internal Policies Policy Department Citizens Rights and Constitutional Affairs.

[7] See web site: http://www.europarl.europa.eu/activities/committees/homeCom.do?language=EN&body=DROI.

Liberties, Justice and Home Affairs (LIBE), entrusted with the protection of citizens' rights, human rights and fundamental rights, including the protection of minorities, as laid down in the Treaties and in the Charter of Fundamental Rights of the European Union.[8]

Reflecting this internal distinction, every year two different reports on the situation of human and fundamental rights are elaborated: (a) the Annual Report on Human Rights in the World prepared by the AFET committee, and (b) the yearly Report on the situation of Fundamental Rights in the European Union prepared by the LIBE committee.[9] In these reports the Strasbourg Assembly offers a global overview of EU's policies and performs a critical analysis of the respect of the right of freedom, democracy, respect for human rights and fundamental freedoms, and the rule of law.[10]

3.1 The Action of the European Parliament in the Field of Human Rights: External Relations

The EP can play an important role in the field of external relations using the bargaining power it enjoys under the assent procedure (when applicable) and influencing the treaty making process under the consultation procedure.

Under the Lisbon Treaty the Council shall obtain the assent of the Parliament for the conclusion of (a) accession agreements[11] (b) association agreements; (c) agreement on Union accession to the European Convention for the Protection of Human Rights and Fundamental Freedoms (d) other agreements establishing a specific institutional framework by organising cooperation procedures; (e) agreements having important budgetary implications for the Community; and (f) agreements covering fields to which either the ordinary legislative procedure applies, or the special legislative procedure where consent by the European Parliament is required.[12]

When applicable, the EP uses the bargaining power it enjoys under the assent procedure. Since the entry into force of the Single European Act, it

---

[8] www.europarl.europa.eu/activities/committees/homeCom.do?language=EN&body=LIBE

[9] F. Geyer, n. 6 above.

[10] The European Parliament has prepared annual reports on human rights since the late Nineties, thereby enhancing its proactive role. In many cases, the Reports are a response to the Council's Annual Report on Human Rights in the World. See 2006 (2007/2020/INI) and 2007 (2007/2274/INI) EP Annual Report on Human Rights. As a matter of fact the EP is not involved in the drafting of the latter report and has been constantly demanding to be associated to the procedure for its elaboration.

[11] Cf. Art. 49 TEU.

[12] Cf. Arts. 217 and 218 (6) letter (a) TFEU (former Arts. 300 and 310 TEC).

has carefully scrutinized new accessions and the conclusion of association agreements. The latter agreements foresee reciprocal rights and obligations under the control of an Association Council, an Association Committee and an Association Conference, composed by members of the European Parliament and members of the relevant national parliament. This framework allows the Assembly to play an active role in the development of these agreements, and its intervention is often focused on the respect of human rights.

The agreements are adopted following the assent procedure and allow the EP to (threaten to) use its veto power when human rights concerns arise during the negotiations. This happened for instance in the process which led to the Association Agreement with Turkey, where the EP denied its assent due to the human rights issue in that country and to the conditions of the Kurdish minority.[13] Indeed, Turkey represents a rather peculiar case since it applied for membership as early as 1987. This explains why the EP has so closely monitored its internal situation and acted consequently. In 1994, for instance, the discrimination against the Kurds and the denial of the Armenian genocide,[14] led the EP to suspend for 2 years the relevant joint parliamentary conference.

The European Parliament's concern for the respect of human rights does not vary when it comes to other international partners. For example, during the procedure for the conclusion of the Euro-Mediterranean Association Agreement with Syria, the EP gave its assent but not before underlining, in a (previous) resolution addressed to the Council, the need to respect democratic values, human rights and civil liberties. In particular, based on the Véronique De Keyser (PSE) Report, the EP Committee on Foreign Affairs called upon the Council to ask the Syrian Government to comply with international human rights standards and to report on the progress regarding the respect of religious rights and other minority rights, namely those of the Kurds.[15]

Although in the negotiation of other international agreements the EP does not have an equivalent power,[16] it is still capable of influencing the decision making process, especially when there is a potential violation of human rights. In 2004 the Parliament opposed the Council decision to conclude the EU/US Agreement on the processing and transfer of passengers

---

[13] [1998] OJ C 13/28.

[14] EP Resolution of 18 June 1987, A2-33/8.

[15] EP Resolution containing the European Parliament's recommendation to the Council on the conclusion of a Euro-Mediterranean Association Agreement between the European Community and its Member States, on the one side, and the Syrian Arab Republic, of the other, 2006/2150(INI).

[16] With the exception of the agreements mentioned in Art. 218 (6) letter (a), TFEU, the European Parliament is required to deliver an opinion during the negotiation of an international agreement (Art. 218 (6) letter (b), TFEU).

name records (PNR)[17] and asked an Opinion from the Court of Justice on its compatibility with the Treaties, claiming a breach of the right to privacy.[18] Failure to protect personal data was after all one of the grounds upon which the EP sought the annulment of Council Decision 2004/496/EC, of 17 May 2004, on the conclusion of this agreement.[19]

The European Parliament had also an important role in the development of the conditionality clause. In fact, in 1978 it pushed for the inclusion of a Human Rights clause in the agreements with the African, Caribbean and Pacific States. After this precedent the EP pressed for a generalisation of the clause to all the international agreements and in 1995 it successfully requested the Council to include a (compulsory) human rights clause in all the international agreements concluded by the Community. Thus, it can be said that the EP plays an active role in the protection of human rights notably influencing the decision making process of international agreements.

The role of the EP in the field of external relations is not confined to its involvement in the conclusion of international agreements. Suffice it here to recall its contribution to the current formulation of EC Regulation No 1889/2006 of the European Parliament and of the Council on establishing a financing instrument for the promotion of democracy and human rights worldwide.[20] On this occasion, the Institution carried out an intensive effort that culminated in the 'adjustment' of the objectives and scope of the envisaged measure. The aim was to enhance its efficiency (i.e. capability to respond to critical situations) and effectiveness (e.g. providing for the support of non-state actors promoting democracy and human rights). In this respect it should also be noted that during the procedure the EP insisted on the need to adopt further measures for the protection and promotion of human rights.[21]

---

[17] Doc. PE, A5-0271/2004, 2004/0064(INI).

[18] See Opinion 1/04 of the European Court of Justice. In particular, the European Parliament submitted to the ECJ the following questions: (a) is the first sentence of the first subparagraph of Art. 300(3) EC the appropriate legal basis for the Council Decision on the conclusion of the proposed agreement between the European Community and the United States of America on the processing and transfer of Passenger Name Record data by air carriers to the United States Department of Homeland Security, Bureau of Customs and Border Protection? and (b) must the above mentioned proposed agreement be regarded as being compatible with the right to protection of personal data, as enshrined in particular in Art. 8 of the European Convention on Human Rights (ECHR), which the Community is required to observe in the same way as the Treaty? The text of the Opinion can be found at the following address: http://www.curia.eu.

[19] Case C-317/04 *Parliament v. Council* [2006] ECR I-4721. In particular, the European Parliament put forward four pleas in support of its action, namely: misuse of powers by the Commission, breach of the fundamental principles of Directive 95/46/EC, breach of fundamental rights and breach of the principle of proportionality.

[20] [2006] OJ L 386/1.

[21] In particular, during the first reading phase, the EP obtained an adjustment of the objectives and scope of the envisaged measures as well as modifications intended to

In addition, the EP often acts on the international scene publicly deploring human rights violations. Resolutions are commonly used for this purpose. Their adoption follows extensive public hearings where the deputies are provided with information and expert assessments on the basis of which they can debate and elaborate an opinion.[22]

As is clear from the reactions by politicians and embassies of the 'accused' countries, these resolutions can have a strong political impact[23] despite their non-binding nature.[24] This allows the EP to play an important proactive role on the international scene even in cases where it has no formal competence. For example, the 2002 Resolution on the EU Strategy towards China – where the EP expressed its concern for the respect of human rights in that country, as well as for the Chinese policy with regard to Tibet[25] – triggered a harsh reaction on the part of the Foreign Affairs Committee of China's Peoples Congress which qualified the position adopted by the EP as 'extremely erroneous'. Moreover, the Chinese Central Government considered the demand for further cooperation between China and the European Union on international and regional

---

guarantee a prompt response in case of sudden events. Most notably, it successfully proposed the introduction of a new Article providing for "ad hoc measures", whereby the Commission would be entitled to allocate small grants on an ad hoc basis to human rights defenders responding to urgent protection needs. Furthermore, during the proceedings the responsible committee proposed a series of amendments designed to flesh out the various categories of action for which support would be provided through civil society, and also added new categories as "the promotion and defence of freedom of expression, including artistic and cultural expression, and the fight against censorship". See the Summary of the EP position in first reading, COD/2006/0116, www.europarl.europa.eu/oeil/resume.

[22]Resolutions in this area are generally based on the EP Rules of procedure (7th parliamentary term, December 2009), notably: Art. 98 (resolutions on breaches of human rights); Art. 110 (resolutions following Statements by the Commission, the Council and the European Council); Art. 115 (resolutions following questions for oral answer with debate); Art. 122 (resolutions following debates on cases concerning breaches of human rights, democracy and the rule of law, also known as "urgent resolutions"). See Beyond Activism, *The impact of the resolutions and other activities of the European Parliament in the field of human rights outside the European Union* (EUIC, 2006), 105. Moreover, it should not go unnoticed that the MEPs can acquire information from a particular person on a specific issue.

[23]Beyond Activism, n. 22 above, at 91.

[24]Case T-346/03 *Krikorian* [2003] ECR II-6037. In this instance the Court affirmed: "It suffices to point out that the 1987 resolution is a document containing declarations of a purely political nature, which may be amended by the Parliament at any time. It cannot therefore have binding legal consequences for its author nor, a fortiori, for the other defendant institutions. 20. That conclusion also suffices to dispose of the argument that the 1987 resolution could have given rise to a legitimate expectation, on the part of the applicants, that the institutions would comply with that resolution" (paras 19–20).

[25]EP resolution on the Commission Communication to the Council and the European Parliament on an EU Strategy towards China: Implementation of the 1998 Communication and future steps for a more effective EU policy– 2001/2045(COS), points 36 and 46.

issues such as Taiwan as a violation of the "EU's solemn commitment to one-China policy" and an undue interference in China's internal affairs'.[26]

Finally, the role of the EP's delegations should not be underestimated as they interact with other regional or interparliamentary assemblies, participate in joint assembly in the context of an association agreement and develop parliamentary relations. In particular, delegations are in charge of the maintenance and the development of the Parliament's international relations. To this end, they work to maintain and enhance the relations with Parliaments of States that are traditionally partners of the European Union and contribute to promoting in third countries the values on which the European Union is founded, namely the principles of liberty, democracy, respect for human rights and fundamental freedoms, and the rule of law.[27] At present there are 35 delegations, which can by and large be divided in two categories: (a) the interparliamentary delegations, whose task is to maintain relations with the parliaments of countries outside the European Union that have not applied for membership; (b) the joint parliamentary committees, which maintain contacts with the parliaments of countries that are candidates for accession to the European Union and States parties to association agreements. Furthermore, the EP has 5 Multilateral Assemblies, which bring together deputies of the EP and parliamentarians from African, Caribbean and Pacific States (ACP-EU JPA), the Mediterranean (EMPA), Latin America (EUROLAT), EU's eastern neighbouring countries (EURONEST), and NATO countries.[28]

3.2 The Action of the European Parliament in the Field of Fundamental Rights: The "Internal Dimension"

The concern for fundamental rights is not limited to the EU's external relations. As already mentioned, the EP prepares annual reports on the situation of fundamental rights in the EU and adopts resolutions in specific areas such as citizenship and discrimination. This has enabled it to play a more proactive role in the internal evolution of the EU legal order.

Following the Treaty of Amsterdam, the Community was entitled to take the appropriate actions to combat any kind of discrimination,[29] to regulate delicate issues such as asylum, refugees and immigration, and to sanction Member States responsible for serious and persistent violations of human

---

[26] Statement by NPC Foreign Affairs Committee on Report on Commission Communication on Europe and Asia: A Strategic Framework for Enhanced Partnerships Passed by European Parliament (2002.09.09). www.china-un.ch/eng.

[27] See Arts. 2, 6 and 11(1), 5th indent, TEU.

[28] See web site: www.europarl.europa.eu/parliament/public/staticDisplay.do?id=45&pageRank=6&language=EN.

[29] See Art. 19 TFEU (former Art.13 TEC, introduced by Art. 2 (7) of the ToA).

rights.[30] By virtue of these new competences, the Council started to prepare Annual Reports on Human Rights replacing the former memorandum on the Union's activity in this domain. These reports were submitted to the Parliament, which in turn started preparing its own Report on Human Rights in the Union.[31] Indeed, the EP has drafted an annual report on fundamental rights in the Union since the early Nineties.[32] Following the suggestion expressed in a 1991 resolution,[33] where it concluded that monitoring the state of human rights in third countries was in itself insufficient, in 1993 the EP adopted its first report on the situation of human rights within the EU.[34]

With the adoption of the Charter in 2000,[35] the Committee on Civil Liberties, Justice and Home Affairs decided to elaborate a Report based on the rights enshrined in the new document, and consequently abandoned the general reference to "human rights". More precisely, this parliamentary Committee is involved in the protection of citizens' rights, human rights and fundamental rights within the territory of the Union, including the protection of minorities, as laid down in the Treaties and in the CFR. The committee is also responsible for the adoption of measures aimed at combating all forms of discrimination, ensuring transparency and the protection of natural persons with regard to the processing of personal data, guaranteeing the free movement of persons, regulating asylum and migration, managing the judicial and administrative cooperation in civil matters and the police and judicial cooperation in criminal matters. Last but not least, the Committee plays an important role in the determining the risk of a serious breach (by a Member State) of the principles common to the Member States.[36]

That being said, the report prepared by the LIBE Committee is intended to offer an overview of the concrete activity carried out by the European Union in order to guarantee compliance with the standards set out in the CFR. This instrument enables the EP to perform a critical analysis of the protection of fundamental rights in the different Members States and to suggest possible courses of action to remedy the deficient situations singled out therein.[37]

---

[30] See Art. 7 TEU.

[31] See, for example, the Report on Human Rights in the Union released in 1999, [2000] OJ C 377/344.

[32] F. Benoit-Rhomer, n. 1 above, at 19.

[33] [1991] OJ C 240/45.

[34] [1993] OJ C 115/115.

[35] [2000] OJ C 364/1.

[36] For a detailed list of the competences of the LIBE Committee, see http://www.europarl.europa.eu/activities/committees/committeesList.do?language=EN

[37] As F. Sylla, rapporteur of the 2002 resolution, noted : "this report constitutes a valuable point of reference for elaborating and implementing EU policies. It is also an open

Indeed, since its adoption the Charter has been used as a parameter of legality of EU acts. In fact, following its solemn proclamation the President of the EP declared that the Charter would become the law guiding the actions of the Assembly and would be the inescapable point of reference for all acts with a direct or indirect impact on the lives of citizens throughout the Union.[38] On its part, the Commission accepted to act in accordance with the Charter[39] and, in 2005, decided to go further issuing a specific notice on the methodology for systematic and rigorous monitoring of all legislative proposals in order to guarantee the respect of fundamental rights.[40] The EP welcomed the proposal and insisted on the opportunity to extend this procedure to the entire legislative process and to the Comitology mechanism.[41]

Again, this reveals a high prioritization of fundamentals rights protection within the European Union.[42] This approach is also reflected in the former Rules of Procedure of the EP (6th parliamentary term). Art. 34, in fact, stated that the Parliament should pay particular attention in ensuring that legislative acts comply with the Charter of Fundamental Rights, and respect the principles of subsidiarity and proportionality and the rule of law.[43] The new Rule of Procedure (7th parliamentary term), edited in accordance with

---

method of coordination which highlights good practices in the Member States and makes it possible to draw a comparison between initiatives and ensure compatibility between them. It provides a means of allowing and supporting the establishment of the prevention mechanism under Art. 7 of the Treaty on European Union. It should also contribute to publicising and sharing the European Parliament's commitment in this specific area and, lastly, it promotes transparency and facilitates dialogue with civil society". EP Report on the situation concerning fundamental rights in the European Union (2002) 2002/2013/INI, OJ C 76 E of 25 March 2004, p. 245.

[38] These are the words of the former President of the European Parliament, Nicole Fontaine, on 7 December 2000 in Nice, during the official proclamation of the Charter of Fundamental Rights of the European Union by the European Parliament, the Commission and the Council of the European Union.

[39] SEC(2001) 380/3.

[40] COM(2005)0172.

[41] EP resolution of 15 March 2007 on compliance with the Charter of Fundamental Rights in the Commission's legislative proposals: methodology for systematic and rigorous monitoring, 2005/2169(INI).

[42] A. Williams, 'Respecting Fundamental Rights in the New Union: A Review', *The Fundamentals of EU Law Revisited: Assessing the Impact of the Constitutional Debate* (Oxford University Press, 2007) 71.

[43] Art. 34 of the EP Rule of Procedure, Examination of respect for fundamental rights, the principles of subsidiarity and proportionality, the rule of law, and financial implications: "During the examination of a legislative proposal, Parliament shall pay particular attention to respect for fundamental rights and in particular that the legislative act is in conformity with the European Union Charter of Fundamental Rights, the principles of subsidiarity and proportionality and the rule of law. In addition, where a proposal has financial implications, Parliament shall establish whether sufficient financial resources are provided".

the new provisions of the Lisbon Treaty, goes further and Art. 36 states that Parliament shall in all its activities fully respect fundamental rights as laid down in the Charter of Fundamental Rights of the European Union and also the rights and principles enshrined in Art. 2 and in Art. 6(2) and (3) TEU. Furthermore, the provision foresees that where the competent committee, a political group of at least 40 members, are of the opinion that a proposal for a legislative act does not comply with rights enshrined in the Charter, the matter shall, at their request, be referred to the committee responsible for the interpretation of the latter. The last part of this provision, whereby the EP could delay the adoption of the act, clearly shows the concern of the Parliament for fundamental rights protection particularly within the EU law making process.

But the powers of control assigned to the EP are not confined to the elaboration of legislative acts. On the contrary, over the years this institution has been progressively recognized (unfettered) standing in actions for annulment,[44] a prerogative which it exercises when fundamental rights issues arise. The *PNR* case offers a good example of the Institution's activism in this field. In 2004, acting under the 1999 Comitology procedure,[45] it adopted a resolution in which it expressed a number of reservations of a legal nature on the approach followed by the Commission in order to provide adequate protection of personal data contained in the Passenger Name Record. In particular, the EP considered that the draft decision exceeded the powers conferred on the Commission and expressed doubts as to its compatibility with fundamental rights. Despite the Parliament's reservations, the decision was adopted.[46] Hence, the EP brought an action for annulment against that measure claiming, inter alia, the breach of the right to private life and of the right to protection of personal data laid down in Art. 8 of the European Convention for the Protection of Human Rights and Fundamental Freedoms (hereafter, ECHR), as applied by the Court of Justice and by the European Court of Human Rights.[47] Although the ECJ refused to carry out a fundamental rights reasoning, it nonetheless decided to annul the decision.

Another interesting example is offered by the 2006 *European Parliament v. Council of the EU* case,[48] where the Parliament sought the

---

[44] See R. Corbett, F. Jacobs and M. Shacklethon, *The European Parliament* (John Harper, 2007) at 300; L. Daniele, 'Parlamento europeo e Corte di giustizia: chi la dura la vince?' (1991) *Foro Italiano* 1.

[45] Art. 8 of the Council Decision of 28 June 1999, 1999/468/EC [1999] OJ L 184/23.

[46] Commission Decision 2004/535/EC of 14 May 2004 on the adequate protection of personal data contained in the Passenger Name Record of air passengers transferred to the United States Bureau of Customs and Border Protection [2004] OJ L 235/11.

[47] On the protection of personal data in the former third pillar and the impact of the Lisbon Treaty in this field see in this volume V. Bazzocchi, "Chapter 10".

[48] Case C-540/03 *Parliament v. Council of the European Union* [2006] ECR I- 5769.

annulment of some Articles of the Council Directive 2003/86/EC[49] arguing that the contested provisions did not respect fundamental rights and in particular the right to family life and the right to non-discrimination. To support its arguments, the EP invoked the ECHR, the constitutional traditions common to the Member States *and* the Charter of Fundamental Rights[50] (Arts. 7 and 21). Although it dismissed the action, the ECJ recognised that:

> While the Charter is not a legally binding instrument, the Community legislature did, however, acknowledge its importance by stating, in the second recital in the preamble to the Directive, that the Directive observes the principles recognised not only by Article 8 of the ECHR but also in the Charter. Furthermore, the principal aim of the Charter, as is apparent from its preamble, is to reaffirm 'rights as they result, in particular, from the constitutional traditions and international obligations common to the Member States, the Treaty on European Union, the Community Treaties, the [ECHR], the Social Charters adopted by the Community and by the Council of Europe and the case-law of the Court . . . and of the European Court of Human Rights.[51]

Therefore, it may be argued that the EP, by insisting on the need to respect fundamental rights within the European Union, acts as a sort of 'European conscience' with respect to the internal dimension of EU law, as well as to EU external relations.[52] The vision of the EP, as the institution representing EU citizens, as a 'champion of EU values',[53] can thus be fully endorsed.

The active role played by the EP can also be appreciated by acknowledging its activism vis-à-vis the petitions received from ordinary citizens. The possibility to react to a specific request on the part of individuals was firstly recognized by the 1952 Rules of Procedure but was included in the Treaty only after Maastricht. Art. 24 (2) TFEU (former Art. 21 TEC) now provides that: 'Every citizen of the Union shall have the right to petition the European Parliament'. As one of the rights inextricably linked to European citizenship (but extended to all persons residing and all

---

[49] Council Directive 2003/86/EC of 22 September 2003 on the right to family reunification [2003] OJ L 251/12. In particular, the Parliament contested the final subparagraph of Art. 4(1), Art. 4(6) and Art. 8 of the Council Directive.

[50] In particular, reference was made to Arts. 7 (non-discrimination) and 21 (right to privacy) CFR.

[51] Case C-540/03 *Parliament v.Council,* n. 48 above, para 38.

[52] This assumption finds further confirmation in a number of events patronized by the European Parliament. Amongst the latter, the yearly conferral of the Sacharov Prize for Freedom of Thought is noteworthy. Since 1998 this prize is awarded to individuals or organisations for their efforts on behalf of human rights and fundamental freedoms. Despite its merely symbolic value, the event can nonetheless give international visibility to the candidates and most importantly to the causes they embraced. See also, *Beyond Activism*, n. 22 above.

[53] F. Benoit-Rhomer, n. 1 above.

undertakings having their legal seat in the Community), it is also enshrined in Art. 44 CFR.[54]

Although frequently underestimated, petitions allow the EP to appreciate the sensitivity of individuals, legal and natural persons, for certain European matters thereby stimulating a direct and open dialogue between the citizens and the institution through calls for action or simple expressions of interest.[55] In addition, they offer private parties the possibility to single out possible inconsistencies of EU legislation, including the non-compliance with fundamental rights.

Petitions may also favour the identification of breaches of EU law by the Member States and allow the EP to pressure the national governments to put an end to the violation without having recourse to the infringement procedure. Of course, this does not prevent the case to be handled by the Commission under Art. 258 TFEU (former Art. 226 TEC), but sometimes the analysis of the petitions by the competent committee can contribute to a modification of the contested situation avoiding further legal action. For example, in 1992 an unemployed French citizen living in Belgium submitted a petition to the EP claiming that he had been refused employment at a public office in the Belgian Municipality of Uccle because the position was reserved to nationals pursuant to a law of 1937. Pressures by the EP Petition Committee (backed by the Commission) led to the amendment of the relevant domestic provisions.

About one-third of the infringement procedures are related to issues submitted by petitioners to the European Parliament.[56] This is particularly important in a system where the right of individuals to bring an action directly before the European courts against measures with a general scope of application is limited. In this sense, the right of petition, coupled with the right to address complaints to the European Ombudsman, tends to (partially) compensate the shortcomings of Art. 263 (4) TFEU.[57]

For example, in 2001, following some petitions concerning the frequent expulsion of Italian citizens from Germany, the Commission brought an enforcement action against the latter Member State, accused of violating the freedom of movement of persons. In this case the ECJ held that the Federal Republic of Germany failed to fulfil its obligations under Art. 39

[54] See also Art. 227 TFEU (former Art. 194 TEC).

[55] The European Parliament has always made use of petitions as a way of gathering privileged information and use it to exercise its political monitoring powers, with a particular focus on serious infringements of Community law, while at the same time giving citizens a chance to express their day-to-day expectations or fears concerning Europe. See EP Resolution on the deliberations of the Committee on Petitions during the parliamentary year 2002–2003, 2003/2069(INI).

[56] Report on the deliberations of the Committee on Petitions during the parliamentary year 2007, Doc. Ref. 2008/2028(INI).

[57] But see in this volume G. Sanna, "Chapter 9".

TEC, Art. 3 of Directive 64/221 and Art. 10 of Directive 73/148.[58] More recently, on the basis of two petitions by Polish and Lithuanian environmental associations that feared that a planned pipeline could harm the marine eco-system in the Baltic Sea, the EP adopted a resolution in which it expressed its concern about the impact of the pipeline project.[59] The European Commission thus activated an infringement procedure against the Polish Republic concerning the incorrect application of Directives 79/409/EEC (Birds) and 92/43/EEC (Habitats).[60]

These examples show the active role played by the EP and the importance of the right of petition, which gives the Institution the possibility to signal breaches of citizen's rights – including fundamental rights – by a Member State.

4 A Possible New Partner of the EP: The Agency for Fundamental Rights

Since it became operative at the beginning of 2008, the European Union Agency for Fundamental Rights – building upon the existing European Monitoring Centre on Racism and Xenophobia – provides the institutions of the European Union (and its Member States when implementing Community law), with information, assistance and expertise on fundamental rights within their respective spheres of competence in order to fully guarantee the observance of fundamental rights.

The agreement between the institutions on the definition of the structure of the new body was not easy to attain. According to the original proposal of the Commission, during the negotiations for the creation of the new Agency the Parliament insisted on the need to extend its competencies to the former Third Pillar matters. This point was contested by the Council and the negotiations proved harder than originally planned. Although the EP was only entitled to issue a non-binding opinion, the Commission proposed to proceed with trilogues in order to reach an agreement. The Council accepted and at the end of 2006 the matter was finally settled.

The difficulties which have characterised the creation of the Agency show the distrust of the Council and call for an intervention of the EP, which could highly benefit from a close cooperation with the new body. This would enable it to play a more active part in the monitoring and promotion of fundamentals rights within the EU institutional framework.

[58] Case C-441/02 *Commission v. Germany* [2004] ECR I-3449.

[59] 2007/2118/INI.

[60] Case C-193/07 *Commission v. Poland Republic*, withdrawn.

Pursuant to the Council Regulation establishing a European Union Agency for Fundamental Rights,[61] the EP will be involved in the activities of the Agency, including the adoption of the Multiannual Framework, and in the selection of the candidates for the post of Director of the Agency.

Furthermore, it should not be forgotten that pursuant to Art. 4 (2) of the establishing regulation, the Agency may formulate conclusions and opinions and elaborate reports concerning proposals from the Commission or positions taken by the institutions in the course of the legislative procedure, but only upon request by the respective institution. The original Commission's proposal excluded any participation of the Agency from stating on EU legislative procedure.[62] This limitation was initially foreseen to prevent the institutions from involving the Agency in the legislative process for political reasons and consequently delaying the procedure.[63] Fortunately, pressures by the EP during the legislative procedure led to the current formulation of the provision[64] making the Agency a possible important ally of the EP when fundamental rights issues arise. This is particularly true in light of the new Art. 36 of the Rules of Procedure by which the Institution shows its willingness to carry out a stringent control over the respect of fundamental rights during the law making process, to begin with legislative proposals.

Despite the absence of any formal link between the EP and the Agency – as is the case with the European Ombudsman – the two can work together to guarantee full observance of the EU fundamental rights standard. The Strasbourg Assembly endorsed this position when it strongly advocated the possibility to ask for the Agency's expertise. It should not be forgotten, in fact, that amongst the main tasks of the latter there is the formulation and publication of opinions on specific topics and of an annual report on issues related to fundamental rights falling within the scope of application of the establishing regulation.

[61] Council Regulation (EC) No 168/2007 of 15 February 2007 establishing a European Union Agency for Fundamental Rights [2008] OJ L 53/1.

[62] Art. 4(2) of the original proposal of the European Commission, COM/2005/0280 final – CNS 2005/0124: "The conclusions, opinions and reports formulated by the Agency when carrying out the tasks mentioned in paragraph 1 shall not concern questions of the legality of proposals from the Commission under Article 250 of the Treaty, positions taken by the institutions in the course of legislative procedures...".

[63] G. N. Toggenburg, 'The role of the new EU Fundamental Rights Agency: Debating the "sex of angels" or improving Europe's human rights performance?' (2008) 3 *European Law Review* 384.

[64] Report of the European Parliament of 26 September 2006 on the proposal for a Council regulation establishing a European Union Agency for Fundamental Rights, A6-0306/2006.

5 The Impact of a Newly Binding Charter of Fundamental Rights on the Activity of the European Parliament

Regardless of the original market oriented nature of the founding treaties and the consequent lack of any formal competence on the subject matter, the European Parliament was able to extend its influence in the field of human and fundamental rights affirming itself (as mentioned above) as a sort of 'European conscience' with respect to the external and the internal dimension of EU law.[65]

As has been illustrated, a number of instruments are available when it comes to promoting and monitoring the respect of a (minimum) common standard of protection. Firstly, the EP can question the activity of the Commission and/or the Council through parliamentary hearings. Secondly – and most notably when its assent is required – it may influence the decision making process of an international agreement trying to foster higher standards worldwide. In this regard the possibility to make its views known through the adoption of resolutions, reports and other non binding documents, should not be underestimated. Thirdly, by virtue of its involvement in the decision making process, it will verify the compatibility with fundamental rights of all legislative proposals falling within the first pillar. Fourthly, it can seek and obtain the annulment of an act arguing that the contested provision is not in compliance with the level of protection required by the EU legal order. As indicated above, petitions are also a viable instrument inasmuch as they allow private parties to single out possible inconsistencies of EU legislation, including non-compliance with fundamental rights.

Against this background it can be argued that the Lisbon Treaty can impact profoundly the position and activity of the European Parliament, enhancing its role as a fundamental rights promoter and guarantor both within and outside the EU legal order. Indeed, as to the former aspect, the Reform Treaty extends the co-decision procedure to several new legal bases, including budgetary provisions, measures adopted in the field of the common agricultural policy and the Area of Freedom, Security and Justice. This enables the EP, acting as co-legislator, to exercise a more extensive control over the respect of fundamental rights in these areas of law.[66]

---

[65] E. Soler, I. Lecha, 'Debating Turkey's accession: National and ideological cleavages in the European Parliament', in M. E. Barbé Izuel and A. Herranz (eds.), *The role of parliaments in European foreign policy: Debating on accountability and legitimacy* (IUEE 2005) 55. The Author uses this expression to qualify the activism of the EP in the field of the enlargement of the European Union.

[66] Furthermore, it should not go unnoticed that the new Treaty foresees the possibility to extend the ordinary legislative procedure to other legal bases for which the application of a special legislative procedure is established. To be sure, Art. 48 (7) TEU provides that: "Where the Treaty on the Functioning of the European Union provides for legislative

But the Lisbon Treaty also strengthens the role of the EP in the field of external relations. Following its entry into force, the Parliament's assent has become necessary whenever the relevant agreement concerns areas of law to which the ordinary legislative procedure (or a special legislative procedure requiring the EP's consent) applies.[67] The same holds true for the (future) agreement on the Union's accession to the European Convention for the Protection of Human Rights (ECHR).[68]

In addition, it should not go unnoticed that the new Treaty assigns a greater role to national parliaments.[69] Suffice it here to recall the right to be informed of all progress in the area of freedom, security and justice, of proposals to amend the treaties and of applications for membership; the involvement in future conventions dealing with Treaty amendments and the possibility to contest (ex ante) the violation of the subsidiarity principle (so-called orange card procedure).[70] Nonetheless, other forms of pre- and post-legislative dialogue between the EP and national parliaments could be envisaged with a view to enhance the control over the correct implementation of EU law and, pursuant to Art. 51(1) CFR, on the compatibility of domestic legislation with fundamental rights.

In this context, the presence of a binding EU Charter of fundamental rights – strongly advocated by the EP during the 2007 IGC – and future accession to the ECHR are particularly noteworthy. On the one side, the breach of rights contained in the CFR, whether by secondary legislation or by international treaties concluded by the Union, amounts to a violation of the Treaty and might be brought before the ECJ as an autonomous ground for annulment or in the context of an action in tort against the Union. On

acts to be adopted by the Council in accordance with a special legislative procedure, the European Council may adopt a decision allowing for the adoption of such acts in accordance with the ordinary legislative procedure".

[67] Under the former treaties, Art. 300 (3) TEC provided that the assent is required for Association Agreements, other agreements establishing a specific institutional framework by organising cooperation procedures, agreements having important budgetary implications for the Community and agreements entailing amendment of an act adopted under the codecision procedure.

[68] Art. 218 TFEU.

[69] R. Passos, 'Recent developments concerning the role of national parliaments in the European Union' (2008) *ERA* 25. P. Kitver, 'The composite case for national parliaments in the European Union: Who profits from enhanced involvement?' (2006) 2 *European Constitutional Law Review* 331.

[70] J. V. Louis, 'National Parliaments and the principle of subsidiarity', in *Ceci n'est pas une Constitution – Constitutionalisation without a Constitution?*, ECLN Conference Sofia, 2008, at 132; S. Rothenberger, O. Govt, 'The "Orange Card": A fitting response to national parliaments' marginalisation in EU decision making?', Paper presented at the conference *Fifty Years of Interparliamentary Cooperation,* 13 June 2007, Bundesrat, Berlin, organised by the Stiftung Wissenschaft und Politik (SWP), accessible at www.swpberlin.org/en/common/get_document.php?

the other side, should the latter fail to comply with the standard set by the ECHR, it would be possible to turn to the Strasbourg Court.[71]

In conclusion, the legal enforceability of the Charter, coupled with external judicial control on the part of the European Court of Human Rights tends to put fundamental rights at the core of the EU legal order thereby granting the European Parliament yet another opportunity to acquire further institutional leadership in their promotion. The action of the EP will have as an ineluctable point of reference the (higher) standard of protection set by the Charter and perhaps find in it new ways of affirming the EU's commitment to human rights protection. In performing this function the EP would undoubtedly benefit from the assistance of the Fundamental Rights Agency, and although concrete signs of a productive cooperation are at this writing yet to be seen, the new Treaty is likely to modify the situation.

[71]On the consequences of the EU accession to the European Convention on Human Rights, see in this volume the contribution by G. Di Federico, "Chapter 2".

Fair Trial, Due Process and Rights of Defence in the EU Legal Order

Marco Borraccetti

1 Preliminary Remarks

The aim of this Chapter is to analyse the relation between Art. 47 of the Charter of Fundamental Rights of the European Union (hereafter CFR or the Charter) and the procedure before the Court of Justice of the European Union, which comprises three judicial instances: the Court of Justice (hereafter ECJ or EUCJ); the General Court (hereafter, GC) and the Civil Service Tribunal. To that end, after having examined the ECJ's case law on the matter, the impact of a legally binding Charter, as provided by Art. 6 TEU as amended by the Lisbon Treaty, will be addressed.

According to Art. 47 CFR, everyone has the right to an effective remedy before a tribunal; is entitled to a fair and public hearing within a reasonable time by an independent and impartial tribunal previously established by law, and shall have the possibility of being advised, defended and represented. Moreover, "Legal aid shall be made available to those who lack sufficient resources in so far as such aid is necessary to ensure effective access to justice".

According to Art. 6(1) TEU, the Charter – including Art. 47 – shall be interpreted in compliance with the general provisions of Title VII and in accordance with the Explanations introduced in 2000 – and updated in 2007[1] – exclusively in order to inform the citizens about the content of

M. Borraccetti (✉)
Faculty of Political Science, Forlì Campus, University of Bologna, Bologna, Italy
e-mail: marco.borraccetti@unibo.it

[1]Pursuant to the most recent version, these Explanations "have been have been updated under the responsibility of the Praesidium of the European Convention, in the light of the drafting adjustments made to the text of the Charter by that Convention (notably to Arts. 51 and 52) and of further developments of Union law". [2007] OJ C 303/17. On this topic, see K. Lenaerts, P. V. Van Nuffel, R. Bray (eds.), *Constitutional law of European Union* (Sweet & Maxwell, 2007); K. Lenaerts, D. Arts, I. Maselis (eds.), *Procedural law of European Union* (Sweet & Maxwell, 2006); V. Constantinesco, Y. Gautier, V. Michel

G. Di Federico, *The EU Charter of Fundamental Rights*, Ius Gentium: Comparative Perspectives on Law and Justice 8, DOI 10.1007/978-94-007-0156-4_5,

those provisions[2] and therefore cannot be considered exhaustive.[3] Since the principles enshrined in this provision can also be found in Art. 6 of the European Convention for the protection of Human Rights and Fundamental freedoms (hereafter, ECHR) and therefore already constitute general principles of EU law, it can be argued that no variation will take place in the way the latter norm is conceived, interpreted and applied.

In the case *Asian Institute of Technology (AIT) v. Commission*, the claimant invoked Art. 47 of the Charter denouncing the infringement of her right to an effective remedy. In her opinion AG Stix-Hackl stated that:

> The precepts which can be inferred from the European Convention on Human Rights and which are also binding on the Community institutions, including the Court, could, at most, be considered as the legal basis for the requirement of an effective remedy.[4]

In relation to the interpretation of the provisions of the Charter, it seems unlikely that the EU's highest Jurisdiction will depart from the case law of the European Court of Human Rights (hereafter, ECtHR). In particular, it is hard to envisage that the former court would ever deny the protection requested by the applicant when the latter has previously granted it in similar cases. However, at least until the European Union accedes to the ECHR, the applicability of the case law of the Strasbourg Court by its counterpart in Luxembourg will remain problematic, especially with reference to the content of Art. 47 CFR.[5]

In the future scenario, situations of potential conflict will have to be approached differently. In this regard, the *Emesa Sugar* order[6] provides a good example of how the situation might evolve in the future. Here the ECJ considered the Strasbourg case law on Art. 6 of ECHR[7] inapplicable to the rules of procedure, specifying that:

(eds.), *Le Traité établissant une Constitution pour l'Europe. Analyses & commentaires* (Presses Universitaires de Strasbourg, 2005); G. Zagrebelsky, *Diritti e Costituzione nell'Unione europea* (Laterza, 2003).

[2]The Explanations set out the background of each Charter Article and try to define its scope. To be sure, pursuant to Art. 6 (1) TEU, as amended by the Lisbon Treaty: "The rights, freedoms and principles in the Charter shall be interpreted [. . .] with due regard to the explanations referred to in the Charter, that set out the sources of those provisions". See J. Ziller (ed.), *Il nuovo Trattato europeo* (Il Mulino, 2007) 112.

[3]For instance, with regard to Art. 47 CFR, no reference is made to the *Vermeulen* judgment by the ECtHR (Appl. No 19075/91, *Vermeulen v. Belgium*, (1996) Reports 1996-I).

[4]Case C-547/03P *Asian Institute of Technology (AIT)* [2005] ECR I-845, AG Stix-Hackl.

[5]On the current and future relation between these two courts in the field of fundamental rights protection, see in this volume G. Di Federico, "Chapter 2".

[6]Case C-17/98 *Emesa Sugar* [2000] ECR I-665. See the contribution by P. Oliver in (2002) 39 *Common Market Law Review* 337.

[7]*Vermeulen v. Belgium*, n. 3 above, and Appl. No 39594/98, *Kress v. France*, (2001) Reports 2001-VI.

> the Advocates General [...] are not public prosecutors nor are they subject to any authority, in contrast to the manner in which the administration of justice is organised in certain Member States. They are not entrusted with the defence of any particular interest in the exercise of their duties.

and that:

> Having regard to both the organic and the functional link between the Advocate General and the Court [...], the aforesaid case law of the European Court of Human Rights does not appear to be transposable to the Opinion of the Court's Advocates General.[8]

Before analysing these aspects, it is important to evaluate the right to a fair trial in the ECJ's case law, including the opinions rendered by the Advocates General.

2 Art. 47 in the Case Law of the European Court of Justice

Reference to Art. 47 CFR is rather unfamiliar in the case law of the ECJ.[9] Although the Charter has been mentioned in the vast majority of the decisions on the matter, the Courts have made reference to the right to an effective judicial protection,[10] to the right to a fair trial,[11] to the right to a hearing within a reasonable time[12] and to the right of defence, which

[8]Case C-17/98 *Emesa Sugar*, n. 6 above, para 13.

[9]On the use of the Charter by National and supranational and international courts, see in this volume V. Bazzocchi, "Chapter 3".

[10]Case 222/84 *M. Johnston v. Chief Constable of the Royal Ulster Constabulary* [1986] ECR 1651, para 18, see L. Dubouis, 'A propos de deux principes généraux du droit communautaire (droit au contrôle juridictionnel effectif et motivation des décisions des autorités nationales qui portent atteinte à un droit conféré par la règle communautaire)', (1988) *Revue française de droit administrative* 691; Case C-50/00 P *Union de Pequenos Agricultores v. Council* [2002] ECR I-6677, para 39, see on this topic the contributions by P. Cassia, 'Quelles perspectives pour la recevabilité du recours en annulation des particuliers?', (2002) *Recueil Le Dalloz Jur.* 2825; P.G. Ludewig, 'A lost opportunity: No new approach to the concept of locus standi under Article 230 EC', (2002) *European Law Reporter* 259; M. Granger, 'Standing for the judicial review of community acts potentially harmful to the environment: some light at the end of the tunnel?', (2003) 5 *Environmental Law Review* 45; F. Ragolle, 'Access to justice for private applicants in the Community legal order: recent (r)evolutions', (2003) 28 *European Law Review* 90; J. Temple Lang, 'Actions for declarations that Community regulations are invalid: the duties of national courts under Article 10 EC', (2003) 28 *European Law Review* 102.

[11]Case C-305/05 *Ordre des barreaux francophone et germanophone and Others* [2007] ECR I-5305, paras 29–31, see G. De Amicis, O. Villoni, 'Mandato d'arresto europeo e legalità penale nell'interpretazione della Corte di giustizia', (2008) *Cassazione penale* 383; Case T-351/03 *Schneider Electric SA* [2007] ECR II-2237.

[12]Cf. Case C-185/95 P *Baustahlgewebe* [1998], ECR I-8417, paras 26–54, see further A. Tizzano, 'Durata "ragionevole" dei processi comunitari e problemi di convivenza a Lussemburgo', (1999) *Il Diritto dell'Unione Europea* 174; H. Toner, 'Case C-185/95

represent specific manifestations of the former. Moreover, the rules of procedure state that the parties are entitled to free legal aid so to ensure access to justice regardless of the citizens' financial resources.[13]

The relevant case law mostly concerns EU competition law, for it is in this field that legal or natural persons risk having their rights violated by the European Commission in the course of an administrative procedure, and can seek judicial review before the GC (Court of First Instance before the Lisbon reform) and, on appeal, before the EUCJ.

2.1 The Right to an Effective Judicial Protection

As the ECJ said in *Johnston*[14]:

> The right to an effective judicial protection of the rights that derive from the Community legal order is one of the general principles of law stemming from constitutional traditions common to the Member State.

Moreover, the Luxembourg judges underlined that this principle is also enshrined in Arts. 6 and 13 ECHR.[15] This interpretation and its implementation has some interesting implications. First of all, the conditions for the admissibility of an action for annulment are not dependent upon

P, Baustahlgewebe GmbH v. Commission', (1999) 36 *Common Market Law Review* 1345; M.C. Baruffi, 'Sul diritto di accesso al fascicolo nei procedimenti giurisdizionali comunitari', (1999) *Diritto pubblico comparato ed europeo* 691; Case C-523/04, *Commission v. The Nederlands* [2006] ECR I-3267, AG Mengozzi, paras 57–60.

[13]The right to legal aid is laid down in Art. 76 of the Rules of Procedure of the Court of Justice and in Art. 94 of the Rules of Procedure of the Court of First Instance.

[14]Case 222/84 *M. Johnston*, n. 10 above, para 18.

[15]Case 50/00 P *Union de Pequenos Agricultores*, n. 10 above, para 39; Case C-263/02 P *Commission v. Jégo-Quéré* [2004] ECR I-3425, para 29, see J. Schwarze, 'The legal protection of the individual against regulations in European Union law', (2004) 10 *European Public Law* 285; B. Jack, 'Locus standi and the European Court of Justice: A faint light on the horizon?', (2004) 6 *Environmental Law Review* 266; C. Brown, J. Morijn, 'Case C-263/02 P, Commission v. Jego-Quere & Cie SA', (2004) 41 *Common Market Law Review* 1639; Case T-228/02 *Organisation des Modjahedines du Peuple d'Iran v. Council* [2006] ECR I-4665, para 110, see further C. Eckes, 'Case T-22802, Organisation des Modjahedines du peuple d'Iran v. Council and UK (OMPI)', (2007) 44 *Common Market Law Review* 1117; O. Cotte, 'Des précisions bienvenues quant aux garanties applicables lors de l'adoption de mesures de gels de fonds dans le cadre de la lutte contre le terrorisme', (2007) 22 *L'Europe des libertés: revue d'actualité juridique* 19; Y. Moiny, 'Le contrôle, par le juge européen, de certaines mesures communautaires visant à lutter contre le financement du terrorisme', (2008) 149 *Journal des tribunaux/droit européen* 137; Case C-432/05 *Unibet Ltd v. Justitiekanslern* [2007] ECR I-2271, see the contributions by G. Anagnostaras, 'The quest for an effective remedy and the measure of judicial protection afforded to putative Community law rights', (2007) 32 *European Law Review* 727; A. Arnull, 'Case C-432/05, Unibet (London) Ltd and Unibet (Internationa l) Ltd v. Justitiekanslern', (2007) 32 *Common Market Law Review* 1763.

the claimant's interpretation of the right to effective judicial protection: the Court stated that an individual who is not directly and individually concerned and whose interests consequently could not be affected cannot invoke the right to judicial protection.[16] Otherwise, the ECJ would exceed the jurisdiction it enjoys under the treaties.[17]

However, the EU legal order guarantees the possibility to address the Court. The latter claims that, by virtue of Arts. 263 (230 TEC) and 277 TFEU (241 TEC), combined with Art. 267 TFEU (234 TEC).

> The Treaty has established a complete system of legal remedies and procedures designed to ensure review of the legality of acts of the institutions, and has entrusted such review to the Community Courts.[18]

However, if they cannot directly challenge EU measures of general application under Art. 263 (4) TFEU (230 (4) TEC), natural or legal persons are able – depending on the case – either to indirectly plead for the invalidity of such acts before the European Union courts under Art. 277 TFEU (241 TEC) or, alternatively, to act before the national courts applying for a preliminary reference to the EUCJ as to their validity.[19] In fact, as argued by AG Kokott in *Roquette Frères*:

> Where no other possibility exists for an applicant to obtain a review of the lawfulness of a Community legal act concerning him, the fundamental right to effective judicial protection requires the indirect route – outlined immediately above – not to be barred to him and his indirect challenge to be admissible in an action before national courts.[20]

---

[16] Case C-260/05 P *Sniace SA* [2007] ECR I-10005, paras 64–65, see B. Cheynel, 'Intérêt à agir et participation à la procédure', (2008) 14 *Revue Lamy de la Concurrence: droit, économie, regulation* 43; E. Fridensköld, 'Locus standi in Article 88(2) cases: No cure for the Plaumann-blues I', (2008) *European Law Reporter* 17; J. Battista, 'Is participation in the Commission's administrative procedure a necessary condition for legal standing?', (2008) *European State Aid Law Quarterly* 317.

[17] Case C-131/03 P *Reynolds Tobacco Holdings Inc.* [2006] ECR I-7795, para 81, see the contributions by D. Simon, 'Non-recevabilité de l'action contre une décision de recours en justice', (2006) 303 *Europe* 10; M. Varju, 'Case C-131/03, Reynolds tobacco and others v. Commission', (2007) 44 *Common Market Law Review* 1101; Case C-167/02 P *Rothley et a. v. EP* [2004] ECR I-3149, para 47.

[18] Case C-50/00 P *Union de Pequenos Agricultores*, n. 10 above, para 40; Case C-263/02 P *Jégo-Quéré*, n. 15 above, para 30.

[19] Case C-263/02P *Jégo-Quéré*, n. 15 above, para 30. It is well known that national courts are not entitled to review the legality of Community acts. Cf. Case 314/85 *Foto-Frost* [1987] ECR 4199, see G. Bebr, 'The reinforcement of the constitutional review of community acts under Article 177 EEC Treaty', (1988) 25 *Common Market Law Review* 667; A. Arnull, 'National courts and the validity of community acts', (1988) 14 *European Law Review* 125; L. Goffin, 'De l'incompétence des juridictions nationales pour constater l'invalidité des actes d'institutions communautaires', (1990) *Cahiers de droit européen* 216 and Case 461/03 *Gaston Schul* [2005] ECR I-513. On the latter judgment, see L. Coutron, 'L'arrêt Schul: une occasion manquée de revisiter la jurisprudence Foto-Frost?', (2007) 43 *Revue trimestrielle de droit européen* 491.

[20] Case C-441/05 *Roquette Frères* [2007] ECR I-1993, paras 30 e 33.

In this case, in fact, the exclusion of the indirect challenge in an action before national courts can only be justified in cases where it would undoubtedly have been open to the individual to bring annulment proceedings before the EU Courts. By contrast, should objective uncertainties remain, the private parties are by and large granted standing under Art. 263 (4) TFEU (230 (4) TEC). Moreover, individuals have the possibility to act before the EUCJ promoting an action for non-contractual liability under Arts. 268 (235 TEC) and 340 TFEU (288 TEC). However, given the strict liability conditions laid down therein, their chances of success are rather limited.[21]

As to the protection of EU rights within the national legal orders, the Court has in more than one occasion underlined that fundamental rights, which form an integral part of the general principles of European Union Law, "must also be observed by the Member States when they implement Community rules."[22] Therefore, Member States have the responsibility to ensure, at the national level, judicial protection against such proceedings with all the guarantees provided for by domestic law.[23] In fact, the EU legal order requires that national legislation not undermine the right to an effective judicial protection.[24]

2.2 The Right to a Fair Trial

To describe the concept of "fair trial", the EU judges have regularly referred to the Strasbourg case law. In *Ordre des barreaux francophone et germanophone et a.*, for instance, they underlined that it constitutes a fundamental right which the European Union respects as a general principle under Art. 6(2) TEU. On other occasions the ECJ clarified that this concept consists of various elements which include the rights of defence, the principle of equality of arms, the right of access to the courts and the right to legal assistance both in civil and criminal law proceedings.[25]

This idea was reaffirmed by the Court of First Instance (now General Court, hereinafter CFI) in *Schneider Electric SA/Commission*, where it stated that:

---

[21]Case C-131/03 P *Reynolds Tabacco Holdings Inc and Others*, n. 17 above, para 82.

[22]Case C-521/04 P (R) *Hans-Martin Tillack* [2005] ECR I-3103, para 38; Joined cases C-20/00 e C-64/00 *Booker Aquacultur Ltd and Hydro Seafood GSP Ltd* [2003] ECR I-7411, para 88.

[23]Case C-521/04P(R) *Tillack*, n. 22 above, para 38.

[24]Case C-13/01 *Safalero Srl* [2003] ECR I-8679, para 50.

[25]Case C-305/05 *Ordre des barreaux francophone*, n. 11 above, paras 29–31 that refers to the following European Court of Human Rights judgments: Appl. No 4451/70, *Golder v. UK*, (1984) A18; Appl. Nos 7819/77 and 7878/77, *Campbell-Fell v. UK*, (1984) A80; Appl. No 12005/86, *Borgers v. Belgium*, (1991) A214-B.

> Observance of all persons' right to a hearing before an independent and impartial tribunal is guaranteed by Article 6(1) of the Convention, to which reference is made by Article 6(2) of the Treaty on European Union and which was reaffirmed by the second paragraph of Article 47 of the Charter of Fundamental Rights of the European Union.[26]

In particular, it has been pointed out that the right to a fair hearing is a rule intended to confer rights on individuals and appears amongst the fundamental rights protected in the EU legal order by the ECJ, which is called upon to ensure its respect by the Institutions while exercising their competences.[27]

This judgment is also relevant because the judges expressly defined the content of Art. 47 of the CFR despite its non-binding nature. To be honest, reference to the Charter (and to some of its provisions) can be found in the opinions of the Advocates General[28]. Art. 47 of the Charter, for example, was mentioned in the opinions delivered in *Maersk Olie & Gas A/S*[29] and in *Pupino*.[30]

In the former case, AG Léger invoked this rule in relation to the (legal) notion of trial. In particular, arguing on the basis of the right to a fair trial, he suggested that in defining the expression " party to proceedings", the safeguards laid down in Art. 6 ECHR and in Art. 47 CFR, according to which

[26]Case T-351/03 *Schneider Electric SA*, n. 11 above, para 181.

[27]Case T-309/03 *Camos Grau* [2006] ECR II-1173, paras 102–103, see the contribution by A. García Ureta, '"Qui custodiat custodes?" Sobre las investigaciones de la Oficina Europea de Lucha contra el Fraude', (2006) 8–9 *Unión Europea Aranzadi* 13.

[28]*Ex multis*, Case C-173/99 *The Queen v. BECTU* [2001] ECR I-4881, AG Tizzano, para 26, underlining for the first time the Charter of fundamental right of the European Union, in particular Art. 31. For an extensive review of the use of the Charter by Advocates General, cf. in this volume V. Bazzocchi, "Chapter 3", and G. Ricci, 'BECTU: An unlimited right to annual paid leave', (2001) 30 *Industrial Law Journal* 401; S. Mouthaan, 'The BECTU Case: A la recherche de la charte oubliée', (2001) 12 *European Current Law* xi.

[29]Case C-39/02 *Mærsk Olie & Gas A/S v. Firma M. de Haan en W. de Boer* [2004] ECR I-9657, para 36.

[30]Case C-105/03 *Criminal proceedings against Maria Pupino* [2004] ECR I-5285, para 66, on this topic see the contributions by J.R. Spencer, 'Child witnesses and the European Union', (2005) 64 *The Cambridge Law Journal* 569; E. Broussy, F. Donnat, C. Lambert, 'L'obligation d'interpréter le droit national conformément au droit communautaire s'applique également aux décisions-cadres, (2005) *L'actualité juridique – Droit Administratif* 2336; M. Fletcher, 'Extending "indirect effect" to the third pillar: The significance of Pupino?', (2005) 30 *European Law Review* 862; A. Weyembergh, P. De Hert, P. Paepe, 'L'effectivité du troisième pilier de l'Union européenne et l'exigence de l'interprétation conforme: la Cour de justice pose ses jalons (note sous l'arrêt Pupino, du 16 juin 2005, de la Cour de justice des Communautés européennes)', (2007) 18 *Revue trimestrielle des droits de l'homme* 269; G. Gebbie, '"Berlusconi" v. "Pupino": Conflict or Compatibility?', (2007) 1 *Journal of European Criminal Law* 31; E. Spaventa, 'Opening Pandora's Box: some reflections on the constitutional effects of the decision in Pupino', (2007) 3 *European Constitutional Law Review* 5.

every person has the right to be heard, must be respected. The right of every person to a fair hearing is indeed a general principle of European Union law.

In *Pupino*, AG Kokott suggested that each Member State must also comply with the right of the accused to a fair trial since, under Art. 6 (1) TEU, the European Union, "that is to say, the Community and the Member States", must respect that right, which is also enshrined in Art. 47 of the Charter. In this regard, the Opinion underlines that Art. 6 ECHR is fully applicable. With the ratification and the entry into force of the Lisbon Treaty this type of reference will no longer be necessary: on the one hand there will be a legally enforceable Charter; on the other, the EU will accede to the ECHR.

2.3 The Right to a Hearing Within a Reasonable Time

The right to a hearing within a reasonable time, which also constitutes one of the general principles of EU law, is enshrined in the second paragraph of Art. 47 CFR, that draws inspiration from the ECHR and its interpretative case law. To analyse those rules and how they must be applied, however, reference can be made to the copious jurisprudence developed over the years by the ECJ and the CFI, especially in the field of competition law. In this sense:

> Observance of a reasonable period has been seen by the Community judicature above all as a test for establishing a possible breach of certain general principles of Community law such as, notably, the principle of the protection of legitimate expectations, the principle of legal certainty, the principle of protection of the rights of the defence, as well as the right to a due process.[31]

Furthermore, the right to a fair trial within a reasonable time represents a criterion by which it may be determined whether the EU institutions have acted in accordance with the principle of sound administration. To use AG Mengozzi's words:

> Regardless of its classification as a general principle of Community law or a mere component of principles that are classified as such, compliance with a reasonable time limit is a requirement imposed on the Community administration as a basis for assessing the legitimacy of action taken by it.[32]

This rule, above all, imposes on the institutions a time limit for exercising the powers entrusted to them, since – in compliance with the principle of legal certainty – an Institution cannot unduly and indefinitely defer the exercise of its duties.

---

[31] Case C-523/04 *Commission v. The Netherlands* [2006] ECR I-3267, AG Mengozzi, paras 57–60.

[32] Ibid., para 59.

In *Baustahlgewebe*,[33] which remains an isolated case, the ECJ recognized the violation of that right by the CFI. This judgment represents a landmark decision on the respect of the right in question by the institutions, both in judicial and administrative procedures. On this occasion, the Court decided on appeal against a judgment of the CFI. In support of its action, the appellant claimed that the time taken by the latter to give judgment had been excessive. By analogy with the ECtHR judgments in *Erkner* and *Kemmache*,[34] the ECJ declared that the reasonableness of the time of the trial must be appraised in the light of: (a) the circumstances specific to each case and, in particular, the importance of the case for the person concerned; (b) the complexity of the case and (c) the conduct of the applicant and of the competent authorities.

In particular, as to the first criterion, it is important to underline that both the economic aspect (i.e., the fact that the economic survival of the appellant is not endangered by the proceedings) and the legal aspect (i.e., the need to ensure legal certainty to the applicant, its competitors and other third parties) must be taken into consideration. The second element that judges might appreciate is the number of applications decided concomitantly and which are formally joined for the purposes of the oral procedure, as well as the different languages of the procedure.

As far as the conduct of the appellant is concerned, the courts may evaluate any delaying tactics. With reference to the conduct of the competent institutions, the ECJ has stated that the structure of the EU judicial system justifies, to a certain extent, that the judge – who is ultimately responsible for establishing the facts and undertaking a substantive examination of the dispute – be allowed a relatively long period to investigate actions calling for a close examination of complex facts. However, this does not relieve the EU Court from the duty to observe reasonable time limits in dealing with cases pending before it, acting in accordance with the rules governing the use of languages and the publicity of judgments.

More precisely, the EU judges considered the plea alleging the excessive duration of the proceedings to be well founded for the purposes of setting aside the contested judgment, in so far as it set the amount of the fine imposed on the appellant company. In fact, in the absence of any indication that the length of the proceedings affected their outcome in any way, the ECJ decided not to set aside the contested judgment. For reasons of procedural economy and in order to ensure an immediate and effective remedy

[33] Case C-185/95 P *Baustahlgewebe*, n. 12 above, paras 26–54.

[34] Appl. No. 9616/81, *Erkner-Hofauer v. Austria*, (1987) A124-D, para 66, "Le caractère raisonnable de la durée d'une procédure s'apprécie suivant les circonstances de la cause et eu égard aux critères consacrés par la jurisprudence de la Cour, en particulier le degré de complexité de l'affaire, le comportement des requérants et celui des autorités compétentes"; Appl. Nos 12325/86 and 14992/89, *Kemmache v. France*, (1991) A-218, para 60; Appl. No 11804/85, *Manzoni v. Italy*, (1991) A 195-B, para 17.

against the procedural irregularity committed by the CFI, the judges opted for a reduction of the amount of the fine imposed by the Commission (and confirmed by the CFI) without specifying any general criterion, but construing a strict connection between fine reduction and compensation for damages.

This position – which limits the possibility to set aside the judgment under appeal to cases where it appears sufficiently clear that the length of the proceedings affected their outcome but in no way conditions the right to compensation for damages – was reaffirmed in *SARL (SGA)*,[35] *Nederlandse Federatieve*[36] and, most importantly, in *Thyssen Stahl AG*[37] where the judges offered further indications on the issue.

In fact, after having repeated that the right to a fair hearing and to have a case tried within a reasonable period are general principles of European Union law,[38] the ECJ claimed that the reasonableness of such period is to be appraised in the light of circumstances specific to each case, and in particular, of the importance of the case for the person concerned, its complexity, as well as the conduct of the applicant and of the competent authorities. In addition, the ECJ held that the list is not exhaustive and that the assessment of the "reasonable time" does not require a systematic examination of each single criterion where the duration of the proceedings appears justified in the light of (just) one of them. More generally, in fact, the average time needed to handle similar cases will be used like a general benchmark.

Of course, the need for prompt decisions has to be balanced against the necessity to fully establish – and with the highest possible exactness – the facts at the origin of the case at hand. As underlined in the *Limburgse Vynil* judgment,[39] the aim of swiftness – which the Union judiciary must seek to attain – must not adversely affect the efforts to establish the facts at issue and to provide the parties with every opportunity to produce evidence and submit observations, and to reach a decision only after close consideration.[40]

---

[35] Case C-39/00P *SARL* [2000] ECR I-11201, para 46.

[36] Case C-105/04P *CEF BV and CEF Holdings Ltd v. Nederlandse Federatieve Vereniging and Technische Unie BV* [2006] ECR I-8725, para 43, see the contribution by F. Zivy, 'Le prolongement excessif de la phase d'instruction peut permettre une violation des droits de la défense', (2006) 4 *Revue des droits de la concurrence* 115.

[37] Case C-194/99 P *Thyssen Stahl AG* [2003] ECR I-10821, paras 154 to156 and 165 to 167.

[38] In Case C-403/04P *Sumitomo Metal Industries Ltd and Nippon Steel Corp.* [2007] ECR I-729, paras 115 to 123, the Court reaffirmed that the right to a fair trial – and in particular the right to a fair trial in a reasonable time – is enshrined in Art. 6 ECHR.

[39] Case C-238/99P, *Limburgse Vinyl Maatschappij NV* [2002] ECR I-8375, para 234.

[40] Appl. No 2122/64, *Wemhoff v. Germany*, (1968) A7 and Appl. No 1936/6327, *Neumeister v. Austria*, (1968) A8.

2.4 The Right of Defence and the Right to Be Heard

The second aspect to be analyzed concerns the principle of the right to a fair hearing. If, originally, it has mainly been invoked in the context of competition law cases and in infringement procedures against Member States, the principle is now characterizing EU procedural law as a whole. On several occasions, its respect was contested by the parties complaining that they had no right to object to the AG's opinion. The request was founded on the respect of Art. 6 ECHR as interpreted by the ECtHR. But before addressing the scope of the right to be heard it is necessary to refer to the right to a fair hearing and to the right of defence.

In this regard, the Court of Justice stated that "the principle of the right to a fair hearing is closely linked to the principle of the right to be heard" and that it must be applied to citizens as well as to Member States.[41] This is one of the fundamental principles of Community law and all national legal orders "in all proceedings initiated against a person which are liable to culminate in a measure adversely affecting that person", must guarantee it, even in the absence of specific domestic rules governing the proceedings in question.[42]

It will be recalled that in *Corus UK*[43] the ECJ insisted on the need to respect the rights of the defence as one of the fundamental principles of EC/EU law, adding that this principle is infringed whenever a judicial decision is based on facts and/or documents which the parties, or one of them, have not had an opportunity to examine and on which they have been unable to comment.

This decision seems to go against what had been affirmed in the *Emesa Sugar*[44] order and in various other occasions. The impossibility to replicate to the solution put forward by the AG has always been "settled" by making reference to Art. 61 of the Rules of Procedure, although this rule assigns to the Court a discretionary power to order the reopening of the oral procedure.[45] If the Court of Justice finds it possible to deliver the judgment without acquiring further information, there will be no need to reopen the procedure. This stance conflicts with the *Corus UK* judgment, as well as with the *Vermeulen* case law of the Strasbourg' Court,[46] which grants

---

[41] Joined cases C-439/05 P and C-454/05 P *Land Oberosterreich and Austria* [2007] ECR I-7141, para 36, see F. M. Fleurke, 'What use for Article 95(5) EC?', (2008) 20 *Journal of Environmental Law* 267.

[42] *Ex multis*, Case C-287/02 *Spain v. Commission* [2005] ECR I-5093, para 37.

[43] Case C-199/99 P *Corus UK Ltd* [2003] ECR I-11177, paras 19–25, 41–43, 50–59.

[44] Case C-17/98 *Emesa Sugar*, n. 6 above.

[45] According Art. 61 of the Rules of Procedure, the Court of Justice "may after hearing the Advocate General order the reopening of the oral procedure".

[46] *Vermeulen v. Belgium*, n. 3 above.

the parties the right to have knowledge of, and comment on, all evidence adduced or observations filed so as to influence the Court's final decision.

This right is not called into question by the *Kress* judgment,[47] where the ECtHR found no breach of the principle of equality of arms. In fact, following the *Commissaire du gouvernement's opinion*, the parties (lawyers, if they wish, can ask the Government Commissioner, before the hearing, to indicate the general tenor of his submissions) may reply to those submissions by means of a memorandum. This being the case, the compatibility of the national legal order with the ECHR is evident, but the same does not apply to the EU system which, on the contrary, provides that after having heard the opinion of the Advocate General in a public hearing the President "shall declare the oral procedure closed".[48]

But the violation of the right to adversarial proceedings resulting from the refusal on the part of the ECJ to allow the reply to the Opinion of the AG was recently argued again before the ECtHR in *Cooperatieve Producentenorganisatie van de Nederlandse Kokkelvissarij v. Netherlands*.[49] Here the Court applied the equivalent protection doctrine elaborated in *Bosphorus* but found that the applicants had failed to prove that the guarantees available to them under the EU legal order were manifestly deficient; consequently, they had not rebutted the presumption that the procedure before the ECJ provides equivalent protection of their rights. Most notably, the ECtHR accepted as "realistic and not merely theoretical" the possibility offered by Rule 61 of the Rules of Procedure. In doing so it cited AG's Opinion in *Government of the French Community and Walloon Government v. Flemish Government*[50] and inferred directly from the decision in *Landelijke Vereniging* that a request for reopening submitted by one of the parties to the proceedings "is considered on its merits".[51]

3 Future Perspectives Arising from the Reform Treaty

It appears useful here to try to assess the consequences of a legally binding Charter and of the future accession of the EU to the ECHR.

As far as the EU procedural law is concerned, it appears evident that individuals will be able to rely exclusively on Art. 47 CFR. This would most

---

47 *Kress v. France*, n. 7 above.

48 Pursuant to Art. 59 of the Rules of Procedure: "The Advocate General shall deliver his opinion orally at the end of the oral procedure" and "After the Advocate General has delivered his opinion, the President shall declare the oral procedure closed".

49 Appl. No 13645/05, *Cooperatieve Producentenorganisatie van de Nederlandse Kokkelvissarij v. The Netherlands*, (2009) unreported.

50 Case C-212/06 *Government of the French Community and Walloon Government v. Flemish Government* [2008] ECR I-1683.

51 Case C-127/02 *Landelijke Vereniging tot Behoud van de Waddenzee and Others* [2004] ECR I-7405.

likely be the only relevant novelty, since – as was stated by the judgment *Baustahlgewebe*[52] – the rights related to the right to a fair trial already receive protection within the EU legal order and the rules on access to justice will remain substantially unaltered.

And yet, some doubts could arise as to the institution individuals should turn to when seeking redress for the violation of the rights deriving from Art. 47 CFR and more precisely the damages deriving from an excessive duration of proceedings. In this regard it can be argued that when the proceeding in question concerns a case pending before the General Court[53] the infringement will be brought before the EUCJ.[54] In other words the approach adopted in *Baustahlgewebe* would remain valid with the difference that individuals could base their appeal on Art. 47 CFR. By contrast, should the EUCJ be responsible for such a violation – judging in the case of appeal against a decision of the General Court or in a preliminary ruling procedure – it is suggested that the competent judge would be the General Court, addressed under Arts 268[55] and 340 (2) TFEU,[56] since this action is not reserved to the former Judge under Art. 51 of the Statute.

As to the accession to the ECHR, it is suggested that not all actions brought before ECtHR – which are admissible only after all internal remedies have been exhausted – would necessarily result in a condemnation of the EU. In fact, should cases concerning the violation of rights protected under the Convention reach the judges in Strasbourg, the latter would presumably (continue to) apply the well known *Bosphorus* precedent evaluating whether the protection of fundamental rights by EU Law can be considered to be – and to have been at the relevant time – "equivalent" to that guaranteed under the ECHR.[57] Only in the event the required protection is deemed to be insufficient, a judgment against the EU legal system could be rendered, underlying the violation of the principles laid down in the ECHR, as interpreted by the European Court of Human Rights.

---

[52] Case C-185/95P *Baustahlgewebe*, n. 33 above.

[53] Under the Lisbon Treaty the CFI is referred to as the General Court (cf. Art. 19 TEU).

[54] The General Court shall have jurisdiction to hear and determine actions and proceedings brought against decisions of the Civil Service Tribunal.

[55] Cf. Art. 235 TEC.

[56] Cf. Art. 288 TEC.

[57] Appl. No 45036/98, *Bosphorus v. Ireland* [2005] 42 EHRR, para 155 and *Cooperatieve Producentenorganisatie*, n. 49 above.

Candidate Countries Facing a Binding Charter of Fundamental Rights: What's New?

Luisa Ficchi

1 Preliminary Remarks

From the perspective of candidate countries the adoption of a newly binding Charter of Fundamental Rights (hereafter CFR or the Charter) certainly raises many interesting questions. This Chapter aims at answering the following: (a) does the binding nature of the Charter affect the accession procedure to the EU? and (b) is the Charter likely to raise the threshold of human rights conditionality with respect to enlargement policy?

Before addressing these core questions, it appears useful to verify the potential of the Charter against the general topic of integration within the EU. The Charter represents one of the main constitutional steps the EU has taken throughout its history, and this entails a major change in the European internal order. It will affect, among other things, the internal scrutiny of the EU Member States with reference to their human rights standards and allow the EU to assess the continuous compliance of the 27 Members with fundamental rights and freedoms. This is not just a matter for "internal" concern; it also affects the integration of new Member States in the EU.[1] These aspects will be analysed in the first section of this Chapter. The second part will analyse the implications of a binding Charter of fundamental rights from the standpoint of the enlargement policy with specific regard to the accession criteria.

L. Ficchi (✉)
Faculty of Political Science, Forlì Campus, University of Bologna, Bologna, Italy
e-mail: luisa.ficchi@gmail.com

[1] M. Cremona, 'EU enlargement: Solidarity and conditionality', (2005) 30 *European Law Review* 3. See also G. De Búrca, 'On enlargement of the European Union: Beyond the Charter: How enlargement has enlarged the human rights policy of the European Union', (2004) 27 *Fordham International Law Journal* 696.

G. Di Federico, *The EU Charter of Fundamental Rights*, Ius Gentium: Comparative Perspectives on Law and Justice 8, DOI 10.1007/978-94-007-0156-4_6,

2 Fostering Integration Through a Binding Charter

The Charter undoubtedly represents a further step towards the progressive constitutionalisation of the EU.[2] The mere fact that the CFR is no longer included in a primary law act – explicitly called "Constitution" or "Constitutional Treaty" – but simply referred to in a Protocol of the Lisbon Treaty, does not affect its binding force[3] nor its symbolic value. As to its legal and political significance, it appears undisputable that it will play an essential role in the EU constitutional construction.

From a purely internal perspective, the CFR can be considered as a synthesis of the values and legacies of the historical, political and legal experiences of the various Member States as well as the result of the process of integration itself. The adoption of a common catalogue of fundamental rights and freedoms is in fact the expression of the intention to create "an even closer union"[4] between the former. It is well known that far from being the first acknowledgment of fundamental rights within the EU/EC legal system, the Charter purports an extensive codification of the latter.[5] In this sense, it represents a starting point towards a further "deepening" of EU integration. The European Council of Cologne, in 1999, also pointed out that making rights visible through a comprehensive codification would enhance the overall legitimacy of the EU within its borders.[6] The European Council was mainly concerned about the perception that citizens had of the EU, promoting the perception of the Union as a legitimate political actor founded on shared values.

The issue of "internal legitimacy" must be put into perspective by taking into account two specific aspects. Firstly, the EU had just completed a revision of the founding treaties, failing to solve the problem of the competence of the Union in the field of human rights protection posed by Opinion 2/94.[7] According to the European Court of Justice, only an amendment

---

[2]L.S. Rossi, 'Verso la Costituzione europea?' in L.S. Rossi (ed.), *Carta dei Diritti Fondamentali e Costituzione europea* (Giuffré, 2002) 249; J.H.H. Weiler, *The Constitution of Europe: "Do the new clothes have an emperor?" And other essays on European integration* (Cambridge University Press, 1999).

[3]And further specified in Protocol No 8 annexed to the Treaty. [2008] OJ C 115/273.

[4]Cf. Preamble of the Charter [2007] OJ C 303/1.

[5]This was the view of the European Council when deciding to draft the Charter. 'There appears to be a need, at the present stage of the Union's development, to establish a Charter of Fundamental Rights in order to make their overriding importance and relevance more visible to the Union's citizens." Cf. Conclusions of the Presidency, Cologne European Council, 3 and 4 June 1999, accessible at http://www.consilium.europa.eu/.

[6]According to the Presidency Conclusions: 'Protection of fundamental rights is a founding principle of the Union and an indispensable prerequisite for her legitimacy".

[7]Opinion 2/94 [1996] ECR I-1759. The Court of Justice did recall, however, that 'fundamental rights form an integral part of the general principles of law whose observance the Court ensures" (para 33). See further, P. Allott, 'Fundamental rights in the EU',

of the Treaties would have allowed accession to the ECHR, but no legal basis for this was included into primary law until recently, when Art. I-9 of the Constitutional Treaty expressly recognised that "[t]he Union shall accede to the European Convention for the Protection of Human Rights and Fundamental Freedoms".[8] The Lisbon Treaty has maintained this provision unaltered.[9] Secondly, the Cologne European Council was facing the widest enlargement the Union has ever experienced: strengthening internal self-representation and legitimacy was of the utmost importance.

Moreover, there was widespread concern about the ability of the Central and Eastern European candidates to fully integrate into the EU legal system. Less than a decade had passed since these countries were on the other side of the Iron Curtain and their transition to democracy and a free market economy had just begun. Against this background, Member States demanded that the move towards the EU Western political model be closely monitored in order to avoid jeopardizing the achievements so painfully attained.[10]

Thus, a certain parallelism can be drawn between the enlargement dynamics and the progressive constitutionalisation of the EU in the field of human rights, even if the "official documents do not show that the enlargement factor played any significant role in the context of drafting the Charter."[11] In this regard, Wojciech Sadursky points out that the European Commission's Communication of 2000[12] "seems to be more of an

(1996) 3 *The Cambridge Law Journal* 409; G. Gaja, 'Opinion 2/94, Accession by the Community to the European Convention for the Protection of Human Rights and Fundamental Freedoms, given on 28 March 1996, not yet reported', (1996) 4 *Common Market Law Review* 973; L.S. Rossi, 'Il parere 2/94 sull'adesione della Comunità europea alla Convenzione europea dei diritti dell'uomo', (1996) 3 *Il Diritto dell'Unione Europea* 839; P. Wachsmann, 'L'avis 2/94 de la Cour de justice relatif à l'adhésion de la Communauté européenne à la Convention de sauvegarde des droits de l'homme et des libertés fondamentales', (1996) 3 *Revue trimestrielle de droit européen* 467; N. Burrows, 'Question of Community accession to the European Conventiondetermined', (1997) 1 *European Law Review* 58.

[8] [2004] OJ C 310/1.

[9] [2008] OJ C 115/1.

[10] K. E. Smith, 'The evolution and application of EU Membership conditionality', in M. Cremona (ed.), *The enlargement of the European Union* (Oxford University Press, 2003) at 106.

[11] W. Sadursky, 'Charter and enlargement', (2002) 3 *European Law Journal* 340. See also W. Sadursky, 'The Role of the EU Charter of Rights in the process of enlargement' in G. Bermann and K. Pistor (eds.), *Law and governance in an enlarged European Union* (Hart, 2004), at 61and C. Pinfell, 'Conditionality and enlargement in the light of EU constitutional development', (2004) 10 *European Law Journal* 354.

[12] Commission Communication on the Charter of Fundamental Rights of the European Union. COM (2000) 559 final, para 12 states that: '[w]ith the Union now developing a real common foreign and security policy, in which respect for fundamental rights will play a key role, the adoption of a catalogue of rights will make it possible to give a clear response

after-thought [...] rather than a motivating factor for launching the work on the Charter."[13]

The Preamble of the Charter makes no reference to the external dimension of the Union. It is stated that:

> The peoples of Europe, in creating an ever closer union among them, are resolved to share a peaceful future based on common values [...]. The Union contributes to the preservation and to the development of these common values while respecting the diversity of the cultures and traditions of the peoples of Europe.[14]

The Member States share common values and are thus willing to deepen their integration precisely through their promotion. No reference is made to the neighbouring countries already involved in the accession process.[15]

The idea of a larger Union may, with a certain interpretative effort, be inferred from the reference to the peoples of Europe and not to the citizens of the EU. After all, it is precisely to these subjects that the Charter will apply. Nonetheless, since the EU was still undergoing an enlargement process, a short reference to "the others" would not have been inappropriate. Of course one could argue that this circumstance does not in itself discard the idea of a "larger Union". And yet the exclusion of any reference to candidate countries is difficult to understand given that representatives from the then ten Eastern Europe candidate countries joined the Convention called upon to draft the Charter, albeit only as "observers".[16]

The fact that enlargement is not explicitly taken into consideration cannot exclude virtuous interrelations between the "widening" of the EU and this (constitutional) "deepening". This becomes evident taking into consideration a specific facet of enlargement and integration, namely the double standard problem. The latter will be addressed in the following section.

---

to those who accuse the Union of employing one set of standards at external level and another internally. The Charter will provide the Union with a clear catalogue of rights that it will have to respect when implementing both internal and external policies."

[13] W. Sadursky, 'Charter and enlargement', n. 10 above, at 345.

[14] [2007] OJ C 303/1.

[15] Neighbouring countries must be understood in a geo-political sense. No reference is made to those countries which, although involved in the Neighbourhood policy of the European Union, have no chance of becoming new members or, rather, are a priori excluded from any admission procedure. The latter statement does not apply to the Balkan countries and Turkey that are formally candidate or potential candidate states. Cf. Conclusions of the Presidency, Santa Maria Da Feira European Council, 19 and 20 June 2000, para 67.

[16] They are not included amongst the observers (two representatives of the Court of Justice of the European Communities to be designated by the Court and two representatives of the Council of Europe, including one from the European Court of Human Rights), but in a separate group labelled 'Exchange of views with the applicant States'. Cf. Annex to the Presidency Conclusions, Tampere European Council, 15 and 16 October 1999.

3 The Double Standard vis-à-vis Member States

The attitude of the EU towards its Member States has often been accused of being much more permissive than the approach developed in evaluating the "new" acceding countries on issues related to the protection of human rights. Some have denounced the schizophrenia afflicting the EU in its internal and external policies;[17] others have spoken about a "bifurcation" in the EU's approach to human rights.[18] As argued by Andrew Williams:

> The scope of human rights so scrutinised in the accession criteria extends some way beyond that which falls within the European Union's internal concerns.[19]

The application of a double standard – one for Member States, the other for candidate countries – undermines the overall credibility of the EU as a human rights actor, ultimately jeopardizing its external legitimacy.

This distinction affects the assessment/enforcement of human rights, within and outside the EU. If we take into consideration the enlargement policy there is a full set of procedures developed by the EU institutions in order to ascertain the actual compliance with accession standards by candidate countries through the Commission's regular reports. Failure to achieve the expected results may entail the suspension of the accession procedure until the country in question has taken the appropriate steps to remedy the situation. This was the case with Bulgaria and Romania, which acceded only in 2007 although originally expected to join in 2004.

However, there is yet another level of conditionality applying to accession. On the one hand, there are conditions, such as the Copenhagen criteria, that must be satisfied in order to start negotiating the accession agreement. On the other hand, there are requirements that follow the conclusion of agreements, heralding the presentation of a candidature (this is the case with potential Member States) or representing an integral part of the pre-accession strategy. These agreements, known as "association agreements", "Europe agreements" or "stabilisation agreements", depending on the countries involved,[20] establish another system for sanctioning the non

---

[17] P. Alston and J.H.H. Weiler, 'An European Union human rights policy' in P. Alston (ed.), *The European Union and human rights* (Oxford University Press, 1999).

[18] A. Williams, *EU human rights policies. A study in irony* (Oxford University Press, 2004).

[19] A. Williams, 'Enlargement of the Union and human rights conditionality: A policy of distinction?', (2000) 25 *European Law Review* 601 and A. Williams, *EU Human Rights Policies. A Study in Irony* (Oxford University Press, 2004).

[20] The European Community has entered into association agreements with a number of countries (for example, with the Mediterranean countries – within the Euro-Mediterranean Partnership – and with countries involved in the European Neighbourhood Policy of South Caucasus and Turkey). These agreements were not conceived as pre-accession instruments, but some of them were progressively re-oriented so to fall within the accession strategy. See E. Lannon, K. Inglis and T. Haenebalke, 'The

fulfilment of certain conditions concerning the respect of democratic principles, human rights and the rule of law. According to the general rules of international law,[21] these conditions are to be considered essential, allowing one of the contracting parties to suspend or terminate the relevant treaty when the other party fails to comply with them.

The mechanism laid down to sanction the behaviour of Member States appears to be far less complex. The first attempt to introduce a monitoring procedure within the EU borders can be found in the Amsterdam Treaty, subsequently amended by the Nice Treaty. Reference is to Art. 7 TEU, stating that the Council, on a reasoned proposal by one third of the Member States, by the European Parliament or by the Commission, after obtaining the assent of the European Parliament, may determine that there is a clear risk of a serious breach by a Member State of the principles mentioned in Art. 6 (1) EU, and address appropriate recommendations to that State. Moreover, the Council, acting unanimously on a proposal by one third of the Member States or by the Commission and after obtaining the assent of the European Parliament, may determine the existence of a serious and persistent breach by a Member State of the principles mentioned in Art. 6 (1) EU and decide to suspend certain of the rights deriving from the application of the Treaty to the Member State in question, including the voting rights of the representative of the government of that Member State in the Council.[22]

This procedure has never been implemented so far and contains an important shortcoming: the rights of the accused Member State are not fully protected for it has no right to reply to the Council's findings. Moreover, the gravity of the violation required de facto limits the use of the provision in

many faces of EU conditionality in Pan-Euro-Mediterranean relations' in M. Marescau and E. Lennon (eds.), *The EU's enlargement and Mediterranean strategies. A comparative analysis* (Basingstoke, 2001) at 110. In line with this new trend, the 90s association agreements concluded with the countries of Central and Eastern Europe (namely, Bulgaria, the Czech Republic, Estonia, Latvia, Lithuania, Hungary, Romania, Slovakia, Slovenia and Poland) were named Europe Agreements and the relations with the Western Balkan countries (namely, Macedonia and Croatia) Stabilisation and Association Agreements. This process has not directly concerned the Association Agreement with Turkey (see Council Decision 64/732/EEC of 23 December 1963 on the conclusion of the Agreement establishing an Association between the European Economic Community and Turkey [1964] OJ L 217/1) that has not been amended despite the strategic importance of fundamental rights protection.

[21] Namely, Arts. 60–62 of the Vienna Convention on the Law of Treaties (1969).

[22] H. Schmitt von Sydow, 'Liberté, démocratie, droits fondamentaux et etat de droit. analyse de l'art. 7 du Traité UE', (2001) 2 *Revue du Droit de l'Union Européenne* 285; A. Verhoeven, 'How democratic need European Union members be? Some thoughts after Amsterdam', (1998) 1 *European Law Review* 217; A. von Bogdandy, 'The European Union as a human rights organisation? Human rights and the core of the European Union', (2007) 4 *Common Market Law Review* 1307.

question.[23] In this respect, the potential of the CFR is remarkable. Firstly, it introduces a comprehensive system of human rights standard for Member States, whereas the control guaranteed so far by Art. 7, in conjunction with Art. 6 (1) TEU, may not cover some basic rights, such as minority rights, taken into great consideration during the accession strategy and then suddenly forgotten once membership is achieved.

Secondly, it can be very useful in helping the institutions set the appropriate threshold of a violation. For instance, according to Art. 52 CFR, if the allegedly violated right corresponds to a right guaranteed by the ECHR, it will have to be interpreted in accordance with the meaning and scope it is granted under the latter convention. The CFR must ensure the same protection as the ECHR. If the Council were confronted with a serious and persistent (alleged) breach, its task would be easier, since it could refer to the case law of the ECtHR concerning that right.

Thirdly, the respect for the rule of law could be enhanced. The judicial review of the Court of Justice of the European Union (hereafter ECJ or EUCJ) does not cover the political decision adopted by the Council pursuant to Art. 7 TEU, but it does extend to the violation of the procedure provided for therein allowing for the annulment of the decision imposing sanctions on the responsible Member State. On the contrary, according to Art. 51 CFR, both aspects (procedural and substantial) fall within the scope of application of the Charter and are subject to the jurisdiction of the EUCJ.[24]

4 The Charter and Candidate Countries: Old *Acquis* or New Burdens?

4.1 A Brief Excursus on Enlargement Conditionality

When dealing with accession conditionality,[25] it should be borne in mind that the standard has substantially varied throughout the years: the first Member States to enter the EC had to comply with far less stringent requirements with respect to the new joining Parties. The conditions for accession

---

[23]B. De Witte and G. Toggenburg, 'Human rights and membership of the European Union', in S. Peers and A. Ward (eds), *The European Union Charter of Fundamental Rights* (Oxford University Press, 2004) at 73.

[24]Unfortunately, this does not mean that the right for individuals to access the Court will be enhanced. The Treaty of Lisbon, in fact, has only brought minor changes to the wording of Art. 230 TEU. Cf. Art. 263 of the Treaty on the Functioning of the European Union. On this particular issue see in this volume the contribution by G. Sanna, "Chapter 9".

[25]On conditionality, see E. Fierro, *The EU's approach to human rights conditionality in practice* (New York, 2003).

were never included in a legally binding document but have nevertheless become one of the most powerful instruments of EU foreign policy.[26]

Political conditionality – linked to the respect of human rights, democracy and the rule of law – has been the main benchmark in evaluating candidatures since the mid-1970s. During those years, three European countries (namely, Spain, Portugal and Greece), after the transition from an authoritarian regime to democracy, manifested their intention to accede to the EC. The European Council did not explicitly impose precise conditions on these candidatures, but limited itself to declare that respect for human rights and representative democracy were essential elements to acquire membership.[27] The elaboration of a more complex and structured set of rules on accession became particularly urgent after the end of the Cold War, when a great number of States that had belonged to the Soviet block applied to join the EC.

The first document spelling out the scope of membership conditionality was drafted by the Copenhagen European Council in 1993.[28] According to the resulting so-called "Copenhagen criteria", each candidate country had to achieve:[29] (a) stability of institutions guaranteeing democracy, the rule of law, human rights and respect for and protection of minorities (political criterion); (b) the existence of a functioning market economy as well as the capacity to cope with competitive pressure and market forces within the Union (economic criterion); (c) ability to take on the obligations of membership including adherence to the aims of political, economic and monetary union (*acquis communautaire* criterion).

The criteria which govern accession can be found in primary law since the 1997 Amsterdam Treaty. In this respect two provisions are noteworthy: on the one hand, Art. 6 (1) TEU states that " [t]he Union is founded on the principles of liberty, democracy, respect for human rights and fundamental freedoms, and the rule of law, principles which are common to the Member States"; on the other, Art. 49 TEU affirms that " [any] European State which respects the principles set out in Art. 6 (1) may apply to become a member

---

[26] M. Cremona, 'Enlargement: A successful instrument of EU foreign policy?', in T. Tridimas and P. Nebbia (eds.), *European Union law for the twenty-first century: Rethinking the new legal order*, vol. *I* (Oxford University Press, 2003) 268.

[27] K. E. Smith, 'The evolution and application of EU membership conditionality', in M. Cremona (ed.), *The enlargement of the European Union* (Oxford University Press, 2003) at 109–110. See also M. Nowak, 'human rights 'conditionality' in relation to entry to, and full participation in, the EU', in P. ALSTON (ed.), *The EU and human rights* (Oxford University Press, 1999) 687; and M. Maresceau and E. Lannon (eds.) *The EU's enlargement and Mediterranean strategies: A comparative analysis* (London, 2001).

[28] Conclusions of the Presidency, Copenhagen European Council, 21–22 June 1993, SN 180/1/93.

[29] On the Copenaghen criteria see also: D. Katz, 'Les 'critères de Copenhague'', (2000) 40 *Revue du Marché Commun et de l'Union Européenne* 483 and D. Kochenov, 'Behind the Copenhagen Facade. The Meaning and Structure of the Copenhagen Political Criteria of Democracy and the Rule of Law', (2004) 8 *European Integration On-Line Papers* 10.

of the Union. [...]. The conditions of admission and the adjustments to the Treaties on which the Union is founded, which such admission entails, shall be the subject of an agreement between the Member States and the applicant State"[30].

Unfortunately, no subsequent amendments provided further indication regarding the above mentioned conditions. This is most regrettable since the Copenhagen criteria lack in transparency leaving open to speculation crucial issues such as the notion of democracy, the scope of human rights or the set of requirements coming under the umbrella of the rule of law.

These shortcomings seem to have been acknowledged by the General Affairs Council in its Conclusions concerning the relations with the States of Former Yugoslavia of 1997 when it was agreed that in evaluating compliance with democratic principles, the following conditions would be verified: the existence of a representative government and of an accountable executive; the presence of a government and public authorities that act in accordance with the constitution and the law; the separation of powers (government, administration, judiciary); the holding of free and fair elections at reasonable intervals and by secret ballot.

Under the heading human rights and rule of law, the Council places freedom of expression, including independent media; right of assembly and demonstration; right of association; right to privacy, family, home and correspondence; right to property; the existence of effective means of redress against administrative decisions; access to courts and right to fair trial; respect for the principle of equality before the law and equal protection by the law; protection from inhuman or degrading treatment and arbitrary arrest. As to minorities, the document recognizes the right to establish and maintain their own educational, cultural and religious institutions, organisations or associations; the need to guarantee adequate opportunities to use their respective language before courts and public authorities as well as an adequate protection of refugees and displaced persons returning to areas where they represent an ethnic minority.[31]

It follows that the conditions for accession are flexible and mutable. They are basically defined on a case-by-case basis as the progress and monitoring reports regularly issued by the European Commission clearly indicate. Each candidate country is considered individually and independently from the others so that some of the requirements for the scrutiny by the Commission vary during the pre-accession phase.[32]

---

[30]To be sure, Art. O of the Maastricht Treaty stated that any European State could apply to become a member of the European Union.

[31]See Annex, European Council Conclusions 'on the principle of conditionality governing the development of the European Union's relations with certain countries of Southern Europe', EU *Bull*. 4-1997.

[32]M. Maresceau, 'Pre-accession', in M. Cremona (ed.), *The enlargement of the European Union* (Oxford University Press, 2003) 9; and M. Maresceau and E. Montaguti,

4.2 The True Scope of the Charter

According to Art. 51 of the CFR: "[t]he provisions of this Charter are addressed to the institutions, bodies, offices and agencies of the Union with due regard for the principle of subsidiarity and to the Member States only when they are implementing Union law". As the Praesidium states,[33] this Article "seeks to establish clearly that the Charter applies primarily to the institutions and bodies of the Union, in compliance with the principle of subsidiarity" and, as far as Member States are concerned, that "it follows unambiguously from the case-law of the Court of Justice that the requirement to respect fundamental rights defined in the context of the Union is only binding on the Member States when they act in the scope of Union law".

This provision removes any possible doubt on the applicability of the Charter to candidate States. As previously suggested, this is not striking: if the applicability of the CFR is limited vis-à-vis the Member States, any interpretation in favour of candidate states should be ruled out. Of course, the fact that an act is not legally binding and is not directly linked to conditionality does not prevent the EU from applying it to the enlargement policy actions it carries out. This has occurred, for instance, with the Copenhagen criteria, which offer the correct interpretative key: as far as the provisions of the CFR can be considered to be part of the *acquis communautaire*, they compel candidate States. The question is whether and to what extent this assumption is correct and verifiable.

And yet, in order to compare the level of protection granted by each right proclaimed in the CFR with the level of protection guaranteed by the *acquis communautaire*, an in-depth analysis of each provision of the Charter would be needed. This goes beyond the scope of this Chapter.[34] Nonetheless, some general observations appear necessary. The CFR does not follow the traditional classification of other human rights instruments: no distinction is made between civil and political rights on the one hand, and economic and social rights on the other.[35] However, these categories will be used for the sake of clarity and simplification.

'The relations between the European Union and Central and Eastern Europe: A legal appraisal', (1995) 6 *Common Market Law Review* 1328.

[33] Explanations Relating to the Charter of Fundamental Rights [2007] OJ C 303/17.

[34] Furthermore, this kind of analysis has been carried out by several scholars: see, for example, S. Koukoulis-Spiliotopoulos, 'Towards a European Constitution: Does the Charter of Fundamental Rights 'maintain in full" the *acquis communautaire*?', (2002) 1 *Revue européenne de droit public* 57; C. Tomushat, 'Common values and the place of the Charter in Europe', (2002) 1 *Revue européenne de droit public*, 159; J. Dutheil de la Rochère, 'Les droits fondamentaux reconnus par la Charte et leurs applications', (2002) 1 *Revue européenne de droit public* 227; P. Craig, 'The Community Rights and the Charter', (2002) 1 *Revue européenne de droit public* 196.

[35] By contrast, rights are listed under the following titles: Dignity, Freedoms, Equality, Solidarity, Citizens' Rights and Justice.

As far as civil and political rights are concerned, a substantial correspondence can be traced between the CFR and the ECHR.[36] Some issues are raised in Art. 2 CFR inasmuch as this provision deals with bioethical questions such as human cloning, which were never addressed before within the EU. Art. 8 (on the protection of personal data) represents a new right, the protection of which is guaranteed by the CFR.

As far as economic, social and cultural rights are concerned, a full, comprehensive equivalence of the CFR with the *acquis* is not as evident. Art. 15, for instance, concerning the right to work, only partially reflects the latter. According to the *acquis*, the right to work is a basic, fundamental social right enshrined in the European Social Charter – whereas Art. 15 of the CFR only concerns the freedom to seek employment, to work and to move throughout the Union.[37]

With reference to accession policy and conditionality, it is perhaps striking that the Charter does not mention minority rights. Art. 21, prohibiting any kind of discrimination, explicitly refers to national minorities, but the numerous concerns linked to the respect of minority rights – which, as a cornerstone of membership conditionality, had a significant impact on national legislation during the pre-accession phase – found no place in the CFR. This does not imply, however, that this acquis has not found any codification in the reshaping of the structure of the EU. According to Art. 2 TEU as reformulated by the Lisbon Treaty, that corresponds to former Art. 6 TEU, stating the values on which the Union is founded, the respect for the rights of persons belonging to minorities is included together with the traditional reference to the values of democracy, respect for human rights and the rule of law. According to Art. 49 TEU, compliance with these conditions represents a necessary step to apply for membership.

Thus, the CFR does not seem to impose new and more onerous conditions on potential and candidate countries.[38] When the first draft of the

---

[36]The participation of acceding countries to the ECHR is, generally speaking, the main criterion EU institutions take into account when assessing the commitment of potential Member States to the protection of human rights.

[37]Other problematic examples are to be found in Art. 14 (Right to education), which is only mentioned in an additional Protocol to the ECHR), in Art. 37 (Environmental protection) and in Art. 38 (Consumer protection), that are not an integral part of the *acquis communautaire*.

[38]J. Czuczai, 'The EU Charter of fundamental rights: Is it a new accession condition for the candidate countries especially in light of the post-Nice IGC?', in T. Tridimas and P. Nebbia (eds.), *European Union law for the twenty-first century: Rethinking the new legal order* (Hart Publishing, 2004, vol. 1); S. Koukoulis-Spiliotopoulos, 'Which Charter of Fundamental Rights was incorporated in the draft European Constitution?', (2005) 1 *Revue Européenne de Droit Public* 295–304; J. Wouters, 'The EU Charter of Fundamental Rights: Some reflections on its external dimension', (2001) 1 *Maastricht Journal of European and Comparative Law* 3; A. J. Menéndez, 'Chartering Europe: Legal status and policy implications of the Charter of Fundamental Rights of the European Union', (2002) 3 *Journal of Common Market Studies* 471.

Charter was adopted, all acceding countries welcomed it but also expressed their concern about the intention to assign a binding force to the CFR. This is because they believed it was going to set a higher standard of protection with respect to the ECHR and that this would have entailed more onerous conditions to comply with in the accession process.[39] The CFR, instead, mainly reflects the widespread *acquis communautaire* in the field of the protection of fundamental rights and freedoms, with, of course, the exceptions described above. The present and future candidate countries will, therefore, have to take it into account if they want to acquire membership. This is not a direct consequence of Art. 51 of the CFR since the latter consolidates and reflects the already existing *acquis communautaire*.

5 The Impact of a Binding Charter of Fundamental Rights on Enlargement Conditionality

Notwithstanding the silence with respect to the issue and the problems concerning its scope of application, the CFR can still be influential on enlargement dynamics. As previously indicated, the Charter mainly reproduces the *acquis communautaire* and therefore does not pose any application problem within the framework of accession conditionality. Certainly, we cannot deny the existence – or better said, the codification – of some new rights (compared to the *acquis*) and should acknowledge that some important issues related to the enlargement conditionality are not mentioned in the CFR.

If we look at the evolution of accession conditionality, the fact that an act or a document is devoid of a binding force does not exclude the imposition of new burdens on candidate countries. This also applies to the Charter. Moreover the main parameter used by the EU in order to assess the progress of the candidates still remains the ECHR. Hopefully this could change with the Lisbon Treaty in force, since the newly binding Charter could prove to be a better and more comprehensive instrument to assess the EU's human rights standard.

A binding Charter can also have a major impact on the "internal scrutiny" under Art. 7 TEU, especially when assessing the gravity of the violation committed by the Member State. This would ensure a better judicial review by the Court of Justice of the European Union. In this respect, the CFR could help overcome the "double standard issue" by contrasting the far too severe scrutiny applied to candidate countries with a more fair procedure against Member States.

[39] K. Lenaerts 'Fundamental rights in the European Union', (2000) 25 *European Law Review* at 599.

As a result, the EU's overall legitimacy towards present and future citizens would be enhanced in so far as the latter would perceive a more equal and fair system to guarantee their rights. Integration would certainly be favoured if the new Member States did not feel that sort of subtle discrimination generated by the existence of a double standard in assessing compliance with the human rights. The same logic applies to the international arena. The credibility of the EU on the international scene would benefit from the presence of a more consistent approach towards members and non-members. Any actor imposing conditions and standards outside its borders that are not fully respected inside its territory cannot be considered to be a reliable and strong player within the international community.

Part II
The Charter of Fundamental Rights Applied

Free Movement of "Needy" Citizens After the Binding Charter. Solidarity for All?

Federico Forni

1 From Market Citizenship to Union Citizenship

The European Court of Justice (herein ECJ or EUCJ) has always liberally interpreted Community law in order to foster the *effet utile* and encompass as many people as possible in the personal scope of application of the provisions on fundamental freedoms. In the beginning, the broad definition of "worker" allowed individuals whose income was below the subsistence level of the host Member State to be included in this notion,[1] so long as their work activities were genuine and effective[2] even if the migrants had requested social assistance.[3] This approach provided a partial solution to the situation outlined by the Treaty of Rome, which conferred free movement rights only to economically active people.

However, extensive interpretation cannot be blamed for broadening rights in order to overcome the restrictions on EU law and hence for creating rights that do not exist.[4] In other terms, the Court could not overturn a situation in which the *Markbürgerschaft* granted free movement and

F. Forni (✉)
University of Bologna, Bologna, Italy
e-mail: fedeforni@libero.it

[1]See, for instance, Case 75/63 *Unger* [1964] ECR 177, para 1; Case 53/81 *Levin* [1982] ECR 1035, para 16; Case 66/85 *Lawrie-Blum* [1986] ECR 2121, paras 21–22; Case C-292/89 *Antonissen* [1991] ECR I-745, para 13; Case C-357/89 *Raulin* [1992] ECR I-1027, para 11; recently Joined Cases C-22/08 and C-23/08 *Vatsouras and Koupatantze* ECR I-4585 [2009], para 28. On the notion of 'worker', see L.S. Rossi, 'I beneficiari della libera circolazione delle persone nella giurisprudenza comunitaria', (1994) 117 IV *Foro italiano* 101–104.

[2]Case C-53/81 *Levin*, n. 1 above, para 17; Case C-456/02 *Trojani* [2004] ECR I-7573, para 29; Joined Cases C-22/08 and C-23/08 *Vatsouras and Koupatantze*, n. 1 above, para 26.

[3]Case 139/85 *Kempf* [1986] ECR 1741, para 14; Case C-237/94 *O'Flynn* [1996] ECR I-2617, para 30.

[4]This critical observation was raised by K. Hailbronner, 'Union citizenship and access to public benefits', (2005) 42 *Common Market Law Review* 1254.

G. Di Federico, *The EU Charter of Fundamental Rights*, Ius Gentium: Comparative Perspectives on Law and Justice 8, DOI 10.1007/978-94-007-0156-4_7,

residence rights only to the *Marktbürger*.[5] Judicial activism must stay within the boundaries determined by the treaties and only modification of the latter or the introduction of new secondary norms can determine new developments. It follows that the evolution of free movement and residence rights could not be left to the ECJ alone.

Thus, at the beginning of the 1990s the Council adopted three Directives which granted free movement rights to students, retired persons and other inactive individuals.[6] But Member States feared social tourism.[7] Free movement and residence was possible only if inactive Member States nationals did not amount to a burden for the host Member State's public finances.[8] In other words, residence rights were accorded only to economically inactive people with sufficient financial means and an adequate health insurance.

The introduction of EU citizenship by the Maastricht Treaty represented the real turning point, transforming Market citizenship into Union citizenship.[9] Such a transformation should have granted free movement to all citizens, regardless of their financial means. But the new provision on EU citizenship conditioned this right to the respect of the existing legislation, i.e. to the free movement Directives and the limits thereof. Originally this

---

[5]The concept of *Marktbürgerschaft* (i.e. Market Citizenship) was introduced by H.P. Ipsen and G. Nicolaysen, 'Haager Kongress für Europarecht und Bericht über die aktuelle Entwicklung des Gemeinschaftsrechts', (1964) 17 *Neue Juristische Wochenschrift* 339–344.

[6]Council Directive 90/364/EEC on the right of residence, [1990] OJ L 180/26; Council Directive 90/365/EEC on the right of residence for employees and self-employed persons who have ceased their occupational activity, [1990] OJ L 180/28; Council Directive 93/96/EEC on the right of residence for students, [1993] OJ L 317/59.

[7]The 1980s were characterized by the increase of migration towards the European Community by third country nationals, including asylum seekers. Therefore, '[t]he member States' delegations could not be persuaded to distinguish between EC-nationals and third country nationals, even though the Commission's proposal only focuses on the former. The preponderant opinion was that a foreigner is a foreigner'. H.C. Taschner, 'Free movement of students, retired persons and other European citizens. A difficult legislative process', in H.G. Schermers, C. Flinterman, A.E. Kellermann, J.C. van Haersolte and G.W.A. van der Meent (eds.), *Free movement of persons in Europe. Legal problems and experiences* (Nijhoff, 1993) 431.

[8]It seems indeed that 'one of the most remarkable aspects of the development of a general right of residence in the Community is the length of time it took to the Community to concede so little.' S. O'Leary, *The evolving concept of community citizenship. From the free movement of persons to Union citizenship* (Kluwer, 1996) 119. The economic limits were reiterated in Directive 38/2004/EC of the European Parliament and of the Council on the right of citizens of the Union and their family members to move and reside freely within the territory of the Member States, [2004] OJ L 158/77, also known as the *Citizen's Directive*.

[9]S. Carrera, 'What does free movement mean in theory and practice in an enlarged EU?', (2005) 11 *European Law Journal* 700.

concept had a rather symbolic value (as opposed to a substantive role),[10] but over the years the ECJ put flesh on the bones of citizenship.[11]

In 2001 the political environment allowed for judicial activism on the part of the ECJ, due to the adoption of the EU Charter of Fundamental Rights (herein CFR),[12] "which, even though [it] d[id] not [...] produce for the Community any binding effects comparable to primary law, may be referred to as a source of legal guidance."[13] In spite of its non binding nature, the Charter mitigated the importance of economic resources as a limit to the free movement of citizens. In fact, the CFR – which improved "[t]he normative-judicial role of the EU human rights"[14] – deals with the fundamental rights of EU citizens separately from the specific rights granted to workers.

According to these main lines of reasoning, the case law shows that EU citizenship confers the right to move, enter and reside without discrimination based on nationality in relation, for instance, to the language used in criminal proceedings,[15] entrance to university education,[16] taxation level,[17] the right to use one's surname according to the laws of the State of origin[18] and to have the name spelled without modification of its pronunciation.[19] Discrimination is prohibited not only on the basis of nationality, but also when it is a consequence of a change in residence.[20] EU citizenship allowed the Court to further consolidate the role of individuals by granting Art. 18 TEC (now Art. 21 TFEU) direct effect.[21] The movement and residence rights could be considered an essential element in the life of every national of the Member States. Therefore, any restriction must be strictly

---

[10] Case C-228/07 *Petersen* [2008] ECR I-6989, AG Colomer, para 26.

[11] This expression is borrowed from S. O'Leary, 'Putting flesh on the bones of European citizenship', (1999) 24 *European Law Review* 68–79.

[12] D. Kostakopoulou, 'European Union citizenship: Writing the future', (2007) 13 *European Law Journal* 635.

[13] Case C-97/08 P *Akzo Nobel NV* [2009] ECR I-8237, AG Kokott, note 63.

[14] G. De Búrca, 'Beyond the Charter: How enlargement has enlarged the human rights policy of the EU', (2003–04) 27 *Fordham International Law Journal* 679.

[15] Case C-274/96 *Bickel and Franz* [1998] ECR I-7637.

[16] Case C-147/03 *Commission v Austria* [2005] ECR I-5969.

[17] Case C-520/04 *Turpeinen* [2006] ECR I-10685.

[18] Case C-148/02 *García Avello* [2003] ECR I-11613; Case C-96/04 *Standesamt Stadt Niebüll* [2006] ECR I-3561.

[19] Case C-168/91 *Konstantinidis* [1993] ECR I-1191.

[20] Case C-224/98 *D'Hoop* [2002] ECR I-6191.

[21] Case C-413/99 *Baumbast* [2002] ECR I-7091, para 84.

interpreted[22] and must be objectively justified and proportionate to the legitimate aim of national norms.[23]

In this regard, legal commentators often quote the paragraph in which the ECJ declared that:

> Union citizenship is destined to be the fundamental status of nationals of the Member States, enabling those who find themselves in the same situation to enjoy the same treatment in law irrespective of their nationality, subject to such exceptions as are expressly provided for.[24]

Even so, EU citizenship complements national citizenship, but does not replace it. The judgement is projected towards the future, underlining how EU citizenship was yet to play a key role in the development of the rights granted to nationals of the Member States by Community Law.[25] Nonetheless, Union citizenship was indisputably *destined to* become the fundamental status of nationals of the Member States. As a consequence, the quoted paragraph could simply indicate the willingness of the judges to progressively recognize the centrality of this condition having taken note that the Community "is an example of the burgeoning of a broader concept of citizenship".[26]

The cautious approach followed by the ECJ in *Grzelczyk* was later confirmed by the case law on the free movement of EU citizens, where the Court seemed to consider Union citizenship only after having evaluated whether the individual could benefit from other Treaty provisions.[27] This

---

[22] See, e.g., Case 67/74 *Bonsignore* [1975] ECR 297, para 6; Case 36/75 *Rutili* [1975] ECR 1219, para 27; Case 30/77 *Bouchereau* [1977] ECR 1999, para 33; Case C-348/96 *Calfa* [1999] ECR I-11, para 23; Joined Cases C-482 and C-493/01 *Orfanopoulos* [2004] ECR I-5257, paras 64–65; Case C-503/03 *Commission v Spain* [2006] ECR I-1097, para 45; Case C-441/02 *Commission v Germany* [2006] ECR I-3449, para 34.

[23] Case C-413/99 *Baumbast*, n. 21 above, para 91; Case C-406/04 *De Cuyper* [2006] ECR I-6947, para 40.

[24] Case C-184/99 *Grzelczyk* [2001] ECR I-6193, para 31. See also Case C-413/99 *Baumbast*, n. 21 above, para 82; Case C-148/02 *García Avello*, n. 18 above, para 22; Case C-200/02 *Chen* [2004] ECR I-9925, para 25; Case C-209/03 *Bidar* [2005] ECR I-2119, para 31; Joined Cases C-11 and 12/06 *Morgan and Bucher* [2007] ECR I-9161, AG Colomer, para 65.

[25] J.-Y. Carlier, 'Case C-200/02, Kunqian Catherine Zhu, Man Lavette Chen v. Secretary of State for the Home Department, with annotation', (2005) 42 *Common Market Law Review* 1124. The third recital of the Directive 38/2004/EC, n. 8 above, uses hypothetical wording affirming that 'Union citizenship should be the fundamental status of nationals of the Member States when they exercise their right of free movement and residence'.

[26] K. Rubenstein, 'Citizenship in a borderless world', in C.G. Weeramantry, A. Anghie and G. Sturgess (eds.), *Legal visions of the 21st century: Essays in honour of Judge Christopher Weeramantry* (Nijhoff, 1998) 203.

[27] This approach was followed for example in Case C-184/99 *Grzelczyk*, n. 24 above; Case C-224/98 *D'Hoop*, n. 20 above; Case C-413/99 *Baumbast*, n. 21 above; Case C-456/02 *Trojani*, n. 2 above; Case C-200/02 *Chen*, n. 24 above. Sometimes the ECJ examined

stance can be traced to the fact that the movement and residence rights of EU citizens are not unlimited and that the norms concerning economically active people are much more favourable than the rights connected to Union citizenship. This situation could be linked to the order in which the relevant preliminary rulings were submitted, but it cannot be excluded that it may reveal an 'unconscious acknowledgement' of the impossibility to state the real centrality of the citizens' prerogatives without substantial changes in primary or secondary legislation.

2 Union Citizenship and Access to Welfare

For the purposes of this Chapter, the most relevant aspect of the case law on EU citizenship is that it gave access to public benefits, stressing the determination of the ECJ to move from a model of economically active residents to a more general entitlement to free movement and residence. The realization of this ambitious goal could be the result of the perception that EU citizenship derives from the recognition of human rights, independently from the enjoyment of the nationality of a Member State.[28] The possession of the resources required by the Directives concerning economically inactive individuals, reproduced in the *Citizens' Directive*, are essential but no relevance is assigned to the origin of those means.[29]

When the individual lacks adequate income, the Court, through Art. 18 TEC (now Art. 21 TFEU), in combination with Art. 12 TEC (now Art. 18 TFEU), nevertheless grants access to social benefits.[30] The need to combine citizenship with non discrimination derives from the respect of fundamental rights[31]; a connection which the ECJ has recently strengthened by allowing access to benefits falling outside the material scope of Community

---

the right of the citizen directly on the basis of Art. 18 TEC (now Art. 21 TFEU) (see for instance Case C-224/02 *Pusa* [2004] ECR I-5763; Case C-148/02 *García Avello*, n. 18 above). This different approach was probably used in these cases because the situation concerned persons that could not, even artificially, be considered 'economically relevant'.

[28] 'Protection of fundamental rights is a founding principle of the Union and an indispensable prerequisite for its legitimacy. [...] The Charter should also include the fundamental rights that pertain only to the Union's citizens', Annex IV of the Conclusions of the Presidency of the Cologne European Council, 3–4 June 1999, European Council Decision on the drawing up of a Charter of Fundamental Rights of the European Union (Bulletin EU 6-1999, para I.64).

[29] See Directive 38/2004/EC, n. 8 above, Art. 7(1), Case C-200/02 *Chen*, n. 24 above, para 30 and Case C-408/03 *Commission v Belgium* [2006] ECR I-2647, para 51.

[30] Case C-85/96 *Martínez Sala* [1998] ECR I-2691, paras 62–65.

[31] K. Lenaerts and E. de Smijter, 'A "Bill of Rights" for the European Union', (2001) 38 *Common Market Law Review* 275.

law on the sole basis of Art. 18 TEC (now Art. 21 TFEU).[32] By doing so, the Court has undoubtedly signalled a move towards the affirmation of an autonomous dignity of EU citizenship.

Nonetheless, it could be argued that the latter still plays a residual role with respect to national citizenship.[33] It seems that EU citizenship does not actually confer new rights; rather, it offers a new legal dimension in which to collocate the existing community rights[34] (which, on the other hand, does not prescribe any restriction of rights and duties connected to nationality). Hailbronner has reacted to the approach endorsed by the ECJ considering that it entailed a circumvention of the limits contained in the relevant Directives[35] and ultimately marked the end of rational jurisprudence.[36] Although it cannot be denied that a formal approach could have some advantages – a narrow interpretation would ensure more legal certainty and avoid unpalatable interferences into the competences of the Member States[37] – the substantial approach followed by the ECJ, despite the risk of 'unexpected' balancing exercises, seems more in line with the central role of EU citizenship. By doing so, the Court influenced the traditional model of national solidarity,[38] clarifying the need for a certain degree of financial support among the Member States and Union citizens.[39] It is not by chance that Title IV of the Charter protects welfare and social rights. Solidarity is an important social force which builds on the concept

---

[32] Case C-192/05 *Tas-Hagen* [2006] ECR I-10451, para 29; Case C-499/06 *Nerkowska* [2008] ECR I-3993, para 30.

[33] Cf. A. Ianniello-Saliceti, 'Cittadinanza dell'Unione', in P. De Cesari (ed.), *Persona e famiglia* (Giappichelli, 2008) 106, note 42, where the right currently stated in Art. 21 TFEU is considered residual as regards the rights of free movement of the economically active persons.

[34] M. Poiares Maduro, 'Interpreting European law: Judicial adjudication in a context of Constitutional pluralism', (2007) 1 *European Journal of Legal Studies* 12.

[35] K. Hailbronner, 'Union citizenship and access to public benefits', n. 4 above, 1247.

[36] K. Hailbronner, 'Die Unionsbürgerschaft und das Ende rationaler Jurisprudenz durch den EuGH?', (2004) 57 *Neue Juristische Wochenschrift* 2185–2189.

[37] J. Snell, 'And then there were two: Products and citizens in Community law', in T. Tridimas and P. Nebbia (eds.), *European Union law for the twenty-first century. Rethinking the new legal order*, Vol. 2: *Internal market and free movement policies* (Hart Publishing, 2004) 69.

[38] See, for instance, M. Dougan and E. Spaventa '"Wish You Weren't Here..." New models' of social solidarity in the European Union', in M. Dougan and E. Spaventa (eds.), *Social welfare and EU law* (Hart Publishing, 2005) 181–218; M. Ferrera, 'Towards an "open" social citizenship? The new boundaries of welfare in the European Union', in G. De Búrca (ed.), *EU law and the welfare state. In search of solidarity* (Oxford University Press, 2005) 11–38; R.W. Davies, 'Citizenship of the Union... rights for all?', (2002) 27 *European Law Review* 121–137.

[39] Case C-184/99 *Grzelczyk*, n. 24 above, para 44. See also N. Reich, 'The Constitutional relevance of citizenship and free movement in an enlarged Union', (2005) 11 *European Law Journal* 680.

of 'membership'. In relation to economic migrants this solidarity was less problematic, due to the fact that this category of persons contributed to the welfare of the host State. In these cases denying access to welfare benefits would be tantamount to an unlawful expropriation.[40] But an individual in need of help cannot play a part in the development of the economic wellbeing of the 'family', although he/she is entitled to enjoy the solidarity of the group.

The ECJ offered constructive interpretations in order to grant free movement and residence rights to economically inactive citizens on the basis of an inclusive paradigm of EU citizenship which reduces the impact of the limits allowed by the free movement Directives.[41] Since *Grzelczyk* and *Baumbast*, the ECJ made it clear that in assessing the compatibility of domestic law with Community law, the proportionality test would be strictly applied so to limit the economic and insurance justifications adduced by the States to restrain free movement. With this substantial reasoning, the Court seems determined to develop citizens' rights fostering its role of interpreter of the fundamental rights inherent in Community law. Some commentators concluded that this interpretation allows non economically active citizens to circulate without discrimination as to their nationality even though they do not own sufficient resources to avoid claiming the social benefits of the host State.[42] However, it appears that a lot needs to be done before affirming a general entitlement to free movement without any economic restraints. The case law is somewhat 'incremental', based on the level of integration of the citizen within the host State[43]: the longer the citizens reside in a host State, the more benefits they can receive on the same grounds as the nationals of that country.[44]

---

[40] C. Tomuschat, 'Case C-85/96, María Martínez Sala v Freistaat Bayern, with annotation', (2000) 37 *Common Market Law Review* 453.

[41] S. Giubboni, 'Free movement of persons and European solidarity', (2007) 13 *European Law Journal* 367. In this regard, it should be recalled that these economic restrictions were foreseen in a legal context which did not include EU citizenship and in which the legislator enjoyed more ample discretion. J.-P. Jacqué, 'Article II-105', in A. Levade, L. Burgorgue-Larsen and F. Picod (eds.), *Traité établissant une Constitution pour l'Europe,* Tome 2: *La Charte des droits fondamentaux de l'Union* (Bruylant, 2005) 575.

[42] This is called the 'perfect assimilation' approach. See, for instance, A. Iliopoulou and H. Toner, 'Case C-184/99, Rudy Grzelczyk v. Centre public d'aide sociale d'Ottignies-Louvain-la-Neuve, with annotation', (2002) 39 *Common Market Law Review* 616; D.H. Scheuing, 'Freizügigkeit als Unionsbürgerrecht', (2003) 38 *Europarecht* 785; S. Friess and J. Shaw, 'Citizenship of the Union: First steps in the European Court of Justice', (1998) 4 *European Public Law* 533.

[43] C. Barnard, 'EU citizenship and the principle of solidarity', in E. Spaventa and M. Dougan (eds.), *Social welfare and EU law*, n. 38 above, 168–175.

[44] A.P. van der Mei, 'Residence and the evolving notion of EU citizenship', (2003) 5 *European Journal of Migration and Law* 431.

As a consequence, long-term residents are assimilated to nationals of the host State,[45] while medium-term inactive citizens receive *almost* the same treatment and they can invoke the principle of transnational solidarity in order to have their situation carefully examined on the basis of the principle of proportionality when they have temporary difficulties.[46] Therefore, the request of social assistance cannot give rise to the withdrawal of their residence rights.

On the contrary, European citizens who are not integrated in the host society have currently no right to access social benefits.[47] This emerges from the *Collins*[48] case, where the Court appeased the Member States' concerns on social tourism[49]: provided the necessity and proportionality criteria are satisfied, it is possible to condition a jobseeker's entitlement to pay to a residence requirement, the latter being able to ensure that a genuine link exists between the beneficiary and the employment market in question.[50] More recently, in *Förster* the ECJ considered a 5 years residence condition proportionate for the purpose of establishing this effective link,[51] narrowing the distinction between short-term and medium-term residents.

To be honest, the impact of *Förster* is yet to be clarified with the consequence that the notion of citizenship can still be viewed as part of an irreversible dynamic process "capable of being added to or strengthened, but not diminished".[52] However, the evolution is not complete and the widening of the scope of free movement of citizens – which has attained the dignity of an autonomous fifth freedom[53] – meets the resistance of the Member States worried of becoming 'welfare magnets', to the detriment of their financial resources. Thus, the right of free movement and residence continues to be conditional upon a certain level of economic

---

[45] Case C-85/96 *Martínez Sala*, n. 30 above. Cf. Art. 16 Directive 38/2004/EC, n. 8 above.

[46] Case C-184/99 *Grzelczyk*, n. 24 above, para 43; Case C-413/99 *Baumbast*, n. 21 above. See also A.P. van der Mei, *Free movement of persons within the European Community. Cross-border access to public benefits* (Hart publishing, 2003) 147–150.

[47] An exception is represented by the grant of social benefits to the recipients of services through the extension of the principle of non-discrimination based on nationality. Cf. Case 186/87 *Cowan* [1989] ECR 195.

[48] Case C-138/02 *Collins* [2004] ECR I-2703.

[49] S. Giubboni, 'Free movement of persons and European solidarity', n. 41 above, 372.

[50] Case C-138/02 *Collins*, n. 48 above, para 67. See also Case C-209/03 *Bidar*, n. 24 above, para 61.

[51] Case C-158/07 *Förster* [2008] ECR I-8507, para 60.

[52] D. O'Keefe, 'Union citizenship', in D. O'Keefe and P. Twomey (eds.), *Legal issues of the Maastricht Treaty* (Wiley, 1994) 106.

[53] J. Kokott, 'Die Freizügigkeit der Unionsbürger als neue Grundfreiheit', in P.-M. Dupuy, B. Fassbender, M.N. Shaw and K.-P. Sommermann (eds.), *Völkerrecht als Wertordnung – Common values in international law, Festschrift für/Essays in honour of Christian Tomuschat* (N.P. Engel Verlag, 2006) 207; Editorial Comments, 'Two-speed European citizenship? Can the Lisbon Treaty help close the gap?', (2008) 45 *Common Market Law Review* 1.

self-sufficiency[54] in spite of the changes in the original normative framework and the described judicial activism of the ECJ. By virtue of economic considerations, the 'needy' EU citizens without an effective link with the host State are today excluded from this right.

Therefore, regardless of the high consideration for fundamental rights, EU citizenship is at present far from favouring the development of the rights of residence of the indigent. Could the Lisbon Treaty and the legal binding value of the Charter reverse the situation? And if so, to what extent?

3 The Impact of Citizenship Provisions of the Lisbon Treaty

The previous considerations exclude more advanced interpretations in the absence of treaty reforms and specific secondary legislation. The modifications brought about by the Lisbon Treaty have divided legal literature. Indeed, the new provisions on EU citizenship have been criticized for being incapable of determining significant advancements in this area. Changes in the formal status of citizens have been deemed to be limited, and labelled as merely "cosmetic".[55] Moreover, it has been argued that "[t]he indicators are that the Court will not, in the current political climate, use the Charter in a more proactive way when it is made legally binding."[56]

It could thus be argued that the case law developed by the ECJ under the former treaties will remain valid and the scope of citizenship unaffected.[57] However, the potential for further enhancing the scope and status of EU citizenship should be analyzed bearing in mind the judicial activism which has characterised the ECJ[58] and, as previously suggested, the possible added value of the newly binding Charter. On the other hand, it should not go unnoticed that unlike Art. 17 TEC – according to which EU citizenship *complemented* national citizenship – Art. 9 TEU specifies

[54] S. Carrera, 'What does free movement mean in theory and practice in an enlarged EU?', n. 9 above, 701.

[55] M. Condinanzi, A. Lang and B. Nascimbene, *Citizens of the Union and free movement of persons* (Nijhoff, 2008) 61. The authors referred to Art. II-112(2) of the Constitution. The Lisbon Treaty, as the Constitutional Treaty before it, leaves the provisions on citizenship substantially unaltered. In this regard it should be noted that there was no Working Group in the Convention on the Future of Europe entrusted with the task of reflecting on EU citizenship. See further C. Ladenburger, 'Fundamental Rights and Citizenship of the Union', in G. Amato, H. Bribosia and B. De Witte (eds.), *Genesis and destiny of the European Constitution* (Bruylant, 2007) 318–319.

[56] P. Syrpis, 'The Treaty of Lisbon: Much ado... but about what?', (2008) 37 *Industrial Law Journal* 232.

[57] S.C. Sieberson, 'Dividing lines between the European Union and its Member States. The impact of the Treaty of Lisbon' (Asser Press, 2008) 95.

[58] J. Shaw, 'The constitutional development of citizenship in the EU context: with or without the Treaty of Lisbon', in I. Pernice and E. Tanchev (eds.), *Ceci n'est pas une Constitution – Constitutionalisation without a Constitution?* (Nomos, 2008) 106.

that "Citizenship of the Union shall be *additional* to national citizenship", although nationality will not be replaced.

Before the entry into force of the Lisbon Treaty, some authors have described the influence of the Charter as minimal since the majority of the rights enshrined in Title V (Citizens' Rights) were already binding as part of Community law.[59] Others highlighted the central role of the CFR in broadening the concept of EU citizenship.[60] In this sense it has been suggested that "a broader and clearer catalogue of fundamental rights may promote greater judicial activism in the review of legislative and administrative acts of the EU institutions".[61] This remark is supported by AG Tizzano who, immediately after the adoption of the CFR, emphasized that "the Charter cannot be ignored [being] a substantive point of reference for all those involved – Member States, institutions, natural and legal persons – in the Community context".[62] However, as recently pointed out by Jacobs, it is puzzling how far considerations of national interest in the allocation of public funds can limit the rights of individuals considering the uncertainty which surrounds the additional guarantees which the Court could legitimately recognize the citizens.[63]

Now that the Lisbon Treaty has become operative the admissibility of economic limitations excluding some persons from the scope of application of a fundamental freedom is debatable in the least.[64] The legal force attributed to the Charter is certainly capable of injecting more coherence in the case law on free movement of EU citizens, where the ECJ appears to be shrouded in the foggy mists of abstraction. In addition, the wording of Art. 9 TEU appears to endow EU citizenship with an autonomous status. Further rights may be added, without removing the existing ones,[65] thereby making it possible to move "towards a more independent Union

---

[59] See J. Rehman, 'International human rights law: A practical approach' (Pearson Education, 2003) 192.

[60] See A. Buzelay, 'Libre circulation des travailleurs en Europe et protection sociale', (2003) 470 *Revue du Marché Commun et de l'Union européenne* 452–453.

[61] M. Poiares Maduro, 'The double constitutional life of the Charter of Fundamental Rights of the European Union', in T. Hervey and J. Kenner (eds.), *Economic and social rights under the EU Charter of Fundamental Rights: A legal perspective* (Hart Publishing, 2003) 281.

[62] Case C-173/99 *BECTU* [2001] ECR I-4881, AG Tizzano, para 28.

[63] F.G. Jacobs, 'Citizenship of the European Union – A legal analysis', (2007) 13 *European Law Journal* 598.

[64] See P. Craig, 'The Treaty of Lisbon, process, architecture and substance', (2008) 33 *European Law Review* 164, stating that 'the very existence of a legally binding formal list of rights will almost certainly significantly increase the number of rights-based challenges to the legality of EU or Member State action'.

[65] J. Shaw, 'The constitutional development of citizenship in the EU context: With or without the Treaty of Lisbon', n. 58 above, 111.

citizenship".[66] This modification is particularly important: the EU citizen should enjoy "dual citizenship, national citizenship and European citizenship; and [shall be] free to use either, as he or she chooses."[67] To attain this objective, political difficulties as well the fear of losing the patriotic sense of belonging has first of all to be overcome within and by the Member States.

That being said, the following sections aim at clarifying whether a binding catalogue of fundamental rights can provide for a unitary notion of EU citizenship capable of removing the limitations to free movement and residence deriving from the lack of appropriate financial means.

4 The Impact of Art. 45 CFR

The evaluation of the impact of the binding Charter on free movement of Union citizens must begin with the analysis of Art. 45 CFR, which confers to "[e]very citizen of the Union [...] the right to move and reside freely within the territory of the Member States". Occasionally this provision has been quoted by Advocates General in their Opinions.[68] Broadly speaking, its use was functional to the consolidation of previous case law on Art. 18 TEC (now Art. 21 TFEU) which the Court considers to affirm a fundamental freedom[69] with a constitutional ranking.[70]

The considerable impact of a binding Charter is supported by some authoritative Opinions. AG Colomer has recently pointed out that it is not advisable to underestimate the impact of fundamental rights on citizens' prerogatives. In his view:

---

[66]A. Schrauwen, 'European Union citizenship in the Treaty of Lisbon: Any change at all?', (2008) 15 *Maastricht Journal of European and Comparative Law* 59.

[67]The European Convention, 'Preliminary draft Constitutional Treaty', CONV369/02, [2002] 9.

[68]Case C-413/99 *Baumbast* [2002] ECR I-7091, AG Geelhoed, para 110; Case C-456/02 *Trojani* [2004] ECR I-7573, AG Geelhoed, note 6; Case C-200/02 *Chen* [2004] ECR I-9925, AG Tizzano, para 119; Case C-209/03 *Bidar* [2005] ECR I-2119, AG Geelhoed, para 32; Case C-408/03 *Commission v Belgium* [2006] ECR I-2647, AG Colomer, note 19; Joined Cases C-11 and C-12/06 *Morgan and Bucher*, n. 24 above, AG Colomer, para 11.

[69]Case C-184/99 *Grzelczyk*, n. 24 above, para 33; Case C-224/98 *D'Hoop*, n. 20 above, para 29; Case C-148/02 *García Avello*, n. 18 above, para 24; Case C-200/02 *Chen*, n. 68 above, AG Tizzano, para 73; Case C-200/02 *Chen* [2004], n. 24 above, para 33. See also S. O'Leary, 'Solidarity and citizenship rights in the Charter of Fundamental Rights of the European Union', in G. De Búrca (ed.), *EU law and the welfare state. In search of solidarity*, n. 38 above, 75.

[70]J. Baquero Cruz, 'Between competition and free movement. The Economic Constitutional Law of the European Community' (Hart Publishing, 2002) 97.

> [a]s an integral part of the status of citizenship, the fundamental rights strengthen the legal position of the individual by introducing a decisive aspect for the purposes of substantive justice in the case concerned. Holding their fundamental rights as prerogatives of freedom, citizens of the Union afford their claims greater legitimacy.[71]

With the Lisbon Treaty in force, Art. 45 CFR is currently a binding primary norm overlapping with Arts. 20(2a) and 21 TFEU. Some scholars have criticized the superimposition of rules arguing that all duplications should have been avoided.[72] This situation could deprive Art. 45 CFR of any innovative character[73] considering that Art. 52(2) CFR clearly indicates that the rights contained in the Charter are to be applied 'under the conditions and within the limits defined by the Treaties.'[74]

On the one hand, this interpretation is consistent with Art. 21 TFEU, where it states that this right is "subject to the limitations and conditions laid down in the Treaties and by the measures adopted to give them effect", even though Art. 45 CFR does not contain any reference to these limits. On the other hand, it is questionable whether the limits defined by the Treaties should also include the conditions defined by secondary legislation. The possible restrictions would in fact be inconsistent with the status of free movement rights.[75] The inclusion of the latter in what can be considered as a *Bill of Rights* should preclude the discrimination of citizens on the sole basis of their economic resources. In fact, the Charter recognizes a sort of 'right to solidarity' without clarifying the duties of the Member States or introducing a solidarity obligation. But, at the same time, it is puzzling how the denial of a right (the right to free movement) to inactive indigent people is justified by the refusal of the Member States to recognize a second right, i.e. the right to solidarity. In the present historical moment, the world is dominated by a new sensitivity with regard to human rights, but it is hard to disagree with the bitter observation that " [f]ree movement is only free as it does not cost money."[76]

---

[71] Case C-228/07 *Petersen*, n. 10 above, AG Colomer, para 27.

[72] A. Torres Pérez, 'La Carta de Derechos Fundamentales de la Unión Europea' (http://www.upf.edu/constitucional/actualitat/PDFs/Torres_Pxrezx_Aida.pdf) 2, para 2; V. Constantinesco, 'La cittadinanza dell'Unione: una "vera" cittadinanza?', in L.S. Rossi (ed.), *Il progetto di Trattato-Costituzione. Verso una nuova architettura dell'Unione europea* (Giuffrè, 2004) 225.

[73] D.H. Scheuing, 'Freizügigkeit als Unionsbürgerrecht', n. 42 above, 788.

[74] See also *Explanations relating to the Charter of Fundamental Rights*, [2007] OJ C 303/29.

[75] M. Poiares Maduro, 'The double constitutional life of the Charter of Fundamental Rights of the European Union', n. 61 above, 288. According to the author this legislation 'would de facto derogate from the constitutional protection assured to these rights by Article 51(1) EUCFR which enshrines the idea that fundamental rights cannot be dependent on or challenged by any other exercise of power'.

[76] J. Tillotson and N. Foster, 'Text, cases and materials on European Union Law' (Cavendish, 2003) 310.

These perplexities are shared by Poiares Maduro who questions "the lawfulness of some conditions currently imposed by Community legislation on the free movement of persons."[77] Still, it is difficult to address the problems stemming from the binding character of the Charter as it is very difficult to determine a priori whether Art. 45 CFR is capable per se of bringing about any change at all. In this event, the rights and the principles contained elsewhere in the Charter could be used as interpretative tools in order to avoid discrimination of citizens on the basis of their economic status. In fact, it cannot be denied that free movement is linked to other fundamental rights included in the Charter.

This position is shared by many Advocates General. For instance, in analyzing the connection between free movement and access to student grants, AG Colomer considered that "Article 14 of the Charter of Fundamental Rights of the European Union proclaims that everyone has the right 'to education and to have access to vocational and continuing training.'"[78] Moreover, AG Sharpston quoted Art. 24 CFR in a case concerning the surname to give to a Danish child resident in Germany.[79]

Furthermore, considering how the use of the solidarity principle allowed the ECJ to partially erode the economic limits of free movement, it would not come as a surprise if some rights contained in Title "Solidarity" of the CFR were used to extend the right of free movement to the indigents. This solution appears reasonable given that the ECJ's efforts have been directed for a long time at connecting the status of citizens to fundamental rights such as, for instance, family life and privacy.[80] In this sense, "movement would simply become a trigger for activating the Charter."[81]

A new impulse towards social rights protection can be found in some ECJ judgments in which solidarity was used to clarify principles included in the notion of Union citizenship.[82] Citizenship should not be considered isolated from the other provisions of the CFR, as suggested by the preliminary reference in *Ruiz Zambrano*.[83] Here the *Tribunal du travail de Bruxelles* asked the ECJ to clarify the rights granted to EU citizens under Arts. 12, 17 and 18 TEC (now Arts. 18, 20 and 21 TFEU) read jointly with Arts. 21,

---

[77] M. Poiares Maduro, 'The double constitutional life of the Charter of Fundamental Rights of the European Union', n. 61 above, 289.

[78] Joined Cases C-11 and C-12/06 *Morgan and Bucher*, n. 24 above, AG Colomer, para 91.

[79] Case C-353/06 *Grunkin-Paul* [2008] ECR I-7639, AG Sharpston, para 9. The reference to this provision is used to strengthen the effects of Art. 3(1) of the United Nations Convention on the Rights of the Child.

[80] Case C-413/99 *Baumbast*, n. 21 above, para 72; Case C-148/02 *García Avello*, n. 18 above.

[81] P. Eeckout, 'The EU Charter of fundamental rights and the federal question', (2002) 29 *Common Market Law Review* 971.

[82] C. Barnard, 'EU citizenship and the principle of solidarity', n. 43 above, 158–161.

[83] Case C-34/09 *Ruiz Zambrano*, pending [2009] OJ C 90/10.

24 and 34 CFR. This demonstrates a new sensitivity towards the Charter which can undoubtedly allow innovative interpretations. The freedom of movement now reserved to active and economically reliable persons could be extended to the indigent. This is perhaps one of the most relevant consequences following an extensive interpretation of EU law in light of the provisions of the Charter not specifically dedicated to "Citizens' Rights".

5 The Impact of Solidarity on Free Movement of Citizens

The importance of solidarity for the regime applicable to free movement of citizens is confirmed by the statement that the EU "shall combat social exclusion and discrimination, and shall promote social justice and protection [...]. It shall promote [...] solidarity among the Member States".[84] The solidarity principle could contribute to erode the two limits that still exist in the field of free movement of persons (i.e. level of economic resources and adequate sickness insurance). In fact, solidarity needs to be supported by legal provisions whereas only charity, being spontaneous, need not be institutionalized by rules and norms.[85] Moreover, solidarity is often connected to economic, but not commercial aspects. As underlined by AG Fennelly, "[s]ocial solidarity envisages the inherently uncommercial act of involuntary subsidization of one social group by another".[86]

The full acceptance of the free movement of EU indigents – i.e. regardless of the burden it entails for the public finances – presupposes the ability to distinguish the notion of 'citizen' from that of 'migrant'.[87] Member States nationals normally use the word 'citizen' to identify an individual coming from their same country whereas the expression 'EU citizen' is often used for persons coming from another EU country. The Charter looks at things from a different perspective setting out the rights of the EU (im)migrant as a citizen.[88] The time seems ripe for the Courts to endorse this viewpoint: "for some basic social, economic, civic and cultural rights of individuals [...] the link to nationality of the Member States may be beginning to seem a little dated."[89]

---

[84] Art. 3(1) TEU.

[85] A.J. Menéndez, 'The sinews of peace: rights to solidarity in the Charter of Fundamental Rights of the European Union', (2003) 16 *Ratio Juris* 379.

[86] Case C-70/95 *Sodemare* [1997] ECR I-3395, AG Fennelly, para 29.

[87] See n. 7 above.

[88] E. Guild, 'Citizens, immigrants, terrorists and others', in S. Peers and A. Ward (eds.), *The European Union Charter of Fundamental Rights* (Hart Publishing, 2004) 234.

[89] F.G. Jacobs, 'Introduction', in E. Guild (ed.), *The legal framework and social consequences of free movement of persons in the European Union* (Kluwer, 1999) 5. See also A.P. van der Mei, 'Union citizenship and the "de-nationalisation" of the territorial welfare state', (2005) 7 *European Journal of Migration and Law* 207, where it is underlined

The CFR contains rights which guarantee social security and social assistance (Art. 34) and access to health care (Art. 35). Its binding nature reassures EU citizens that the EU institutions and Member States will comply with the rights enshrined therein and possibly allow for an extension of the personal scope of free movement. In this regard, it should be recalled that the UK, Poland, and more recently the Czech Republic, have obtained a Protocol on the Charter. Art. 1(2) of Protocol No 30 states that "nothing in Title IV of the Charter [Solidarity] creates justiciable rights applicable to Poland or the United Kingdom except in so far as Poland or the United Kingdom has provided for such rights in its national law". The UK European Union Committee and the UK Constitution Committee affirm that this Protocol is not an *opt-out* but only an instrument capable of clarifying the Charter's scope of application.[90] On the one hand, this 'explanatory protocol' will cause a certain embarrassment for the national and EU judges.[91] On the other hand, it could be argued that the fears of social tourism advanced by these two Member States demonstrate that the 'needy' EU citizens would actually be entitled to invoke the Title on Solidarity in order to be recognized (full) free movement rights. Therefore, access to public benefits and health care can hardly be considered a utopia.

The indication that these rights are not justiciable could simply indicate that individuals cannot invoke Arts. 34 and 35 before national courts in Poland and in the United Kingdom, but does not prevent the respective domestic judges from declaring that the sufficient economic resources and the medical insurance requirements set out in the Directive, or other national provisions, are inconsistent with primary EU law. Furthermore, if we take into consideration that enlargement conditionality includes not only civil and political rights, but also economic, social and cultural rights,[92] the refusal to respect these rights could represent a violation of the principle of loyal cooperation.

---

that '[r]esidence requirements, not nationality requirements, constitute the proper tools for regulating cross-border access to social assistance, student aid and other tax-funded social benefits schemes'.

[90]House of Lords, Constitution Committee, 6th Report of Session 2007–08, 'European Union (Amendment) Bill and the Lisbon Treaty: Implications for the UK Constitution' (The Stationery Office Ltd, 2008) 35, para 136. However, the aim of this Protocol is mainly ideological, contributing to remove the constitutional value of the Charter since principles not shared by all the Member States cannot be defined as constitutional. From a practical point of view the effects seem to be less important (L.S. Rossi, 'L'integrazione differenziata nel Trattato di Lisbona', (2008) 1 *Sud in Europa*, n. 1, http://www.sudineuropa.net/articolo.asp?ID=317&IDNumero=31).

[91]S. van Raepenbusch, 'La réforme institutionnelle du Traité de Lisbonne: l'émergence juridique de l'Union européenne', (2008) 43 *Cahiers de Droit Européen* 578.

[92]A. Albi, 'Ironies in Human Rights Protection in the EU: Pre-accession conditionality and post-accession conundrums', (2009) 15 *European Law Journal* 49.

This view is not in contrast with Art. 52(5) CFR, which states that the provisions of the Charter containing principles "shall be judicially cognizable only in the interpretation of [legislative and executive acts taken by institutions, bodies, offices and agencies of the Union, and by acts of Member States when they are implementing Union law] and in ruling on their legality". Likewise, the distinction between rights and principles cannot stop national judges from discarding inconsistent internal provisions, even in the absence of direct effect[93]; principles "should instead act merely as useful yardsticks against which to measure the relative success (or otherwise) of Union/national regulatory activity."[94]

The following sections will consider whether Arts. 34(2) and 35 CFR can be invoked, if necessary in combination with Arts. 45 CFR, 20(2a) and 21 TFEU, in order to guarantee a general right to free movement of EU citizens.

5.1 *Access to Public Benefits: Art. 34 CFR and the Limit of Sufficient Resources*

Art. 34(2) of the Charter states that "[e]veryone residing and moving legally within the European Union is entitled to social security benefits and social advantages in accordance with Union law and national laws and practices". This Article, which has never been mentioned by the Advocates General or by the ECJ, could protect the rights related to free movement granting the same treatment to all EU citizens regardless of their economic status. Indeed this provision seems to contrast with the case law according to which short-term residents are excluded from access to public benefits. In the future the norm could be used as a *lex specialis* vis à vis Art. 21 TFEU[95] to improve the free movement jurisprudence that, on the basis of Art. 18(1) TFEU, reserves the benefits granted to host State nationals to some Union citizens only. By the same token, it appears that access to student grants should be requested relying on Art. 34(2) CFR as well, even though, under the Lisbon Treaty, the EUCJ could consider the case pursuant to Art. 14 CFR, concerning the right to education.[96]

---

[93]M. Cartabia, 'I diritti fondamentali e la cittadinanza dell'Unione', in F. Bassanini and G. Tiberi (eds.), *Le nuove istituzioni europee. Commento al Trattato di Lisbona* (Il Mulino, 2008) 105.

[94]M. Dougan, 'The Treaty of Lisbon 2007: Winning minds, not hearts', (2008) 45 *Common Market Law Review* 663.

[95]D.H. Scheuing, 'Freizügigkeit als Unionsbürgerrecht', n. 42 above, 788.

[96]It is difficult to foretell the possible interpretation of situations falling in different Titles of the CFR. However, the choice of organising the Charter in 'values' could have concrete effects in balancing, interpreting and limiting fundamental rights (M. Cartabia, 'I diritti fondamentali e la cittadinanza dell'Unione', n. 93 above, 95).

It is noteworthy that the *Citizen's Directive*, which codifies the most recent case law on the matter, indicates the cases in which an expulsion is allowed, clarifying the scope and grounds of the relevant measures. Giving priority to the individual rather than to the public finances, Art. 27(1) states that: "[t]hese grounds shall not be invoked to serve economic ends." It follows that solidarity goes beyond national frontiers, which allows and promotes social inclusion of an EU citizen who is eager to move even if he/she is lacking economic resources.

The new TEU Preamble confirms the attachment to fundamental social rights, the will to deepen the solidarity between EU citizens and the need to facilitate free movement of persons. Therefore, Art. 34 CFR should be invoked in free movement cases to make this right truly effective. In fact, without the protection of social rights, the protection of other rights, such as civil and political rights, would remain theoretical.[97] Union legislative acts must comply with these rights, since "respect for human rights is a condition of the lawfulness of Community acts".[98]

Although the Member States show deference towards human rights, they have always contested the enforcement of social rights, denying residence rights to EU 'needy' citizens. This is not that surprising taking into account that national rules excluding EU citizens from social benefits granted to third country nationals have recently been declared consistent with Community law.[99] In this regard, the Charter could bring about innovative interpretations capable of addressing the critical issues which still affect social protection in and by the EU.

Art. 34 CFR can also protect the Member States from abuses since it refers to persons moving *legally* within the European Union. Even though commentators suggest that the rationale of the expression is to exclude illegal third country nationals,[100] the provision should be interpreted in such a way as to exclude Union citizens who have circumvented the law. The fact that the provision is also directed at EU citizens is confirmed by the circumstance that the text takes into consideration not only persons who are residing legally but also persons who are moving legally.

However, once a citizen is residing in another Member State, he/she should receive all the benefits granted to nationals of the host country or to other Member States nationals integrated within its society. A different solution would be in contrast with the principle of equality

---

[97] B. Brandtner and A. Rosas, 'Human rights and the external relations of the European Community: An analysis of doctrine and practice', (1998) 9 *European Journal of International Law* 490.

[98] Opinion 2/94 [1996] ECR I-1759, para 34.

[99] Joined Cases C-22 and C-23/08 *Vatsouras and Koupatantze*, n. 1 above, para 53.

[100] M. Borgetto and R. Lafore, 'Article II-94', in A. Levade, L. Burgorgue-Larsen and F. Picod (eds.), *Traité établissant une Constitution pour l'Europe,* Tome 2: *La Charte des droits fondamentaux de l'Union*, n. 41 above, 452.

and would downgrade the short-term resident to a sort of "second-class citizen",[101] who could legally reside but to whom the minimal financial means necessary to live in the society would not be granted.

5.2 Access to Health Care: Art. 35 CFR and the Limit of Sickness Insurance

In the *Decker* and *Kohll* cases, the Court established that health care services provided as economic services to patients fall within the scope of the provisions on the free movement of services.[102] In principle, Union citizens have a right, as service recipients, to access health care in another Member State which is financed by the public social insurance system. In this way the Court established a general right of access to health care in another Member State at the expense of the country where the subject is insured.

However, contradictions still remain, since some less important treatments could not be included in the medical services which can be reimbursed by the public health systems.[103] As a consequence, the EUCJ must seek and find coherence because the limits imposed by EU law on the right of the State to define the situations in which the public funding could reimburse the cost of the treatment still need further clarification.[104]

Health care is an inviolable human right which should not be limited to nationals of the host State.[105] Art. 35 CFR states that everyone has the right to access medical care, subordinating that right to the conditions determined by national legislation and practice. AG Colomer has recently emphasized this aspect underlining that "although the case law takes as the main point of reference the fundamental freedoms established in the Treaty, there is another aspect which is becoming more and more important in the Community sphere, namely the right of citizens to health care, proclaimed in Article 35 of the Charter of Fundamental Rights of the European Union [and] perceived as a personal entitlement, unconnected to a person's relationship with social security, and the Court of Justice cannot overlook

---

[101] K. Lenaerts and T. Heremans, 'Contours of a European social Union in the case-law of the European Court of Justice', (2006) 2 *European Constitutional Law Review* 107.

[102] Case C-120/95 *Decker* [1998] ECR I-1831 and Case C-158/96 *Kohll* [1998] ECR I-1931.

[103] Case C-385/99 *Müller-Fauré* [2003] ECR I-4509, para 98.

[104] The need of coherence is more than justified since the 2008 Proposal for a Directive of patients' rights in cross-border healthcare [COM(2008) 414 final] is based on the principles of free movement as an alternative mechanism to the authorisation procedure of Council Regulation (EEC) 1408/71 on the application of social security schemes to employed persons and their families moving within the Community, [1971] OJ L 149/2–50.

[105] Appl. No 30240/96, *D. v. The United Kingdom*, (1997) ECHR Reports 1997-III.

that aspect."[106] Therefore, the main concern of the health care system is not the capacity of the citizen to pay, but only his medical needs.

This approach suggests that the limit of health insurance could be inconsistent with the fundamental right stated in Art. 35 CFR. Therefore, the case law related to access to health care must take into account the fundamental right of the EU citizen and examine the case on the basis of the free movement of citizens and no longer relegate nationals of the Member States to the legal limbo of service recipients. In the future similar cases should not be analysed on the basis of Art. 56(1) TFEU,[107] but pursuant to Art. 21 TFEU, in combination with Art. 35 CFR. The Charter could then strengthen the role of Union citizenship and provide it with an effective and definitive fundamental status.

Finally, even though Art. 35 CFR does not make a clear reference to legal intra-community movement, the analogy with Art. 34 CFR and the general prohibition contained in Art. 54 CFR[108] should prevent abusive conduct: a citizen cannot benefit from free movement *only* to obtain in another Member State medical treatment which his State of residence does not reimburse.[109]

6 Conclusions

AG La Pergola explained that the ultimate aim of the citizenship provisions was to establish an "increasing equality between citizens of the Union, irrespective of their nationality".[110] This statement suggests that under the previous regime one could expect a certain degree of financial solidarity, but differences would still exist between nationals and Union citizens. As illustrated at the beginning of this contribution, access to public benefits is not based on the equality of Union citizens. A first discrimination exists between 'needy' citizens who could artificially be included in the Treaty

[106]Case C-444/05 *Stamatelaki* [2007] ECR I-3185, AG Colomer, para 40.

[107]Art. 56(1) TFEU states that "restrictions on freedom to provide services within the Union shall be prohibited in respect of nationals of Member States who are established in a Member State other than that of the person for whom the services are intended".

[108]Art. 54 CFR reads: "[n]othing in this Charter shall be interpreted as implying any right to engage in any activity or to perform any act aimed at the destruction of any of the rights and freedoms recognised in this Charter or at their limitation to a greater extent than is provided for herein". On the notion of abuse of law, see generally M. Gestri, 'Abuso del diritto e frode alla legge nell'ordinamento comunitario' (Giuffrè, 2003), in particular Chapter 1.

[109]K. Coldron and L. Ackers, '(Ab)using European Citizenship? EU retired migrants and the exercise of healthcare rights', (2007) 14 *Maastricht Journal of European and Comparative Law* 299.

[110]Joined Cases C-4 and C-5/95 *Stöber and Pereira* [1997] ECR I-511, AG La Pergola, para 50.

provisions concerning economically active people and indigents for whom inclusion is excluded. A second discrimination derives from the 'incremental approach' which links the rights of EU citizens to their period of residence in the host country.

This situation could change with the entry into force of the Lisbon Treaty since it appears to be in contrast with Art. 9 TEU, which states that "[i]n all its activities, the Union shall observe the principle of the equality of its citizens, who shall receive equal attention from its institutions, bodies, offices and agencies". The principle of equality can play an important role by influencing the EUCJ's case law concerning 'reverse discriminations',[111] but also by allowing Union citizens free movement regardless of their income. The emphasis on equality of citizens will avoid situations in which the principle of proportionality is applied strictly, like in *Petersen,*[112] and cases in which it is used very loosely,[113] like in *Förster,*[114] causing disparities of treatment.

In fact, the codification of EU fundamental rights in the Charter enhances the role of the EUCJ, acting as a constitutional judge, giving the latter the possibility to further broaden the personal scope of application of EU citizens' right to free movement. With a binding Charter, the EUCJ will be able to rely on concrete rights contained in both the Title on Citizens' Rights and in the Title on Solidarity, rather than on indefinite principles such as the principle of proportionality.

A first step towards abandoning any consideration as to the individual's degree of integration within the host society can be found in a recent case concerning the Dutch legislation and administrative practice on the residence right of non-active citizens of the Union.[115] Here, the EUCJ found that the Netherlands had violated Community law by requiring that inactive and retired EU citizens demonstrate the ability to afford a stay of at least 1 year in the host Member State. Of course, more advanced interpretations based on the binding Charter provisions are possible and could determine further protection for other categories of inactive persons.

[111] L.S. Rossi, 'Uguaglianza-Cittadinanza', in L.S. Rossi (ed.), *Carta dei diritti fondamentali e Costituzione dell'Unione europea* (Giuffrè, 2002) 113–114.

[112] Case C-228/07 *Petersen* [2008] ECR I-6989.

[113] D. Martin, 'Comments on *Förster* (Case C-158/07 of 18 November 2008), *Metock* (Case C-127/08 of 25 July 2008) and *Huber* (Case C-524/06 of 16 December 2008)', (2009) 11 *European Journal of Migration and Law* 100.

[114] Case C-158/07 *Förster*, n. 51 above.

[115] Case C-398/06 *Commission v Netherlands* [2008] ECR I-56 (summary publication).

Internal Market Derogations in Light of the Newly Binding Character of the EU Charter of Fundamental Rights

Stephen J. Curzon

1 Preliminary Remarks

The establishment of a common market, formerly prescribed by Arts. 2, 3 and 14 of the "Treaty establishing the European Community" (herein TEC), is one of the cornerstones of the European Union (herein EU) and is based upon the protection of four fundamental economic freedoms, i.e. the free movement of goods, persons, capital and the free provision of services. Such free movement provisions have played a pivotal role in the evolution of the EU and appear to have assumed what some consider to be a constitutional value in the EU legal order.[1] To this end, the European Court of Justice (herein ECJ or EUCJ) has described them as "fundamental freedoms",[2] "fundamental principles of the Treaty"[3] or even as "fundamental rights".[4]

The weight ascribed to the liberal free-market principles by the constituting treaties and the ECJ has not limited the development of the EU. On

S.J. Curzon (✉)
University of Bologna, Bologna, Italy
e-mail: scurzon@cirdce.unibo.it

[1] See M. Poiares Maduro, 'Striking the elusive balance between economic freedom and Social Rights in the EU', in P. Alston, M. Bustelo and J. Heenan (eds.), *The EU and Human Rights* (Oxford University Press, 1999) 452. Also see M. Lindfelt, *Fundamental Rights in the EU – Towards a higher Law of the Land?* (Abo: Abo Akademi University Press, 2007) at 196.

[2] Case C-286/06 *Commission v. Spain* [2008] ECR I-8025.

[3] Cf. Case C-49/98 *Finalarte Sociedade de Construção Civil Ldª* [2001] ECR I-7831, para 31.

[4] Certain authors have advanced the consideration that the fundamental economic freedoms can themselves be considered fundamental rights. See, for example, P. Oliver and W.-H. Roth, 'The internal market and the four freedoms', (2004) *Common Market Law Review* 41; A. Biondi, 'Free trade, a mountain road and the right to protest: European economic freedoms and fundamental individual rights',(2004) *European Human Rights Law Review* 1. Interesting considerations are also made by V. Skouris, 'Fundamental rights and fundamental freedoms: The challenge of striking a delicate balance', (2006) *European Business Law Review* 227.

G. Di Federico, *The EU Charter of Fundamental Rights*, Ius Gentium: Comparative Perspectives on Law and Justice 8, DOI 10.1007/978-94-007-0156-4_8,

the contrary, it is the creation of the internal market which kick started the European integration process, progressively leading the EU to be concerned with issues which go well beyond those traditionally associated with a purely economic community. Issues of identity, social values and fundamental human rights have all come to the fore.

Particularly interesting for the purposes of this Chapter is the ever increasing need for EU institutions, and above all the EUCJ, to reconcile fundamental rights with the fundamental freedoms set by the founding treaties.[5] Despite appearances, until recently the underlying tendency, at least from a theoretical point of view, was to subordinate the former to the latter. This is apparent if one assesses the case-law of the Court of Justice in which, notwithstanding the development of a system of protection of fundamental rights, there is a general failure to bestow them with hierarchical priority, the internal market often being preferred. It is to such case-law that we shall turn our attention in the first part of this chapter.

---

[5]There is certainly no lack of academic material on the subject matter. See, for example, T. Ackermann's 'Case-note on Omega', (2005) 42 *Common Market Law Review* 1107; F.R. Agerbeek, 'Freedom of expression and free movement in the Brenner corridor: The Schmidberger case', (2004) 29 *European Law Review* 255; A. Alemanno, 'Libertés fondamentales et droits fondamentaux', (2004) 4 *Revue du Droit de l'Union Européenne* 731; M. Avbelj, 'The European Court of Justice and the question of value choices', Jean Monnet Working Paper 06/04, accessibe at www.jeanmonnetprogram.org.; A. Biondi, 'Free trade, a mountain road and the right to protest: European economic freedoms and fundamental individual rights', n. 4 above; M.K. Bulterman and H.R. Kranenbourg, 'What if rules on free movement and human rights collide? About laser games and human dignity: The Omega case', (2006) 31 *European Law Review* 93; C. Brown, 'Case C-112/00, Eugen Schmidberger, Internationale Transporte und Planzüge v. Austria', (2003) 40 *Common Market Law Review* 1499; R. Conti, 'La Dignità Umana Dinanzi alla Corte di Giustizia', (2005) 4 *Corriere Giuridico* 488; J. Coppel and A. O'Neill, 'The European Court of Justice: taking rights seriously?', (1992) 29 *Common Market Law Review* 669; G. Chu, 'Playing at killing freedom of movement', (2006) 33 *Legal Issues of Economic Integration* 85; G. Facenna, 'Eugen Schmidberger: Freedom of expression and assembly vs. free movement of goods', (2004) 1 *European Human Rights Law Review* 73; M. E. Gennusa, 'La Dignità umana vista da Lussemburgo', (2005) *Quaderni Costituzionali* 174; C. Kombos, 'Fundamental rights and fundamental freedoms: A symbiosis on the basis of subsidiarity', (2006) 12 *European Public Law* 433; J. Morijn, 'Balancing fundamental rights and common market freedoms in Union Law: Schmidberger and Omega in light of the European Constitution', (2006) 12 *European Law Journal* 15; M. Orlandi, 'Libera circolazione delle merci e deroghe giustificate da esigenze di tutela dei diritti fondamentali', (2003) *Il Diritto dell'Unione Europea* 903; E. Pellecchia, 'Il caso Omega: La dignità Umana e il delicato rapporto tra diritti fondamentali e libertà fondamentali nel diritto comunitario', (2007) 1 *Europa e Diritto Privato* 181; A. Rizzo, 'Il problema della tutela dei diritti fondamentali nell'Unione Europea', (2001) *Europa e diritto privato* 59; V. Skouris, 'Fundamental rights and fundamental Freedoms: The challenge of striking a delicate balance', n. 4 above; G. Tesauro, 'I diritti fondamentali nella giurisprudenza della Corte di Giustizia', (1992) *Rivista Internazionale dei Diritti dell'uomo* 426; A. Tizzano, 'La protection des droits fondamentaux en Europe: la Cour de justice et les juridictions constitutionnelles nationales', (2006) 1 *Revue du Droit de l'Union Européenne* 9.

On the other hand, the second part of this chapter will reflect upon the effects that the entry into force of the Treaty of Lisbon may have on the relationship between the two mentioned interests. In this context, one may envisage that the transformation of the EU Charter of fundamental rights (herein the Charter or CFR) from a mere political declaration to binding primary law might grant constitutional force to fundamental rights, placing them on a par with the fundamental economic freedoms enshrined in the Treaty on the functioning of the European Union (herein TFEU). If such an assessment were to reveal itself as correct, potential conflicts between the interests in issue would need to be appraised in a manner substantially different from that currently reflected in the case-law of the ECJ.

2 The Internal Market and Fundamental Rights Pre-Lisbon

As is well known, the original treaties establishing the European Communities contained no specific reference to the protection of fundamental rights. It had not been envisaged that Community acts could be challenged on the basis of such interests and the main concern seemed to be the prevention of human rights violations by States,[6] an aim openly pursued by the European Convention on Human Rights 1950 (herein ECHR).

Nevertheless, with the gradual expansion of Community competences and the general recognition of the supremacy of EC law[7] it was not long before the undesirability of such a state of affairs became apparent. It is against this background that the Court proceeded to develop the concept of fundamental rights stating that their respect, whilst inspired by the constitutional traditions of member States, forms an integral part of the "general principles of law protected by the ECJ".[8] The *Nold*[9] and *Hauer*[10] judgments further affirmed that international treaties for the protection of human rights are sources of inspiration, highlighting the particular significance of the European Convention on Human Rights in this respect (express reference to such a text being made in *Hauer*).[11]

---

[6]See F.G. Jacobs, 'Human Rights in the European Union: The role of the Court of Justice', (2001) 26 *European Law Review* 331.

[7]Case 6/64 *Costa v. ENEL* [1964] ECR 585.

[8]Case 11/70 *Internationale Handelsgesellschaft* [1970] ECR 1125, para. 4. Also see Case 29/69, *Stauder* [1969] ECR 419.

[9]Case 4/73 *Nold* [1974] ECR 491.

[10]Case C-44/79 *Hauer* [1979] ECR 3727.

[11]Although beyond the scope of this contribution, it must be noted that in parallel with the developments of the Court's case-law there has also been a gradual political recognition of human rights. The first example of such an attitude can be traced to the joint declarations of the Parliament, Council and Commission of 5th April 1977 and 1986.

Although the language used in the aforementioned cases evokes respect for fundamental rights, an in-depth analysis demonstrates that the ECJ was actually taking the steps necessary to avoid judicial review by national constitutional courts. It was the need to uphold the principle of supremacy and the need to guarantee the uniform application of EC law that persuaded community judges to refer to, and apply, fundamental rights.[12]

The "ancillary" attitude to the rights under discussion, however, is even more noticeable in the context of the internal market where the Court of justice has for decades clearly prioritised the fundamental economic freedoms. In line with editorial constraints, and keeping in mind the objective of the present article, the following paragraphs shall be devoted to a brief reconstruction of the relevant case-law.

3 A "Right of Way" for the Fundamental Freedoms?

The first signs of internal market prioritisation date-back to the *Wauchauf*[13] and *ERT*[14] cases. Although the former extends the respect of fundamental rights to Member States' implementation of EC law (now EU law) and the latter gives rise to a duty for derogations from the fundamental

---

These were followed by the enactment of the Single European Act which, for the first time, contained provisions regarding fundamental rights. The latter's preamble stated that the member States were "determined to work together to promote democracy on the basis of the fundamental rights recognised in the constitutions… in the convention for the protection of human rights and… the European Social Charter". On 9th December 1989 a further step was taken with the signing of the Community Charter of Fundamental Social Rights by 11 of the then 12 member States. This was followed, in 1992, by the adoption of the Treaty of European Union (herein TEU) which resulted in the insertion of Art 6(2) TEU. The Article provided that the "Union shall respect fundamental rights as guaranteed by the European Convention for the Protection of Human Rights and Fundamental Freedoms signed in Rome on 4 November 1950 and as they result from the constitutional traditions common to the member states, as general principles of Community law". Such an Article was later amended by the Treaties of Amsterdam and Nice giving rise to Arts. 6 and 7 TEU which allowed the Council to adopt measures against member States who seriously and persistently breach fundamental rights. Finally, the political commitment of the EU to fundamental rights culminated in the solemn proclamation of the European Union's Charter of Fundamental Rights in December 2000, subsequently incorporated into the Lisbon Treaty. For a more detailed analysis see G. Di Federico, Chapter 2.

[12]To this effect see, notably, J. Coppel and A. O'Neill, 'The European Court of Justice: Taking Rights Seriously?', n. 5 above; L.S. Rossi, 'How fundamental are fundamental principles? Primacy of the EU Law and fundamental rights after Lisbon', (2008) *Yearbook of European Law* 65.

[13]Case C-5/88 *Wachauf* [1989] ECR 2609.

[14]Case C-260/89 *ERT* [1991] ECR I-2925.

economic freedoms to comply with fundamental rights,[15] it is suggested that this does not imply that such rights are to be given priority. On the contrary, an analysis of the ECJ's methodology shows that in *Wachauf* the Court's reasoning discounts the protection of fundamental rights in the name of "community objectives" necessary for the common organization of a market.[16] The former are therefore likely to be subordinated to EU acts giving effect to the latter.[17] Similarly, in *ERT* the Court uses fundamental rights as an instrument to enforce the internal market, limiting the possibility for member State derogation to measures which comply with fundamental rights. The latter are thus subordinated to the demand of market integration and their protection is of a merely incidental nature.[18]

In a separate line of cases the Court has even gone as far as showing an unwillingness to deal with fundamental rights issues, concentrating solely on the free movement provisions of the Treaty. In *Cinetheque,*[19] for example, the distribution of cinematographic works was appraised in light of the free movement of goods without considering, or attempting to reconcile it with, the freedom of expression. Analogous reasoning may be observed in *Grogan,*[20] where the ECJ refused to examine whether the protection of the right to life, expressed by the Irish constitution, could limit the application of the freedom to provide services. The economic objective of the internal market thus seemed to outweigh the fundamental right in issue. Yet, it must be noted that the case was decided neither in favour of the former nor of the latter, with the Court resorting to a formal approach, claiming that the measure in issue could not be considered a restriction within the meaning of Art. 49 (ex Art. 59) TEC (now 56 TFEU). Nevertheless, the ruling still appears fundamentally flawed in so far as it also fails to recognise the freedom of expression, enshrined in Art. 10 of the European Convention on Human Rights. In this regard, a subsequent ruling of the European Court of Human Rights found the Irish prohibition on the distribution of information on clinics carrying out voluntary terminations of pregnancy in other

---

[15]Ibid., para. 43. Such reasoning has been applied in numerous judgments: Case C-62/90 *Commission v. Germany* [1992] ECR I-2575; Case C- 459/99 *MRAX* [2002] ECR I-6591; Case C-60/00 *Carpenter* [2002] ECR I-6279.

[16]See Case C-5/88 *Wachauf*, n. 13 above, para. 18.

[17]Consequently it is likely that an EU measure will be found to be compatible with fundamental rights whilst the national implementing measure may not be (as in *Wachauf*).

[18]From a legal point of view it also seems very odd that, once it has been established that a restriction is justified from the perspective of Community law, that restriction can still be subject to a scrutiny as to the respect of fundamental rights. See A. Biondi, 'Free trade, a mountain road and the right to protest…', n. 4 above, 55.

[19]Joined Cases C-60 and C-61/84 *Cinéthèque* [1985] ECR 2605. Also see Joined Cases 50–58/82, *Administrateur des Affaires Maritimes, Bayonne and Procureur de la République* [1982] ECR 3949 and Case C-168/91, *Konstantinidis* [1993] ECR 1191.

[20]Case C-159/90 *Grogan* [1991] ECR I-468.

member States, i.e. the main issue brought before the Court in *Grogan*, to infringe such an Article.[21]

The Court's willingness to consider fundamental economic freedoms and avoid dealing with fundamental rights is indicative of the consideration it gives the two competing interests. The objectives linked to the creation of the internal market are clearly guaranteed a privileged status which is no doubt a consequence of the unbreakable bond which exists between the ECJ and the founding treaties which created it. In fact, if one considers that the Court must act within the limits set by the treaties its rather dogmatic protection of the fundamental freedoms of the internal market is not surprising.

4 From *Schmidberger* and *Omega* to *Laval* and *Viking*: A Balancing Act

In *Schmidberger*[22] and *Omega*[23] the Union judges were for the first time called to deal with a straightforward reliance by member States on fundamental human rights[24] as a limit to the fundamental economic freedoms. In this context, the Court unequivocally confirmed that the protection of fundamental rights is a legitimate interest which, in principle, can justify a restriction of the obligations imposed by EC law.[25] In each case it proceeded to determine whether such a justification could subsist by weighing the competing interests through the application of the proportionality test, ultimately ruling in favour of the fundamental rights invoked.[26]

That being so, it is difficult to affirm that such a balancing exercise ensures an adequate protection of the rights in issue. To begin with, there is a persisting presumption that the economic freedoms guaranteed by the treaties are supreme, whereas fundamental rights are mere justifications for breaches of those freedoms. A close analysis of the cases reveals a "mechanical application"[27] of the concept of restriction of the free movement provisions, with the national action (*Omega*) and omission (*Schmidberger*) being considered a restriction regardless of the fact that fundamental rights were being pursued. Given the significance of such rights, should it not

---

[21] Appl. No. 14234/88, *Open Door and Dublin Well Woman*, (1992) ECHR 68.

[22] Case C-112/00 *Schmidberger* [2003] ECR I-5659.

[23] Case C-36/02 *Omega* [2004] ECR I-9609.

[24] Respectively the freedom of expression/assembly and human dignity.

[25] Case C-112/00 *Schmidberger*, n. 22 above, para. 74; Case C- 36/02, *Omega*, n. 23 above, para. 35.

[26] Also see the recent Case C-244/06 *Dynamic Medien* [2008] ECR I-00505 confirming the *Omega* precedent.

[27] See A. Alemanno, 'Libertés fondamentales et droits fondamentaux', n. 5 above, at 731.

instead be presumed that measures based upon them are prima facie compatible with the treaty rules on free movement, subsequently proceeding, if necessary, to balance the competing interests without any sort of bias? As Brown states:

> [...] using the language of prima facie breach or restriction of economic rights suggests that, even if the restriction is ultimately justified, it remains something which is at heart 'wrong', but tolerated.[28]

The outcome of the Court's approach is once again clearly market-oriented. On the one hand, States are warned that measures not compatible with the internal market will need to be justified regardless of the legitimacy of the interest they pursue.[29] On the other hand, the burden of proof rests with the party relying on fundamental rights, a stance which would not be conceivable if the Court adequately protected them as hierarchically superior norms. In this context, although language reminiscent of the European Court of Human Rights is used to conclude that fundamental rights are a primary concern which can, "in principle",[30] justify a restriction to the fundamental economic freedoms, the ECJ fails to take its analysis to a logical conclusion. Rather than finding that restrictions to fundamental rights are exceptional in so far as these are superior norms, it maintains its classic internal market approach re-focusing its attention on whether the restrictions placed upon intra-community trade are proportionate in light of the legitimate objective pursued.[31]

Thus, whilst giving *effective* protection to fundamental rights by finding, in both *Schmidberger* and *Omega*, that they justified restrictions to intra-community trade, the ECJ's approach also highlights that it is fearful to confirm their independence and primacy. In fact, the *theoretical* protection of such rights vanishes in the Court's multi-track endeavour to reconcile the constitutional traditions of member States, the normative

[28] C. Brown, 'Case C-112/00, Eugen Schmidberger, Internationale Transporte und Planzüge v. Austria', n. 5 above, at 1508.

[29] This may lead a State to become so intent on complying with EU obligations that it neglects the protection of fundamental constitutional principles which it would otherwise have guaranteed.

[30] For an analysis of what is meant by the words "in principle" see M. Avbelj, n. 5 above, at 64.

[31] Case C-112/00 *Schmidberger*, n. 22 above, para. 82; Case C- 36/02 *Omega*, n. 23 above, para. 36. It must be noted, however, that the Court leaves a wide margin of discretion to member States as regards the determination of the level of protection to be applied. Such an approach, particularly apparent in *Omega*, is certainly a consequence of the Court's cautiousness when dealing with the constitutional traditions of member States. Moreover, it implicitly acknowledges the fact that there are important differences in the catalogues of rights enshrined in national constitutions (for a similar reading see A. Alemanno, n. 5 above, at 740 and Opinion of Advocate General Jacobs in *Schmidberger*, at para. 97).

systems external to the EU (such as the ECHR) and the protection of the fundamental freedoms of the Treaty.

The Court's discomfort is highlighted by the fact that neither the analysis adopted in *Schmidberger* nor that applied in *Omega*, establish the precise type of justification that fundamental rights embody in the complex framework of rules applicable to the free movement provisions. In the former case, reference is made to Art. 30 TEC (now 36 TFEU) and mandatory requirements alike without further clarifying the heading under which they fall.[32] What seemingly results is the recognition of a new and "autonomous" justification.[33] Contrariwise, in the latter case, the Court allows human dignity to be protected via recourse to the public policy heading of Art. 46 TEC (now 52 TFEU). Such reasoning is difficult to reconcile with the restrictive interpretation of the same, which pervades decades of case-law.[34] Moreover, as is apparent from *Bouchereau,*[35] public policy is a concept based on the collective and it is not easy to envisage how the protection of fundamental individual rights can be based upon it.[36] Accordingly, as supported by wealth of literature the finding that the public policy exception can safeguard human dignity is probably best interpreted as not implying that all fundamental rights can be protected under it.

Although from a practical point of view the determination of whether fundamental rights are to be considered within one ground of justification, as opposed to another, is pointless (since effective protection is ensured either way), the lack of such a determination emphasises the Court's unease when it comes to expressly recognising the independent status and importance to be attributed to fundamental rights.

It is suggested that the problem of internal market prioritisation or, more correctly, fundamental rights "ancillarity", has not been solved by the recent *Viking*[37] and *Laval*[38] cases. Although expressly recognising that the right to strike is a fundamental right, these cases do so in a "defensive"[39] manner. In fact, the trade unions involved in the court proceedings

---

[32]F.R. Agerbeek (n. 5 above), notes: "the advocate general is not entirely clear about the nature of the derogation either" (at 265). See, in this respect, paras. 86–89 of the Advocate General's Opinion in *Schmidberger* (n. 22 above).

[33]See A. Alemanno, above n. 5, at 736; C. Brown, 'Case C-112/00, Eugen Schmidberger, Internationale Transporte und Planzüge v. Austria', n. 5 above, at 1504.

[34]Case C-154/85 *Commission v. Italy* [1987] ECR 2717; Case C- 239/90 *SCP Boscher, Studer et Fromentin* [1991] ECR I-2023.

[35]Case C-30/77 *Regina* [1977] ECR 1999, para. 35.

[36]In support of such a statement it should be noted that the concept of public policy is enshrined in the European convention on Human Rights as a limit to fundamental rights.

[37]Case C-438/05 *Viking* [2007] ECR I-10779.

[38]Case C-341/05 *Laval* [2007] ECR I-11767.

[39]A.C.L. Davies, 'One step forward, two steps back? The Viking and Laval Cases in the ECJ', (2008) 37 *Industrial Law Journal* 139.

were found to be in breach of the fundamental freedoms of the Treaty and were allowed to invoke the right to strike as a justification. It should come as no surprise that the statement of principle made in *Schmidberger* and *Omega*, to the effect that fundamental rights may in principle justify restrictions to fundamental freedoms, is therefore expressly recalled.[40] Similarly, when turning its attention to the justificatory phase, the ECJ followed the *Schmidberger* analysis, holding that the most appropriate way to reconcile the competing interests was through their "balancing" via the application of the proportionality test. In that context, it fell to the trade unions to demonstrate that their industrial action, carried out under the auspices of a legitimate interest (the right to strike), was proportionate in relation to the employer's rights of free movement.

Without dealing with additional issues such as horizontal direct effect or the recognition that fundamental rights embody overriding requirements in the public interest, it is sufficient to note that in *Viking* and *Laval* – though with different outcomes for the two cases in issue[41] – fundamental rights are once more subordinated to the economic objectives of the internal market. In both cases the right to strike is treated as a mere justification which must comply with the principle of proportionality. Not only does this re confirm the problems already verified in the framework of *Schmidberger* and *Omega*, but it is also raises some questions in the specific context of industrial action.

As noted by Davies:

> When we think about proportionality in the context of the right to strike, we generally mean the proportionality of the State's restrictions on that right.[42]

It is also generally acknowledged that the more strike action restricts the choices of an employer, the greater its effectiveness and chances of success. Nonetheless, in the cases in issue, the ECJ requested that the strike carried out by the relevant trade union's be proportional with regard to the economic rights that employer's were granted by virtue of the Treaty. By doing so, the Court effectively negates the inherent objective of the right to strike, subordinating it to the fundamental freedoms of the internal market.

---

[40]Case C-438/05 *Viking*, n. 37 above, para 45, Case C-341/05 *Laval*, n. 38 above, para. 93.

[41]In both cases the Court recognises the right to collective action represents a fundamental right capable of justifying a breach of Treaty provisions. As in *Schmidberger* and *Omega* the Court highlights that the exercise and scope of such a right must therefore be determined via a balancing of interests, namely against the fundamental economic freedoms of the Treaty. The difference between *Laval* and *Viking* is that whilst in the former the Court carries out the assessment itself, ruling that the actions of the Swedish trade union were not proportionate and thus contrary to Art. 49 TEC (notwithstanding the legitimate objective pursued), in the latter it merely sets out a series of guidelines, leaving the final determination to the referring Court.

[42]See A.C.L. Davies, 'One step forward, two steps back? ...', n. 39 above, at 145.

In fact, the greater the restrictions caused to the employer's rights of free movement, the less likely will the strike action be justified. In this respect, striking without impinging on the free movement rights of employers may turn out to be a very hard task indeed.[43]

It is thus suggested that *Schmidberger*, *Omega*, *Viking* and *Laval* do not square the circle, leaving the problem of the relationship between rights and the internal market largely unaltered. The timidity of the Court to adopt a firm position to the protection of fundamental rights results in their inability to have direct effect as legal rules or to create direct legal effects, their application being limited by the medium of the fundamental freedoms. In adopting such an approach, however, the Court cannot be criticised for acting in bad faith. In fact, being an EU institution it must act within the scope of the Treaty and ought not operate outside the limits set. It is not surprising, therefore, that the court feels bound by those economic freedoms and objectives which have formed the basis of the European evolution and have been instrumental in the creation of the EU.

That being so, one must question whether, and to what extent, the newly binding character of the EU Charter of Fundamental Rights can modify the approach so far described. Section 5 is dedicated to the presentation of possible outcomes resulting from the entry into force of the Treaty of Lisbon.

5 The Internal Market and Fundamental Rights Post-Lisbon

Although the Luxembourg Court is in certain cases willing to guarantee the *effective* protection of fundamental rights, i.e. protection in practice, via an evaluation *casu ad casum* (see *Schmidberger* and *Omega*), its *theoretical* protection of such rights is still ill-defined or lacking. In this regard, the system of protection of fundamental rights so far laid down can be compared to a jigsaw puzzle. Whilst the Court has taken all the essential steps to complete the puzzle, by considering fundamental rights as "general principles of Community law" and by showing respect for the priorities of member States and national constitutional courts, it seems unable to place the final piece, failing to expressly assert the relative importance of the said rights and prioritising economic freedoms. It is suggested that such an attitude can be neither conducive to an adequate justiciability of fundamental rights nor to legal certainty.

Moreover, the references made to other systems of protection, namely the ECHR and the constitutional traditions of member States, further

[43] For a more detailed analysis see A.C.L. Davies 'One step forward, two steps back? ...', n. 39 above.

contribute to the quandary. At present the interaction and intertwining of such systems is far from certain, making the Court's reasoning difficult to interpret and reflecting negatively on the protection of fundamental rights.

With the entry into binding force of the Charter and the future accession of the EU to the ECHR it is envisaged that the Court's logic will need to be modified. As a result of the new legal framework the EUCJ is expected to assume a fully constitutional role, adopting a conceptually clear and unambiguous approach to the pre-eminence of fundamental rights[44] and resolving the ambiguities surrounding the coordination of the various systems of protection.

6 The Effects of a Newly Binding Charter of Fundamental Rights

The Treaty of Lisbon represents a landmark in so far as the Charter is concerned, as Art. 6 of the new Treaty of European Union (ex Art. 6 TEU) recognises that the rights, freedoms and principles set out therein shall be guaranteed the same value as the Treaties.[45] It follows that the CFR, as adapted at Strasbourg on the 12th December 2007, will become part of primary EU law, thus acquiring legally binding force. Such a transformation, long awaited by EU institutions and human rights lawyers, is a welcome development for the protection and preservation of fundamental rights in Europe. Although open to debate, it is respectfully suggested that the new character of the CFR may have important consequences in reshaping the delicate balancing process carried out by the EUCJ when dealing with conflicts between the fundamental economic freedoms of the TEC, now re-baptised Treaty on the functioning of the European Union, and fundamental rights.

It must be noted that at present fundamental economic freedoms have a "constitutional" status within the EU similar to that of fundamental rights in national constitutions. This is immediately apparent from the extensive

---

[44]In this context, reference is being made not only to the hierarchical classification of fundamental rights but also to the issue regarding the existence of core fundamental rights in the EC. In *Schmidberger* the Court stated that "unlike other fundamental rights" freedom of expression and freedom of assembly are subject to certain limitations. This is an implicit acknowledgement of the fact that in certain cases fundamental rights can be absolute. The existence of such rights also seems confirmed by references to the constitutions of member States and to the ECHR. Their paramount importance in the EU legal order has been confirmed in the recent Kadi appeal judgement (Case 402/05 P *Kadi*, accessible at http://curia.europa.eu/) where the ECJ considered them to be a parameter of legality of secondary law passed in the CFSP (paras 283–284). See further the contribution in this volume by L. Paladini, Chapter 14.

[45]On the meaning and legal effects of such an 'equation' see G. Di Federico, n. 11 above.

control exercised by EU institutions, particularly the Court of Justice, over national measures with the potential of negatively affecting such freedoms. Moreover, and precisely in light of such a control, fundamental freedoms have assumed a pivotal role in the evolution and advancement of the European Union, resulting in the downward percolation of rights and objectives of market integration into national law.[46]

On the contrary, the same cannot be said of fundamental rights which were initially imported into EC law as a means of avoiding accusations that EU expansion would lead to a reduction in the protection of the rights of individuals. Their subordination to the "*Grundnorm*",[47] in the form of the fundamental economic freedoms, currently pursued by the European Court of Justice, is therefore unsurprising (notwithstanding the fact that even prior to the entry into force of the Treaty of Lisbon the general formulation of Art. 6 TEU appeared to request the respect of fundamental rights at all levels – executive, legislative and judicial). Nevertheless, there seem to be good political and legal reasons to suggest that a binding CFR may shift the demarcation line between the two mentioned values leading the ECJ to a *revirement jurisprudentiel*.

From a political point of view, the proclamation of a binding Charter is a clear value statement which grants visibility and signals that the objectives pursued therein are one of the top priorities of the EU. Since the Court does not operate in a vacuum, it is envisaged that when dealing with fundamental rights it will have to recognise their importance, ensuring a proper interpretation and justiciability. In other words it is possible that the mere political significance of a binding CFR, coupled with the future accession of the EU to the ECHR will be able to guarantee a strengthening of the protection of fundamental rights.

On the other hand, from a legal point of view the fact that the CFR "shall have the same legal value as the Treaties" implies its incorporation into the EU legal order (as primary law) and its subordination to the principles and rules of the same. Amongst such principles, that of *effet utile* is of particular significance for the present discussion.

Union norms have a certain propensity to create rights for individuals and must be interpreted pursuant to the *effet utile* principle. This is normally achieved via the concept of direct effect but, on a more general level, EU norms must be interpreted in a manner functional to their scope, prohibiting member States from adopting measures of an inconsistent nature which could potentially deny their effectiveness. Finally, a necessary corollary is the need for existing EU norms to be interpreted in

---

[46] See to this effect M. Poiares Maduro, 'Striking the elusive balance between economic freedom and Social Rights in the EU', n. 1 above.

[47] See M. Lindfelt, *Fundamental Rights in the EU – Towards a higher Law of the Land?*, n. 1 above.

an evolutionary way, taking new exigencies, subsequently inserted into EU law, into account.

On the basis of the principle of *effet utile*, the insertion of the Charter into primary law will connote a duty for the EUCJ to ensure that the rights and principles contained therein are given full effect. Moreover, and perhaps more fundamentally, the said principle will force the Court to interpret existing norms, be they of primary or secondary law, in conformity with the new developments of the EU legal order. Although fundamental rights have been present since the 1970's, and as such cannot be considered an entirely new exigency, the legally binding character of the CFR represents an important change in the inclinations of the EU. Therefore, it is presumed that in light of the principle of *effet utile*, Union judges will need to modify their current benchmark, interpreting the fundamental economic freedoms in an evolutionary way and keeping in mind that these no longer represent the only element in the formation of a European polity. The upshot should be the consideration of fundamental rights as being as worthy of respect as other values already inscribed into primary EU law.

The political and legal evaluations carried out above would suggest that a binding Charter has the potential to trigger a new approach by the EUCJ when weighing competing values. In particular, when faced with a conflict between internal market obligations and fundamental rights, it is likely that it will strive towards a non-hierarchical approach whereby the two competing values are weighed without any sort of predetermined priority.[48] In this regard, the current stance according to which fundamental rights are seen as a hindrance to free movement, often being construed as mere derogations to the economic freedoms, would have to be abandoned for a more genuine balancing of interests, especially taking into account the (future) international liability of the EU vis à vis the ECHR. Placing fundamental rights on a par with fundamental freedoms would require the EUCJ to preserve both interests, maximising their protection without sacrificing either. As noted by De Schutter:

> There should be, for each situation of conflict, one solution from which any deviation would entail more losses than gains for the two values considered together, which are both equally worthy of respect.[49]

This approach is further justified if one studies the actual text of the CFR. Although reference to fundamental economic freedoms is only made in the

---

[48]Ibid., at 302 where a similar statement is made with reference to the now abandoned Constitutional Treaty.

[49]O. De Schutter, 'The implementation of the EU Charter of Fundamental Rights through the open method of coordination', Jean Monnet Working Paper 07/04, (2004) *New York School of Law*, at 40.

preamble of such a document,[50] it goes without saying that some of the rights it lists are linked to those freedoms. Thus, since the Charter includes fundamental rights of an economic and of a non-economic nature, without distinguishing between them, the need for a non-hierarchical approach when balancing the two sets of rights becomes evident.

In light of the above, it is obvious that the CFR may lead the EUCJ to a *revirement jurisprudentiel* triggering the development of case-law based on an equal balancing of fundamental rights and economic freedoms. Abandoning the subordination of the former to the latter will have the long-awaited consequence of ensuring that the effective protection of fundamental rights, already apparent in cases such as *Schmidberger* and *Omega*, be backed by a sufficiently solid legal and theoretical framework. This will guarantee an independent and adequate justiciability of those rights, simultaneously assuring a more satisfactory level of legal certainty.

Before concluding, a question which deserves a few remarks, and which is being fiercely debated in the academic world, is how and to what extent the opting out of Poland and the UK will affect the CFR.[51] As noted elsewhere in this volume the outcome may well be that the EUCJ will continue to resort to Art. 6 TEU to protect fundamental rights. In effect, nothing in the new Treaties prevents the Court from continuing to develop its case-law on the basis of such an Article. Contrariwise, Art. 6(3) of the reformed TEU re-affirms that fundamental rights remain "general principles of the Union's Law" and the explanations relating to Art. 52 CFR, which are formally granted and interpretative status by Arts. 6 TEU and 52(7) CFR, suggest that the Union's competences remain unaltered even following the entry into force of the Charter. In a similar vein, Protocol no. 30 expressly states that the Charter does not extend the competences of the Court of Justice of the European Union, implicitly confirming that the Court retains all the powers and competences it already possessed.[52]

That being so, a continued reliance on Art. 6 is unlikely to reverse the conclusions reached above regarding the balancing of economic freedoms and fundamental rights. The latter would most probably still assume a "constitutional" role within the EU legal order and be balanced fairly and equally against the former in cases of conflict. The reason for such a conclusion is that the "constitutional process" in this field of law is now unstoppable. In addition, such a conclusion would seem to stem from the structure of

---

[50]"The Union .... seeks to promote balanced and sustainable development and ensures the free movement of persons, services, goods and capital, and the freedom of establishment".

[51]See Protocol No 30 on the application of the Charter of Fundamental Rights of the European Union to Poland and to the United Kingdom. Also see Declarations 61 and 62 by Poland, [2007] OJ C 306/156.

[52]The exercise of such powers must obviously be carried out in conformity with the ECHR as interpreted by the European Court of human rights in Strasbourg.

new Art. 6 of the Treaty on EU. Given that Art. 6(1) of the new Treaty on EU states that the Charter will have the same value as the Treaties, it is highly unlikely that in developing its case-law on the basis of the new Art. 6(3) the EUCJ will not take this into consideration. On the contrary, the Charter will most definitely inform and be instrumental in the Court's rulings on fundamental rights as general principles of law. This is even more so if one considers that at least half of the Charter rights have already been recognized by the ECJ.

Besides confirming that the rights contained in the Charter are to be regarded as general principles of law, the Luxembourg Court may also employ Art. 6(3) to protect unlisted fundamental rights. In such circumstances the member States would be bound by the primacy of EU law and would have to accept the extended protection enacted by the ECJ. Insofar as Poland and the United Kingdom are concerned, their opting out would thus become devoid of any practical effect.

Article 47 of the EU Charter of Fundamental Rights and Its Impact on Judicial Cooperation in Civil and Commercial Matters

Giangiuseppe Sanna

1 Preliminary Remarks

It is well known that one of the most important innovations of the Lisbon Treaty is the binding force attributed to the EU Charter of Fundamental Rights (hereinafter, CFR or the Charter).[1] Art. 6 TEU, as amended by the Reform Treaty, confers to the latter the same legal value of the treaties. This formal incorporation in the new "EU constitutional legal order" – which is addressed to Member States and their nationals and is based on the rule of law – implies that by acquiring the status of primary law, the CFR will prevail over conflicting national legislation and practice. Moreover, provided the relevant conditions obtained, its provisions, such as Art. 47, will be recognized with direct effect and will thus be invoked by citizens before national authorities.

From a general standpoint, the change seems to indicate that the European Union is evolving into a political entity with the characteristics of a modern federal State. In this context, the Charter would play the same role as the catalogues of fundamental rights contained in the national constitutions, making it possible to assimilate the European Court of Justice (hereinafter ECJ or EUCJ) to the highest domestic courts, with a new and extensive human and civil rights jurisdiction in the vast area now covered

G. Sanna (✉)
Studio Legale Sutti, London, UK
e-mail: giangiuseppe.sanna@sutti.com

[1]On the Charter, reference must be made to F. Benoït-Rohmer, *La Charte des droits fondamentaux de l'Union européenne*, (2001), 19 Chronique, 1483; F. Benoït-Rohmer (ed.), 'La Charte des droits fondamentaux de l'Union européennes', (2000) 12 *Revue Universelle des droits de l'Homme*, 1; G.F. Ferrari (ed.), *I diritti fondamentali dopo la Carta di Nizza. Il costituzionalismo dei diritti* (Giuffré, 2001); L.S. Rossi (ed.), *Carta dei diritti fondamentali e costituzione europea* (Giuffré, 2002); M. Wathelet, 'La Charte des droits fondamentaux: un bon pas dans une course qui reste longue', (2000) 5–6 *Cahiers de Droit Européen* 584; and S. Weatherill, *The EU Charter of Fundamental Rights: Politics, law and policy* (Oxford, 2004).

G. Di Federico, *The EU Charter of Fundamental Rights*, Ius Gentium: Comparative Perspectives on Law and Justice 8, DOI 10.1007/978-94-007-0156-4_9,

by EU law.[2] This means that all EU legislative, judicial and executive acts will have to be consistent with the Charter. It is arguable that the latter will impose an obligation on the Union not just to avoid breaching the rights therein, but also to take positive action in order to promote them.[3]

The specific aim of this Chapter is therefore to verify whether and to what extent a newly binding Charter will influence the scope of the principles of effective judicial protection and effective access to justice. To that end, a brief outline of the nature, scope of application and implementation of the right to an effective judicial remedy before a judge, and of the measures aimed at ensuring access to justice on the part of individuals, will be necessary. These guarantees are inherent to a "Community based on the rule of law", as the EC was depicted by the ECJ.[4]

The contribution will then focus on the impact of the Charter on the standing of private applicants before the CFI and ECJ when challenging acts with a general scope of application. It is well known that the restrictive interpretation followed by the ECJ in defining "individual concern" and the right to an effective remedy under Art. 230 (4) TEC caused some preoccupation. In this regard, it will be argued that the binding force of the Charter, combined with the modifications resulting from Art. 263 (4) TFEU, effectively addresses the mentioned concerns.

The last yet central aspect to be analysed is represented by the possible repercussions of a legally enforceable Charter in the field of judicial cooperation in civil law matters, with particular reference to the principle of mutual recognition of judgments and of extra-judicial decisions.[5] The practical and theoretical repercussions of a binding Charter on the creation and the development of an Area of Freedom, Security and Justice (hereinafter, AFSJ) is yet to be assessed although it can already be predicted with a reasonable degree of certainty that the principle of access to justice enshrined therein will become a major yardstick in this field of action of the European Union.

2 Effective Judicial Protection: An Old Concept with a New Vest

The principle of an effective judicial protection is codified by Art. 47 of the Charter ("Right to an effective remedy and to a fair trial") which reads:

---

[2]For a similar opinion, cf. the contribution in this volume by S. Curzon, Chapter 8.

[3]On the distinction between positive and negative rights in Charter, cf. in this volume the contribution by O. Zetterquist, Chapter 1.

[4]Case C-294/83 *Parti écologiste "Les Verts"* [1986] ECR 1339.

[5]Cf. Art. 65 TEC.

> Everyone whose rights and freedoms guaranteed by the law of the Union are violated has the right to an effective remedy before a tribunal in compliance with the conditions laid down in this Article. Everyone is entitled to a fair and public hearing within a reasonable time by an independent and impartial tribunal previously established by law. Everyone shall have the possibility of being advised, defended and represented. Legal aid shall be made available to those who lack sufficient resources in so far as such aid is necessary to ensure effective access to justice.

The fundamental rights enshrined in this Article find their origin in the traditional "right to a judge". All these guarantees – i.e. the right to a legal remedy, to an independent and impartial tribunal, to a fair hearing and to be judged within a reasonable time and to legal aid – are all functional to an effective access to justice, necessary in a "Community governed by the rule of law".[6]

To begin, it should be noted that the Charter merely reaffirms and consolidates fundamental rights which the ECJ already respects. It is well known that the ECJ established the duty to respect fundamental rights in the late 1960s, despite the fact that this obligation had not been enunciated in the founding treaties.[7] More precisely, the principle of effective judicial protection was first proclaimed in the 1986 *Johnston* case[8] as a

---

[6]See Case C-294/83 *"Les Verts"*, n. 4 above; Case C-26/62 *van Gend & Loos* [1963] ECR 1 and Opinion 1/91 [1991] ECR I-6079, where the ECJ affirms that: "the EEC Treaty, albeit concluded in the form of an international agreement, none the less constitutes the constitutional charter of a Community based on the rule of law. The Community treaties established a new legal order for the benefit of which the States have limited their sovereign rights and the subjects of which comprise not only Member States but also their nationals. The essential characteristics of the Community legal order which has thus been established are in particular its primacy over the law of the Member States and the direct effect of a whole series of provisions" (at para 1). On the "right to a judge", cf. L.P. Comoglio, 'Il "giusto processo" civile nella dimensione comparatistica', (2002) 57 *Rivista di Diritto Processuale* 702; J.-P. Jacqué, 'Charte des droits fondamentaux et droit à un recours effectif. Dialogue entre le juge et le "constituant"', (2002) *Il Diritto dell'Unione europea* 1.

[7]Case 29/69 *Stauder* [1969] ECR 419; Case 11/70 *Internationale Handelsgesellschaft* [1970] ECR 1125; Case 4/73 *Nold* [1974] ECR 491; Case C-44/79 *Hauer* [1979] ECR 3727. There is a plethora of critical academic doctrine on the topic. See *ex pluribus* M. Avbeij, 'The European Court of Justice and the question of value choices' (2004) *Jean Monnet Working Paper 06/04*, accessible at http://www.jeanmonnetprogram.org.; T. Ballarino, 'Diritti fondamentali dell'Unione europea', in S. Cassese, *Dizionario di diritto pubblico* (Giuffré, 2006) 1892; F.G. Jacobs, 'Human rights in the European Union: The role of the Court of Justice', (2001) 26 *European Law Review* 331; A. Rizzo, 'Il problema della tutela dei diritti fondamentali nell'Unione Europea', (2001) *Europa e diritto privato* 59; G. Tesauro, 'I diritti fondamentali nella giurisprudenza della Corte di Giustizia' (1992) *Rivista Internazionale dei Diritti dell'Uomo* 426; A. Tizzano, 'La protection des droits fondamentaux en Europe: la Cour de Justice et les juridictions constitutionnelles nationales' (2006) 1 *Revue du Droit de l'Union Européenne* 9.

[8]Case 222/84 *Johnston* [1986] ECR 1651. See also Case 222/86 *Unectef* [1987] ECR 4097; Case C-97/91 *Borelli* [1992] ECR I-6313 and Case C-185/97 *Coote* [1998] ECR I-5199.

general principle stemming from the constitutional traditions common to the Member States and to the international agreements on the protection of human rights, namely to the European Convention on Human Rights and Fundamental Freedoms (hereinafter, ECHR).

Indeed, Art. 47 issues directly from Arts 6 (Right to a fair trial) and 13 (Right to an effective remedy) ECHR but presents some distinctive features. Firstly, since the CFR provisions will apply whenever the implementation of EU law (both at a supranational and domestic level) is at stake,[9] Art. 47 provides a more extensive protection with respect to Art. 13 ECHR. In fact, while the former expressly guarantees an effective remedy before "a tribunal", the scope of application of the latter is restricted to "a national body". Moreover, contrary to Art. 6 (1) ECHR, which limits the right to a fair trial to civil and criminal law cases, Art. 47, (2) CFR applies to all contentious matters.

Regardless of these specific differences, it should be recalled that pursuant to Art. 52 (3) CFR:

> In so far as this Charter contains rights which correspond to rights guaranteed by the Convention for the Protection of Human Rights and Fundamental Freedoms, the meaning and scope of those rights shall be the same as those laid down by the said Convention. This provision shall not prevent Union law providing more extensive protection [...]

Also, it is important to underline that the principle of effective judicial protection will have to be respected by the EU Institutions as well as by the Member States, when implementing EU law. Despite this normative levelling of responsibilities, the case law developed under the former treaties by the ECJ – which is ultimately called upon to ensure the legality of all action taken in the field of EU law – indicates that the respect of the principle of effective judicial protection was presumed at the Community level, but closely scrutinized when it came to domestic legislation and practice.[10]

The double standard applied by the Luxembourg judges clearly emerges in the *Unibet* case,[11] where the Court reaffirmed, with a "surprising"[12] direct reference to Art. 47 of the Charter, that the detailed procedural rules governing actions for the protection of individual rights under Community law must not be less favourable than those applicable to similar domestic actions (principle of equivalence) and must not render practically impossible or excessively difficult the exercise of rights conferred by EC law

[9] Cf. Art. 51 CFR.

[10] See *infra*, para 2.

[11] Case C-432/05 *Unibet* [2007] ECR I-2271.

[12] Cf. M. Bulterman, 'Case C-540/03, Parliament v. Council, Judgment of the Grand Chamber of 27 June 2006, [2006] ECR I-5769', (2008) 45 *Common Market Law Review* at 256, where the author observes that "the ECJ is now also willing to refer to the Charter in situations where the Community legislature has not acknowledged its relevance for the Community measure under review".

(principle of effectiveness). Adopting a case by case approach, the ECJ will assess whether these principles are respected taking into consideration the procedural context in which the relevant provision applies but also its specific features and its interpretation by the competent national authorities.[13]

Of course, it is for the national courts to implement the procedural rules governing actions brought before them so to enable, inasmuch as possible, the effective protection of the rights guaranteed under EC law. In this regard it should also be noted that in order to ensure full and effective protection of the rights granted under EC law Member States are obliged to provide for interim relief whenever the compatibility of a national measure is questioned.[14]

3 The Standing of Private Applicants in the EU and the Effective Access to Justice: A Second Round Forthcoming?

The judicial protection of private parties in the EU today often falls short of the standard set by the legal orders of the Member States.

The *locus standi* conditions required under Art. 230 (4) TEC – which represented, at least in theory, the main legal avenue for individuals to obtain judicial review – required that when challenging EU acts with a

---

[13] *Ex pluribus*, see Case 34/67 *Lück* [1968] ECR 245, 251; Case 33/76 *REWE* [1976] ECR 1989, para 5, Case C-54/96 *Dorsch Consult* [1997] ECR I-4961, para 40; Joined Cases C-279, 280 and 281/96, *Ansaldo* [1998] ECR I-5025, para 27; Case C-111/97 *Evobus* [1998] ECR I-5411, para 15. See A. Barav, 'Effectiveness of judicial protection and the role of national courts', in *Judicial protection of rights in the Community legal order* (Bruylant, 1997) 259; A. Biondi, 'The European Court of justice and certain national procedural limitations: not such a tough relationship', (1999) 36 *Common Market Law Review* 1271; L. Flynn, 'When national procedural autonomy meets the effectiveness of Community law, can it survive the impact?', (2008) 9 *Era Forum scripta iuris europaei*, 245; M. Hoskins, 'Tilting the balance: supremacy and national procedural rules', (1996) 21 *European Law Review* 365; C. Kakouris, 'Do the member States possess judicial procedural autonomy?', (1997) 34 *Common Market Law Review* 1389; P. Oliver, 'Le droit communautaire et les voies de recours nationales', (1992) 3–4 *Cahiers de Droit Européen* 348; A. Saggio, 'Incidenza della giurisprudenza della Corte di Giustizia sulle norme processuali', (2001) *Corriere Giuridico* 114; H. G. Schermers and D. F. Waeibroek, *Judicial protection in the European Union* (The Hague/London/New York, Kluwer Law International, 2001); E. Szyszczak, 'Making Europe more relevant to its citizens: Effective judicial process', (1996) 21 *European Law Review* 351; A. Tizzano, S. Fortunato, 'La tutela dei diritti', in A. Tizzano (ed.), *Il diritto privato dell'Unione Europea*, XXVI, II, 1271, in M. Bessone (ed.) *Trattato di diritto privato* (Torino, 2000).

[14] Cf. Case C-213/89 *Factortame* [1990] ECR I-2433, para 22, Case 432/05, *Unibet*, n. 11 above, paras 67 ff. The same holds true for the case in which the validity of a Community law is doubtful, see Joined Cases C-143/88 and C-92/89, *Zuckerfabrik* [1991] ECR I-415 and case C-465/93 *Atlanta* [1995] ECR I-3761.

general scope of application natural and legal persons demonstrate direct and individual concern. Such conditions have been tangled within the restrictive interpretation given by ECJ in the landmark case *Plaumann*,[15] where the requirement was deemed to be met only if the applicant could demonstrate that despite the general scope of application of the provision in question he/she was individually concerned because of certain features or characteristics capable of distinguishing his/her position with respect to all other potential addressees.

For the past 50 years the *Plaumann* test has limited access to justice on the part of individuals and has long been criticized.[16] The debate on the annulment procedure reached its peak in 2002[17] when the CFI tried to reinterpret the condition laid down in Art. 230 (4) TEC with a view to enhance the judicial protection of individuals within the EC legal order. In *Jégo-Quéré*,[18] it was held that only a new interpretation of "individual concern" could ensure adequate access to justice for private applicants, expressly referring to Art. 47 CFR.[19] The judgment was indeed propitiated by the revolutionary approach taken by Advocate General Jacobs in his opinion

[15]Case 25/62 *Plaumann* [1963] ECR 95.

[16]Cf., amongst others, A. Arnull, 'Private Applicants and the action for annulment under Art. 173 of the EC Treaty', (1995) 32 *Common Market Law Review* 7; P. Craig, 'Legality, standing and substantial review in Community law', (1994) 14 *Oxford Journal of Legal Studies* 507; R. Greaves, '*Locus Standi* under Art. 173 EEC when seeking annulment of a regulation', (1986) 11 *European Law Review* 119; C. Harding, 'The private interest in challenging Community action', (1980) 5 *European Law Review* 345; C. Harlow, 'Towards a theory of access for the European Court of Justice', (1992) 12 *Yearbook of European Law* 213; N. Neuwahl, 'Article 173 Paragraph 4 EC: Past, present and possible future', (1996) 21 *European Law Review* 112; H. Rasmussen, 'Why is Article 173 interpreted against private plaintiffs?', (1980) 5 *European Law Review* 112. It should also be noted that some Authors (P. Craig and G. De Búrca, *EU law: Text, cases and materials* (Oxford University Press, 2003) at 489) have described the Plaumann test as "a mirage in the desert, ever receding and never capable of being grasped".

[17]See A. Albors-Llorens, 'The standing of private parties to challenge community measures: has the European court missed the boat?', (2003) 62 *Cambridge Law Journal* 72; E. Biernat, 'The *locus standi* of private applicants under Article 230 (4) EC and the principle of judicial protection in the European Community' (2003) *Harvard Jean Monnet Working Paper no. 12/03*, accessibile at http://www.jeanmonnetprogram.org/papers/03/031201.html; C. Kombos, 'The recent case law on *locus standi* of private applicants under Art. 230 (4) EC: A missed opportunity or a velvet revolution?', (2005) *European Integration Online Paper*, accessibile at http;//eiop.or.at/eiop/texte/2005-017a.htm; V. Kronenberger and P. Dejmek, '*Locus standi* of individuals before community courts under Article 230 (4) EC: Illusions and disillusions after the Jégo-Quéré (T-177/01) and Unión de Pequeños Agricultores (C-50/00) judgments', (2002) 5 *European Legal Forum* 257; F. Ragolle, 'Access to justice for private applicants in the community legal order: Recent (r)evolutions', (2003) 28 *European Law Review* 90.

[18]Case T-177/01 *Jégo-Quéré* [2002] ECR II-2365.

[19]*Ibid.*, para 47.

in *Unión de Pequeños Agricultores* pending at that time before the ECJ.[20] The opinion is of great importance, as it argues for a wider interpretation of the requirement of individual concern, making for the first time specific reference to Art. 47 CFR. This could have resulted in an extension of the standing in actions brought before the courts against secondary EC legislation. After focusing on whether Art. 234 TEC offered a valid alternative to Art. 230 (4) TEC, the Advocate general suggested a milder interpretation of the requirement, which will obtain when the measure has, or is able to have, a substantial adverse effect on a person concerned.[21]

These efforts were nonetheless vain since in *Unión de Pequeños Agricultores (UPA)*[22] the ECJ reaffirmed the traditional *Plaumann* test. The Court claimed that the Treaty provided for an exhaustive system of legal remedies designed to ensure judicial review of the legality of the acts adopted by the EC institutions through the existence of alternative avenues enabling effective protection, as the preliminary reference procedure laid down in Art. 234 TEC or the plea of illegality under Art. 241 TEC. Although it was accepted that the requirement of individual concern did limit the right to an effective judicial protection, the Court went on to say that it could not simply disregard the wording of Art. 230 (4) TEC making it clear that any change in its case law would have to be preceded by an amendment to the Treaty in accordance with Art. 48 TEU.[23] Subsequently, on the

---

[20] Case C-50/00 *Unión de Pequeños Agricultores v. Council* [2002] ECR I-6677, AG Jacobs.

[21] See F.G. Jacobs, 'Effective judicial protection of individuals in the European Union, now and in the future', (2002) *Il Diritto dell'Unione europea* 203. In his opinion in UPA AG Jacobs found that Art. 234 TEC is not an effective alternative to Art. 230 (4) TEC. In particular, while pursuant to the latter provision the institution responsible for adopting the relevant act will be a party to the proceedings, under the former norm that would not necessarily be the case. Moreover, the national court: (a) may lack the expertise that the ECJ has in specific areas covered by the contested measure; (b) is prevented from declaring the measure as invalid (cf. Case 314/87 *Foto-Frost* [1987] ECR 4199) and (c) may encounter more difficulties in granting the interim relief available to the ECJ pursuant to Arts. 242 and 243 TEC. As to the latter aspect, it should be recalled that: (i) not always domestic legislation provides for the necessary remedies; (ii) the substantial delays and increased costs related to preliminary references are not present to the same extent in direct actions for annulment; (iii) the action for annulment allows for a more intense scrutiny of the contested measure since the applicants autonomously put forward their pleas and invoke the relevant grounds of invalidity whereas under Art. 234 TEC they can (only) intervene submitting written observations and presenting oral arguments before the ECJ and (iv) Art. 234 TEC is subject to the CILFIT jurisprudence (Case 283/81 *Srl CILFIT and Lanificio di Gavardo SpA v. Ministry of Health* [1982] ECR 3415) on the doctrine of '*acte claire et eclairé*' and, in any case, always depends on the willingness of the national Court to make the reference.

[22] C-50/00 *Unión de Pequeños Agricultores* [2002] ECR I-6677.

[23] *Ibid.*, para 45. In doing so the Court appears to acknowledge that, although "complete", the system of protection is not perfect.

appeal against the CFI ruling in *Jégo-Quéré*[24] the ECJ confirmed again its position notwithstanding the arguments put forward by AG Jacobs.[25]

And yet, as the Romans would have put it, *Roma locuta, causa soluta*? In the light of the modifications envisaged by the Constitutional Treaty[26] and more recently introduced by the Lisbon Treaty, access to justice seems to have a new shiny vest given the legal force attributed the Charter. A twofold level of reasoning, both political and legal, strongly suggests that a newly binding Charter would significantly alter the interpretation of the notion of standing by the EUCJ.

In a political and perhaps symbolic sense, the incorporation of the Charter into the EU legal order demonstrates that the "Masters of the Treaties" (i.e the Member States) have taken into greater consideration the need to protect the rights of individuals and more in general the effective access to justice. Thus, it is argued that in the new scenario, the *modus operandi* of the EU courts will change. In this regard, it should not go unnoticed that when the Court of Justice intervenes to promote integration, it acts, from a functional perspective, not only as a judicial body, but also as a political one.

The legal force attributed to the Charter could be understood as the Member States' response to the critical analysis conducted by the ECJ in *Unión de Pequeños Agricultores.* Nonetheless, it is suggested that in this instance the judges were questioning the suitability of the individual requirement test rather than the wording of Art. 230 (4) TEC. In this respect, it is well know that the Lisbon Treaty has removed the "individual concern" requirement only when individuals seek to challenge the validity of "a regulatory act which is of direct concern to them and does not entail implementing measures".[27] This leaves open to speculation the issue

---

[24]Case C-263/02 P *Jégo-Quèrè* [2004] ECR I-3425.

[25]In particular, in his opinion concerning the *Jégo-Quéré* case, Jacobs argued that the CFI erred in law when it departed from the traditional interpretation of individual concern, in breach of the fourth paragraph of Art. 230. He found the strict standing test highly problematic because capable of jeopardizing the individual's right to challenge the validity of secondary legislation. Moreover, the only way to bring a case before a national court and obtain judicial review through a preliminary reference might be to infringe the law, which is not admissible. In addition, the alternative remedy of Arts. 235 and 288 (2) TEC are inadequate, but the situation is an unavoidable consequence of the limitations stemming from the wording of Art. 230 (4) TEC. Interestingly, unlike the Opinion in UPA and perhaps as a consequence of the ECJ's decision in that case, there is no express reference to the right to effective judicial protection nor reference to the inadequacy of Art. 234 TEC as an alternative remedy.

[26]Treaty Establishing a Constitution for Europe, [2004] OJ C 130/1.

[27]Cf. Art. 263 TFEU. The provision removes the "individual concern" requirement only when individuals seek to challenge the validity of "a regulatory act which is of direct concern to them and does not entail implementing measures". However, it should be noted that no definition of "regulatory act" has been provided leaving the question open to

of whether and how a binding Charter would affect the *Plaumann* formula when acts of a general scope of application are contested by private applicants. Ultimately, it is an interpretative problem to be solved by the EUCJ under Art. 19 TEU but it is respectfully submitted that the possibility of a *revirement jurisprudentiel* on the matter can not be excluded a priori. Of course, the answer to the question mainly depends on the reading the EU judges will give to the amendment agreed upon by the Member States during the 2007 IGC.

On the one hand, in fact, the EUCJ could consider the changes to be a confirmation of the will to prevent private parties from bringing an action against legislative measures (as is the case in certain Member States) and consequently deny *locus* standing on grounds of general (constitutional) policy. On the other hand, it can be argued that as any other Treaty provision, Art. 47 CFR will be subject to the traditional teleological, dynamic and functional rules of interpretation used by the EUCJ when applying EU law.

The scope of Art. 47 CFR should therefore be appraised keeping in due consideration the *effet utile* doctrine, whereby norms must be interpreted according to their wording but in a way that ensures full effectiveness of EU law and, in particular, the protection of individual rights.[28] It follows that, since the Charter acquired legal force, the EU courts might change their approach in assessing the individual concern requirement focusing more on the need to respect the principle of effective judicial protection (via the principle of *effet utile*) than on the wording of Art. 263 (4) TFEU, read in light of the *Plaumann* precedent.

Despite the circumstance that the relationship between Art. 47 CFR and Art. 263 TFEU is yet to be clarified, the legal force attributed to the Charter

---

speculation. On the possible notion of "regulatory act", see J. Usher, 'Direct and individual concern – An effective remedy or a conventional solution', (2003) 28 *European Law Review* 575; A. Dashwood and A. Johnston, 'The institutions of the enlarged EU under the regime of the Constitutional Treaty', (2005) 42 *Common Market Law Review* 1481; J. Rideau, 'Présentation des actes juridiques dans la Constitution', in E. Álvarez Conde and V. Garrido Mayol (eds.), *Comentarios a la Constitución Europea*, Vol. I (Tirant lo Blanch, 2004) at 333; R. Bray (ed.), *Procedural law of the European Union* (Sweet & Maxwell, 2006) at 327. Now that the Lisbon Treaty has entered into force, the ECJ will be soon called upon to clarify this point.

[28] Cf. Case 187/87 *Land de Sarre* [1988] ECR 5013, para 19; Case C-223/98 *Adidas* [1999] ECR I-7081, para 21; Case C-440/00 *Kühne & Nagel* [2004] ECR I-787, para 59. On the principle of '*effet utile*' see M. Cartabia, *Princìpi inviolabili e integrazione europea* (Giuffré, 1995); R. Monaco, 'Les principes d'interprétation suivis par la Cour de Justice des Communautés Européennes', in author? *Mélanges offerts à Henri Rolin* (Pedone, 1964); M. Pechstein and C. Drechler, in K. Reisenhuber (eds.), *Europäische Methodenlehre. Handbuch für Ausbildung und Praxis* (De Gruyter Recht, 2006) 172; P. Pescatore, 'Monisme, dualisme et effet utile» dans la jurisprudence de la Cour de Justice de la Communauté européenne', in N. von Colneric, D. Edward, J. Puissochet and D. R. Colomer (eds.), *Une communauté de droit. Festschrift für Gil Carlos Rodríguez Iglesias* (Berliner Wissenschafts-Verlag, 2003) 329.

could possibly result in a new judicial approach towards individual standing. Given that under the Lisbon Treaty both norms have a primary law status, and having in mind the suggested parallelism between the EUCJ and the highest courts of the Member States, the former could assign a prevailing force to the Charter provision enabling effective access to justice (at least in cases where the denial of judicial review could hinder individual rights). By contrast, wearing a 'constitutional vest', the Court of Justice could be tempted to recognize and stigmatise the 'constitutional limit' set out by Art. 263 TFEU and declare the action inadmissible.

4 Effective Access to Justice and Judicial Cooperation in Civil and Commercial Matters

The fundamental rights enshrined in Art. 47 CFR will play a significant role in the context of the judicial cooperation in civil matters and, ultimately, in the developing of an Area of Freedom, Security, and Justice.

In this regard it should be noted that the intention to create such an area led the Member States to grant more competences to the Community, including, in particular, the power to pass legislation with a view to promote the compatibility of the rules concerning conflict of laws and jurisdiction, traditionally left to the national parliaments.[29] Accordingly, the Community has adopted several measures with a cross-border impact to the extent necessary for the proper functioning of the internal market (as, for instance, the well known Brussels Regulation), with an extraordinary and unique legislative activism[30] characterized in the first period by a lack of organicity and coordination. On its part the ECJ recently delivered an Opinion[31] emphatically praising Regulation No 44/2001 inasmuch as it institutes a unified and coherent system of rules on jurisdiction and enforcement of judgements.

The Lisbon-Reform Treaty strengthens the role of the Community legal order in the field of conflict of laws and jurisdiction. Among the several

[29] Reference is made to the amendments introduced by the Amsterdam Treaty. Cf., in particular, Arts. 61, 65 TEC.

[30] Amongst the many acts adopted in this field, cf. EC Regulation 1346/2000, [2000] OJ L 160/1; EC Regulation 1348/2000, [2000] OJ L 160/37; EC Regulation 44/2001, [2001] OJ L 12/1 (Brussels I, on jurisdiction, recognition and enforcement of judgments in civil and commercial matters), and EC Regulation 2201/2003 (Brussels II *bis*, on matrimonial matters), [2003] OJ L 338/1. In the field of conflict of laws, cf. EC Regulation 864/2007 (Rome II, on the extra-contractual obligations), [2007] OJ L 199/40 and Regulation 593/2008 (Rome I, on contractual obligations, amending the 1980 Rome Convention), [2008] OJ L 177/6, see also http://ec.europa.eu/justice_home/doc_centre/civil/acquis/doc_civil_acquis_en.htm

[31] Opinion 1/03 2006 ECR 1145 according to which the conclusion of the new Lugano convention falls entirely within the sphere of exclusive competence of the European Community.

law changes introduced by Art. 81 TFEU, which it would be inappropriate to examine in this Chapter, it must be stressed that such cooperation may now include the adoption of measures for the approximation of the laws and regulations of the Member States aimed at ensuring an effective access to justice.[32] This indirect reference to Art. 47 CFR should not be underestimated. Of course, being part of the wider category of fundamental rights, the protection was already granted in the EU civil judicial cooperation domain, even before the comunitarization brought about by the Amsterdam Treaty.

For the purposes of the present analysis, it is sufficient to recall that under Regulation Brussels I – which, based on the principle of mutual trust in the administration of Justice within the Community, allows for judgments rendered in a member State to be automatically recognised in other Member States[33] – the unsuccessful party will be able to contest, in an adversarial procedure, the declaration of enforceability issued by a national court on the grounds that his/her rights of defence were violated.[34]

At the same time, given the formal abolishment of the three pillar structure,[35] it seems fair to state that with the entry into force of the Lisbon Treaty the scope of the principle of effective access to justice in the AFSJ will be further clarified, fully benefiting from the preliminary reference mechanism laid down in Art. 267 TFEU.[36]

From a general standpoint, it should be underlined that effective access to justice, together with the mutual recognition and trust principles, legal certainty and the autonomy of the parties, provides a posteriori evidence of the actual existence of a system which the Court (correctly) considers to be coherent.

Particular attention should be paid to the circumstance that the effective access to justice is capable of significantly affecting EU cross-border litigation, both in a positive and negative way. On the one hand, in fact, the need to ensure access to justice will have repercussions on the EU legislative

---

[32] Art. 81, lett. e TFUE.

[33] See Chapter III of Regulation 44/2001, n. 30 above, dealing with recognition and enforcement.

[34] Cf. Arts. 33 and 36 of Regulation 44/2001, n. 30 above, respectively.

[35] It is nonetheless true that the common foreign and security policy will maintain its specificity. Cf. in this volume the contribution by L. Paladini, Chapter 14.

[36] In addition, it should be recalled that the Protocol on the Statute of the ECJ has recently been amended by Council Decision 2008/79/EC/Euratom, [2008] OJ L 24/42, which allows for a fast-track procedure. The Rules of Procedure of the Court of Justice have been amended accordingly ([2008] OJ L 24/39) by inserting a new Art. 104b that sets out the new procedure. The referring national court may request that the speedy procedure be applied or the ECJ may decide to apply it ex officio in exceptional cases. The parties to the national proceedings, the member State of the referring court (but not all member States) and the EU institutions may submit written observations within a short deadline set by the Court.

policy in this field. More precisely, it is suggested that regulations will be adopted to reduce the many obstacles private parties still face in exercising this fundamental right. In this regard, suffice it to recall the problems posed by the different legal aid regimes applicable in the Member States.[37] In addition, it should not be forgotten that individuals involved in litigation in a foreign Member State (i.e. an EU country of which they are not citizens) often have to meet nationality or residence requirements and incur in extra costs which ultimately may limit access to justice. The quality and economic accessibility (perhaps through public funding) of legal services are essential conditions to guarantee observance of the 'constitutional' standard of protection affirmed by Art. 47 CFR.[38] Indeed, the will to promote a legislation capable of ensuring effective access to justice can already be appreciated taking into account the latest regulations on the Small Claims procedure and the EU Order for Payment Procedure,[39] both aimed at ensuring (effective and efficient) access to justice by creditors.[40] As far as the former act is concerned, it is interesting to observe that the Recital No 9 makes reference to the fundamental rights and principles enshrined in the Charter. Pursuant to the EU Small Claims Procedure, the court or tribunal must respect the right to a fair trial and to an adversarial trial, in particular when deciding on the need for an oral hearing.

On the other hand, effective access to justice represents a limit vis-à-vis the principle of mutual recognition of judgments and other decisions, recognised as being a cornerstone of judicial cooperation in civil matters at the October 1999 European Council meeting in Tampere. According to this principle, originally developed in the Common Market, a judgement should have the same authority and effectiveness in the country where enforcement is sought and in the country where it was adopted. The ultimate goal is the automatic recognition and execution of judicial decisions among the Member States of the European Union.[41]

---

[37] For further details, see Commission *Green Paper* of 9 February 2000: *Legal aid in civil matters: The problems confronting the cross-border litigant* (COM (2000) 51 final).

[38] In that respect it can be useful to draw a parallelism between the concept of "access to justice" and the (far-reaching) notion of "access to market" elaborated by ECJ in the most recent case law on the freedom of establishment (Case C-442/02 *Caixa-Bank France* [2004] ECR I-8961, para 12). On the free movement of capital, see, in particular, the golden-share saga, considered an obstacles to access (even if only potential) to the financial market of another member State, cf. Case C-367/98 *Commission v Portugal* [2002] ECR I-4731; case C-483/99 *Commission v France* [2002] ECR I-4781; Case C-503/99 *Commission v Belgium* [2002] ECR I-4809; Case C-463/00 *Commission v Spain* [2003] ECR I-4581 and Case C-98/01, *Commission v United Kingdom* [2003] ECR I-4641.

[39] Respectively, EC Regulation 861/2007, [2007] OJ L 199/1 and EC Regulation 1896/2006, [2006] OJ L 399/1.

[40] See Recital No 7 of EC Regulation 861/2007 (n. 39 above) and Recital No. 8 of EC Regulation 1896/2006 (n. 39 above).

[41] In practice, this is done by abolishing all formalities required in the national legal systems in order to enforce the judgments rendered in other Member States and by prohibiting any substantive review of the latter, without any *ordre public* clause.

The binding nature of the Charter appears capable of jeopardising the attainment of this objective. Art. 47 CFR and the described mutual recognition principle are difficult to combine although the former should prevail over the latter. As recognized by the ECJ in *Krombach*,[42] the protection of effective access to justice may in some (exceptional) cases require the refusal to enforce a judgement by a court in another Member State. Pursuant to the classic definition of *ordre public international* in international private and procedural law, this can be justified on grounds of public policy since national and community judges must abide by the fundamental values protected under EU Law.[43] Of course, the legal force attributed to the Charter by the Lisbon Treaty can only strengthen the need to ensure the full effectiveness of its provisions.

Ultimately, it is up to the ECJ to define the contours of the notion of "European public order".[44] It is not difficult to predict that under the new treaties it will carry out this pivotal function by making extensive use of the Charter. In this sense, the effective access to justice affirmed in Art. 47 CFR is likely to become the main benchmark for assessing compliance with fundamental rights in the field of judicial cooperation.

Last but not least it is important to stress the impact of such a strengthened principle of effective access to justice on the national jurisdictions of EU Member States, in particular on their procedural rules. As already indicated, the latter are bound to respect the principles of equivalence and effectiveness so that national laws may not discriminate according

---

Cf. Regulation 805/2004, [2004] OJ L 143/15. See N. Boschiero, 'The forthcoming European enforcement order. Towards an European law-enforcement area', (2003) 86 *Rivista di Diritto Internazionale* 688.

[42]Case C-7/98 *Krombach* [2000] ECR I-1935, para 37. See also H. Muir Watt, 'Evidence of an emergent European legal culture: Public policy requirements of procedural fairness under the Brussels and Lugano Conventions', (2001) 36 *Texas International Law Journal* 539. In this regard, cf. Cour de Cassation, Judgment 16 March 1999, no. 17598 (for a comment see. G.A.L. Droz, 'Variations Pordea (à propos de l'arrêt de la Cour de Cassation; 1er Chambre civile du 16 mars 1999)', (2000) 89 *Revue Critique du Droit International Privé* 181 ff.). Nevertheless, even before the *Krombach* judgment, some Authors pointed out the link between the notion of *ordre public* and the protection of fundamental rights, cf. T. Ballarino, *Costituzione e diritto internazionale privato* (CEDAM, 1974); G. Beitzke, *Grundgesetz und international privatrecht* (Berlin, 1961); P. Hammje, 'Droits fondamentaux et ordre public', (1997) 86 *Revue Critique du Droit International Privé* 1.

[43]Case C-126/97 *Eco Swiss China* [1999] ECR I-3092. The case acknowledged the existence of an *ordre public international* of European source. See S. Poillot Peruzzetto, 'L'ordre public international en droit communautaire. A propos de l'arrêt de la Cour de Justice des Communautés du 1er juin 1999 (affaire Eco Swiss China Tima Ltd)', (2000) 2 *Journal de Droit International* 299. For a different view, cf. M.R. Moura Ramos, 'Public policy in the framework of the Brussels Convention. Remarks on two recent decisions by the European Court of Justice', in M.R. Moura Ramos (ed.), *Estudios de derecho international privado e de derecho processual civil internacional* (Coimbra, 2002) 283.

[44]The elaboration of the notion of *ordre public* cannot be left to the national judicial authorities without hindering the uniform application of EC law (cf. Case C-7/98, *Krombach*, n. 42 above).

to whether the claim is based on domestic or EU law and must guarantee effective and adequate redress for violations of Community law. In this respect, the approach taken by the ECJ in *Leffler* is rather indicative of the far reaching effects of these principles in the field of judicial cooperation,[45]

But with Art. 47 CFR acquiring supremacy and direct effect, it is suggested that all the mechanisms envisaged by the numerous acts passed in civil judicial cooperation matters – which are capable of deeply affecting the Member States' normative systems[46] – will enhance their effectiveness by virtue of the functional integration of national rules into the Area of Freedom, Security and Justice. The latter shall in fact be interpreted in light of the result pursued by the single Regulation under consideration (*effet utile* doctrine), of the objectives of the judicial cooperation in civil and commercial matters and with a view to ensure effective access to justice; when choosing the national adversarial procedure for the *exequatur* of a foreign decision (Arts. 43, 45 of Brussels I Regulation and Art. 31 of Brussels II*bis* Regulation) Art. 47 will become a strong interpretative instrument to say the least. This should also be true for the conflict of laws rules as established by the Rome regulations.

In other words, the circumstance that Art. 81 TFEU refers to effective judicial protection (and should thus, it is submitted, be read jointly with Art. 47 CFR), might lead the European and domestic courts to adjust their interpretative stance when dealing with EU legislation in the field of civil and commercial judicial cooperation and national procedural norms. The potential spill-over effect is notable as a multitude of supranational and, consequently, domestic provisions (broadly) falling within the scope of application of Art. 81 TFEU will be subject to this higher hermeneutical standard.[47]

In any event, it remains to the EUCJ to establish a clear hierarchy or a scale of values to be observed when dealing with judicial cooperation in

---

[45]Case C-443/03 *Leffler* [2005] ECR I-961. It is well known that in this instance, the ECJ (following AG Stix-Hackl's opinion) considered inter alia that "the principle of effectiveness must lead the national court to apply the detailed procedural rules laid down by domestic law only in so far as they do not compromise the *raison d'être* and objective of the Regulation" (para 50).

[46]Suffice it here to recall the domicile determination or the registered office of a company (Arts. 59 and 22, No. of EC Regulation 44/2001), the grant of precautionary measures (Art. 31 of EC Regulation 44/2001) or the determination of the certain date of the beginning of a legal proceeding (Art. 9 (2) of EC Regulation 1348/2000 or Art. 30 of the Brussels I Regulation).

[47]For an example of the possible impact of EU principles on the Italian domestic rules of civil procedure concerning the *quaestio iurisdictionis*, see P. Franzina, 'Il coordinamento fra *lex fori* e norme uniformi nell'accertamento del titolo di giurisdizione secondo il regolamento (CE) n. 44/2001', (2004) 2 *Rivista di diritto internazionale* 384.

civil matters, most notably between those enshrined in Art. 6 ECHR and those contained in Art. 47 CFR supported, of course, by the cornerstone principles of mutual recognition and trust between the Member States.

5 The Impact of a Binding Charter on Enforcement Policy in the Area of Freedom, Security and Justice…and Beyond. Some Brief Considerations *de iure condendo*

In light of the above, some important conclusions can be drawn on the impact of a binding Charter on the legislative policy and judicial approach to be followed in the future. Firstly, it has been argued that the legal enforceability of the Charter of Fundamental Rights might lead the Court to reconsider its traditional approach on private standing in actions against measures with a general scope of application. Acting similarly to a supreme national court, the EUCJ would have to carefully balance Art. 263 TFEU and Art. 47 CFR, as the status of primary law is recognised for both provisions. Nevertheless, should the ECJ decide to follow its 'constitutional vocation' and interpret the last sentence of Art. 263 (4) TFEU as an implicit refusal (on the part of the Member States) to recognise the right for individuals to contest measures which are legislative in nature, an extensive interpretation of the individual concern requirement is highly unlikely.

Secondly, as to the need to ensure effective judicial protection within the EU legal order, it can be observed that Arts. 47 and 51 CFR, read jointly, will undoubtedly contribute to eliminate the double standard issue mentioned at the beginning of this chapter.[48] From a practical point of view it is possible to envisage a decrease in the EUCJ's workload following preliminary references, the (sole) standard being already fixed at a normative level by the EU.

Thirdly, with regard to judicial cooperation in civil and commercial matters, it appears that the reference to effective judicial protection (and therefore, indirectly, to Art. 47 CFR) contained in Art. 81 TFEU will impinge on the lawmaking process in the Area of Freedom, Security and Justice forcing the Council to take court access in the utmost consideration when passing legislation in this field. Not to mention the impact it is likely to have on the case law. In fact, it is suggested that under the new framework the ECJ will have to enhance its fundamental rights reasoning while guaranteeing the "free circulation of judicial decisions". In doing so it will be able to rely on Art. 6 ECHR and on the common traditions of the Member States but most notably (and effectively) on Art. 47 CFR, which appears to be one of the values framing a true European *ordre public* clause.

---

[48] See Section 2 above.

The European Charter of Fundamental Rights and the Area of Freedom, Security and Justice

Valentina Bazzocchi

1 Preliminary Remarks

This Chapter explores the many innovations introduced by the Lisbon Treaty in the Area of Freedom, Security and Justice (hereafter AFSJ) in order to assess the potential of Art. 6 TEU, insofar as it grants the EU Charter of Fundamental Rights (hereafter CFR or Charter) "the same legal value as the treaties".

First, the scope of the relevant new provisions will be considered and evaluated against the previous legal framework. Second, the current state of affairs will be confronted and critically examined with a view to single out the criticalities in three particularly sensitive areas, namely due process, judicial review and data protection. Finally, it will be possible to establish whether and to what extent the newly binding Charter is capable of enhancing the protection of fundamental rights within the EU legal order.

2 The Area of Freedom, Security and Justice Before and After the Lisbon Treaty

2.1 Scope of Application and Competences

The Lisbon Treaty marks the fall of the 'pillar structure' with significant changes in the new institutional framework, but some peculiarities continue to characterize the Justice and Home Affairs Area.[1]

V. Bazzocchi (✉)
CIRDE (Interdepartmental Research Centre on European Law), University of Bologna, Bologna, Italy
e-mail: vbazzocchi@cirdce.unibo.it

[1] In some areas of criminal law and policing a special legislative procedure will be enforced. See Art. 86 of the Treaty on Functioning of the European Union (TFEU) concerning the establishment of a European Public Prosecutor's Office; see Art. 87

G. Di Federico, *The EU Charter of Fundamental Rights*, Ius Gentium: Comparative Perspectives on Law and Justice 8, DOI 10.1007/978-94-007-0156-4_10,

After its creation by the Maastricht Treaty, its partial 'communitarisation' pursuant to the Treaty of Amsterdam and the reforms introduced by the Treaty of Nice, the Third Pillar comes to an end. Although – as in the original Treaty on the European Union – the latter 'reunites' under the same general regime the heterogeneous nature of the matters falling within the AFSJ (immigration, asylum, civil law, criminal and police law), it brings about notable changes with respect to the more recent versions of the treaties.

As far as the allocation of powers is concerned, is should be noted that according to Art. 4 TFEU the AFSJ is included among the shared competences and Member States shall exercise their competence to the extent that the Union has not exercised its own or has decided to cease exercising it.

From an institutional viewpoint, the Justice and Home Affairs Council of Ministers retains general competence, but the reasons for having two Commissioners (one for Justice, Fundamental Rights and Citizenship, the other for Home Affairs) remain unclear. This solution can be justified on account of the fact that it is capable of enhancing efficiency; nevertheless, is can cause confusion regarding the respective aims and responsibilities.

Unfortunately, the overwhelming complexity of the Union system in the AFSJ is only partly reduced by the abolishment of the pillar structure because the special regimes granted to the United Kingdom, Ireland and Denmark remain. Indeed, the price paid for the communitarisation of the Third Pillar was the extension of the opt-out regime applicable to the UK and Ireland with regard to the entire area of EU Freedom, Security and Justice, including police cooperation and criminal law. However, according to Protocol No 21, they are free to exercise an opt-in right in relation to a new measure or to a measure amending a pre-existing act which they have already accepted. Moreover, they may refuse to accept an amendment concerning a non-Schengen binding measure. However, if the Council determines that the non-participation of the United Kingdom or Ireland makes the application of that measure inoperable for other Member States or the Union, it may urge them to exercise their opt-in right. Following a period of two moths and in the absence thereof, the Council may determine that Ireland and/or the United Kingdom shall bear the direct financial consequences, if any, necessarily and unavoidably incurred as a result of their choice.

In addition, the Schengen Protocol[2] allows these countries not to participate in a Schengen building measure even if it is covered by the Schengen

---

TFEU concerning the operational cooperation between competent authorities, including police, customs and other specialised law enforcement services in relation to the prevention, detection and investigation of criminal offences.

[2]Protocol No 19.

acquis they have accepted. The situation is further complicated by the absence of a clear-cut distinction between Schengen building measures and non-Schengen building measures. For instance, it is difficult to establish with certainty whether access to information contained in a national police database by agents from another Member State amounts to a Schengen building measure or not.[3]

After a transitory period of 5 years,[4] the United Kingdom and Ireland will be subject to the expanded jurisdiction of the Court of Justice (hereafter ECJ or EUCJ) as regards asylum and civil law legislation which they have accepted, or will accept in the future, as well as any future police and criminal law measure which they will opt into. At the latest 6 months before the expiry of this transitional period, the United Kingdom may notify the Council its non-acceptance, with respect to acts adopted in the field of police and judicial cooperation in criminal matters before the entry into force of the Treaty of Lisbon, of the powers of the institutions, including the competence of the Court of Justice.[5] This privileged condition allows it to accept at any time acts which have ceased to apply to it.[6]

The so called 'variable geometry' that continues to characterize European integration in this Area[7] is also determined by the particular position of Denmark, which remains unaltered in relation to the Schengen *acquis*. According to Protocol No 22, "none of the provisions of Title V of Part Three of the Treaty on the Functioning of the European Union, no measure adopted pursuant to that Title, no provision of any international agreement concluded by the Union pursuant to that Title, and no decision of the Court of Justice of the European Union interpreting any such provision or measure or any measure amended or amendable pursuant to that Title shall be binding upon or applicable in Denmark".[8] But this State remains free to opt-in.

The flexible participation of these three States makes it difficult to consider the AFSJ fully within the competence of the Union. The complexity of the system also suffers from the new flexibility arrangements, such as the Prüm Treaty. Signed initially by seven Member States,[9] since

---

[3]See R. Baratta, 'Le principali novità del Trattato di Lisbona', (2008) *Il Diritto dell'Unione europea* 69. See Protocol No 21.

[4]Protocol No 36, Art. 10.

[5]Protocol No 36, Art. 10(4).

[6]Protocol No 36, Art. 10(5).

[7]This variable geometry does not only characterize the Area of Freedom Security and Justice policy but also the rights because the Protocol No 30 on the application of the Charter of fundamental rights in the EU to the United Kingdom and to Poland provided specific derogations concerning in particular the social rights. On the scope of Protocol No 30, see in this volume G. Di Federico, Chapter 2.

[8]Protocol No 22, Art. 2.

[9]Belgium, Germany, Spain, France, Luxembourg, the Netherlands and Austria.

November 2009 the latter has been in force in fourteen Member States.[10] This international agreement provides for the exchange of a wide range of personal information, including fingerprints, DNA and other sensitive data. Relevant parts of this Treaty, namely the provisions designed to improve the exchange of information, are transferred into the legal framework of the European Union by two Decisions adopted by the Council.[11] Like the Schengen Convention, the Treaty of Prüm is seen as a "laboratory for Europe", the goal of which is to push European integration forward. But the idea to develop new mechanisms that operate above and beyond the EU level confirms that Member States have not lost their taste for conventional intergovernmentalism.[12] The adoption of an international instrument and its partial incorporation into the treaties implies that all Member States will become bound by measures decided by a limited number of countries without the participation of the European Parliament.

To conclude, the Lisbon Treaty tried to fully resolve all problems that arise from the Third Pillar, but the difficulties caused by the signaled specificities, namely the 'flexible participation approach', remain.

2.2 Sources of Law and Primacy

With the entry into force of the Lisbon Treaty, the EU measures concerning the AFSJ will take the form of Regulations and Directives, adopted by the EU Council by a qualified majority according to the ordinary legislative procedure. This compensates the shortcomings of the previous regime, where unanimity and the absence of direct effect and primacy raised concerns in terms of efficiency and effectiveness.[13] The most important consequence is that the principle of primacy and the principle of direct effect, affirmed by the Court of Justice in relation to acts adopted under the First Pillar, will be applicable in any area where the EU can generate law, including the measures on police and judicial cooperation in criminal matters.

Before the entry into force of the Lisbon Treaty the Court of Justice has tried to overcome the limits affecting the Third Pillar either by broadening

---

[10]Belgium, Germany, Spain, France, Luxembourg, the Netherlands, Austria, Finland, Slovenia, Hungary, Bulgaria, Romania, Slovakia and Estonia.

[11]Council Decision 2008/615/JHA of 23 June 2008 on the stepping uo of cross-border cooperation, particularry terrorism and cross-border crime, [2008] OJ L 210/1; Council Decision 2008/616/JHA of 23 June 2008 on the implementation of the Decision 2008/615/JHA, [2008] OJ L 210/12.

[12]E. Baker, C. Harding, 'From past imperfect to future perfect? A longitudinal study of the Third Pillar', (2009) 34 *European Law Review* 47.

[13]C. Ladenburger, 'Police and criminal law in the Treaty of Lisbon. A new dimension for the community method', (2008) 4 *European Constitutional Law Review* 21.

its competences or by extending the applicability of principles elaborated in the First Pillar to situations falling within the Third Pillar. In *Pupino*[14] the Court affirmed for the first time that the duty of consistent interpretation also applied to framework decisions: although prevented from acting *contra legem*, the national court should interpret domestic rules in light of the wording and purpose of the framework decision in order to comply with Art. 34(2)(b) TEU.[15] Building upon its traditional case law, the ECJ affirmed that:

> it would be difficult for the Union to carry out its task effectively if the principle of loyal cooperation, requiring in particular that Member States take all appropriate measures, whether general or particular, to ensure fulfillment of their obligations under European Union law, were not also binding in the area of police and judicial cooperation in criminal matters, which is moreover entirely based on cooperation between the Member States and the institutions.[16]

The Court therefore concluded that its jurisdiction would be deprived of most of its useful effect if individuals were not entitled to invoke framework decisions in order to obtain a conforming interpretation of national law before the courts of the Member States.[17]

The indirect legal effect of EU framework decisions, however, did not attract the principle of primacy, which was never extended by the Court of Justice to the Third Pillar. On the other hand, in *Segi*[18] the Court affirmed that the right to make a reference for a preliminary ruling existed in respect of all measures adopted by the Council, whatever their nature or form, which are intended to have legal effects in relation to third parties. As a result it was possible to review a common position intended to produce legal effects in relation to third parties even in the absence of any express indication to that effect in Art. 35 (1) TEU. According to the Court, the fact that its jurisdiction was less extensive under Title VI of the Treaty on European Union than it was under the EC Treaty, and the fact that there was no complete system of actions and procedures designed to ensure the legality of the acts of the institutions in the context of Title VI, did not invalidate the conclusion that the appellants could not validly argue that they were deprived of all judicial protection.

[14] Case C-105/03 *Pupino* [2005] ECR I-5285.

[15] According to a consolidated case law, the principle of consistent interpretation is based on the binding character of directives, provided by Art. 249 TEC, and on the principle of loyal cooperation between the Member States and the Community, provided by Art. 10 TEC. See Case C-106/89 *Marleasing* [1990] ECR I-4135; Case C-334/92 *Wagner Miret* [1993] ECR I-6911, Case C-91/92 *Faccini Dori* [1994] ECR I-3325.

[16] Case C-105/03 *Pupino*, n. 14 above, para 42.

[17] For further developments of the Pupino precedent, see Case C-467/05 *Giovanni Dell'Orto* [2007] ECR I-5557.

[18] Case C-355/04 P *Segi* [2007] ECR I-1657.

Unlike the Treaty establishing a Constitution for Europe, the Lisbon Treaty confines the principle of primacy in a Declaration.[19] However, this does not affect its binding nature: according to the opinion of the Council Legal Service,[20] the Treaties and the law adopted by the Union on the basis of the Treaties have primacy over the law of Member States, under the conditions laid down by the first case returned by the Court.[21] In the recent *Filipiak* case[22] the latter, ruling on income tax legislation, affirmed that the national court must apply Community law and refuse to apply conflicting provisions of national law, irrespective of the judgment of the national Constitutional court which had deferred the date on which those provisions, held to be unconstitutional, were to lose their binding force. This judgment exemplifies the ongoing dialogue between European and national courts which has characterized the most important steps of European integration.

In recent times, the principle of primacy came into play before some national Constitutional Courts when deciding on the European Arrest Warrant Framework Decision,[23] confronting the latter with the potential clash between an EU provision and the (constitutionality of) the measure adopted to implement it into the national legal order. Albeit for different reasons, in none of these instances did the national courts invoke the well known counter-limits doctrine, a circumstance which could not be taken for granted. In fact, Constitutional courts have often stressed their role of ultimate guarantors of the basic national fundamental principles. Suffice it here to recall the judgment of the German Constitutional Court on the Treaty of Lisbon.[24] In line with the "Solange jurisprudence",[25] the judges

[19] Declaration concerning privacy No 17.

[20] Opinion of the Council Legal Service of 22 June 2007, 1197/07 attached to the Declaration concerning privacy.

[21] Case 6/64 *Costa v. ENEL* [1964] ECR 585.

[22] Case C-314/08 *Filipiak* [2009] nyr.

[23] German Constitutional Court, *Bundesverfassungsgericht*, judgment 18 July 2005, 2 BvR 2236/04, in www.bverfg.de/entscheidungen/rs20050718-2bvr223604.html; Poland Constitutional Court, *Trybunal Konstytucyjny*, judgment 27 April 2005, No P 1/05, in www.trybunal.gov.pl/eng/summaries/documents/P-1-05-GB.pdf; Cypriot Constitutional Court, judgment 7 November 2005, No 294/2005; Belgian Constitutional Court, Cour d'Arbitrage belge, judgment 13 July 2005, No 124/2005, in *www.arbitrage.be*; Czech Constitutional Court, judgment 8 May 2006, in http://test.concourt.cz/angl-verze/doc/pl-66-04.html

[24] German Constitutional Court, judgment 30 June 2009, No BvR 2 BvE 2/08 2 BvE 5/08 -2 BvR 1010/08 -2 BvR 1022/08 –2 BvR 1259/08 – 2 BvR 182/09, para 35. For an exhaustive analysis of this judgment, see M. Poiares Maduro, G. Grasso, 'Quale Europa dopo la sentenza della Corte costituzionale tedesca sul Trattato di Lisbona', (2009) *Il Diritto dell'Unione europea* 503.

[25] Cf. German Constitutional Court, judgment 29 May 1974, No BvR 52/71 (Solange I); German Constitutional Court, judgment 22 October 1986, No 2 BvR 197/83 (Solange II). See also German Constitutional Court, judgment 12 October 1993, No 2 BvR 134/92

claimed that "With Declaration no. 17 Concerning Primacy annexed to the Treaty of Lisbon, the Federal Republic of Germany does not recognise an absolute primacy of application of Union law, which would be constitutionally objectionable, but merely confirms the legal situation as it has been interpreted by the Federal Constitutional Court".[26] They significantly added that: "the values codified in Art. 2 TEU Lisbon, whose legal character does not require clarification here, may in the case of a conflict of laws not claim primacy over the constitutional identity of the Member States, which is protected by Art. 4 (2) sentence 1 TEU Lisbon and is constitutionally safeguarded by the identity review pursuant to Article 23.1 sentence 3 in conjunction with Article 79.3 of the Basic Law".[27]

Even supporting an extensive interpretation of the scope of primacy, capable of covering the principle of loyal cooperation, it was impossible before the entry into force of the Lisbon Treaty to impose its observance given the inapplicability of the infringement procedure in the field of police and judicial cooperation in criminal matters. This amounted to a significant restriction on judicial protection.[28] It is thus possible to fully appreciate the impact of the Lisbon Treaty: the extension of judicial control over, and the application of the principle of primacy to, measures falling within the scope of the former Third Pillar undoubtedly constitute important steps in the process of European integration.

2.3 *Judicial Review*

The fall of the pillar structure attributes general jurisdiction to the Court of Justice and most notably removes the limitations concerning preliminary rulings in the Area of Freedom, Security and Justice. It will be remembered that in the field of visas, asylum, immigration and judicial cooperation in civil matters, only higher national courts were entitled to refer cases to the ECJ pursuant to Art. 68 TEC,[29] which undoubtedly compromised the

---

(Maastricht) and German Constitutional Court, judgment 7 June 2000, No 2 BvR 1/97 (Banenmarktordnung).

[26]German Constitutional Court, judgment 30 June 2009, n. 24 above, para 331.

[27]Ibid., para 332.

[28]V. Bazzocchi, 'Il Mandato d'arresto europeo e le corti supreme nazionali', (2007) *Il Diritto dell'Unione europea* 663.

[29]According to certain authors higher courts could (i.e. were not under an obbligation) request a preliminary ruling to the Court of Justice (H. Labayle, 'Un espace de liberté, de sécurité et de justice', (1997) *Revue trimestrielle de Droit européen* 863, P. Wachsmann, 'Les droits de l'homme', (1997) *Revue trimestrielle de Droit européen* 890; K. Leanaerts,, E. De Smijter, 'Le Traité d'Amsterdam', (1998) *J. Trib. Droit européen* 30 and B. Nascimbene, 'L'incorporazione degli Accordi di Schengen nel quadro dell'Unione europea e il futuro ruolo del Comitato parlamentare di controllo', (1999) *Rivista Italiana di Diritto Pubblico Comunitario* 738). Other commentators opine that higher national judges were required to submit a preliminary ruling to the Court of Justice (L.S. Rossi,

uniform application of EC law. Moreover, the different standard afforded to EU and foreign citizens was hard to combine with the need to guarantee the protection of fundamental rights within the EC legal order. Finally, it should not be forgotten that, unlike the Member States, the Council and the Commission, the European Parliament was prevented from asking the ECJ to rule on the interpretation of measures adopted on the basis of Title IV of the EC Treaty.

On the other hand, pursuant to Art. 35 EU each Member State was free to accept the jurisdiction of the Court of Justice by making a declaration in which it would specify whether the latter applied to all domestic courts, or to last instance tribunals only. This situation was in contrast with the principle of equality, the uniform interpretation of the Law and ultimately fundamental rights. Furthermore, Art. 35 TEU did not grant the European Parliament and individuals standing in annulment actions against Third Pillar acts. Lastly, the provision lacked any reference to the infringement procedure and actions for failure to act.

Under the Lisbon Treaty, these specificities disappear with positive repercussions on the right to an effective judicial remedy and to a fair trial, enshrined in Art. 47 CFR. In this sense, the restrictive conditions set out in Art. 230 (4) TEC have been partially compensated by the new wording of Art. 263 (4) TFEU, which provides that natural and legal persons may bring proceedings against a regulatory act if they are directly affected by it and if it does not entail implementing measures without needing to demonstrate "individual concern".

As anticipated, this full jurisdiction of the Court will become operative only in 2014.[30] In addition it should not go unnoticed that the limitations provided in Art. 68 (2) TEC and Art. 35 (5) EU, are confirmed in Art. 276 TFEU, according to which:

> In exercising its powers regarding the provisions of Chapters 4 and 5 of Title V of Part Three relating to the area of freedom, security and justice, the Court of Justice of the European Union shall have no jurisdiction to review the validity or proportionality of operations carried out by the police or other law-enforcement services of a Member State or the exercise of the responsibilities incumbent upon Member States with regard to the maintenance of law and order and the safeguarding of internal security.

'Verso una parziale "comunitarizzazione" del terzo pilastro', (1997) *Il Diritto dell'Unione euopea* 249; C. Curti Gialdino, 'Schengen et le troisième pilier: le contrôle juridictionel organisé par le traité d'Amsterdam', (1998) *Revue du Marché de l'Union européenne* 105 and H. Bribosia, 'Liberté, sécurité et justice: l'imbroglio d'un nouvel espace', (1998) *Revue du Marché de l'Union européenne* 34.

[30] Art. 10 of Protocol No 36 on transitional provisions. It is provided that, as a transitional measure, the powers of the Court of Justice are to remain the same with respect to acts in the field of police cooperation and judicial cooperation in criminal matters which have been adopted before the entry into force of the Treaty of Lisbon. This transitional measure is to cease to have effect 5 years after the date of entry into force of the Treaty of Lisbon.

3 Fundamental Rights Protection in Police and Judicial Cooperation in Criminal Matters: Legal Framework

The fall of the pillar structure and the binding character of the Charter favors a more appropriate balance between the different founding elements of the AFSJ with respect to what occurred in the past. Before the Lisbon Treaty the limited competences of the Court of Justice and the intergovernmental method used to pass legislation were capable of seriously impinging on the liberty of citizens.[31] The main measures adopted in the Third Pillar aimed at enhancing cooperation between police and judicial authorities in combating serious crimes,[32] the so-called security aspect of the AFSJ, but this was not accompanied by a higher degree of protection of the rights of defense of individuals.[33] Most probably, the European Commission and the Member States felt that national legislations would have been sufficient in this regard (!).

The majority of the acts adopted in this area is the expression of the principle of mutual recognition between Member States[34]; a principle created by the Court of Justice in the First Pillar and extended to the Third Pillar also thanks to the European Council of Tampere. On this occasion the Heads of State and Government considered it as the cornerstone of judicial cooperation in both civil and criminal matters, together with the harmonization of the procedural rights and access of justice. As a consequence, the Commission and the Council were invited to act consequently ensuring an adequate level of legal aid in cross-border cases throughout the Union.

---

[31] E. Baker, C. Harding, n. 12 above, at 40.

[32] See the European Arrest Warrant and the surrender procedures, Council Framework Decision 2002/584/JHA of 13 June 2002, [2002] OJ L 190/1, that has replaced the extradition procedures; see the European Evidence Warrant for the purpose of obtaining objects, documents and data for use in proceedings in criminal matters, Council Framework Decision 2008/978/JHA of 18 December 2008, [2008] OJ L 350/72. See also Council Framework Decision 2003/577/JHA of 22 July 2003 on the execution in the European Union of orders freezing property or evidence; Council Framework Decision 2008/675/JHA of 24 July 2008 on taking account of convictions in the Member States of the European Union in the course of new criminal proceedings, [2008] OJ L 220/32; Council Framework Decision 2008/909/JHA of 27 November 2008 on the application of the principle of mutual recognition to judgements in criminal matters imposing custodial sentences or measures involving deprivation of liberty for the purpose of their enforcement in the European Union, [2008] OJ L 327/27; Council Framework Decision 2008/947/JHA of 27 November 2008 on the application of the principle of mutual recognition to judgments and probation decisions with a view to the supervision of probation measures and alternative sanctions, [2008] OJ L 337/102.

[33] According to E. Baker, C. Harding, "in a context where the Union's legal regime to protect fundamental rights is widely regarded as inadequate, its deficiencies with respect to the Third Pillar are particularly acute", n. 12 above, at 45.

[34] Among these acts the most important is the European Arrest Warrant.

In the period following the Tampere Summit, however, the focus was on 'repression' rather than on procedural guarantees. European criminal law must be understood as a law used not only against persons, but also to protect persons. The protection of fundamental rights is an unfailing necessity in all areas of EU action and not only as a limit to optimal cooperation in criminal matters. The subordinate position that rights have instead assumed in recent years certainly does not match the 'constitutionalization' of the Charter of Fundamental Rights.

Judicial cooperation mainly depends on mutual trust between the Member States concerning their criminal systems; the harmonization of procedural rights thus becomes a priority. In order to facilitate the implementation of the principle of mutual recognition, action should be taken to guarantee common minimum standards. This explains why, on the one side, the European Commission submitted a proposal for a Framework Decision on five basic procedural rights in criminal proceedings.[35] On the other hand, in spite of wide academic support, this proposal remained stalled in the Council for more than 5 years. And this independently of the fact that its contents have been substantially diluted in the quest for unanimous consent. Moreover, the Multiannual Hague Programme on the strengthening of the Area of Freedom, Security and Justice has underlined that "the realization of mutual recognition implies the development of equivalent standards for procedural rights in criminal proceedings". The adoption of the proposal was obstructed by those States fearing a duplication of the ECHR content, with possible repercussions on the consistency between the case law of the Strasbourg and Luxembourg Courts, as well as on legal certainty for EU citizens and Member States.[36]

Although all Member States are parties to the Convention, experience shows that this in itself does not always provide a sufficient degree of trust in the criminal justice systems of other Member States. To enhance mutual trust within the European Union, it is important to establish EU standards for the protection of procedural rights. In 2009, probably because of the imminent entry into force of the Lisbon Treaty, the need to balance security and justice became a priority for all European Institutions. The strengthening of rights is seen as the essential element not only to develop confidence

[35] European Commission, Proposal for a Council Framework Decision on certain Procedural Rights in Criminal Proceedings throughout the European Union, COM(2004)328, 24 April 2004. The five rights mentioned in the proposal of Framework Decision were: right to legal advice, right to interpretation and translation for non-native defendants, right to specific attention for persons who cannot understand or follow the proceedings, right to communication and/or consular assistance, the way in which the suspect/defendant is notified of his rights.

[36] There are the same fears that accompanied the elaboration and adoption of the Charter.

between national criminal authorities, but also to increase the confidence of European citizens in the European Union.

The Council decided to use a step-by-step approach, focusing its attention on each individual measure. In a resolution on a roadmap for strengthening procedural rights of suspected or accused persons in criminal proceedings it included a non exhaustive list of measures to be adopted.[37] It is important to note that the Council specified that any new EU legislative acts in this field should be consistent with the minimum standards set out in the ECHR, as interpreted by the European Court of Human Rights. In accordance with this roadmap, the Commission presented a proposal for a Framework Decision on the right to interpretation and to translation in criminal proceedings, that constituted the right which appeared to be the least controversial in the preceding discussions.

With the entry into force of the Lisbon Treaty this proposal needs to be transformed into a Directive which will be adopted pursuant to the ordinary legislative procedure and will be subject to full judicial scrutiny by the EUCJ. It seems that a number of Member States want to take initiative in this regard; but it cannot be excluded that the Commission will advance its own autonomous proposal. If that were the case, the responsible committee within the European Parliament will have to deal with both draft bills, but, according to Art. 44 of the Rules of Procedure, it will draft a single report indicating "to which text it has proposed amendments and it shall refer to all other texts in the legislative resolution". This act would be the first to be adopted by the Council acting by a qualified majority together with the European Parliament. Certainly, for the first time in this area the European Parliament can play a key role and can therefore promote fundamental rights protection in the European Union.

Following the Tampere European Council of 1999, the Lisbon Treaty explicitly underlines the importance of fundamental rights in the Area of Freedom, Security and Justice.[38] A compromise had to be found between mutual recognition of judicial decisions and the harmonization of criminal law and the Lisbon Treaty appears to have acknowledged the complementary nature of these objectives.[39] Moreover, unlike the previous Art. 29 TEU, Art. 67 (3) TFEU provides that the approximation of criminal law

---

[37] Resolution of the Council of 30 November 2009 on a Roadmap for strengthening procedural rights of suspected or accused persons in criminal proceedings,[2009] OJ C 295/1. The measures included into the roadmap are: translation and interpretation, information in Rights and Information about the Charges, Legal Advice and Legal Aid, Communication with Relatives Employers and Consular Authorities, Special Safeguards for Suspected or Accused Persons who are Vulnerable, and finally a Green Paper on Pre-Trial Detention.

[38] Art. 61 TFEU.

[39] C. Ladenburger, 'Police and criminal law in the Treaty of Lisbon. A new dimension for the community method', n. 13 above, at 35.

is supported by, and no longer subordinated to, the needs of judicial cooperation in criminal matters,[40] assuming therefore an autonomous importance.

4 Some Criticalities: Due Process, Judicial Review and Data Protection

As previously seen, the limited role played by the Court in the Third Pillar was due to the intergovernmental character of judicial cooperation in criminal matter. In *Segi*, the Court acknowledged these limits, affirming that "there is no complete system of actions and procedures designed to ensure the legality of the acts of the institutions in the context of Title VI".[41] Nevertheless, it argued that the appellants had not been "deprived of all judicial protection".[42] In reaching the same conclusion, AG Mengozzi claimed that in the Third Pillar the right to judicial protection was ensured because "the judicial system of the Union [...] does not consist solely of actions that can be brought before the Court of Justice but also of those that can be brought before national courts". In other words, in a multilevel system of protection of fundamental rights, the possibility to obtain justice at a national level is regarded as capable of compensating the signaled deficiencies of the Third Pillar.

This approach was followed by the Court of First Instance in *Ayadi*,[43] concerning the freezing of funds of persons/entities included in a black list. But in the subsequent *Kadi* case[44] the Court of Justice required the Council and the Commission to take the appropriate measures in order to guarantee the protection of fundamental rights and in particular of the right to a fair trial.[45] It is beyond doubt that the Lisbon Treaty offers a concrete answer to this need: the extension of the competencies of the EUCJ and the legal force attributed to the Charter will lead the former to assume the role of a constitutional court having the last word on the compatibility of EU legislation with the procedural rights enshrined in the latter.[46]

---

[40] C. Sotis, 'Il Trattato di Lisbona e le competenze penali dell'Unione europea', (2009) *La Magistratura* 27.

[41] Case C-105/03 *Pupino*, n. 14 above, para 35.

[42] Case C-355/04 P *Segi*, n. 18 above, para 51.

[43] Case T-253/02 *Ayadi* [2006] ECR II-2139.

[44] Joined cases C-402/05 P and C-415/05 P *Kadi and Al Barakaat* [2008] ECR I-6351.

[45] See further in this volume L. Paladini, Chapter 14.

[46] On the external supervision carried out by the Strasbourg Court upon accession to the European Convention on Human Rights, see in this volume G. Di Federico, 'Chapter 2'. It is important to note that some limitations continue to characterise the right to an effective remedy within the EU judicial system, due to the restrictions resulting from Art. 263 (4) TFEU.

Moreover, the fall of the pillar structure eliminates one of the main problems that the Legislator was called to handle in adopting acts within the Area of Freedom, Security and Justice; i.e. the choice of the correct legal basis. The Court of Justice ruled on this issue many times in fact. In some cases it demanded the adoption of the act under the First Pillar, in others under the third. In the celebrated *PNR* judgment, the Court annulled both the Council decisions on the conclusion of an Agreement between the European Community and the United States of America on the processing and transfer of Passenger Name Records (PNR) data and the Commission Decision on the adequate protection of personal data contained in the PNR given that their objective was not to develop functioning of the internal market, but to prevent and to fight against terrorism.[47]

In this instance, the Court did not consider all pleas presented by the European Parliament, namely those concerning the respect of the right to data protection, but tackled the problems connected to the division between pillars, and to the exchange of personal data, essential for the development of the European Area of Freedom, Security and Justice (AFSJ).[48]

It is also worth mentioning that the Court[49] ruled on the on the correct choice of the legal base of Directive 2006/24/EC on the retention of data generated or processed in connection with the provision of publicly available electronic communications services or of public communications networks.[50] Unlike the previous PNR case, the action brought by Ireland relates solely to the choice of the legal basis and not to any possible infringement of fundamental rights arising from interference with the exercise of the right to privacy contained in Directive 2006/24.

Moreover, unlike the decision on the processing and transfer of PNR, which concerned a transfer of personal data within a framework instituted by the public authorities in order to ensure public security, Directive 2006/24 covers the activities of service providers in the internal market and it does not contain any rule governing the activities of public authorities for law-enforcement purposes. The Court therefore affirmed that the

---

[47]Joined cases C-317/04 and C-318/04 *European Parliament v. Council and Commission* [2006] ECR I-4721.

[48]The different understanding of data protection and privacy further complicate the issue, since the US approach to privacy protection relies on industry-specific legislation, regulation and self-regulation, whereas the European Union relies on a comprehensive privacy legislation. In particular, the judicial system of the United States does not provide effective remedy because it only provides for administrative redress.

[49]Case C-301/06 *Ireland v. Parliament and Council* [2009] ECR I-593.

[50]Directive 2006/24/EC of the European Parliament and of the Council of 15 March 2006 on the retention of data generated or processed in connection with the provision of publicly available electronic communications services or of public communications networks and amending Directive 2002/58/EC, [2006] OJ L 105/54.

provisions of this Directive are essentially limited to the activities of service providers and do not govern access to data or the use thereof by the police or judicial authorities of the Member States. Furthermore, the measures provided for by Directive 2006/24 do not, in themselves, involve intervention by the police or law-enforcement authorities of the Member States. In fact, the service providers are to retain only data that is generated or processed in the course of communication services and is closely linked to the exercise of the commercial activity of the service providers. For these reasons, the Court dismissed the action concluding that Directive 2006/24/EC was directed essentially at the activities of service providers in the relevant sector of the internal market.

With the Lisbon Treaty and the collapse of the pillar structure, the issue of the incorrect legal base becomes less dramatic. The two judgments mentioned above regarded the collection and the exchange of personal data, an aspect that has assumed progressive importance in the AFSJ. Preliminary to any further consideration on the matter is the difference between data protection and privacy, although both are fundamental rights. Art. 7 and Art. 8 of the Charter represent this distinction well. Art. 7, concerning privacy, reflects an updated version of the content of Art. 8 ECHR; Art. 8 instead is based on the European Convention No. 108/1981 and the following Directive 95/46/EC on data protection. It is important to underline that the scope of application of Art. 8 is wider than that of the Directive, which is limited to internal market situations only.

The system of data protection within the AFSJ is a patchwork of provisions, comprising an ever increasing number of instruments: international conventions,[51] bilateral agreements,[52] community instruments,[53] ad hoc provisions.[54] The proliferation of crime and non crime data bases as well as the promotion of their interoperability;[55] the importance of delivering quick responses; the absence of a comprehensive regulation due to the difficulty to legislate under the unanimity voting rule; the exchange

[51] European Convention of Fundamental Rights, European Convention No 108/1981 for the Protection of Individuals with regard to Automatic Processing of Personal Data.

[52] Agreement between the EU and the USA on PNR, Agreement between the EU and the USA on SWIFT; Agreement between the EC and Australia on PNR, Agreement between the EC and Canada on PNR; Agreement between Europol and third countries (Europol-USA, Canada, Iceland, Switzerland), and Treaty of Prüm.

[53] Directive 95/46/EC on the protection of individuals with regard to the protection of personal data and on the movement of such data, [2005] OJ L 281/31; Directive 97/66/EC concerning the processing of personal data and the protection of privacy in the telecommunication sector, [1998] OJ L 24/1; Directive 2002/58/EC on privacy and electronic communications, [2002] OJ L 201/37.

[54] Eurodac, Schengen Information System (SIS), System of Information of Europol, System of Information of Eurojust Visa Information System (VIS).

[55] According to the Communication of the Commission, COM (2005)597, interoperability is the ability of IT systems and of the business processes they support to exchange data and to enable the sharing of information and knowledge.

of sensitive data between national law enforcement authorities under the principle of availability; the broader use of biometric data; the involvement of the private sector in the collection of personal data and the exchange with third countries – all of these factors show how the exchange of information has become progressively an inescapable need.[56] The reason for this can be traced to the fact that the development of data bases (e.g. VIS and Eurodac), and their interoperability, is no longer solely linked to the development of community policies (in particular for immigration purposes), but is used for enforcement purposes alike. [57] It is precisely this condition that raises doubts about the respect of the principle of limited purposes, which constitutes one of the fundamental principles of data protection contained not only in the European Convention No 108/1981,[58] but also in the Directive 95/46/EC.

Stronger needs to fight against terrorism and organized crime pressed the Community legislator to adopt measures of surveillance of movements and communications of European citizens and foreigners which reveal the particular importance that the European Union, greatly influenced by the US,[59] attributes to the security aspect of the AFSJ. Such measures were not accompanied by the adoption of a specific act for the protection of data in the Third Pillar.

Only recently, after many years of discussion within the Council, a "partial" change in the balance between security and freedom/justice is represented by the adoption of the framework decision of the data protection in the Third Pillar.[60] Indeed, although this act tries to offer a comprehensive framework of data protection in the field of police and judicial cooperation, it ultimately amounts to a race to the lowest common denominator and has raised some criticism.[61] Its scope is limited: first, it does not cover internal situations and processing operations by Europol and Eurojust; second, the use of personal data is subject to a special regime. So, even if the EU legislator adopted a specific act concerning data protection in the Third Pillar, the legal framework continues to be a patchwork.

---

[56] V. Mitsilegas, 'The third wave of Third Pillar law. Which direction for EU criminal justice?', (2009) 34 *European Law Review* 557.

[57] An example is Council Decision 2008/633/JHA concerning access for consultation of the VIS by designated national authorities and Europol for the purposes of the prevention, detection and investigation of terrorism and other serious criminal offences.

[58] For many years this convention represented the text of reference for EU instruments in the Third Pillar, providing the minimum standard of data protection.

[59] P. Pawlak, 'Made in the USA? The influence of the US on the EU's data protection regime', accessible at http://www.ceps.be. The author affirms that "while the EU is convinced of the supremacy of ist data protection system, many aspects oft he US approach to data protection could be beneficial to EU citizens", at 21.

[60] Council Framework Decision 2008/977/JHA of 27 November 2008 on the protection of personal data processed in the framework of police and judicial cooperation in criminal matters, [2008] OJ L 350/60.

[61] The European Data Protection Supervisor adopted three opinions in 2005, 2006, 2007.

The most important step towards the balance between security and freedom/justice is made by the Lisbon Treaty with the introduction in primary law of a general provision on data protection, Art. 16 of the TFEU[62]. The data protection provision will be applicable to all areas of EU law, including the area of police and judicial cooperation. It is important to note that Art. 16 (1) TFEU, by reflecting the content of Art. 8 of the Charter, gives additional value to fundamental rights.[63] Moreover, the use of the ordinary legislative procedure in laying down rules on data protection, prescribed in Art. 16 (2), entails that the European Parliament can strongly influence the adoption of acts that have implications for data protection. Moreover, the European Parliament could trigger the adoption of security measures: according to Art. 87 (2)(a) and Art. 88 (2)(b) TFEU, it establishes, together with the Council, measures concerning the collection, storage, processing, analysis and exchange of relevant information in police cooperation and include them among tasks of Europol.

The limitations that characterized the Third Pillar and marginalized the role of the European Parliament were overcome by the Treaty of Lisbon. The ordinary legislative procedure reflects the need to obtain the European Parliament's consent for the conclusion of international agreements, as will be the case with the new agreement on PNR between the EU and the US and the new SWIFT agreement. Having a final say in the conclusion of international treaties covering data protection and data access for security purposes, the European Parliament acquires an important power in the context of the internationalization of data access.

But the mere entry into force of the Lisbon Treaty does not in itself change the state of affairs since it will be necessary to specify the right to data protection amending or modifying Directive 95/46/EC and Framework-Decision 2008/977/JHA. In fact, Art. 9 of Protocol No 36 provides that the legal effects of the acts adopted prior to the entry into force of the Treaty of Lisbon shall be preserved until those acts are repealed, annulled or amended in implementation of the Treaties.

Moreover, Declaration No 21 of the Lisbon Treaty notes that specific rules on the protection of personal data and the free circulation of such data in the area of judicial and police cooperation in criminal matters may prove necessary because of the specificities of this particular field of law. In addition, it should not be forgotten that the scope of Art. 16 TFEU considering the particular position of the United Kingdom and Ireland. According to Art. 6a of Protocol No 21 annexed to the Treaty, these States shall not be bound by the rules adopted pursuant to that provision where they are

[62] Art. 16 TFEU states: "everyone has the right to the protection of personal data concerning them".

[63] H. Hijmans, A. Scirocco, 'Shortcoming in EU data protection in the third and second pillars: Can the Lisbon Treaty be expected to help?', (2009) 46 *Common Market Law Review* 1485, at 1517.

not bound by the relevant rules governing the forms of judicial and police cooperation in criminal matters or police cooperation.

Moreover, even if Art. 16 TFEU covers all areas of EU law, a particular situation concerns the Common Foreign and Security Policy (CFSP). Art. 39 TEU now states that:

> In accordance with Article 16 of the Treaty on the Functioning of the European Union and by way of derogation from paragraph 2 thereof, the Council shall adopt a decision laying down the rules relating to the protection of individuals with regard to the processing of personal data by the Member States when carrying out activities which fall within the scope of this Chapter, and the rules relating to the free movement of such data. Compliance with these rules shall be subject to the control of independent authorities.

This means that even if the pillar structure has been repealed, a specific procedure (not the ordinary one) will apply to Member States while implementing measures falling within the scope of the Common Foreign and Security Policy. In spite of these remaining elements of the pillar structure, the Treaty of Lisbon marked the inclusion of data protection in the filed of CFSP. In fact, the Second Pillar lacked a legal regime concerning data protection. This vacuum was particularly important considering that the "blacklists" of persons suspected of terrorism are created collecting data and they are publicized in order to subject them to freezing measures. In this regard, it is interesting to note that in the judgments by the Court of First Istance (hereafter CFI or GC) CFI and the ECJ concerning these "blacklists", no reference was made to data protection, probably because it was not invoked by the applicants. Only in the *Hassan* case[64] did the CFI recognize the right to privacy (not specifically the right to data protection) as a part of *jus cogens*. In this particular case, however, it considered that there had clearly been no such interference with the applicant's exercise of the right to respect for private life. In spite of the lack of any express reference to the respect of data protection by the Court of Justice, the elements of data protection (the right of access to personal data, the right to be informed, the right to receive compensation for damage suffered, the data quality, the right to a judicial remedy) are used to ensure the right to defence and judicial protection.[65]

To conclude, the Stockolm programme on the AFSJ (2010–2014) and the provisions of the Treaty of Lisbon seem to urge the European Union to develop not only the exchange of data to improve police and judicial cooperation in criminal matters, but also to give prominence to the data

---

[64] Case T-49/04, *Hassan* [2006] ECR II-52.

[65] Case C-266/05 P *Sison* [2007] ECR I-1233; Case T-284/08, *Organisation des Modjahedines du people d'Iran* [2008] ECR II-3487; H. Hijmans, A. Scirocco, 'Shortcoming in EU data protection in the third and second pillars: Can the Lisbon Treaty be expected to help?', n. 63 above, 1509.

protection of individuals. But this intention must translate itself into legislative activity in this direction and it is still too early to express a conclusive assessment in this regard.

5 The Effects of a Binding EU Charter of Fundamental Rights in the Area of Freedom, Security and Justice After Lisbon

The Lisbon Treaty places fundamental rights at the core of the realization of an Area of Freedom, Security and Justice. According to Art. 67 TFEU: "[T]he Union shall facilitate access to justice, in particular through the principle of mutual recognition of judicial and extrajudicial decisions in civil matters".[66] Although security continues to represent an essential feature, the focus on individual liberties derives from the newly binding nature attributed to the Charter. In the Preamble of the latter, in fact, it is clearly stated that "the Union places the individual at the heart of its activities by creating an area of freedom, security and justice".

The innovations described in the previous section compensate the many gaps which characterized the protection of fundamental rights in the former Third Pillar. For example, the Data Protection Framework Decision fails to meet the criteria laid down in Art. 8 CFR and Art. 16 TFEU and will thus need to be substituted by a directive. However, it may be wiser to adopt a more general legislative measure on data protection (i.e. not limited to the ASFJ), for example by amending Directive 95/46/EC. The prescriptions which can be found in Title VI of the Charter must be observed and call for the adoption of specific rules under the new legislative mechanism foreseen for the harmonization of procedural guarantees.

The EU action in the field of substantive and procedural criminal law has raised doubts regarding the respect of the principle of legality, one of the cornerstones of modern criminal law. In this regard, the Framework Decision on combating terrorism[67] and the Framework Decision on European Arrest Warrant are particularly noteworthy. As to the former, legal commentators have indicated that the definition of the constitutive elements of the crime of terrorism are too vague and general.[68]

[66] Art. 29 TEU (Nice Treaty) stated that: "Without prejudice to the powers of the European Community, the Union's objective shall be to provide citizens with a high level of safety within an area of freedom, security and justice by developing common action among the Member States in the fields of police and judicial cooperation in criminal matters and by preventing and combating racism and xenophobia".

[67] Council Framework Decision on combating terrorrism, 13 June 2002, 2002/475/JHA, [2002] OJ L 164/3.

[68] A. Weyembergh, V. Santamaria, 'Lutte contre le torrorisme et droits fondamentaux dans le cadre du trosième pilier. La décision-cadre du 13 juin 2002 relative à la lutte

This seems difficult to combine with the aforementioned principle insofar as it fails to offer a sufficient degree of legal certainty. In relation to the Framework Decision on the European Arrest Warrant, it may be recalled that the Belgian Constitutional Court submitted a preliminary ruling on its validity in which it considered that the offences indicated therein (Art. 2(2)) were vague inasmuch as they were not accompanied by any legal definition.[69]

The Court of Justice, having asserted that the Union is founded on the principle of the rule of law, affirmed that the principle *nullum crimen, nulla poena sine lege*, one of the general legal principles common to the constitutional traditions of the Member States, enshrined in various international treaties (including the European Convention on Human Rights) and in Art. 49 CFR, was not infringed because the Framework Decision did not seek to harmonize the criminal offences in relation to their constituent elements or the penalties which they attract. The definition of those offences and of the applicable penalties are left to national law.

On the other hand, the democratic deficit characterizing the decision making process applicable to Third Pillar acts cannot be ignored. As indicated, the possible infringement of formal aspects of the principle of legality is partially remedied following the entry into force of the Lisbon Treaty, which provides for the ordinary legislative procedure involving the Council of Ministers and the Parliament alike.

In the future, the need to comply with the principle of legality is even more important. First, the latter is expressly mentioned in Art. 49 CFR, which shall be observed in light of its newly binding force. Second, the extended competence of the Court of Justice will ensure adequate judicial control over possible violations thereof. Third, it should be noted that directives defining criminal offences and sanctions in areas of particularly serious crime with a cross-border dimension, if clear, precise and unconditioned, will have direct effect.[70]

In adopting new legal measures, the Institutions have to systematically assess the compatibility of EU legislation with fundamental rights. The same holds true for Member States when adopting the relevant implementing measures. Citizens are provided with a system of redress against acts of misadministration or the abuse of power across the whole range of EU activity. After a 5 year transitional period, the Court of Justice will have

---

contre le terrorisme et le principe de la légalité', in J. Rideau, (ed.), *Les droits fondamentaux dans l'Union européenne. Dans le village de la Constitution européenne* (Bruylant, 2009) 200; see M.L. Cesoni, 'La mise en œuvre ne droit européen des dispositions internationals de lutte contre le terrorisme', (2004) *Revue Générale de Droit Public International* 475.

[69] Case C-303/05 *Advocaten voor de Wereld* [2007] ECR I-03633.

[70] On the criminal competences of the EU, see C. Sotis, 'Il Trattato di Lisbona e le competenze penali dell'Unione europea', n. 40 above, at 20.

full competences in the AFSJ and, similarly to what happens with national Constitutional Courts, may be called upon to balance conflicting interests and rights. In doing so it will not be forced to outsource, being able to rely directly on a binding Charter of Fundamental Rights, which finally has the status of primary law.

The binding nature of the Charter will also allow the development of a more coherent Human Rights policy, promoting a common standard of fundamental rights protection independently of the internal or external projection of the specific policy under consideration.[71] In particular, the binding nature of the Charter implies that the external action in police and judicial cooperation in criminal matters is fully subject to fundamental rights. Most notably, the external *volet* of the AFSJ will be confronted with the right to life and the prohibition of the death penalty, the integrity of the person and the prohibition of torture and inhuman or degrading treatments, all of which are explicitly protected by the Charter.

In spite of the growing importance of the external dimension of the AFSJ, the Lisbon Treaty took it into consideration only in two provisions: Art. 78(2)(g) TFEU declares that special attention should be paid to cooperation with third countries for the purpose of managing inflows of people applying for asylum or subsidiary or temporary protection; Art. 70(3) TFEU states that the EU may conclude agreements with third countries for the readmission of illegal immigrants into their country of origin or provenance. But the significant changes introduced by the Lisbon Treaty concerning the nature of the Charter, the abolition of the pillar structure and the application of the ordinary legislative procedure, may have a highly positive impact on the external dimension of the AFSJ.

Nevertheless, a number of factors are likely to compromise the Union's ability to act consistently and to speak with one voice on the international scene: the position of Ireland, Denmark and the United Kingdom; the "emergency brake" mechanism which can be invoked to prevent the application of the ordinary legislative procedure[72] and the admissibility of enhanced cooperation between at least nine Member States.[73] But the most dangerous attack on "the political project of having a sole and unique area

---

[71] See also L. Ficchi, 'EU Member States and candidate countries facing a binding Charter of Fundamental Rights: What's new?'.

[72] According to Art.s 82(3) and 83(3) TFEU, where a member of the Council "considers that a draft directive (...) would affect fundamental aspects of its criminal justice system, it may request that the draft directive be referred to the European Council. In that case, the ordinary legislative procedure shall be suspended. After discussion, and in case of a consensus, the European Council shall, within 4 months of this suspension, refer the draft back to the Council, which shall terminate the suspension of the ordinary legislative procedure".

[73] See Art. 82(3), 83(3) and 87(3) TFEU.

where a common level of all its elements is guaranteed"[74] is represented by the United Kingdom and Polish Protocol on the Charter. The risk of creating different standards of fundamental rights protection, however, is mitigated by the fact that the Charter merely codifies rights and principles which are common to the constitutional traditions of the Member States, included in the ECHR, and that constitute general principles of the Union.[75]

This situation may affect the external dimension of the AFSJ. Correctly, the European Parliament in a resolution on the Stockholm Programme,[76] speaking on the need to promote the respect and the protection of human rights and fundamental freedoms, stated that in order to acquire and retain the necessary external credibility, it would be necessary to assure an adequate and consistent internal human rights policy.

In such a context, to ensure coherence and the sustainability of the AFSJ it will be necessary that Commission, European Parliament and Court use the powers that the Lisbon Treaty has attributed them most effectively. Having become legally binding, the Charter demands that individual rights are adequately balanced against the interest of the Union, which undoubtedly strengthens the freedom and judicial dimensions of the AFSJ.

[74]S. Carrera, F. Geyer, 'The Reform Treaty and Justice and Home Affairs: Implications for the Common Area of Freedom, Security and Justice', in E. Guild, F. Geyer, (eds.), *Security versus Justice? Police and Judicial Cooperationin the European Union* (Ashgate, 2008) 303.

[75]L.S. Rossi, 'How fundamental are fundamental principles?', in G. Venturini, S. Bariatti (eds.), *Individual rights and international justice* – Liber Fausto Pocar (Giuffré, 2009) 801.

[76]European Parliament, resolution 25 November 2009 on Multi-annual programme 2010–2014 regarding the area of freedom, security and justice (Stockholm programme), P7_TA-PROV(2009)0090.

Social Rights in the European Union: The Possible Added Value of a Binding Charter of Fundamental Rights

Serena Coppola

1 What Are Social Rights?

The expression "social rights" cannot be fully understood without considering civil and political rights, which are all inherent to citizenship. In particular, as T.H. Marshall notes, "the civil element is composed of the rights necessary for individual freedom-liberty of the person, freedom of speech, thought and faith, the right to own property and to conclude contracts, and the right to justice."[1] Political rights, instead, embody "the right to participate in the exercise of political power, as a member of a body invested with political authority or as an elector of the member of such body."[2] Finally, social rights comprehend "the whole range, from the right to a modicum of economic welfare and security to the right to share to the full in the social heritage and to live the life of civilized being according to the standards prevailing in the society."[3]

Hence, while civil and political rights can be defined and listed, social rights are difficult to identify, and the relative standard of protection varies over time. It follows from the above that social rights, which are intended to guarantee adequate conditions of life to citizens, do not operate on the basis of universally recognised minimum standards. Rather, they belong to an open catalogue, which constantly evolves according to the changes that occur within the society. On the one hand, this means that social rights are flexible and capable of responding to the needs of society, thus contributing to ensure a high standard of life to citizens. On the other hand, their vagueness and the consequent difficulty of translating objectives into binding norms conditions their justiciability and their effectiveness.

S. Coppola (✉)
University of Bologna, Bologna, Italy
e-mail: serena.coppola@studio.unibo.it

[1] T. H. Marshall, *Citizenship and social class* (Pluto Press, 1992).

[2] Ibid., 8.

[3] Ibid.

G. Di Federico, *The EU Charter of Fundamental Rights*, Ius Gentium: Comparative Perspectives on Law and Justice 8, DOI 10.1007/978-94-007-0156-4_11,

During the nineteenth century, social rights were progressively recognized as such, thus contributing to the elimination of inequalities. In particular, this was possible by enabling individuals to claim for the respect of those rights by public authorities.[4] And yet, social rights are regarded as relative, without a universal character. Citizens are entitled to be protected by the State when, in a given situation, they are discriminated[5] and only inasmuch as social rights have been implemented through domestic legislation.[6]

Broadly speaking, social and economic rights, the so-called "second generation rights", are programmatic rather than directly enforceable and they are addressed to the community rather than to the individual.[7] On the contrary, civil and political rights, which are undoubtedly complementary to social rights, are often qualified as negative freedoms. Endowed with a constitutional status, they presuppose non-intervention by the State. Social rights specify a number of guarantees which characterize the modern welfare State, ranging from adequate income standards to education, from housing to health care, from collective bargaining to workplace safety. The legislator's intervention will determine the scope and the extent to which welfare services are to be granted to the Community, taking in due consideration the social and cultural traditions which characterize the national context.[8]

2 Social Rights in the Constitutions of the EU Member States

All EU Member States protect social rights at a statutory level by fixing labour conditions and regulating the social security system. Hence, the level of protection is far from uniform, as opposed to what happens in relation to civil and political rights, which enjoy a constitutional rank. In fact, social rights are not regarded as fundamental in all Member States and similar concepts are treated differently in the various legal systems. Moreover, even when social rights are recognised by the Constitution, they often amount to policy clauses. They are therefore relegated to the rank of

---

[4]See further L. Principato, 'I diritti sociali nel quadro dei diritti fondamentali', (2001) *Giustizia Costituzionale* 873, and P. Carretti, *I diritti fondamentali. Libertà e diritti sociali* (Giappichelli, 2005).

[5]See M.V. Ballestrero, 'Europa dei mercati e promozione dei diritti', (2007) 55 *WP CSDLE "Massimo D'Antona"* 2.

[6]See J. P. Costa, 'Vers une protection jurisdictionelle des droits économiques et sociaux en Europe?', in *Les droits de l'homme au seuil du troisième millénaire: Mélange en hommage à Pierre Lambert* (Bruylant, 2000).

[7]See G. S. Katrougalos, 'The implementation of social rights in Europe', (1996) 2 *Columbia Journal of European Law* 277.

[8]G. Majone, 'The EC between social policy and social regulation', (1993) 31 *Journal of Common Market Studies* 153 at 161.

general, public objectives, which leave the legislator free to determine their scope of application.[9]

A brief overview of the constitutional systems of the EU Member States allows us to classify the latter in three general categories, based on the rank assigned to social rights. Some countries, such as United Kingdom and Austria, do not include social rights in their Constitution: they prefer a market-oriented solution, leaving social regulation to statutory law. Southern States, like Italy, Greece, Spain and Portugal, instead, have opted for constitutional catalogues of social rights, albeit rarely provided with direct effect. In this regard, an exception can be traced in the Fundamental Law of the ex-Communist new Member States where, pursuant to the concept of "social market economy", social rights are considered to be rights of the individual.[10] Finally, a third group of Member States combines the two said approaches by differentiating among individual social rights, social objectives and social policy clauses.[11]

The lack of an immutable bill of social rights is not necessarily detrimental to their protection as flexibility allows the legal order to adjust to the cultural, economic and social developments of the society.[12] In fact, regardless of the different approaches elaborated at a domestic level, it can be maintained that throughout the Member States minimum guarantees encompass "old age pensions, sickness and invalidity allowances, unemployment benefits, minimum subsistence benefits, educational grants, the provision of healthcare, and maternity and child-raising allowances".[13] In particular, it seems that in order to allow citizens to conduct a decent and dignified life, all constitutional systems envisage the right to economic resources necessary for subsistence, to be ensured through the arrangement of social aids schemes.[14]

Judicial review is often left to the national Constitutional Courts, pursuant to domestic legislation. The rules governing the scope of the relative judgment vary substantially throughout the Member States. Some countries

---

[9]To be sure, references to "adequate standards of protection" are of little use without implementing provisions. See further A. Manessis, in J. Iliopoulos-Strangas(ed.), *La protection des droits sociaux fondamentaux dans les États membres de l'Union européenne: Étude de droit comparé* (Bruylant, 2000) 19.

[10]See C. Costello (ed.), *Fundamental social rights: Current European legal protection and the challenge of the UE Charter of Fundamental Rights* (Irish Centre for European Law, 2001).

[11]The welfare State clause of the German Basic Law offers a good example of this approach. See further C. Fabre, 'Social rights in European Constitutions', in G. De Búrca, B. De Witte, *Social rights in Europe* (Oxford University Press, 2005) 22.

[12]See C. Fabre, n. 11 above, at 15.

[13]See S. O' Leary, 'Solidarity and citizenship rights', in G. De Búrca (ed.), *EU Law and the Welfare State – In search of solidarity* (Hart Publishing, 2005) 39.

[14]The underlying rationale being that all individuals should be guaranteed a decent and dignified life. See G. S. Katrougalos, n. 7 above.

provide for an ex post control whilst others establish an ex ante judicial review mechanism, following the request of the legislator or, in some instances, as a result of popular referenda.[15]

Just as the criminal and fiscal domains, welfare is thus perceived as a national priority, a very expensive one actually, because of the investments it requires (in terms of premises, infrastructures, personnel, etc.). *A contrario*, it could be argued that the natural resistance of Member States to give up sovereignty in the field of social security can be traced to the will to preserve their own distinctive features. Certainly, despite the many differences which characterize the European legal landscape in this area, it can be nonetheless stated that EU Member States guarantee a rather high standard of living to their citizens.[16]

3 Social Rights in the EU Legal Order: Retrospective Analysis

If the protection of social rights is one of the distinctive functions of the State, it is quite natural that, pursuant to the founding treaties, the Community was devoid of any competence in this respect. Nevertheless, the "raising of the standard of living" and the "quality of life, and economic and social cohesion and solidarity among Member States" were listed amongst the goals to be pursued by the Community.[17]

As a consequence, Community legislation dealing with the rights of workers was mainly aimed at removing all obstacles to economic integration within the common market.[18] Initially, basic social rights were thus able to emerge through the case law of the Court of Justice (hereafter ECJ or EUCJ) ECJ on the provisions relating to the four fundamental freedoms, which had progressively been granted direct effect.[19]

Unfortunately history shows that contemporary States periodically face market failures which need to be confronted through public intervention[20].

[15]See A. Eide, 'Future protection of economic and social rights in Europe', in A. Bloed, L. Leicht, M. Nowak, A. Rosas (eds), *Monitoring human rights in Europe: Comparing international procedures and mechanism* (Martinus Nijhoff, 1993) 187.

[16]See G. S. Katrougalos, n. 7 above.

[17]Art. 2 TEC.

[18]See T. Faist, 'Social citizenship in the European Union: Nested membership', (2001) 39 *Journal of Common Market Studies* 37, at 38 and M. Luciani, 'Diritti sociali e integrazione europea', (2000) 3 *Politica del Diritto* 367.

[19]See K. Lenaerts and P. Foubert, 'Social rights in the case-law of the European Court of Justice: The impact of the Charter of Fundamental rights of the European Union on standing case-law', (2001) 28 *Legal Issues of European Integration* 267.

[20]See M. E. Butt, 'Fundamental social rights in Europe', (2000) *Social Affairs Series*, SOCI 104-02/2000.

The first European document which expressly enumerates and protects social rights is the European Social Charter (hereinafter ESC) adopted by the Council of Europe in 1961, later revised in 1986. This document has the same status as the European Convention on Human Rights (hereinafter ECHR) and is complementary to it.[21] The ESC covers a number of fundamental social and economic rights such as housing, health, education, employment, legal and social protection, free movement of persons and non-discrimination, but, most importantly, establishes a supervisory mechanism guaranteeing their respect by the Contracting Parties. In this regard, the European Committee of Social Rights verifies whether the contracting Parties comply with the Charter.[22]

The monitoring procedure is based on national reports. States submit a yearly report indicating how they have implemented the Charter in law and in practice.[23] The Committee examines the reports and decides whether or not the national situation complies with the provisions of the Charter[24]. Should a breach of the Charter be found, and the position of the Social Committee disregarded by the addressee, the Committee of Ministers may issue a recommendation demanding that the violation be remedied through a modification of law and/or practice.[25]

Although the will to equate civil and political rights, enshrined in the ECHR, and economic and social ones, included in the ECS, seems to prevail, only the former covenant has been ratified. This appears to indicate that social rights are relegated to the periphery of the EU legal order. In addition, the ECS has a relatively ineffective system of control and the EU is not a member of the Council of Europe. However, it should not go unnoticed that the latter instrument significantly contributed to the elaboration of concepts later included in the Community Social Charter of 1989.

The latter, which is a community act, encompasses the fundamental social rights of workers and defines the general framework for the

[21] S. Evju, 'The European social Charter', in R. Blanpain (ed.), *The Council of Europe and the social challenges of the XXI century* (Kluwer Law, 2001) 19.

[22] Its fifteen independent and impartial members are elected by the Committee of Ministers of the Council of Europe for a period of 6 years, renewable.

[23] The report will only concern the provisions which have been accepted by the submitting member State.

[24] The conclusions of the Committee are published every year and posted on the website of the Council of Europe (http://www.coe.int/t/dghl/monitoring/socialcharter/Conclusions/ConclusionsIndex_en.asp)

[25] The Committee of Ministers' work is prepared by a Governmental Committee comprising representatives of the governments of the States Parties to the Charter, assisted by observers representing European employers' organisations and trade unions which, since 1995, have the possibility to lodge complaints of violations of the Charter to the European Committee of Social Rights See further J. F. Akandji-Kombé, 'L'application de la Charte sociale européenne: La mise en oeuvre de la procédure de réclamations collectives', (2000) *Droit social* 888.

development of European labour law. Many of the economic and social rights protected by the ECS received a first formal acknowledgment by the EC legal order through the Social Charter. Initially, it was intended to be part of the Single European Act, but remained a mere political declaration after the refusal of the United Kingdom to confer binding force upon it. This opposition also explains why the Social Charter foresees mere guidelines in the field of employment for the national and supranational legislators .

Although not formally binding, some authors consider this Charter an instrument of soft law, used by the Court of Justice as a catalogue of social rights, and by the European legislator during the nineties as an inspiration for some labour related directives.[26] The adoption of the Social Charter by eleven Member States favoured the debate on social rights at the Community level. In fact, during the drafting of the Maastricht Treaty, those eleven States reached an agreement with the United Kingdom on the Community social policy. Despite the lack of a formal competence in this field, the EC was entrusted with the task of defining minimum standards of protection, the application of which pertained to the Member States. For example, the Community had to guarantee minimum standards of remuneration, which were however concretely established by each Member State. Also, the right to strike and the freedom of association remained questions of national law and escaped the Community regulatory powers.

Even the Amsterdam Treaty disappointed those who expected a triumphal entry of social policy in the realm of Community competences. On the one hand, the Amsterdam Treaty made explicit reference to the Community Charter and to the ECS introducing guidelines for a social European policy through Art. 136 TEC. On the other hand, it did not create well defined rights, and in particular it failed to establish an effective system of protection. The right to equality between men and women constituted an exception being recognised by Art. 141 TEC, a provision which was soon declared of direct effect.[27]

One of the major achievements of the Amsterdam Treaty was the removal of the opt-out of the United Kingdom on social policy. Protocol no. 14 of the Maastricht Treaty was repealed and the content of the Agreement on social policy included in Arts. 136 to 145 of the revised EC Treaty. However, action taken at a supranational level was only intended to "complement and support" Member States policies in this area and the aforementioned provisions, with the notable exception of Art. 141 TEC, were devoid of direct effect.

---

[26]See, for instance Directive 92/56/EEC on the approximation of the laws of the Member States relating to collective redundancies, [1992] OJ L 245/73; Directive 98/50/ECC on the approximation of the laws of the Member States relating to the safeguarding of employees'rights in the event of transfers or undertakings, businesses or part of undertakings or businesses, [1998] OJ L 201/88.

[27]Case 43/75 *Defrenne* [1996] ECR 455, para 42.

Although only a very small part of the EU budget was specifically devoted to the development of a social policy, many expenditures included therein were nonetheless able to indirectly affect the social policies of the Member States, namely those provided for within the Common Agricultural Policy, as well as Structural and Social funds. In addition, it should not be forgotten that a growing number of positive social obligations were being imposed on the Member States pursuant to the EC Treaty: an example of this is the improvement of labour conditions for mothers and the guarantee of a safe and healthy working environment.[28]

National welfare law and social policies were subject to the basic tenets of EU law, including those relating to fundamental freedoms, competition, state aids and, of course, those on equality between men and women in the workplace.[29] In the field of social welfare, the result of this symbiotic relationship between EU and national law is a contribution to the development of a multilevel system of social welfare. Welfare governance took place at two and perhaps more levels, depending on the protection-oriented remedies offered at the community level.

4 The Open Method of Coordination

As previously seen, the allocation of competences between the EU and the Member States remained of central importance for the full recognition of social rights at the Union level. The European Council of March 2000 set up the so-called Lisbon strategy: a strategic plan aimed at turning the EU into "the most competitive and dynamic knowledge-based economy in the world capable of sustainable economic growth with more and better jobs and greater social cohesion."[30]

The Lisbon strategy indicates two objectives: the improvement of European competitiveness and the development of the European social method through social cohesion. The implementation of those policies entails integration via coordination of the Member States' legal orders, the so called Open Method of Coordination (OMC). The OMC – which appears to be an alternative to the harmonization approach – is based on three elements: flexibility, the use of non regulatory instruments and the partial delegation of powers. It was used for the first time in the late 1990s as an

[28]See for example Joined Cases C-397 to 303/01 *Pfeiffer* [2004] ECR I-8835 and Case C-207/98 *Mahalburg* [2000] ECR I-549.

[29]See M. Dougan and E. Spaventa, 'Wish you weren't here: new models of social solidarity in the European Union', in M. Dougan and E. Spaventa (eds.), *Social welfare and EU law* (Hart Publishing, 2005).

[30]See Lisbon European Council, 23–24th March 2000, Presidency Conclusions, accessible at http://www.consilium.europa.eu/uedocs/cms_data/docs/pressdata/en/ec/00100-r1.en0.htm, para 5.

alternative to the community method to guarantee a minimum coordination of the Member States' policies in the field of employment. The so-called EES, the European Employment Strategy, was created in 1997 during the Luxembourg Council in order to properly address the problems concerning the different employment policies of the Member States and their compatibility with the single market. A dialogue between the Member States had to be ensured in order to develop a common approach in guaranteeing high employment standards within the European single market.

European Employment Guidelines are issued yearly and are to be taken into account by the Member States when developing and implementing national employment policies. The latter are also required to submit an annual report (NAP) illustrating what measures were adopted to implement the guidelines. The role of the Commission is to analyse the results of the annual reports in order to draft subsequent guidelines, so that the Council can make non-binding recommendations to Member States.[31]

The OMC provides a model of integration that does not entail a delegation of competences to the EU. The foreseen mechanisms of coordination are represented by administrative and political networking as well as sharing practices, knowledge and experience, assisted by the cooperation between the different social actors at the European level. Hence, the OMC leaves untouched the subsidiarity principle and does not involve any transferral of competence from the national to the supranational level.

The OMC also provides an adequate framework of mutual learning through the exchange of experiences and good practices and particularly by the involvement of all stakeholders, including social NGOs, in the process of preparing, implementing and evaluating action plans in the field of the fight against poverty and social exclusion. Moreover, the OMC favours exchanges and contacts between organizations at the European level and regional and local social actors.[32] In this respect it is a multilevel instrument of governance which creates a balance between the need to respect diversity among Member States and the coherence of EU action in the social field.

Concretely, the main procedures of this method are: common guidelines to be reflected in the national policy, combined with periodic monitoring, evaluation and peer reviews. These mechanisms are organized as mutual learning processes based on predetermined indicators and benchmarks as additional means of comparing best practices.[33] The OMC is therefore a

[31] For a more detailed description of the OMC mechanism see S. Smisman, 'Reflexive law in support of directly deliberative polyarchy: Reflexive-deliberative polyarchy as normative frame of the OMC', in O. De Schutter and S. Deakin (eds.), *Social rights and market forces: Is the Open Method of Coordination of employment and social policies the future of social Europe?* (Bruylant, 2005).

[32] Such as employers, unions and NGOs.

[33] Ibid., para 37.

sort of soft law instrument first of all because it does not provide a coercive mechanism and secondly because the Court of Justice is not involved. The OMC is a flexible benchmark which refers to fundamental social rights as parameters used to improve social policies. The role for the open co-ordination method in the field of social protection and social cohesion has been strengthened in the last decades. By virtue of the positive results achieved through the EES, the use of the OMC was further extended to areas such as social inclusion and pensions.[34]

Although at present the real impact of the OMC on the EU legal order is hard to assess, the European actors seem to have recognized it as a viable way of achieving harmonization. Perhaps this is why the Lisbon Treaty (indirectly) refers to it in some provisions dedicated to social policy. Most notably, Art. 168 (2) TFEU expressly assigns to the EU the task of encouraging *cooperation between the Member States to improve the complementary of their health services in cross- border areas*, and imposes on the latter an obligation to *coordinate among themselves their policies and programmes* in this domain.

As previously stated, the effectiveness of this method in coordinating the different national legal systems remains uncertain, but can still offer a viable alternative approach to the problem, favouring the creation of new employment and a new social policy without generating further bureaucratic burdens.[35]

The OMC is based on recommendations and opinions which are not directly challengeable under Art. 263 TFEU. The role of social rights can nevertheless be appreciated taking into consideration that Member States are allowed to invoke fundamental rights in order to depart from EU law.[36] A clear example of this is offered by the recent *Viking* and *Laval* cases, where the ECJ recognized that important labour rights, such as the right of collective bargaining and the right to collective action, amounted to legitimate interests which, in principle, can justify a restriction of one of the fundamental freedoms guaranteed by the Treaty.[37] A logical consequence of this is that the results of the OMC could amount to derogations, in the sense

---

[34]See D. M. Trubek and L. G. Trubek, 'Hard and soft law in the construction of Social Europe: The role of the Open Method of Coordination', (2005) 3 *European Law Journal* 343.

[35]See D. Ashiagbor, 'EMU and the shift in the European labor law agenda: From Social Policy to Employment Policy', (2001) 7 *European Law Journal* 311.

[36]Although the Court has recognized fundamental social rights as part of the general principles of Community law, they have rarely found their way into the case law, and there is no case in which the Court has required the Member States or the EU to take positive action in order to respect an 'unwritten' fundamental social right. See Section 11.6 .

[37]Case C-438/05 *Viking* [2007] ECR I-10779 and Case C-341/05 *Laval* [2007] ECR I-11767. On the relation between fundamental rights and fundamental freedoms see further in this volume S. Curzon, Chapter 8.

that they "promote the application of the rights and principles enshrined in the Charter."[38]

The OMC does not operate in a legal vacuum. It is based on the coordination of the different national systems by defining minimum requirements and the EES demonstrates that this may happen in practice. The marginal role recognized to the workers' and employers' associations, and the absence of participation of NGOs are mainly responsible for the scarce success obtained by the Social European Charter and by the system that this Charter has created. On the contrary, the potential of the OMC mechanism lies in the possibility to determine "a high level of political participation",[39] through the involvement of the civil society. In this respect the OMC could be an important instrument to plan, define and direct the European social policy.

5 Social Rights and the EU Charter of Fundamental Rights

In 1999 the Cologne Council agreed to elaborate a catalogue of rights recognized within the EU legal order. Comprising civil, political and social rights, the aim of such a document was to codify principles expressed in the existing case law on the matter and to provide the latter with more visibility. As to social rights it was decided to take into account those protected by the ECHR, the ECS and the International Labour Organisation (ILO) conventions.

The task was assigned to a special body, the Convention, that drafted the Charter as if it were to have a binding character. This is apparent in the language used in the text, which is often similar to that of the American Declaration of Independence, the UN Declaration of Human Rights, the ECS and the Community Charter of Social Rights. On the other hand, some of the Member States, in particular the United Kingdom, were worried about the possibility that such a change in the legal status of the Charter could cause a significant increase of EU competences, in particular in the field of social policy. This is one of the reasons why Art. 51 CFR explicitly clarifies that the provisions contained in the Charter do not extend the field of application of Union law.

The circumstance that, on the one side, social legislation has a major impact on the life of citizens and that, on the other, the level of protection varies considerably from one State to another (partially) explains why some governments are worried about losing competences in the field of social rights to the advantage of EC/EU legislation and creative case law by

---

[38] Art. 51 CFR.

[39] See S. Borrás and K. Jacobsson, 'The Open Method of Coordination and new governance patterns in the EU', (2004) 11 *Journal of European public policy* 185.

the ECJ. According to Antonio Vitorino, social rights such as the right to education (Art. 14 CFR), the right to social security and social assistance (Art. 34 CFR) and the right of collective bargaining and action (Art. 28 CFR) could enlarge the tasks of the Community, violating the principle of conferral of powers enshrined in Art. 5 (1) TEC.[40]

Thus, it should not come as a surprise that the "horizontal provisions" of the Charter, such as Arts. 51, 52, 53 and 54 divided Member States between those hoping for a more extensive control by the EUCJ over fundamental rights protection and those fearing that such a control may have widened the Community competences in this sensitive area. As expected, the final text is a compromise: Arts. 51 and 52 CFR state that EU tasks and powers are not extended or modified, and that the Charter can be invoked to review European acts and national legislation, but only when implementing EU law.

Notwithstanding the fact that during the 2000 European Council in Nice the Charter was solemnly proclaimed by the European Parliament, the Council and the Commission, it remained a non-binding political declaration. The EU institutions committed themselves to respect the Charter when proposing or adopting legislation, but the Charter's legal status was postponed and left to the general debate on the future of the European Union.[41]

During the preparatory works of the newly created Convention for the elaboration of a Treaty establishing a Constitution for Europe, it was decided to give the Charter binding force by integrating it in Part II of that text. To limit the expansion of the EU fields of intervention via the promotion/protection of social rights, during the negotiations which led to the signature of the Constitutional Treaty some Member States pressed for an amendment of the Charter obtaining a clear distinction between rights and principles.[42] The United Kingdom in particular conditioned its acceptance of the latter to the explicit indication of such a distinction. The reason for this is quite simple: principles are not justiciable, or at least not in the same way as rights can be. In fact principles come into play only in the interpretation of EU primary and secondary law, or of domestic legislation (and practice) when implementing the former. Only the social rights of the individual are 'fully reviewable'. The Chapter on Solidarity covers individual rights, guiding principles and objectives.[43] According to this distinction Art. 34 CFR (Social security and social assistance) is considered as a mere

---

[40] See Document 03, 5-VII-2002 accessible at www.european-convention.eu.int

[41] See in particular Laeken European Council, 14–15th December 2001, Presidency Conclusions, accessible at http://www.consilium.europa.eu/uedocs/cms_data/docs/pressdata/en/ec/68827.pdf

[42] See Art. 52 CFR.

[43] It should not go unnoticed that other social rights, such as non discrimination and equality between men and women, are included in other parts of the Charter. See Art. 20

objective; Art. 28 CFR (collective bargaining) is a guiding principle[44] since its practical specification is left to national legislation while provisions such as Art. 29 CFR (right to access to placement services) and Art. 31 (2) CFR (maximum working hours), are considered justiciable.

With the failure of the Constitutional Treaty, the issue of the legal nature of the Charter remained unsettled and continued to represent one of the central issues to be discussed during the 2007 IGC, after the so-called period of reflection. In the meantime the opposition to its binding force became more evident, so that in the end it was decided not to incorporate it in the Lisbon Treaty. However, pursuant to the new formulation of Art. 6 TEU, the Charter has the same legal value as the Treaties. As a consequence, it becomes a (formal) parameter of legality of EU acts.

It is well known that one of the most distinctive features of the Charter is that it postulates the indivisibility of fundamental rights. Civil, political and social rights are in fact regarded as equivalent (i.e. not hierarchically organized), and inherent to all human beings. Another characteristic is that, with the notable exception of those specifically directed at EU citizens, rights are generally referred to all persons present on the EU territory, regardless of their nationality. This undoubtedly strengthens the idea that fundamental rights are perceived as universal.

Furthermore, the provisions of the CFR dealing with social rights must be read jointly with those included in Title X of the TFEU, devoted to social policy, and in particular with Art. 151 TFEU. The latter provides that, when implementing its policies and actions, the Union must take into account the promotion of employment as well as the need to guarantee an adequate social protection, to fight social exclusion and to increase the standard of education, training and human health. In addition, Art. 168 TFEU acknowledges the role of social parties by increasing the debate on employment.[45] This is particularly important considering that although social rights are not self-executing and need to be implemented through positive domestic measures,[46] they may play an important role in other domains of EU competence.

Those who oppose the Charter's legal enforceability claim that this would allow the EUCJ to "have substantial new power to review and change

CFR (Equality), Art. 21 CFR (Non discrimination), Art. 23 (Equality between women and men).

[44]In this respect is should also be noted that Art. 137 (2) TEC expressly excluded collective bargaining and action from EU legislative competences.

[45]Gil y Gil J.L., 'Los derechos sociales en la Carta de los derechos fundamentales de la Union Europea', (2003) 8 *Relaciones laborales: Revista Critica de Teoria y Pratica* 93.

[46]An example of this particular role of social rights can appreciated in the Directive 96/71/EC on the protection of posted workers, [1997] OJ L 18/1, which is formally based on Art. 57 (2) EC Treaty (now 64 (2) TFEU), but nonetheless affects the social rights of employees.

national laws."[47] Of course this is an extreme view, but on the other hand it cannot be ruled out that the Court, through its case law, could extend the effective protection of fundamental rights. Under the former treaties, the ECJ viewed the Charter as a codification of those social rights which were already part of the EU legal order[48] and used it as a source and inspiration for the interpretation of social policy measures taken by EU institutions when acting under Art. 137 TEC.[49] Against this background it is well known that the United Kingdom, Poland and the Czech Republic have negotiated what appears to be an opt-out from the Charter, expressed in Protocol No. 30 of the Lisbon Treaty.

6 Social Rights vs. Economic Freedoms: The Balancing of Interests in the Case-Law of the European Court of Justice

In order to better understand the hostility of some countries towards the adoption of a binding Charter, it appears useful to analyze the attitude of the Court of Justice regarding social rights. With the entry into force of the Lisbon Treaty social rights assume a new role in the *aquis* due to their equation with the economic and civil rights. This means that also social rights shall be balanced with the economic freedoms when they enter in conflict with them.

To date social rights have generally been regarded as 'secondary rights' and the four economic freedoms have tended to prevail over social rights. In performing this balancing of interests the Court uses the proportionality test and accepts limitations to the former only when: (a) mandatory requirements are at stake (e.g. protection of workers); (b) the restriction is effectively capable of protecting the (legitimate) objective pursued and (c) the restriction is strictly necessary in order to attain that objective.

Indeed the Court has recognised the right to paid vacation, the right of dignity, the right of freedom of thought and the right of meeting,[50] thereby showing a preference for individual social rights. By contrast, collective rights, and in particular the right to strike, were addressed for the first time

---

[47] See 'Guide to the Constitutional Treaty', accessible at www.open-europe.org.uk

[48] See Case C-173/99 *BECTU* [2001] ECR I-4881, AG Tizzano. See further in this volume V. Bazzocchi Chapter 10.

[49] See Case C-84/94 *UK v Council* [1996] ECR I- 5755 para 15.

[50] See Case C-36/02 *Omega* [2004] ECR I-9609; Case C-112/00 *Schmidberger* [2003] ECR I-5659, Case C-71/02 *Karner* [2004] ECR I-3025; Case C-210/03 *Swedish Match* [2004] ECR I-11893.

in *Viking*[51] case. In this case, as in *Laval*[52] and *Rüffert*,[53] the Court was called to balance the protection of workers' rights and working conditions together with the safeguard of fundamental freedoms as they are established by primary and secondary EU law. Here it was a matter of determining whether it was legitimate for an international trade union to use a collective action to force a ferry company to abandon its plans to re-flag a ship from Finland to Estonia. Viking argued, inter alia, that the threat of a collective action by the Finnish Union, and the coordination activities within the relevant association of trade unions (ITF), were incompatible with its right of establishment as guaranteed by Art. 43 TEC. The Laval case, instead, concerned the possibility for a Swedish Trade Union to use a collective action in order to force a Latvian company to enter into a collective agreement fixing work and pay conditions which went beyond the core mandatory rules established in the Posting of Workers Directive. Finally, Rüffert was about the scope of public procurement rules in a German Land Law and more precisely whether they could impose on a Polish undertaking wages higher than those set by the universally applicable federal collective agreement.

These cases focus on the conflict between the freedom of establishment (Art. 43 TEC, now 49 TFEU) and the freedom to provide services (Art. 49 TEC, now 56 TFEU), and collective actions taken by Trade Unions in order to pressure undertakings and avoid social dumping.[54] According to the Court the need to balance these potentially conflicting rights rests on the following considerations: (a) collective social rights, included in the Charter, fall within the constitutional heritage of the Member States and are thus principles of EU law[55] and (b) it is necessary to combine political and economic integration, the four freedoms representing a 'constitutional limitation' to social rights.

Hence, the right to strike appears to amount to a mandatory requirement capable of justifying a derogation to economic freedoms. On the other hand, the fact that their regulation falls within the competence of the Member States does not entail that the latter are free to limit the freedom to provide services and the freedom of establishment. To use the words of the Court:

---

[51]Case C-438/05 *Viking*, n. 37 above. See also Case C-265/95 *Commission v France* [1997] ECR I-6959.

[52]Case C-341/05 *Laval*, n. 37 above.

[53]Case C-346/06 *Rüffert* [2008] ECR I-1989.

[54]One of the main problems here is represented by the fact that according to the constitutional traditions of the Member States, Trade Union agreements are autonomous in nature and amount to a constitutional prerogative, but are formally not attributable to the State. On the other hand, it should be noted that social dumping is not regulated in EU secondary legislation.

[55]Case C-438/05 *Viking*, n. 37 above, para 44 states that: "The right to take collective action, including the right to strike, must therefore be recognised as a fundamental right which forms an integral part of a general principles of Community law the observance of which the Court ensured [. . .]"

> even if, in the areas which fall outsides the scope of the Community's competences, the Member states are still free, in principle to lay down the conditions governing the existence and exercise of the rights in question, the fact remains that, when exercising those competences, the Member States must nevertheless comply with Community law.[56]

All conflict between economic freedoms and social rights must respect the principle of proportionality, an assessment which is normally left to the national judge. However, in all the above mentioned cases, the ECJ considered that the actions taken by the trade unions went beyond what was necessary to protect the workers involved. More notably, before applying a strict proportionality test, the Court 'wisely' conditioned the lawfulness of the collective action to the circumstance that "the job or conditions of employment at issue are in fact jeopardised or under serious threat."[57]

In conclusion, what emerges from these cases is that: (a) the right to strike and collective actions were granted the status of fundamental rights even before the Charter acquired full legal force; (b) by reason of the extensive reading of Art. 137 (5) TEC, now 151 (5) TFEU, the lack of legislative competences in the field of social rights does not relieve the Member States from the duty to ensure their respect; (c) as all mandatory requirements, social rights may justify a restriction to economic freedoms only insofar as their exercise complies with the principle of proportionality.

Now that the Charter has entered into force, it is suggested social rights will no longer be viewed as mandatory requirements, but – at least inasmuch as they are (directly) enforceable – as fundamental rights having the same status of Arts. 49 and 56 TFEU.

7 The UK and Polish Protocol on the Charter: A Real Opt-Out?

There has been particular concern in Britain that some of the rights and principles in the Charter could allow the EUCJ's case law to impinge on British law, especially in the field of employment law. This was considered to be particularly true for Art. 28 CFR on the right of workers to be consulted by their employers, the right of collective bargaining and the right to strike. However, these preoccupations are believed to be ill-founded since the Charter applies to EU institutions and to Member States, not only when they implement EU law. As the EU has no competence to pass legislation on the right to strike, the Charter cannot be used as a picklock for widening the scope of such a right.[58]

---

[56] Ibid.

[57] Case C-438/05 *Viking*, n. 37 above, para 81.

[58] *A Constitutional Treaty for the EU: The British Approach to the European Union Intergovernmental Conference 2003*, CM 5934, September 2003, para. 102.

Many authors claim that, in spite of the wording of Arts. 51 and 52, the Charter is capable of modifying national legislations in the sense of establishing a single standard of European protection, under the supervision of the Court of Justice.[59] The debate on the Charter at the time of the first draft of the Constitutional Treaty showed that those 'safeguards' were not sufficient to allow the British government and other countries to accept the Charter as legally binding. For this reason the United Kingdom asked for and obtained a specific Protocol on the Charter, annexed to the Lisbon Treaty.[60] The ultimate purpose of the latter is to avoid any possible interference by the EU on labour and entrepreneurial rights recognized under British national law.[61] Poland adhered to this Protocol given the entrenched notion of 'family' under domestic law. With respect to social rights, instead, the government feared a decrease in the level of protection of workers with respect to the guarantees they receive pursuant to national legislation as a consequence of the activism of Solidarnosc.[62] Lastly, in 2009, upon ratification, also the Czech Republic obtained the possibility to be included in the Protocol concomitantly to the next accession Treaty.[63]

However, it appears that the Protocol leaves the situation (and the competences of the EUCJ) substantially unaffected since, on the one side, the British and Polish courts are in any case obliged to respect the primacy of EU law[64] and, on the other, it merely reasserts what is already clear from Arts. 51 and 52 CFR. In addition, it is commonly accepted that the Court of Justice could continue to elaborate on social rights as general principles of EU law, a category which survives the Lisbon Treaty. Indeed, it is too early to assess the real impact of the Protocol, but the possibility for the EU law to interfere with the social model of its Member States cannot be excluded a priori. The refusal to concede an important portion of their sovereignty currently impedes any attempt to harmonize the legislation in this area. As a consequence, a different approach to the problem founded on the co-operation between the Member States could be a viable solution.

---

[59] See 'The EU Charter of Fundamental Rights: Why a fudge won't work', accessible at www.openeurope.ork.uk

[60] See Protocol No 7 annexed to the Lisbon Treaty.

[61] On the scope of Protocol No 30, see further in this volume G. Di Federico, Chapter 2.

[62] Solidarnosc is a particular trade-union characterized by a major Catholic component. It was born during the 1980s and during the 1990s it became the antagonist of the Communist party, and led the movement for the liberal-democratic development in that country.

[63] The enlargement to Croatia and Iceland will most probably take place in 2012.

[64] See *Garland v British Rail Engineering Ldt* [1983] 2 AC 751, *Pickston v Freemans plc* [1989] AC 66 and *Litster v Forth Dry Dock & Engineering* [1990] 1 AC 58.

8 Final Remarks

In conclusion it can be said that social rights involve and are involved in many aspects of the EU legal order. While Member States recognize social rights to various extents, the EU has limited competences in this field. On the other hand, the ECJ actively contributed to their promotion, affirmation and development, thereby raising concerns as to the possible widening of supranational competences through judicial activism.

Given the opposition by many Member States to give up sovereignty on social matters, an alternative to the traditional community method was elaborated; a compromise aimed at guaranteeing the (most effective) protection of social rights. The OMC promotes a common understanding of the problems posed by the social rights dimension and stresses the need for common employment standards within the EU through a method of mutual accord. Although devoid of an effective mechanism of control, this alternative method has proven to be effective in addressing a variety of issues, ranging from the ESS macro-economic policy to employment policy and from social inclusion to enterprise policy. In this sense it has been suggested that in the absence of binding social norms at the EU level, the OMC could influence national social policies and promote a more uniform approach, thus reducing the risk of a *race to the bottom* effect due to regulatory competition.[65]

With the entry into force of the Lisbon Treaty, social rights are equated to civil and political rights as the newly binding Charter postulates the indivisibility of fundamental rights. However, social rights are not necessarily (directly) enforceable; nor, a fortiori, will their violation entail sanctions. What is clear is that they have entered the judicial arena and that in the future the EUCJ will face an ever increasing number of cases presupposing a balancing of economic freedoms and social rights. For the moment one can only hope in the emergence of a new "heroic jurisprudence".[66]

---

[65] See S. Smismans, 'The Open Method of Coordination and fundamental social rights, in G. De Búrca and B. De Witte, n. 11 above, at 237.

[66] See R. Bifulco, M. Cartabia, A. Celotto, 'Introduzione', in R. Bifulco, M. Cartabia, A. Celotto (eds.), *L'Europa dei diritti* (Il Mulino, 2001) 12.

The Charter of Fundamental Rights and the Environmental Policy Integration Principle

Marco Lombardo

1 Preliminary Remarks

Environmental issues have been so far confined within the limits of Arts. 174, 175 and 176 TEC (now 191, 192 and 193 of the Treaty on the Functioning of the European Union, hereafter TFEU), which attribute to the Union a specific normative competence in this field of law. Nevertheless the development of an effective policy at a supranational level goes beyond the elaboration of a set of rules aimed at enhancing the protection of the environment. Albeit necessary, such provisions must be supported by the enactment of a wider strategy capable of removing this 'legal fence' and, consequently, allowing the affirmation of a more comprehensive approach towards this topic. As will be demonstrated, the Environmental Policy Integration principle (hereafter the EPI principle) precisely addresses these objectives and aims at guaranteeing the coherence and the coordination of EU action in the field of environmental protection with the exercise of other EU competences.

This contribution focuses on Art. 37 of the Charter of Fundamental Rights (hereafter, CFR or the Charter) and more precisely on the EPI principle. If compared with other well known principles developed in this area of law (such as the sustainable development principle, the precautionary principle, the principle of preventive action, the polluter-pays principle), the latter calls for a closer analysis as to its scope and possible impact on the development of the EU environmental policy and on the protection of individuals, especially in light of the binding force assigned to the Charter by the Lisbon Treaty.

By way of introduction, it can be said that the EPI principle plays both a *substantial role*, as a parameter of legality of EU acts having a

M. Lombardo (✉)
CIRDE (Interdepartmental Research Centre on European Law), University of Bologna, Bologna, Italy
e-mail: mlombardo@cirdce.unibo.it

G. Di Federico, *The EU Charter of Fundamental Rights*, Ius Gentium: Comparative Perspectives on Law and Justice 8, DOI 10.1007/978-94-007-0156-4_12,

direct/indirect effect on the environmental policy, and a *procedural role*, as a governance criterion to be followed when deciding environmental issues. In the latter sense, the EPI principle can be intended as comprising a horizontal dimension – which can be traced to the capacity of *greening* the EU policies, translating ecological concerns into operative law – and a vertical dimension – mainly related to the multilevel governance (local, national and supranational) in the field of environmental protection, calling for a more extensive participation of citizens and stakeholders in the law making process.

Moving from these premises, the chapter pinpoints some major shortcomings of the EPI principle, as it is currently construed: the different doctrinal elaborations, the unclear legal enforceability, the evolution of its scope of application from the market to the security area (particularly relevant for the implications that the fight against climate change might have on EU external relations), the potential conflict of competencies between the institutions called upon to ensure its respect and the possible inconsistencies in the case law of the Luxembourg and Strasbourg Courts.

2 The Protection of Environmental Law in the EU Legal Order: A Brief Overview

Before addressing the provisions contained in the CFR concerning the EPI principle it should be recalled that the subject-matter has undergone substantial developments in primary and secondary legislation, as well as in the case law of the Court of Justice (hereafter ECJ or EUCJ).

The deepening of European integration runs parallel to the *greening process* of the EU legal order. Environmental protection was timidly referred to in the Treaty of Rome and included amongst the EEC competences by the Single European Act,[1] but became a genuine EC policy only at Maastricht.[2]

---

[1] References could be found in the 'Preamble' and in Arts. 2, 100 (now 114 TFEU) and 235 (now 352 TFEU).

[2] See Title XVI (Arts. 130 R, 130 S, 130 T) of the TEC as amended by the Maastricht Treaty. In the TEU, environment became an objective of the EU included in Arts. 2 and 3, let. k). For a more detailed reconstruction of the environmental protection in a European constitutional law perspective, see L. Krämer, *EC environmental law*, 6th ed. (Sweet & Maxwell, 2007); J. Scott (ed.), *Environmental protection: European law and governance* (Oxford University Press, 2009); M. Lee, *EU Environmental Law: Challenges, change and decision-making* (Hart Publishing, 2005); J. H. Jans, H. B. Vedder, *European Environmental Law*, 3rd ed. (Europa Law Publishing, 2000); N.S.J. Koeman (ed.) *Environmental law in Europe* (Kluwer Law, 1999); L. Krämer, 'Droit communautaire et état de l'environnement en Europe', (2007) 1 *Revue du droit de l'Union européenne*, 127.

Subsequently, the Amsterdam Treaty, besides confirming the competence of the Union in the field,[3] turned the sectorial EPI principle into a general and founding principle (via Art. 6, paragraph 2 of EC Treaty) of the EU legal order.

While the Nice Treaty simply consolidated the objectives and principles of what had become EU environmental law,[4] the Lisbon Treaty makes some (little) steps further placing the EPI principle in Art. 11 TFEU and opening new horizons, given the recognition of the de facto competence on energy[5] (Art. 194 TFEU) and of the unprecedented competence in the fight against climate change (Art. 192 TFEU).

If environmental integration is just a frame of the kaleidoscopic deepening process of European integration, the horizontal scope of application of the EPI principle, which applies to both the internal and external dimension, allows for a widening of environmental concerns which shall be duly taken into account when acting in fields of EU competence such as transport, energy, public health, social and territorial cohesion. Notwithstanding the fact that EU environmental law has progressively affirmed itself as an autonomous area of the EU legal order, it fails, alone, to solve all the problems deriving from the lack of coordination and coherence among the various policies developed therein. For the purpose of this contribution, the analysis will focus on the EPI principle in the attempt to ascertain whether it responds to the aforementioned needs thus allowing a true and effective 'greening' of the EU system.

3 The Environmental Policy Integration (EPI) Principle in the Charter of Fundamental Rights (CFR)

Firstly, it is necessary to clarify the notion of the EPI principle. For this purpose, the relevance of the environmental protection within the constitutional framework of the Member States will be analyzed, since the *common constitutional traditions* have been used as a source of inspiration in the drafting process of Art. 37 CFR.

Secondly, the legal consequences deriving from the inclusion of environmental protection in the catalogue of fundamental rights will be examined, both in substantive and interpretative terms.

---

[3] See Title XIX (*sub* Arts. 174, 175 and 176 TEC).

[4] Arts. 174 and 175 TEC.

[5] Although the EPI principle has 'general application', reference to the latter in the EU Energy policy signals the *special* relation between energy and environment.

3.1 The Drafting of Art. 37 CFR

The Charter provisions in the field of environmental protection do not originate from a legal vacuum. On the contrary, they draw inspiration from the Member States' common constitutional traditions and have been the object of numerous EU acts and of a consistent case law on the part of the ECJ.[6] This is particularly important because it confirms that the latter shares the same roots and recognizes the necessity to protect fundamental rights.[7]

With specific reference to environmental protection, though, the heterogeneity characterizing the different national legal orders made it impossible to draft Art. 37 CFR on a comparative basis. In some countries, it is understood as a right while in others it only amounts to a political objective or an ethical value.

From a comparative law perspective it is possible to roughly divide national systems into three categories,[8] according to the rank and nature that environmental protection is awarded in the relevant constitutional order.

In some countries environmental protection is expressly mentioned in the Constitution as an individual right.[9] This does not necessarily presuppose a genuine concern for environmental issues: it could also depend on external historical and legal reforms which strongly influenced the

---

[6]See L. Krämer, *Casebook on EU environmental law*, 2n ed. (Hart Publishing, 2002).

[7]From a general legal theory perspective, the notion of fundamental rights has been addressed by both *jus* naturalists and positivists. Broadly speaking, while *jus* naturalism operates on an axiological level, singling out the minimum criteria necessary to identify the content of fundamental rights (i.e. which rights 'are' or 'should be' fundamental), *jus* positivism operates on a prescriptive and normative level.

[8]This classification is clearly not free from the risk of over-simplification. For an assessment of the environmental protection in a comparative perspective, cf. S. Grassi, 'Costituzioni e tutela dell'ambiente', in S. Scamuzzi (ed.), *Costituzioni, razionalità, ambiente*, (Bollati Boringhieri, 1994) 404; L. Iapichino, 'L'environnement en tant que droit individuel dans l'Union européenne' in J. Rideau (ed.), *La protection des droits fondamentaux dans l'Union européenne, Actes du Colloque de Nice,* (Bruylant, 2009); F. Haumont, 'Le droit constitutionnel belge à la protection d'un environnement sain: état de la jurisprudence', (2005) 41 *Revue juridique de l'environnement* 41; M. Fitzmaurice, 'Environmental Human Rights Before the English Courts', (2006) *Annuaire international des droits de l'homme* 351; H. Smets, 'L'environnement dans les Constitutions des quinze et de la Suisse, (2003) *Revue juridique de l'environnement* 139.

[9]See Art. 45 of the Spanish Constitution; Arts. 7 and 35 of the Czech Republic's Charter of fundamental rights and freedoms (read jointly); Art. 115 of the Latvian Constitution; Art. 53 of the Estonian Constitution; Art. 66 of the Portuguese Constitution; Art. 18 of the Hungarian Constitution; Art. 72 of the Slovenian Constitution; Art. 5 of the Polish Constitution; Arts. 20, 44 and 45 of the Slovakian Constitution (read jointly). The right to environment has been inserted into Art. 23 of the Belgium Constitution only in 1994, as a result of a constitutional review procedure. In France the acknowledgment of the right to environment as a constitutional right arrived as late as 2003 with the adoption of the Environmental Charter.

elaboration of the most recent Constitutional Charters. This is particularly true for the former communist States that joined the EU in 2004, which had to take into account the constitutional trend in favor of the recognition of the so called 'third generation' fundamental rights, such as environmental rights.

In other States environmental protection is not conceived as a constitutional *right* but, rather, as a constitutional *value*.[10] The Scandinavian area is particularly sensitive towards environmental protection and has played a proactive role in the negotiations leading to the adoption of the Charter. The efforts of Sweden, Finland and Denmark were intended to avoid that the environmental protection guaranteed by the European Union be lower than the standard set at a national level.[11]

Lastly, there are countries in which environmental protection is not present in the formal constitutional text but 'lives' in the *material constitution*[12] via the (constitutional) courts' case law.[13] It follows that Art. 37 CFR is the result of a compromise which saves the symbolic value of the Charter,[14] but impeded the elaboration of a clearly formulated norm. As stated in the *Explanatory notes* annexed to the Charter,[15] in drafting this

---

[10] See Art. 20 of the German Federal Constitution; Arts. 10–12 of the Austrian Constitution; Art. 21 of the Dutch Constitution; Art. 24 of the Greek Constitution; Art. 2 of the Swedish Constitution and Art. 18 (3) of Chapter II of the Law of 24 November 1994, amending the Instrument of Government; Art. 20 of the Finnish Constitution.

[11] The prominent role of the Scandinavian countries in raising the EU's concerns in the field of environmental protection has been (indirectly) acknowledged by deciding (in 1995) to place the European Environment Agency in Copenhagen.

[12] In this sense, see C. Mortati, *La Costituzione in senso materiale* (Giuffrè, 1940). More recently, see E. Paciotti (ed.), *Per un'Europa costituzionale* (Ediesse, 2006).

[13] In countries such as Italy and Spain the affirmation of environmental rights within their constitutional legal framework has been the result of judicial activism. With specific reference to Italy, before the amendment of title V of the Constitution, the environment found protection under Art. 2, then under Art. 9 (2) and, finally, according to a consistent case law of the Constitutional Court, under Art. 32 (right to health), as the right to live in a healthy environment. With the Constitutional law no. 3/2001, the environment has been explicitly recognized in Art. 117 (2) lett. s), entrusting the State with the exclusive competence in the protection of the environment (although pursuant to Art. 117 (3), the valorization of environmental goods falls within the domain of the competencies shared with the Regions). On the right to environment in the Italian constitutional text (in particular, Art. 117), see B. Caravita, 'Costituzione, principi costituzionali e tecniche di normazione per la tutela dell'ambiente', in S. Grassi M. Cecchetti, A. Andronio (eds.), *Ambiente e Diritto* (Olschki, 1999) 175; B. Caravita, *Diritto dell'ambiente* (Il Mulino, 2001); A. Crosetti, *Diritto dell'ambiente* (Laterza, 2005).

[14] More generally, because of the UK's and Poland's reservations to the Charter, some Authors talked about "une charte à la carte". In this regard, see A. Moriceau, 'Le traité de Lisbonne et la Charte des droit fondamentaux', (2008) 519 *Revue du Marché Commun et de l'Union Européenne* 361.

[15] [2007] OJ C 303/17. The Explanatory notes adopted by the *Praesidium* have no legal effect, though they may be of assistance when interpreting the Charter. It is still highly

provision the Convention drew inspiration from Arts. 2, 6 and 174 of TEC (now amended by Art. 3 (3) of the TEU, and Arts. 11 and 191 e TFEU), as well as from some constitutions of the Members States (but with no further indication as to the relevant countries).[16]

3.2 Art. 37 of the Charter of Fundamental Rights: Substantive and Interpretative Issues

Environmental protection is enshrined in Art. 37 CFR, under the Chapter "Solidarity".[17] By contrast with the other provisions contained therein, the norm does not mention the term "right". This suggests (and marks) the (unclear) difference between "rights" and "principles". It is left to the interpreter – namely, the EUCJ – to clarify this distinction.

From a general standpoint, it is evident that while "rights" can be invoked directly by individuals before the courts, "principles" bind European and national institutions when they exercise their legislative and executive competencies in areas covered by EU law and only indirectly affect individuals. To be sure, the violation of such principles can determine (only) the annulment of the relevant acts.[18]

---

controversial whether the Explanatory notes will have the effect of crystallizing the content of the rights enshrined therein, thus limiting judicial activism on the part of the EUCJ, or rather may be used to up-date the content of the provisions included in that text. In this sense, climate change policies could be included within the scope of application of Art. 37 CFR see further Section 7).

[16]There is of course a direct link between the elaboration of the integration principle in the CFR and the inclusion of the Environmental Charter in the French constitutional order. In this regard, see S. Doumbe-Bille, 'Charte ET the droit international', (2005) *Revue juridique de l'environnement* 191; M. Prieur, 'La Charte, l'environnement et la Constitution', (2003) *Actualité juridique. Droit administratif* 353; Y. Jegouzo, 'La genèse de la Charte constitutionnelle de l'environnement', (2003) *Revue juridique de l'environnement* 23; P. Billet, 'La constitutionnalisation du droit de l'homme à l'environnement. Regard critique sur le projet de loi constitutionnelle relatif à la Charte de l'environnement', (2003) *Revue juridique de l'environnement* 35; R. Romi, 'Les principes du droit de l'environnement dans la 'Charte constitutionnelle':'jouer le jeu' ou mettre les principes 'hors-jeu'?', (2003) *Revue juridique de l'environnement* 46 and 'La Charte de l'environnement, l'avatar constitutionnel?', (2004) *Revue du droit public et de la science politique en France et à l'étranger* 1485; L. Verdier, 'Vers une constitutionnalisation du droit de l'environnement: prolégomènes sur la Charte de l'environnement' (2003) *Bulletin du droit de l'environnement industriel* 4.

[17]One of the major innovations of the CFR consists in considering fundamental rights as indivisible: civil, political, social and economic rights are all included in one single text. Such conception reflects the linkage between (and the evolving nature of) the rights enshrined therein allowing for a 'dynamic interpretation' of the latter.

[18]Pursuant to the *Explanatory notes*, rights which are identified as 'principles' include: the rights of the disabled (Art. 26); the rights to social security and social assistance

Pursuant to Art. 37 CFR:

> A high level of environmental protection and the improvement of the quality of the environment must be integrated into the policies of the Union and ensured in accordance with the principle of sustainable development.

As already mentioned, the formulation of this provision is far from satisfactory and it is hard to appreciate any added value with respect to what is already affirmed in Art. 6 TEC (now Art. 11 TFEU). Moreover, the inclusion of environmental protection in the Charter raises many interpretative questions.[19]

Firstly, what are the legal consequences of this choice? In this regard, it should be noted that while the reference to environmental protection in the TEU[20] and in the TFEU[21] can be explained with the need to state a fundamental value on which the Union is founded and to clarify the objectives to be pursued by the legislator, respectively, the re-statement of the principle in a Bill of Rights such as the Charter is less convincing. Far from affirming the existence of an individual right to environmental protection, Art. 37 CFR only entails political obligations.

The situation would be quite different if the provision had been construed in the following terms:

> Everyone has the right to environmental protection. The content and limits of the right to environment shall be prescribed by EU law and national law, according to Article 5 TEU.

A similar formulation would have allowed individuals to bring an action in law for violation of the right to the protection of their natural environment. Of course, as a citizen's right, such a provision should have appeared amongst the first Articles of the Charter. This would also have contributed to increase its visibility vis à vis EU citizens.

(Art. 34); the right to healthcare (Art. 35) and the right to environmental protection (Art. 37). Rights which are not identified as principles include the freedom to choose an occupation and to engage in work (Art. 15); the rights of the elderly to dignity and independence and to participate in social life (Art. 25); the rights of workers to information and consultation (Art. 27); the right to protection from unjust dismissal (Art. 30); the right to fair and just working conditions (Art. 31); the prohibition on child labour and the protection of young people at work (Art. 31) and the right to family life, and to economic and social protection of the family (Art. 33).

[19]The difficulties intrinsic to the formulation of the environmental rights were already present at the 1999 Cologne European Council. It will be remembered that the Convention's mandate was deliberately wide and flexible in the field of social rights so to avoid ideological conflict amongst its members. In this regard it should not go unnoticed that the only clear indication was that economic, social or solidarity rights should not be reduced to mere political objectives. Something that, prima facie, seems to have occurred with environmental protection.

[20]Cf. Arts. 3, n. 3, and 21 let. d) TEU.

[21]Cf. Arts. 4, n. 2, let. e), 11, 13, 114, 191, 194 TFEU.

Secondly, can environmental protection be considered a (real) fundamental right? In this respect, it can be observed that the Charter does not conceive the rights enshrined therein in hierarchical terms. As Win Griffiths, the House of Commons representative on the drafting body, pointed out:

> Some of the rights are fundamental and we can all agree on them. However, should we include a right to a healthy environment, or is that just a worthy political objective? Might consumer rights be included? Are the rights to safety and health, to fair remuneration, to paid holidays, to a pension and to training at work and to social security fundamental, or are they matters that Governments and political parties have as worthy objectives, which should not be included in such a declaration?[22]

The inclusion of environmental protection in the catalogue of fundamental rights has various important legal effects. On one side, it reinforces procedural rights in the field of environmental law (access to documents, right to participate in the law making process, effective access to justice); on the other side, it protects European citizens by preventing the adoption of EU acts, and national implementing measures, without taking into due consideration their environmental impact.[23]

The right to environment as a fundamental right obviously affects other rights like consumer rights and health care. The enhancement of the horizontal dimension of environmental rights clearly emerged in other drafting projects, such as the compromise Braibant-Meyer (from the name of its proponent), according to which Arts. 35 (Health care), 37 (Environmental protection) and 38 (Consumer protection) CFR should have been unified in one single provision; this proposal was formally rejected on the basis that each right deserved autonomous treatment.

Thirdly, can we qualify the environmental protection represented in Art. 37 CFR as a human right? If the answer is in the positive, what effects would this circumstance have on the scope and nature of that provision? In recent times the elaboration of a true "human rights approach" to environmental rights has become the object of an intense legal debate.[24] Although it is commonly accepted that certain rights (such as the right to life, the right to health, the right to develop) are at the core of international human rights law, the legal consequences of this *status* are less evident. In fact, from a universal and humanistic perspective, the right to environment should be considered as a corollary of the right to life, encompassing the right of living. As a consequence, there is a legal and moral duty to preserve the planet in conditions which allow for the survival of mankind. By contrast, from an ecological perspective, the right to health presupposes the right to live in an healthy environment with the result of creating positive and negative

---

[22]House of Commons, 16 February 2000, c228WH. See further L.S. Rossi, 'How fundamental is a fundamental principle? Primacy and fundamental rights after the Lisbon Treaty', *Yearbook of European Law* (Oxford University Press, 2008) 65.

[23]Cf. Section 4.

[24]Cf. Section 10 below.

obligations – inter-generational and intra-generational – for environmental protection. From a social and economic perspective, instead, the right to develop as a human being entails the right to access natural resources[25] and, most notably, basic energy services.[26] In this context, the latter should be construed as an individual fundamental right forming part of the more general category of human rights, which must be protected regardless of any further qualification. This approach undoubtedly restricts the scope of application of the right to environment, but can have major practical consequences.[27]

Even in the absence of a shared conception of the right to environment as a human right, the circumstance that the access to natural resources is a necessary precondition to the enjoyment of all other human rights – from the right to live, to the respect of human dignity, from the right to develop to the right to live in peace and security – cannot be neglected.[28]

4 Art. 37 and the EPI Principle

As already stated, Art. 37 CFR requires environmental policies to be integrated into the Union policies.[29] The legal *status* of the EPI principle remains unclear and somewhat ambiguous. This is because of the

---

[25] The right to access natural resources is indeed a corollary of the principle of non discrimination. Of course the relation with other principles/rights does not impinge on the autonomous nature of the latter.

[26] See further L. Dell'Agli, 'L'accesso all'energia elettrica come diritto umano fondamentale per la dignità della persona umana', (2007) 5 *Rivista Giuridica dell'ambiente* 713. According to the Author, if access to basic energetic services is considered to be a human right, individuals should be granted the same kind of protection allowed for when human dignity is violated, as would be the case when full enjoyment of their primary needs is denied.

[27] The inclusion of the right to environment in the category of human rights would have important implications. More precisely, it would place on the institutions the duty to guarantee non discrimination in the enjoyment of environmental resources within the territory of the European Union.

[28] See further Section 9 below.

[29] K. Hectors, 'The Chartering of environmental protection: Exploring the boundaries of environmtenal protection as human right', (2008) *European Energy and Environmental Law Review* 165; A. Lucarelli, 'Articolo 37' in R. Bifulco, M.Cartabia, A. Celotto (eds.), *L'Europa dei diritti. Commento alla carta dei diritti fondamentali dell'Unione Europea* (Il Mulino, 2001) 261; S. Grassi, 'La Carta dei diritti e la tutela dell'ambiente (art. 37)', in G. Vettori (ed.), *Carta europea e diritti dei privati* (CEDAM, 2002); B. Pozzo, 'L'articolo 37 e la tutela dell'ambiente come diritto fondamentale', in M. D. Panforti (ed.), *I diritti fondamentali in Europa* (Giuffrè, 2002) 171; C. Coffey, 'The EU Charter of Fundamental Rights: The place of the environment', in K. Feus (ed.), *The EU Charter on Fundamental Rights: Text and commentaries* (Federal Trust, 2000) 132; A. C. Kiss, 'The European Charter of fundamental rights and freedoms, environment and consumer protection', in S. Peers and A. Ward (eds.), *The EU Charter of Fundamental Rights* (Oxford University Press, 2004).

vagueness of its notion, which leaves the interpreter with the difficult task of construing it.[30]

Briefly, it is possible to isolate different conceptions of the EPI principle. Firstly, the latter can be viewed as a principle or, rather, an objective (as opposed to being a legal concept per se), which must inspire the Union in developing its environmental policy. Secondly, it may be understood as a parameter designed to keep the Union in line with international law. Lastly, it could be considered a legal principle with an autonomous normative value. Some authors suggests that the EPI principle could also play the three abovementioned functions at once.[31]

Adopting a functional approach, the EPI principle can also be understood as a parameter of legitimacy of EU acts, or as a new governance criterion. In the former sense, it could be used by judges to uphold the invalidity of a measure openly conflicting with the need to protect the environment. In the latter sense, it should inspire all European legislative action in this area of law, making it possible to attain a high level of protection of the environment and, possibly, to improve its current condition. These aspects will be considered separately below.

5 The Legal Enforceability of the EPI Principle in the Light of ECJ Jurisprudence

In order to function as a parameter of legality, the EPI principle must be acknowledged to possess full legal force. This inevitably places a notable responsibility on the EUCJ, which is called upon to recognize the latter as an autonomous normative principle.

The ECJ has referred to the EPI principle on a number of occasions. Suffice it here to recall the *PreussenElektra AG*,[32] *Commission v. Austria*[33] and *Commune de Mesquer v. Total France SA*[34] cases (the

[30]For an historical reconstruction of the EPI principle in the EU integration process see, among others, A. Jordan (ed.), *Environmental Policy in the European Union* (Earthscan, 2005). See also P. Brumber-Coret, N. Pourbaix, 'La communication interprétative de la Commission européenne relative à l'intégration des exigences environnementales dans le droit des marchés publics', (2001) 3 *Revue du droit de l'Union européenne* 739. More recently see A. Jordan, A. Lenschow (eds.), *Innovation in environmental policy? : integrating the environment for sustainability* (Edward Elgar, 2008).

[31]A. Nollkaemper, 'Three conceptions of the integration principle in international environmental law', in A. Lenschow (ed.), *Environmental Policy Integration. Greening sectoral policies in Europe* (Earthscan, 2002).

[32]See Case C-379/98 *PreussenElektra AG* [2001] ECR I-2099.

[33]Case C-320/03 *Commission v. Austria* [2005] ECR I-09871.

[34]See Case C-188/07 *Commune de Mesquer* [2008] ECR I-4501.

latter mainly concerning the interpretation of the *polluter-pays principle*).

In the first of the above mentioned cases, Advocate General Jacobs stated that:

> As its wording shows, Article 6 is not merely programmatic; it imposes legal obligations.[35]

The suggested legal enforceability of the EPI principle calls for a closer examination of the practicable legal avenues for ensuring its observance. Under Art. 263 TFEU the Court should declare the invalidity of EU acts whenever the environmental implications thereof have not been taken in due consideration.[36] As a parameter of legality for both legislative and executive measures, the EPI principle limits the discretionary powers of the EU legislator. The same result could be achieved via the preliminary ruling procedure laid down in Art. 267 TFEU, in so far as the EUCJ would quash any EU act contrasting with Art. 11 TFEU and Art. 37 CFR, or interpret the latter provisions as precluding (or not precluding) a specific EU or national legislation in the field of environment.

The EPI principle comes into play during the decision-making process and it can only be applied to situations in which the Union has taken positive measures. It follows that it cannot be relied upon in the context of a procedure for failure to act on the part of the institutions. On the other hand, because the EPI principle forms an integral part of the EU legal order, it can be argued that when its encroachment is ascribable to the Member States, the Commission shall activate an infringement procedure for failure to respect the environmental protection in the EU system.

6 The EPI Principle as a Method of Governance

Recognizing the existence of the EPI principle based on Art. 11 TFEU and Art. 37 CFR, however, is not enough to affirm that environmental law issues shall prevail over other EU interests. Although the institutions enjoy wide discretionary power in balancing potentially conflicting values, the legal force of the principle in question ensures that environmental interests are not disregarded or misapplied. From this perspective, the EPI principle

[35]See Case C-379/98 *PreussenElektra*, n. 32 above, AG Jacobs, Case C-277/02 *EU-Wood-Trading GmbH* [2004] ECR I-11957, AG Léger, para 9; Case C-87/02 *Commission v. Italy* [2004] ECR I-05975, AG Colomer, para 36.

[36]The concrete application of the EPI principle as parameter of legality of acts adopted by the EU institutions prevents the rights enshrined in the CFR from becoming boilerplate provisions. Pursuant to the Communication of the Commission "*Compliance with the Charter of Fundamental Rights in Commission legislative proposals*" (COM (2005) 172), when submitting its proposals, the latter institution must respect fundamental rights regardless of the entry into force of the CFR.

serves as a criterion in the elaboration and implementation of EU policies; it can impact significantly the balancing method for the composition and/or reconciliation of divergent interests. This implies that European institutions must take into account the effects of the adopted measures, reshaping the governance of the EU environmental policy.

As a method of governance, the EPI principle has a horizontal dimension, which requires legislation to respond to the environmental concerns, regardless of the field in which it is passed. This dimension certainly represents the core essence of the EPI principle, but the enforcement of environmental protection suggests the presence of a vertical dimension via an extensive interpretation of the latter. As a result all interested parties shall be involved in the decision making process leading to the adoption of acts that have a direct or indirect impact on the environment.

6.1 The Horizontal Integration

As far as the horizontal dimension is concerned, it must be noted that Art. 11 TFEU and Art. 37 CFR allow for the integration of environmental issues in all the EU policies and actions.[37] The added value of these two provisions can be easily appreciated by recalling that, traditionally, the need to act in line with the environmental concerns was limited to acts adopted pursuant to Art. 174 ECT (now Art. 191 TFEU), dealing specifically with environmental matters.

The development of the EPI principle into a guideline for EU action ensures a uniform approach with regard to the protection of the environment. As a consequence, the latter seems to imply an obligation on the part of the European institutions to promote a *"greening of EU policies"*.[38]

To *green* EU policies means to insist on the need to protect the environment throughout the various other areas of law via the application of the EPI principle.[39] Political and judicial support for the EPI integration

---

[37] D. Grimeaud, 'The integration of environmental concerns into other policies: a genuine policy development?', (2000) 9 *European Environmental Law Review* 216; M. Wasmeier, 'The integration of environmental protection as a general rule for interpreting community law', (2001) 38 *Common Market Law Review* 159; N. Dhondt, *Integration of environmental protection into other EC policies: Legal theory and practice*, (Europa Law Publishing, 2003).

[38] U. Collier, 'EU Energy policy in a changing Climate', in A. Lenschow (ed.), *Environmental Policy Integration: greening sectoral policies in Europe*" (Earthscan, 2002) 175.

[39] With regard to the integration of environmental needs in the European internal market, see P. Brumter-Coret, N. Pourbaix, 'La communication interprétative de la Commission européenne relative à l'intégration des exigences environnementales dans le droit des marchés publics', n. 30 above.

principle necessarily implies that environmental protection should become a major benchmark for the assessment of the quality of EU legislation, possibly evolving into the standard against which the coherence and uniformity of the EU legal order is measured.

Moreover, it should not go unnoticed that the EPI principle can play an important role in guaranteeing better regulation since it enhances the simplification and the coherency of legislation.[40]

6.2 The Vertical Integration

A true integrated approach requires environmental concerns to be carefully taken into consideration in all areas covered by the EU policies *and* at all stages in the decision-making process, from their drafting to their implementation, including consultation with the interested parties.

In its vertical dimension, the EPI principle calls for a closer coordination between European, national and local levels in order to adopt global, integrated and coherent environmental policies. Allowing environmental concerns to permeate other policy areas, the EPI principle will presumably lead European institutions to recognise ample participation in the decision making process. This means that the legislative proposal should be based on a thorough impact assessment and follow open discussions with Member States, environmental organizations, stakeholders and other interested parties.

The EPI vertical dimension should also reinforce, in a 'constitutional sense', many environmental procedural rights. A conscious participation of environmental stakeholders in the law making process and in the application of EU acts in environmental matters implies the right to access environmental documents,[41] the right to receive information on environmental issues, the individual's right to participate in the making of

[40]On the negative impact of the deregulation in the field of European environmental law envisaged by the Notice on "Better Regulation" (COM (2002) 275), see L. Krämer, 'Mieux légiférer et déréglementation du droit de l'environnement européen', (2007) 4 *Revue du droit de l'Union européenne*, 801. For a concrete application of the EPI principle in its procedural dimension, see the recent Directive proposal on the promotion of use of renewable energy sources (COM (2008) 19). The latter, which also fixes a 10% minimum target for bio-fuels in transport, will substitute the two previous directives in the field of renewable energy (concerning, respectively, electricity and bio-fuels). In addition, it should be noted that the decision-making-process leading to the final proposal followed an impact assessment process with widespread consultation of the various interested parties (Member States, citizens, stakeholder groups, NGOs).

[41]EC Directive 2003/4, [2003] OJ L 41/26.

environmental plans or programs.[42] It should also be observed that effective access to justice is to be guaranteed in the presence of a violation of environmental procedural norms.[43]

The enhancement of deliberative democracy in the field of environmental protection at the EU level should determine a strict interpretation of the derogations to the full accessibility of environmental documents rule, an approach which finds no confirmation in the current practice[44] but that seems to be imposed by Art. 15 (3) TFEU and Art. 47 CFR.

Last but not least, the procedural dimension of the EPI principle affects a growing number of European companies in so far as the latter are encouraged to promote their corporate social responsibility (CSR) integrating, on a voluntary basis, social and environmental concerns with business strategy and operations; from this perspective, the European Commission can foster the EPI principle favouring the elaboration of a binding normative framework on CSR at the EU level. At present there are some proposals on the communication with the public of enterprises, paving the way for the introduction of specific information duties on the respect of minimum environmental standards in the production process of European undertakings and the adoption of a Charter on ecological accountability of commercial information.[45] The debate is now open on the future adoption of European legislation on the Social accountability of EU enterprises in cases of damages produced outside the European territory.

---

[42] EC Regulation 1367/2006, [2006] OJ L 264/13. For an international law perspective on this point, see M. Iovane, 'La participation de la société civile à l'élaboration et à l'application du droit international de l'environnement', (2008) 3 *Revue Général de Droit International Public* 465.

[43] Rights enshrined in the Äarhus Convention, transposed into the EU legal order by virtue of Decision 2005/370, [2005] OJ L124/1. The procedural burdens of Art. 263 TFEU are particularly limiting in the field of the environmental rights due to the fact that environmental interests are often 'rarefied' and it becomes extremely difficult for environmental associations to demonstrate of being directly and individually affected by the relevant EU act. On the *locus standi* attributed to environmental associations access, see, among others, Case T-105/95 *WWF* [1997] ECR II-313 and Case T-585/93 *Greenpeace* [1995] ECR II-2205.

[44] D. Obradovic, 'EC rules on public participation in environmental decision-making at the European and national levels', (2007) 32 *European Law Review* 839; L. Krämer, 'Mieux légiférer et déréglementation du droit de l'environnement européen', n. 40 above, at 813.

[45] See http://ec.europa.eu/enterprise/csr/index_en.htm. See also the 'Grenelle Environment Round Table', called by the French President, Nicolas Sarkozy, and its online reports accessible at http://www.legrenelle-environnement.fr/grenelle-environnement/IMG/pdf/G6_Synthese_Rapport.pdf

7 From Nice to Strasburg: A Missed Opportunity to Reform Art. 37 CFR?

Seven years passed between the proclamation of the Charter of Fundamental Rights in Nice, on the 7th December 2000, and the (re-)proclamation of the Charter in Strasbourg, on the 12th December 2007. Over this period of time, environmental policies evolved by virtue of the "Stern Review"[46] and the 2007 IPCC Panel,[47] and the awareness of social and economic costs created by climate change grew significantly. Despite the attention of the media and the inclusion in the Lisbon Treaty of a specific provision on climate change,[48] the close link between the latter and environmental protection was not sufficiently reflected in the Charter.

According to Art. 191 TFEU, the EU's environmental policy should pursue a number of objectives, amongst them, the promotion, at an international level, of measures to combat the effects of climate change. Still, the will to insert such a norm directly in the Treaty was not accompanied by an amendment of the Charter, which remains silent in this respect. This is not free from consequences, as otherwise (i.e., if the Charter had been amended) issues related to climate change should have been taken into due consideration, via the EPI principle, in sectors such as transport, agriculture, energy and tourism, which are largely responsible for the polluting emissions. On the other hand, the recent legislative proposal package presented by the European Commission on the application of the EPI principle in areas related to climate change suggests that this omission could be the result of negligence more than a conscious choice.[49]

---

[46] N. Stern, *The Economics of Climate change. The Stern Review* (Cambridge University Press, 2006).

[47] IPCC, 'Summary for Policymakers', in M. L. Parry (ed.), *Climate change 2007: Impacts, Adaptation and Vulnerability. Contribution of Working Group II to the Fourth Assessment Report of the Intergovernmental Panel on Climate Change* (Cambridge University Press, 2007) 7.

[48] It is not by chance that under the Lisbon Treaty energy is among the areas of shared competence (see Arts. 4 and 194 TFEU). Art. 191 TFEU is closely linked to Art. 194 TFEU on energy, demanding that European institutions, in the interest of citizens, take into account climate change issues in the development of the EU energy policy.

[49] Indeed there has been an intense activity on the part of the Commission in the development of an integrated approach on climate and energy issues as confirmed by the adoption of the *third energy package* (Directive 2009/72/EC concerning common rules for the internal market in electricity, [2009] OJ L 211/55; Directive 2009/73/EC concerning common rules for the internal market in natural gas, [2009] OJ L 211/94; Regulation (EC) No 713/2009 establishing an Agency for the Cooperation of Energy Regulators, [2009] OJ L 211/1) and the *new* ETS Directive (Directive 2009/29/EC of the European Parliament and of the Council of 23 April 2009 amending Directive 2003/87/EC so as to improve and extend the greenhouse gas emission allowance trading scheme of the Community, [2009] OJ L 140/63).

The situation could be remedied by referring to the *Explanatory notes*, which explicitly invoke Art. 3 (3) TEU and Arts. 11 and 191 TFEU. In particular, it is suggested that the latter provision – insofar as it lists the fight against climate change amongst the environmental priorities – suggests that climate change falls under the scope of application of the EPI principle.

8 The Integrated Approach Between Climate Change and EU Energy Law

So far, the integration of environmental priorities in other EU policies has been systemically invoked, but never implemented. To a large extent this can be explained by the absence of an effective control system on the respect of environmental law. In this regard, the legal enforceability of the EPI principle, coupled with the emerging competencies in the field of energy and in the fight against climate change competences, can bring about many important changes.[50]

Recently, the Commission proposed a legislative package based on an integrated approach to energy and climate related measures, thus demonstrating to take seriously in account the binding nature of the EPI principle.[51] This is particularly evident when examining the exhaustive analysis carried out with respect to the need to comply with the subsidiarity principle. In addition, on the institutional level, it should be recalled that the EPI principle led the EP to set up a temporary committee on climate change.[52] The CLIM Committee was vested with the power to formulate proposals to the EP standing's committee, making recommendations as to measures and initiatives to be taken on climate change issues.

In practical terms, a true integrated approach requires that when adopting legislative and non-legislative acts, the EU institutions take in the

---

[50] K. MacDonald, 'A right to a healthful environment – humans and habitats: Re-thinking rights in an age of climate change', (2008) 17 *European Energy and Environmental Law Review* 213.

[51] See the Commission's Green Paper on the adaptation to climate changes (COM (2007) 534). See further, L. Eccher, 'Il libro verde della Commissione europea sull'adattamento ai cambiamenti climatici', (2007) 5 *Rivista giuridica dell'ambiente* 933, especially for the impact that the external dimension of climate change actions might have on the Common Foreign and Security Policy (CFSP).

[52] See European Parliament, Decision of 25 April 2007, [2008] OJ C 74E/652) setting up a temporary committee on climate change (CLIM Committee). The CLIM Committee was composed of 60 MEP's, and was operative between May 2008 and May 2009. As a result of its work the Plenary adopted on February 2009 a Resolution entitled "2050: The future begins today – Recommendations for the EU's future integrated policy on climate change" (2008/2105(INI)) OJ C74E/106.

utmost consideration the risks for climate change. As a consequence they must provide for measures capable of preventing the damages to the environment deriving from pollution and conceived to avoid, limit or, at least, internalize all costs associated with climate change.[53]

9 The Impact of Climate Change Policies on EU External Relations

As a priority of the EU Environmental policy, the fight against climate change deeply affects EU external relations. This is particularly evident when reading the motivation for the award of the 2007 Nobel Prize for Peace to the IPCC for *The Fourth Assessment Report on Climate Change*. Passages of the document highlight the link between climate change policies and international security, insisting on the fact that acknowledging the threats to stability and human security which are inherent to climate change is the necessary precondition for the elaboration of adequate responses.

As the President of IPCC, R. K. Pachauri, pointed out:

> In recent years several groups have studied the link between climate and security. These have raised the threat of dramatic population migration, conflict, and war over water and other resources as well as realignment of power among nations. Some also highlight the possibility of rising tensions between rich and poor nations, health problems caused particularly by water shortages, and crop failures as well as concerns over nuclear proliferation [...]. Peace can be defined as security and the secure access to resources that are essential for living. A disruption in such access could prove disruptive for peace [...].[54]

By extending the application of the EPI principle to the domain of climate change, the measures intended to mitigate the negative effects

---

[53] In International law, the expression *climate change* covers every change in the climate, directly or indirectly attributed to human activities and/or to natural causes, such as to determine a modification of the composition of the global atmosphere. In turn, *adaptation* entails the ability of a system to adapt to climate changes in order to reduce potential damages or to anticipate the consequences thereof. *Mitigation*, instead, identifies all human activity capable of reducing climate change risks; these measures – adopted by national governments or international organizations (according to field of competence in the fight against climate change) – are intended to combat the social and economic costs deriving from global warming as well as to reduce the risks of natural disasters. The adaptation and mitigation measures facing global warming would have to take in due consideration the interaction between environmental protection and other key sectors like energy, public health, agriculture, tourism, economic and fiscal policies. International organizations and States should elaborate comprehensive, global and effective solutions in accordance with the EPI principle.

[54] R. K. Pachauri, *Acceptance speech for the Nobel Peace Prize awarded to the Intergovernmental Panel on Climate Change* (IPCC), online publication accessible at: http://www.ipcc.ch/graphics/speeches/nobel-peace-prize-oslo-10-december-2007.pdf

thereof will acquire greater visibility in the field of EU external relations.[55] Consequently, the Cooperation Agreements, the Common Foreign and Security Policy (CFSP), the European Neighborhood Policy (ENP) and the Common Commercial Policy (CCP) should take into account the implications of the actions adopted for the protection of climate as well as those aimed at maintaining international security and peace. On the international level, the EU is called to face new challenges deriving from climate change effects, such as displacement, for the protection of "climate refugees".[56]

Of course, including the right to access natural resources in the category of human rights would reinforce the ethical commitment and the legal obligation of the EU to cooperate with the developing countries in the fight against poverty, ensuring access to those natural resources that meet the basic needs of human beings.[57]

10 The Different Roles of the Fundamental Rights Agency and the European Environment Agency

The inclusion of the EPI principle in the Charter could also affect the institutional level, and most notably the sharing of competencies between the bodies responsible for ensuring its respect.

The European Environment Agency (hereinafter EEA), created in 1993 with a view to provide sound and independent information on the EU environmental legislation,[58] has limited powers in the elaboration and the

[55] One of the main tasks of the CLIM Committee was to "collect and coordinate the opinions of the various committees concerned, so that the Parliament can play a key role in raising awareness and placing the challenge of climate change at the very top of the international agenda". In this regard it should not go unnoticed that the CLIM Committee took part in the EP-delegation to the 13th Conference of Parties of the United Nations Climate Change Conference held in Bali in December 2007.

[56] On this point, see D. Corlett, *Stormy Weather: The Challenge of Climate Change and Displacement*, (Sidney University of New South Wales Press, 2008).

[57] The multifold nature of environmental protection calls for a clearer distinction between external trade and environmental policies and the growing need to ensure the coherence between the pillars. In this regard, see P. Koutrakos, 'Development and foreign policy: where to draw the line between the pillars', (2008) 33 *European Law Review* 289.

[58] EEC Regulation 1210/90, [1990] OJ L 120/1. It is noteworthy that the regulation on the establishment of the EEA was based on Art. 130 s (now 174) TEC. EC Regulation 1641/2003, [2003] OJ L 245/03 has partially modified the EEA without substantially altering the situation described above.

dissemination of data relating to environmental issues, mainly in the form of non binding reports.[59]

The intergovernmental body charged with the task of guaranteeing the respect of European environmental law is IMPEL (European Union Network for the Implementation and Enforcement of Environmental Law).[60] Unfortunately, though, the Commission, the EEA and the IMPEL are devoid of any inspective powers to verify the correctness of the information contained in the Annual National Reports on the implementation of environmental measures.

Whether the enforceability of the EPI also presupposes the need to lay down new (formal) control mechanisms is debatable, but it is argued that in the future the Fundamental Rights Agency (hereafter FRA) could play a role in covering the enforcement of EU environmental provisions by European and national bodies. Any overlap between the activities carried out by the FRA and the EEA could be easily avoided by a strict respect of the respective mandates. In particular, the FRA would guarantee compliance with the EPI principle in those areas directly linked to the protection of fundamental rights (such as the right to environmental information, the right to access environmental law and the right to access environmental justice), while the EEA would monitor the implementation of the EPI evaluation framework by the Member States. A joint involvement of the two Agencies would undoubtedly enhance the commitment to environmental protection, with a positive impact on the operational solutions and best practices endorsed at a domestic level. Ultimately, this would facilitate the development of a common administrative culture and contribute to the cooperation invoked by Art. 197 TFEU.

11 . . .and the Possible Inconsistencies in the Case Law of the Luxembourg and Strasbourg Courts

With the entry into force of the Lisbon Treaty, the development of a coherent enforcing policy requires a coordination between the case law of the Court of Justice and the Strasbourg court, especially since the latter has interpreted the right to privacy enshrined in Art. 8 ECHR as including environmental rights.

---

[59] See EEA, *Environmental Policy Integration in Europe. Technical Report*, (2005) 5 *EEA* 1.

[60] 'Implementation and enforcement of environmental law', 5th Environmental Action Program, [1993] OJ C 138/5.

In fact, even in the absence of an explicit normative reference to environmental rights, the European Court of Human Rights (hereinafter ECtHR), conceiving the Convention as a living instrument, has gradually interpreted Arts. 2[61] and 8[62] ECHR as including such rights.[63] In its case law, the

[61] The case *Öneryildiz v. Turkey* concerned a methane explosion at the municipal rubbish tip in Ümraniye which occurred on 28 April 1993 that caused the destruction of rudimentary dwellings, built without any authorization in the area surrounding the rubbish tip, and the death of thirty-nine people (Appl. No 48939/99, (2004) Reports 2004-XII). In the Court's view, the State's responsibility was engaged under Art. 2 ECHR since Turkish authorities knew or ought to have known that there was a real and immediate risk to a number of persons living near the Ümraniye municipal rubbish tip and they consequently had a positive obligation to take such preventive operational measures as were necessary and sufficient to protect those individuals especially in the context of "dangerous activities" (as the operation of waste-collection sites). From a procedural standpoint, the liability of the State derived from the lack of adequate protection 'under the law' for the right to life, deterring similar life-endangering conduct in the future and failing to comply with the State duty to inform the inhabitants of the risks they were taking by continuing to live near a rubbish tip.

[62] The right to a healthy environment is included in the concept of the right to respect for private and family life. In the *Powell and Rayner v. the United Kingdom* case (Appl. No 9310/81, (1990) Series A no. 172) the Court declared Art. 8 applicable because "[i]n each case, albeit to greatly differing degrees, the quality of the applicant's private life and the scope for enjoying the amenities of his home ha[d] been adversely affected by the noise generated by aircraft using Heathrow Airport". The *López Ostra* case (Appl. No 16798/90, *López Ostra v. Spain*, (1994) Series A no. 303-C) concerned the releasing of gas fumes with a harmful effect which created an unlawful interference with the health of the families living in the vicinity of the plant. The Court of Strasbourg held that the presence of fumes, smells and noise did itself amount to a breach of the right to the inviolability of the home. The Court stated that there had been a violation of Art. 8 ECHR since, despite the margin of appreciation left to the respondent State, the Court considered that the State did not succeed in striking a fair balance between the interest of the town's economic well-being – that of having a waste-treatment plant – and the applicant's effective enjoyment of the right to the respect of the home and to private and family life. The Guerra Case (Appl. No 14967/89, *Guerra and others v. Italy*, (1998) RD 1998-I), instead, concerned the direct effect of toxic emissions produced by the Enichem Agricoltura Company's chemical factory on 420 Manfredonia (Foggia) residents rights' to respect for their private and family life under Art. 8 ECHR. In this case the Court observed that: "The direct effect of the toxic emissions on the applicants' right to respect for their private and family life means that Article 8 is applicable".

[63] Recently, in *Giacomelli* (Appl. No 59909/00, *Giacomelli v. Italy*, (2006) unreported), the Court, after indulging on the scope of Art. 8, considered that the individual right to the protection of the home covers the physical area and the quiet enjoyment of that area. The Court found that breaches of the right to respect for the home are not confined to concrete or physical breaches, but also include those that are not concrete or physical, such as noise, emissions, smells or other forms of interference. The breach of a person's right to respect for his/her home will amount to a serious infringement if it prevents him/her from enjoying the amenities of the home (see para 76 of the judgment). In this instance, notwithstanding the margin of appreciation left to the respondent State, the Court considered that the latter had failed to strike a fair balance between the interest of the Union in having a plant for the treatment of toxic industrial waste and the applicant's

Strasbourg Court reiterates that Art. 8 may apply to environmental cases when the pollution is directly caused by the State (positive duty) or when State responsibility arises from the failure to regulate private-sector activities properly (interference doctrine). Whether the case is analyzed in terms of a positive duty on the State to take reasonable and appropriate measures to secure the applicants' rights under Art. 8 (1) or in terms of an interference by a public authority to be justified in accordance with paragraph 2 (justification test), the applicable principles are broadly similar. In both contexts regard shall be paid to the fair balance that must be struck between the competing interests of the individual and of the community as a whole; and in both contexts the State enjoys a certain margin of appreciation in determining the steps to be taken to ensure compliance with the Convention.

In *Hatton I* [64] the applicants invoked the violation of Art. 8 by virtue of the increase in the level of noise caused at their homes by aircraft using Heathrow airport at night after the introduction of the "1993 Scheme". Here the competent Chamber strengthened the environmental protection afforded by the ECHR thus creating the "minimum interference with fundamental rights" rule, according to which in the particularly sensitive field of environmental protection, the States are required to minimize, as far as possible, interference with Art. 8 rights by trying to find alternative solutions in the least onerous way as regards human rights. Furthermore the minimum interference approach implies that the justification test of Art. 8 (2) ECHR is not fulfilled by the mere reference to the economic well-being of the country which is not sufficient, in itself, to outweigh the individual's right to a sound and healthy environment.[65] By contrast, in *Hatton II*[66] the Grand Chamber avoided adopting a "special approach" by reference to a "special status of environmental human rights" and has recognized to the States a wide margin of appreciation.

The Strasbourg Court case law on Art. 8 ECHR illustrates a two step approach: a substantive one and a procedural one. As to the substantive aspects, the Court scrutinizes the merit of the government's decision, whether the alleged violation is the result of an illegal behavior

right to an (effective) enjoyment of the right to the respect of her home and her private and family life. The Court found that there had been a violation of Art. 8 ECHR because the State authorities failed to comply with domestic legislation on environmental matters and subsequently refused to enforce national judicial decisions in which the activities at stake had been found to be unlawful, thereby rendering inoperative the procedural safeguards previously available to the applicant and breaching the principle of the rule of law (see paras 93–98 of the judgment).

[64] Appl. No 36022/97, *Hatton and Others v. the United Kingdom*, (2001) Report 2001-IX.

[65] Ibid., para. 97.

[66] Appl. No 36022/97, *Hatton and Others v. the United Kingdom*, (2003) Report 2003-VIII.

(e.g. carrying out dangerous activities without a license) or of an irregularity (e.g. failure to comply with the statutory obligation to provide information on health risks related to dangerous activities) at the domestic level, and, lastly, whether paragraph 2 applies. In performing such an assessment, the Court will ascertain the fairness of the balance struck by the national authorities. But according to the Strasbourg Court's case law, Art. 8 also establishes procedural requirements: the decision making process leading to the adoption of measures of interference must be fair, involving appropriate investigations and studies on the health risks of dangerous activities, so as to guarantee due respect to the individual's interests falling within the scope of application of Art. 8 ECHR.

The risks of inconsistencies – if not of open conflict – between the case law of the ECtHR and of the EUCJ cannot be ruled out. In particular, problems may arise from the different approaches used by the two courts in ensuring environmental protection: while Art. 8 ECHR is individually oriented, Art. 37 CFR is socially oriented, as confirmed by its collocation under the category of "solidarity rights". On the other hand, it is possible that a more strict interpretation of Art. 37 CFR on the part of the EUCJ will influence the Strasbourg Court's jurisprudence, thereby levelling the protection offered under the two regimes.

More precisely, in order to avoid this potential overlapping, the EUCJ should streamline the environmental protection through the proposed new interpretation of Art. 37 CFR, taking into account the procedural and substantial contents of the EPI principle (an interpretation which, as previously suggested, keeps in due consideration the individual component of this "third generation right"). This could determine a change in the Strasbourg Court case law on environmental protection[67] leading the latter to adopt a more restrictive approach towards Art. 8 (2) ECHR by: (a) softening the test applied in establishing a direct link between the damage and the harmful effect on individuals and (b) narrowing down the margin of appreciation left to the State by virtue of the recognized fundamental nature of environmental rights.[68] Such a stance would necessarily entail a *revirement* of the *Hatton* jurisprudence.

[67] The ECR and the ECHR systems should not be conceived as separate monads, not linked to each other; this is confirmed from the continuous references that judges of the Strasbourg made to the Art. 37 CFR. Also, judges and General Advocates of the ECJ quote the ECtHR jurisprudence on environmental matters to support their opinions (on the latter sense, see the case law quoted by AG Colomer in his opinion in Case C-176/03 *Commission v. Council* [2005] ECR I-7879).

[68] As stated in the Joint dissenting opinion of judges Costa, Ress, Türmen, Zupančič and Steiner in the Hutton II case, in the particularly sensitive field of environmental protection, mere reference to the economic well-being of the country is not sufficient to outweigh the rights of others. The margin of appreciation of the State should be narrowed because of the fundamental nature of the right to sleep, which may be outweighed only by the real, pressing (if not urgent) needs of the State.

This could allow for a competition of rights in environmental principles, which most likely will prove to be highly beneficial for EU citizens.[69]

12 Some Final (But Not Conclusive) Remarks

The environmental protection stated in Art. 37 CFR undoubtedly confirms the progressive "greening" of the EU legal system. The entry into force of the Lisbon Treaty makes it very difficult for European and national Courts to ignore this primary law provision. Nonetheless, the formal recognition of the EPI principle must be accompanied by concrete measures to prevent it from turning into a paper tiger.

Taking fundamental rights seriously[70] means creating a coherent and integrated environmental law complying with Art. 11 TFEU and Art. 37 CFR. This will avoid reducing the EPI principle to a mere boilerplate provision with little more than a placebo effect, which is of the utmost importance if the EU as a whole wants to play a leading role (i.e. be assumed as a model) in the governance of environmental protection. The Union is facing a "global challenge on the protection of rights"; to succeed, domestic and European Courts will have to guarantee the effectiveness of environmental rights (also) through the recognition of the EPI principle as a parameter of legitimacy of acts adopted in environmental matters.

The consequences of a binding Charter on the EPI principle are twofold: in its horizontal dimension, the principle fosters the greening of EU legislation by extending environmental protection to all EU policies with an impact on the environment; in its vertical dimension, it may act as a new governance method in the environmental law making process.

During the initial phase of the legislative process, the EPI principle mainly concerns the Commission since it is the latter that enjoys the power of initiative. When drafting the proposal for a directive the institution should ensure transparency by allowing stakeholders, including representatives from the industrial sector and environmental organizations, to participate in the preparatory work. The regulation of the relevant consultation operations would provide the EPI principle with a third – transversal – procedural dimension, guaranteeing an effective participation of the civil society to the environmental law making process. This would also favour the increased awareness of European public opinion with regard

---

[69] For a reconstruction of the ECtHR jurisprudence on environmental rights see F. Sudre and others (eds.), *Les grands arrêts de la Cour européenne des droits de l'homme*, (Presses Universitaires de France, 2007), 479–487.

[70] See R. Dworkin, *Taking rights seriously* (Duckworth, 1978).

to environmental issues and consequently the enhancement of democracy in European governance.

The circumstance that climate change concerns have not been included in the wording of Art. 37 CFR has no preclusive effect. It is in fact possible to attain the same result by an extensive interpretation of the latter provision based on the reference that the *Explanatory notes* make to Art. 191 TFEU.

To be sure, climate change priorities and the impact of environmental consequences on security issues will become an important point of reference in ascertaining the effectiveness of the EPI principle. A permanent judicial control over its respect and the political/institutional commitment towards environmental protection regardless of the specific area of intervention will contribute to making the Union, at a regional level, a guardian of the right of EU citizens to live in an healthy environment and, at a global level, a promoter of stability by guaranteeing that future generations will live in an environment that allows them to develop in an (ever more) equal and balanced way.

The EU Charter of Fundamental Rights and the Social Dimension of International Trade

Valeria Bonavita

1 Preliminary Remarks

The purpose of the present Chapter is to explore whether and, if so, to what extent, the entry into force of a legally binding EU Charter of Fundamental Rights (hereafter, Charter or CFR) will influence the attitude of the European Union in the relation between social rights and international trade, particularly within the World Trade Organisation (hereafter WTO).

The issue must be contextualised in the broader framework of the ongoing debate on the phenomenon of social dumping and the subsequent proposals for the inclusion of social clauses in trade agreements as a viable instrument to promote the respect of core labour standards as defined by the International Labour Organization (hereafter ILO). From the point of view of EU law, attention will be devoted to Title IV of the CFR dealing with "Solidarity" and, in particular, to workers' rights.

The analysis will address the possible impact of the social rights contained in the Charter on the Common Commercial Policy (hereafter CCP) in order to ascertain whether the legally binding force of the latter prescribed by the reformed Art. 6 (2) TEU will influence the EU contribution to the aforementioned debate, and more broadly EU practice in international trade. In this sense, the analysis will show that it is doubtful whether the entry into force of the Lisbon Treaty will cause a significant redirection of the EU's positions vis-à-vis the social dimension of international trade.

V. Bonavita (✉)
University of Bologna, Bologna, Italy
e-mail: valeria.bonavita@unibo.it

G. Di Federico, *The EU Charter of Fundamental Rights*, Ius Gentium: Comparative Perspectives on Law and Justice 8, DOI 10.1007/978-94-007-0156-4_13,

2 Social Dumping and the Debate on the Inclusion of a Social Clause in Multilateral Trade Agreements

International trade is currently characterized by the progressive reduction of tariff barriers and by the liberalisation of exchanges based on multilateral negotiations, as well as on the parallel decrease of distance-related costs due to advancement in the fields of transportation and communications. Social factors, mainly labour, have become one of the few variables a country can fine-tune in order to face international competition, particularly in those sectors of its economy that are exports-oriented. That being so, the reduction of production costs through the lowering of social standards often replaces the updating of production-planning schemes as a tool to gain further competitiveness in the global market.[1]

The rush to diminish labour standards in order to reduce the costs of production and increase international competitiveness accounts for the ongoing competition amongst social systems, and gives rise to a phenomenon often referred to as *social dumping*. This notion refers to the production and commercialisation of products whose international price is lower than the price resulting from the costs of production that the exporting country would bear should it abide by fundamental social rights and core labour standards. In other words, the price of the exported good does not reflect the social costs of production as assessed through the parameters of the importing country. Therefore the phenomenon of social dumping results in a distortion of international competition, since it confers an artificial comparative advantage upon those countries that do not respect fundamental social rights. By granting low standards of social

---

[1]For an exhaustive overview of the debate on the social dimension of international trade, see C. Di Turi, 'Globalizzazione dell'economia e diritti fondamentali in materia di lavoro' (2000) *Rivista di diritto internazionale* 113, and 'Liberalizzazione dei flussi commerciali internazionali, norme di diritto internazionale del lavoro e promozione della dignità umana' (1998) 37 *Diritto comunitario e degli scambi internazionali* 51; R. Howse and M. Mutua, 'Protecting human rights in a global economy. Challenges for the World Trade Organization' (2000), accessible at http://lic.law.ufl.edu/~hernandez/Trade/Howse.pdf; V. A. Leary, 'The WTO and the social clause: Post-Singapore', (1997) 8 *European Journal of International Law* 118; F. Maupain, 'La protection internationale des travailleurs et la libéralisation du commerce mondial: un lien ou un frein?' (1996) *Revue Générale de Droit international Publique* 45; Y. Moorman, 'Integration of ILO core rights labor standards into WTO' (2001) 39 *Columbia Journal of Transnational Law* 555; A. Perulli, 'La promozione dei diritti sociali fondamentali nell'era della globalizzazione' (2001) 02 *Diritto delle Relazioni Industriali* 157; E.-U. Petersmann, R. Howse and P. Aston, 'Trade and human rights: An Exchange', *Jean Monnet Working Papers* WP 12/2002; S. Sanna, 'Diritti fondamentali dei lavoratori: ruolo dell'OIL e dell'OMC' (2004) 78 *Diritto del lavoro* 147; J.-M. Siroën, 'Organisation mondiale du commerce, clause sociale et développement' (1997) 98 *Mondes en Developpement* 29; M. Balboni, 'Diritti dei fanciulli e commercio equo: clausola sociale o altro?', in L.S. Rossi (ed.), *Commercio internazionale sostenibile?: WTO e Unione europea* (il Mulino, 2003) 119.

protection, these countries bear lower production costs vis-à-vis their commercial partners which, on the contrary, acknowledge and guarantee those rights. Commercial advantages of developing countries,[2] which derive from extremely low levels of labour costs, would therefore be gained as a result of the maintenance of working conditions in violation of core labour standards. Many countries, namely developed ones, maintain that the above mentioned economic argument accounts for the need to link multilateral trade negotiations to the promotion of core labour standards.

The objectives of setting up minimum conditions of social protection and promoting the respect of core labour standards have been pursued for the last 15 years mainly via the proposal of inserting a so-called *social clause* in multilateral agreements liberalising international trade. This legal instrument outlines conventional norms identifying internationally recognised social rights that must be respected in order to enjoy advantages deriving from negotiated trade liberalisation. Should a country fail to comply with such norms, trade partners would be entitled to impose commercial sanctions to be determined in the framework of WTO procedure.[3]

The value of the social clause lies in the introduction of a criterion of social conditionality in the context of multilateral trade governance, involving WTO in the enhancement of working conditions worldwide. It allows the limitation of importations, including importations under preferential regimes, of goods produced by countries where labour conditions do not abide by conventional standards. The insertion of a social clause in multilateral trade agreements would thus promote the foundation of a social dimension of international trade. The sanctioning mechanism underpinning the clause makes the latter far more effective than international instruments currently in force. In fact, from the point of view of enforcement, the social clause significantly differs from conventions such as those adopted in the context of the ILO, whose effectiveness is undermined by the fact that the sanctioning apparatus they put in place is solely based upon persuasion and the high moral value of the commitments contained therein.

---

[2] The link between the non respect of core labour standards and developing economies, namely the circumstance that violations thereof mainly take place in developing countries, is widely accepted. As far as the European Union is concerned, in its Communication of 2001 on the promotion of core labour standards in the context of globalisation, the Commission for instance noted that «In many developing countries, a large part of the local economy is informal and unregulated. Poorer people are heavily reliant on the informal sector, both as workers and consumers, and they consequently tend to be less well protected by core labour standard agreements», Commission of the European Communities, Communication from the Commission to the Council, the European Parliament and the Economic and Social committee "Promoting core labour standards and improving social governance in the context of globalisation", COM(2001) 416 final, 18.7.2001, 11–12.

[3] Reference is herein made to Art. XX of the WTO Agreement.

On the other hand, the need to guarantee a social dimension of international trade does not exclusively stem from purely economic considerations, the latter also being complemented by ethical and legal reasons. With regard to legal considerations, it has been maintained that within the international community there is an established *opinio juris* according to which certain core labour standards are of universal application,[4] thus acting as fundamental human rights. Economic reasons cannot therefore be invoked in order to set such standards aside.[5]

Insofar as the origin of basic social rights is concerned, the latter can be traced back to certain ILO Conventions, to the Universal Declaration of Human Rights[6] and to the UN Covenants on Civil and Political Rights[7] and on Economic and Social Rights.[8] Core labour standards were also recognised in the 1995 Copenhagen Declaration on Social Development[9] and finally acknowledged in the Declaration adopted by the International Labour Conference during the 86th Session of 18 June 1998.[10]

These conventional instruments are based on four main principles: freedom of association and collective bargaining, prohibition of forced labour, non-discrimination, eradication of any form of exploitation of child labour. As previously stated, the international community looks at these principles as fundamental human rights. The ILO Declaration of 1998 makes clear that all members, even if they have not ratified the relevant conventions, are under a duty, merely by virtue of belonging to that organisation, to observe the above mentioned principles. Therefore, these are the standards the social clause would refer to and which would function as the parameters of social conditionality to which the enjoyment of benefits deriving from the liberalisation of international trade would need to conform. However, since the aforementioned basic workers' rights are commonly accepted, the

---

[4]In its Communication of 2001 the Commission states that agreement on the universality of core labour standards has been reached within the international community and that the universal application of those standards must be promoted, Communication "Promoting labour standards", n. 2 above, at 13.

[5]C. Di Turi, 'Globalizzazione dell'economia e diritti fondamentali in materia di lavoro', n. 1 above, at 131.

[6]General Assembly of the United Nations, Universal Declaration of Human Rights, UNGA Resolution 217 A (III) of 10 December 1948.

[7]General Assembly of the United Nations, International Covenant on Civil and Political Rights, UNGA Resolution 2200A (XXI) of 16 December 1966.

[8]General Assembly of the United Nations, International Covenant on Economic, Social and Cultural Rights, UNGA Resolution 2200A (XXI) of 16 December 1966.

[9]Report of the UN World Summit for Social Development (also includes the Copenhagen Declaration and Programme of Action), *A/CONF.166/9.*

[10]ILO Declaration on Fundamental Principles and Rights at Work – 86th Session, Geneva, 19 June 1998.

social clause amounts to a codification of principles already in force under customary international law.[11]

The debate revolving around the insertion of a social clause in multilateral trade agreements is characterized by diverging views put forward by developed and developing countries. The former consider the clause to be an instrument for the restoration of fair conditions in international trade competition, whereas the latter view it as a form of disguised protectionism. Developing countries are the main beneficiaries of the comparative commercial advantages resulting from low levels of the cost of labour allowed by the disregard of core labour standards, and believe that the aim of the social clause is not the wholehearted promotion of decent working conditions for all but rather represents the attempt by developed countries to raise the costs of production, particularly the cost of labour, undermining competitiveness margins via the eliminations of the very source of comparative advantage for developing countries.[12]

These different positions are reflected in the final Declaration of the first WTO ministerial conference held in Singapore in December 1996. After reaffirming their commitment "to the observance of internationally recognized core labour standards", delegates of Member States expressed the view that "[t]he International Labour Organisation (ILO) is the competent body to set and deal with these standards" and granted their "support for its work in promoting them". However, in Art. 4 of the Declaration, which is devoted to core labour standards as such, the Conference intended to balance the previous statement by rejecting "the use of labour standards for protectionist purposes" and agreeing that "the comparative advantage of countries, particularly low-wage developing countries, must in no way be put into question".[13] Concerns expressed by developing countries in relation to how social conditionality could undermine their competitiveness emerge also from Art. 5 of the above mentioned ILO Declaration of 1998.

---

[11] C. Di Turi, 'Liberalizzazione dei flussi commerciali internazionali, norme di diritto internazionale del lavoro e promozione della dignità umana', n. 1 above, at 64.

[12] Developing countries also criticize the fact that the introduction of a social clause would imply a de facto discrimination of their product vis-à-vis competing ones. However, Howse and Mutua offer an interesting interpretation of the national treatment principle under WTO law, which rules out such an argument. One of the WTO members' basic obligations is to provide treatment as favourable to imports as that provided to domestic products. Therefore they assume that a country that has banned slave labour in domestic production, for instance, could equally ban imports of products from facilities that use slave labour. This would amount to equal treatment of both domestic and imported products, with reference to the requirement that slave labour not be used. The authors conclude that requiring a country to accept imported products produced with slave labour, regardless of the treatment of similar domestic products under its law, would amount to demanding more favourable treatment for imports. See R. Howse and M. Mutua, n. 1 above.

[13] WTO Doc. WT/Min(96) Dec./W., 18 December 1996, point 4.

While the Preamble of the Declaration links economic growth to social development, Art. 5 clarifies that such a link does not contemplate recourse to international labour standards "*à des fins protectionnistes*" which would reduce "*l'avantage comparatif d'un quelconque Pays*".[14]

These documents show what sort of clash of opinions revolves around the involvement of the WTO in the enhancement of working conditions in developing countries via the subordination of further trade liberalisations to the respect of core labour standards. This being the general framework, understanding what position the EU has maintained so far with regard to the promotion of labour standards in international trade is essential to analyse the effects that the internal recognition of workers' rights via a binding Charter might produce on the EU approach to such issues.

3 The EU and the Promotion of Core Labour Standards

The European Union actively takes part in the debate on how to provide international trade with a social dimension. On the one hand, positions expressed by European institutions on several occasions show commitment to the promotion of trade liberalisation schemes which respect human dignity and enhance compliance with human rights in the work place.[15] More concretely, these positions have been transposed into the EC Common Commercial Policy (CCP), particularly via the conditionality enshrined in the General System of Preferences, which is the main instrument of the preferential trade arrangements adopted by the Community to the advantage of developing and least developed countries.

In this regard, the EU follows the principles set out in the October 1999 Council Conclusions, namely the universality of core labour standards, the rejection of any sanctions-based approach and the support for the work of the ILO and for the co-operation between the latter and other international organisations such as the WTO. The attitude of the EU towards social rights and international trade is inspired by these three elements, and policy-making in this domain develops accordingly.

As stated in a series of Communications by the European Commission, the basic assumption of the European approach is the close relationship between trade liberalisation, economic development and social progress.

---

[14] ILO Declaration on Fundamental Principles and Rights at Work, *supra*, point n. 5, which in particular states that: "*[La Conférence international du travail] souligne que le normes du travail ne pourront servir à des fins commerciales protectionnistes et que rien dans la présente déclaration et son suivi ne pourra être invoqué ni servir à des pareilles fins; en outre, l'avantage comparatif d'un quelconque Pays ne pourra, en aucune façon, être mis en cause du fait de la présente déclaration et son suivi*".

[15] C. Di Turi, 'Liberalizzazione dei flussi commerciali internazionali, norme di diritto internazionale del lavoro e promozione della dignità umana', n. 1 above, at 69.

In the Communication on fair trade issued in view of the WTO Millennium Round, the Commission stresses that the EU will pursue trade liberalisation while respecting sustainable development and contributing to the enhancement of social standards worldwide.[16] In particular, trade liberalisation should help to achieve goals such as high growth, full employment, poverty reduction and the promotion of decent work.[17] The strategic economic and social policy goals of the EU are underpinned by the recognition that sustainable economic growth goes hand in hand with social cohesion, which also implies respect for core labour standards.[18]

The European Parliament expressed similar views by stressing that the objective of the multilateral trading system is to produce a long-term positive development of trade and economic reforms,[19] considering that this system is primarily meant to play an important role in the creation of prosperity in all parts of the world. International trade should therefore be one of the preferential channels for introducing social change in order to ensure the observance of labour rights.[20]

The first principle inspiring the EU approach is the recognition of the universality of core labour standards as defined in the 1998 ILO Declaration on fundamental rights at work.[21] In line with the content of the Declaration, European institutions often make reference to the fact that core labour

---

[16]Communication from the Commission to the Council on 'fair trade', COM(1999) 619 final, 14.

[17]Communication from the Commission to the Council, the European Parliament and the Economic and Social Committee: "Promoting decent work for all. The EU contribution to the implementation of the decent work agenda in the World", COM(2006) 249 final, 8.

[18]Communication from the Commission to the Council, the European Parliament and the Economic and Social Committee, "Promoting core labour standards and improving social governance in the context of globalisation", COM(2001) 416 final, 1. See also Communication from the Commission to the Council: "The trading system and internationally recognised labour standards", COM(1996)0402 final.

[19]European Parliament Resolution on the Communication from the Commission to the Council on the trading system and internationally recognised labour standards (COM(96)0402 C4-0488/96), [1999] OJ C104/63, point B. See also Resolution on the compliance with and consolidation of international labour standards [1987], OJ C 99/11, as well as Resolutions of 9 September 1986, [1986] OJ C255/69, 18 November 1988, [1988] OJ C 326/315,11 October 1990, [1990] OJ C 284/152, 30 September 1993, [1993] OJ C 279/16, 28 October 1993, [1993] OJ C 315/242, 9 February 1994, [1994] OJ C 61/89, 14 December 1995, [1995] OJ C 17/175, 15 May 1997, [1997] OJ C 167/158 and 15 January 1998, [1998] OJ C 34/156, calling for guaranteed minimum standards with regard to freedom of association, freedom to engage in collective bargaining, working hours, the minimum age for employment, security of employment, industrial safety and inspection of working conditions and the introduction of a code of good conduct for European multinational undertakings.

[20]Ibid., point C.

[21]Communication 'Promoting core labour standards and improving social governance in the context of globalisation', n. 2 above, 1.

standards are to be considered as fundamental rights and their respect is seen as a *conditio sine qua non* for achieving social development. In fact, citizens perceive that an equitable global economic system should *both* promote social development *and* fundamental rights. The Union considers that the protection of fundamental rights, including core labour standards, must be integrated in the global trade regulatory system if the latter is to accomplish the task of promoting development.

As the Commission observes, while European citizens are protected by Community and national laws governing areas such as health and safety at work as well as employers' and employees' statutory rights and obligations, in many developing countries similar statutory rights are still in the making, and even where they are fully recognised, economic or other conditions may impede compliance with the relevant provisions.[22] Therefore, the EU is committed in enhancing working conditions by remedying the inadequacies which currently affect core social standards throughout the world.[23]

The approach connecting core labour standards to fundamental rights was clearly defined in the 2001 Communication entitled "Promoting core labour standards and improving social governance in the context of globalisation", whose objective was to outline a strategy for the improvement in social governance and the promotion of core labour standards, with a view to enhancing the contribution of globalisation to social development and to the respect for fundamental rights.[24]

The recognition by the Union of core labour standards as fundamental rights is particularly relevant to the present analysis because it points out how the EU Charter came into play so far, notwithstanding the lack of binding force, in relation to the Union's approach to the social dimension of international trade. In the above mentioned Communication, the Commission sets out the linkage between the internal and the external projection of the rights proclaimed in the Charter. Referring to the long standing commitment of the Union in favour of social development and to its role in the promotion of core labour standards throughout the world, the Commission states that:

> The EU itself rests on the respect of fundamental rights. The Charter of Fundamental Rights of the European Union, proclaimed in Nice in December 2000 confirms the EU's aim to promote and fully integrate fundamental rights – including core labour standards – in all its policies and actions.[25]

---

[22] Communication on 'fair trade', n. 16 above.

[23] Ibid., 11.

[24] Communication 'Promoting core labour standards and improving social governance in the context of globalisation', n. 2 above.

[25] Ibid., at 10.

Since all policies and actions of the Union aim at promoting fundamental rights, even before acquiring legal force the Charter has been regarded as a guideline for policy-making in relation to external aspects of internal policies and to external policies as such, including the CCP. Indeed, the European Parliament underlines the link between the affirmation of fundamental rights in the EU and the duty to respect those rights when setting up Community external policies[26] by consistently referring to fundamental rights and to the EU Charter, in particular when dealing with the promotion of core labour standards. In its 2003 Resolution on the Commission's Communication, the Parliament makes direct reference to the Charter.[27] Not only the reference in itself, but also its placement at the very beginning of the document is meaningful. The Charter is mentioned therein right after the Communication constituting the very object of the Resolution, and before every other document adopted at the European and international level. This being so, it can be said that the Parliament considers the Charter as one of the major sources of inspiration for policy-making, even when it comes to principles governing the external action of the Union and the CCP in particular. On this basis, the Parliament states that greater respect for fundamental rights and other social rights requires fairer international trade policies which take into account the existence of unequal partners. It also underscores current difficulties in tackling the problem of fundamental social standards in the framework of the WTO. It therefore encourages the Commission to define new strategies to properly place social standards in a new international trade-regulatory architecture, so as to enhance the contribution of the EU trade policy to sustainable development.[28]

The second element of the EU position on the social dimension of international trade governance concerns how to put in practice the "ideals" indicated so far and consists in the rejection of any sanction-based approach. Instead of sanctioning violations of core labour standards, the EU tends to incorporate the principle of awarding trade incentives for

[26]European Parliament Resolution on the Communication on the trading system and internationally recognised labour standards cited, point P, where the Parliament considers that the affirmation of fundamental rights in the European Union treaties imposes obligations on both the developed and the emerging countries.

[27]European Parliament Resolution on the Commission Communication to the Council, the European Parliament and the Economic and Social Committee entitled "Promoting core Labour Standards and Improving Social governance in the context of globalisation" (COM(2001) 416 — C5-0162/2002 — 2002/2070(COS)), OJ C271E/598. Before the Charter was proclaimed in 2000, the European Parliament used to make reference to the Social Charter adopted by 11 Member States at the Strasbourg European Council on 8 and 9 December 1989 as shown in the European Parliament Resolution on the Communication on the trading system and internationally recognised labour standards cited, point II.

[28]Ibid., points 10 and 11.

compliance with minimum social standards into its legislation on external trade. The rationale of such a choice lies in the fact that, by favouring reforms in the beneficiary countries, incentive clauses are more suitable than penalties to achieve development, poverty reduction and equality.

The support for positive measures to encourage respect of core labour standards and a firm opposition to any sanctions-based policy has been confirmed by the Commission throughout the years.[29] Incentive clauses represent the main device in the Generalised System of Preferences (GSP) and other Community unilateral preferential arrangements towards developing countries aiming at the enforcement of the fundamental rights component of such a trade scheme.

The incentives-based approach is the corollary of the fact that the Union's support for social conditionality in international trade serves no protectionist purpose. In its 1999 conclusions, the Council agreed that the comparative advantage of countries, particularly low-wage developing countries, must in no way be put into question, and the Commission confirmed such a stance by maintaining that the need to ensure full respect of core labour standards is complementary to the necessity to avoid any risk of abuse by unilateral, protectionist measures.[30]

The support for ILO and for the strengthening of the latter's relationship with the WTO, deemed unable to avoid the issue of compliance with minimum social standards in the long run, represents the third element of the European position. In its Communication of 2001, the Commission notes that the international community has not yet found adequate ways of addressing the interface between globalisation, trade and social development, notwithstanding the growing need to do so. The ILO enforcement mechanism, being limited to ratified conventions, is said to have limited effectiveness.

By comparison, the World Trade Organisation, with its rules-based system and binding dispute settlement mechanism, appears to be endowed with more appropriate tools for ensuring compliance with core labour standards. Nonetheless, the Commission expresses the view that ILO must remain the competent organisation to set and deal with labour standards, and that a rebalancing of the global trading system should strengthen the social pillar by taking its starting point in the ILO mechanisms, not within the WTO. What has to be sought is therefore not the replacement of the ILO by the WTO but, rather, enhanced coordination between the two

[29] See Communication on 'fair trade', n. 16 above, and Communication "Promoting core labour standards and improving social governance in the context of globalisation", n. 2 above, 11. Also the European Parliament favours this approach, as shown in the Resolution on the Commission Communication "Promoting core Labour Standards and Improving Social governance in the context of globalisation", n. 2 above, point 13.

[30] Communication "Promoting core labour standards and improving social governance in the context of globalisation", n. 2 above.

organisations. In other words, WTO rules could be borrowed to make ILO instruments more effective in promoting core labour standards.[31]

The European Economic and Social Committee gave its advisory opinion of the matter suggesting that the WTO must help to resolve these issues by encouraging positive measures and incorporating provisions to exclude members that breach international labour standards from the benefits of membership in its implementing system. It also called on the WTO to collaborate with ILO ensuring substantive involvement, for instance by granting the latter observer status not only at its ministerial conferences, but also within its other bodies.[32]

These being the operational principles endorsed by the EU for the promotion of fundamental rights at work, one can wonder whether the policies developed in this field are in line with the former. Since 1992 all agreements concluded between the EC and third countries have been required to incorporate a clause defining human rights as an essential element thereof. This clause encompasses also core labour standards as set out in the mentioned ILO Conventions. Furthermore, the 2000 Cotonou Agreement between the EC and the 77 ACP states represented a step forward in this area, as it includes a specific provision on trade and labour standards, which confirms the parties' commitment to their respect.[33] In fact, the EU considered it essential that a social clause be included not only in the trade and cooperation agreements concluded by the EU with third countries, but also in all financing conventions between the Commission and European undertakings benefiting from the various instruments to encourage investment in third countries.[34]

Having regard to the specific measures adopted in the framework of the Union's trade policy, the main instrument for promoting core labour standards is the new Generalised System of Preferences (herein GPS) and its special incentive for sustainable development and good governance GSP+,[35] whereby the EU requires conditionality unilaterally without

---

[31] Ibid.

[32] Opinion of the European Economic and Social Committee: "For a WTO with a human face: the EESC's proposals" of 26 March 2003.

[33] Title II: Economic and trade co-operation, Chapter 5: Trade-related areas, Article 50: Trade and labour standards.

[34] European Parliament Resolution on the Communication from the Commission to the Council on the trading system and internationally recognised labour standards, n. 19 above, point 24.

[35] Council Regulation (EC) No 732/2008 of 22 July 2008 Applying a Scheme of Generalised Tariff Preferences for the period from 1 January 2009 to 31 December 2011 and amending Regulations (EC) No 552/97, (EC) No 1933/2006 and Commission Regulations (EC) No 1100/2006 and (EC) No 964/2007, [2008] OJ L 211/1, replacing Council Regulation (EC) No 980/2005 of 27 June 2005 Applying a Scheme of Generalised Tariff Preferences, [2005] OJ L 169/1.

negotiations with third countries. However, it should be noted that the conditionality enshrined in the GSP scheme does not consist only of incentives for the Community's virtuous trade partners. On the contrary, positive conditionality in the GSP appears to be ancillary in a scheme primarily based on the provision of sanctions in case of violations of fundamental rights. This arrangement mirrors the very practical need to balance a positive approach with more pragmatic sanctioning provisions.

Since 1971 the EC has unilaterally granted trade preferences, implemented through periodically updated Council regulations based on Art. 133 EC, to developing and least developed countries. These preferences are granted voluntarily and not by virtue of a binding legal obligation under WTO law. This being so, since 1994 EC Regulations setting up the GSP contain conditionality clauses which make the granting of preferential trade treatment to beneficiary countries subject to the respect of international provisions on human rights and labour standards by the latter.

Arts. 9 and 15 to 19 of Council Regulation 732/2008 contain a withdrawal clause which applies *inter alia* to serious and systematic violations of sixteen core UN and ILO human and labour rights conventions.[36] The ILO conventions referred to in the withdrawal clause include Convention No. 138 concerning minimum age for admission to employment; Convention No. 182 on the prohibition and immediate action for elimination of the worst forms of child labour; Convention No. 105 on the abolition of forced labour; Convention No. 29 concerning forced or compulsory labour; Convention No. 100 concerning equal remuneration of men and women workers for work of equal value; Convention No. 111 concerning discrimination in respect of employment and occupation; Convention No. 87 concerning freedom of association and protection of the right to organise; Convention No. 98 concerning the application of the principles of the right to organise and to bargain collectively.[37]

These conventions clearly aim at protecting those rights defined as core labour standards in the 1998 ILO Declaration. Violations of these conventions by beneficiary countries conferred upon the Union the power to temporarily withdraw preferential access treatment foreseen by the Regulation. Acting upon these provisions, the Council suspended preferential access to the Community market for products coming from Myanmar in 1997 and from Belarus in 2007, because of systematic violations of the prohibition of forced labour in the case of Myanmar and of the freedom of association as for Belarus.

Such a penalty clause coexists with a special regime contained in the GSP+ scheme, which includes special incentives for sustainable development and good governance. According to this scheme, products of

[36] Council Regulation (EC) No 732/2008, Chapter III "Temporary withdrawal and safeguard provisions", particularly Art. 15.

[37] Ibid., Annex III, Part A "Core human and labour rights UN/ILO Conventions".

vulnerable countries are granted duty-free access if the country fulfils certain requirements, which include the implementation of twenty-seven key international conventions on political, human and labour rights. The aim of this additional scheme is to help beneficiary countries to achieve development by setting up more advanced social policies.

The various GSP have already accelerated the ratification of ILO core labour standards conventions. However the Commission has suggested that, in the context of future reviews of the GSP scheme, consideration should be given to enhancing the possibilities to use GSP incentives to further promote core labour standards. In particular, the social incentive scheme should be strengthened by extending the basis to all of the four core labour standards in the 1998 Declaration. The Commission has also proposed that provision for temporary withdrawal be extended by broadening the basis to severe and systematic violations of any of the core labour standards. More in general, the EC and Member States should improve the link between the GSP scheme and development programmes to help countries make better use of the incentive schemes for the promotion of core labour standards.[38] Finally, the Commission suggested to make better use of Sustainability Impact Assessments (SIA) in relation to future trade negotiations and agreements, in order for the EC to be aware of the effect of trade policy on social development and the promotion of core labour standards in third countries, particularly developing ones.[39]

4 Workers' Rights in the EU Charter

The Charter contains a number of provisions which can be considered as the translation into the European legal order of social rights protected by core international conventions. Provisions having an impact on the social dimension of individuals' life are present throughout the Charter.[40] However, Chapter IV (Arts. from 27 to 38) deals in particular with solidarity rights, whereas the Preamble defines solidarity as one of the indivisible and universal values founding the European Union, together with human dignity, freedom and equality.

---

[38] Communication "Promoting core labour standards and improving social governance in the context of globalisation", n. 2 above.

[39] Ibid.

[40] It has been submitted that the Charter contains a myriad of rights which could fall under the "social" heading, which demonstrates how difficult it is to establish boundaries in this sphere. See P. Lorber, 'Labour Law', in S. Peers and A. Wards (eds.), *The EU Charter of Fundamental Rights* (Hart Publishing, 2004) 211, at 218. For the purposes of the present analysis the focus is on social rights connected to working activities, namely labour rights referring to individual and collective rights of workers.

Keeping in mind the ILO Declaration of 1998, it is possible to ascribe some of the social rights proclaimed in the Charter to four macro areas corresponding to the core labour standards set out in the Declaration, namely freedom of association and collective bargaining, prohibition of forced labour, non-discrimination and prohibition of exploitation of child labour.

Starting from the freedom to associate and bargain collectively, both aspects are covered in the Charter by two different provisions. The first is Art. 12 CFR recognising the freedom of assembly and association. Under the first paragraph of that provision everyone is entitled to the right to freedom of peaceful assembly and to freedom of association at all levels, including at the European level. In particular, the provision makes reference to freedom of association in relation to trade union matters, which implies the right of everyone to form and to join trade unions for the protection of his/her interests. This provision corresponds to Art. 11 of the European Convention on Human Rights and has the same meaning.[41] Therefore, as stated in the explanations by the *Praesidium* relating to the text of the Charter,[42] and in accordance with Art. 52(3) of the Charter itself,[43] limitations on the right of association may not exceed those considered legitimate by virtue of Art. 11(2) of the ECHR, namely those restrictions which are necessary in the interest of national security or public safety, for the prevention of disorders or crime, for the protection of health or morals or for the protection of the rights and freedoms of others.

The second provision is contained in Art. 28 CFR dealing with the right of collective bargaining and action. Workers and employers have the right to negotiate and conclude collective agreements and, in cases of conflicts of interest, to take collective action to defend their interests, including strike action. This provision is based on Art. 6 of the European Social Charter and on points from 12 to 14 of the Community Charter of the Fundamental Social Rights of Workers. The right of collective action was recognised by the European Court of Human Rights as one of the elements of trade union

[41] This right is also based on Art. 11 of the Community Charter of the Fundamental Social Rights of Workers.

[42] Text of the explanations relating to the complete text of the Charter as set out in CHARTE 4487/00 CONVENT 50, CHARTE 4473/00 CONVENT 49. Even if not endowed with legal binding force, the explanations by the *Praesidium* are a valuable instrument for the interpretation of the provisions of the Charter. In particular, they are granted interpretative value by Art. 52(7) CFR.

[43] Art. 52(3) CFR reads as follows: "Insofar as this Charter contains rights which correspond to rights guaranteed by the Convention for the Protection of Human Rights and Fundamental Freedoms, the meaning and scope of those rights shall be the same as those laid down by the said Convention. This provision shall not prevent Union law providing more extensive protection".

rights laid down in Art. 11 ECHR and is thus subject to no limitations except those enlisted therein.

Secondly, Arts. 5 and 31 CFR contain provisions prohibiting forced labour. Art. 5 foresees that no one shall be held in slavery or servitude (paragraph 1), or shall be required to perform any form of forced or compulsory labour (paragraph 2). The wording of Art. 5(1) and (2) corresponds to that of Art. 4(1) and (2) of the ECHR. The two provisions have the same meaning and scope by virtue of Art. 52(3) of the Charter. Consequently no limitation can legitimately affect the right provided for in paragraph 1. Moreover, the expression "forced or compulsory labour" under paragraph 2 must be understood taking into account the "negative" definitions contained in Art. 4(3) ECHR. Under the latter provision the term does not include: compulsory work in the ordinary course of a legitimate detention or during conditional release from such detention; any service of a military character or, in case of conscientious objectors, service exacted instead of compulsory military service; any service exacted in case of an emergency or calamity threatening the life or well-being of the community; any work or service which forms part of normal civic obligations. Art. 31 CFR recognises the right to fair and just working conditions, which are meant to respect the health, safety and dignity of every worker. The provision also sets out the right to limitation of maximum working hours, to daily and weekly rest periods as well as to an annual period of paid leave.[44]

On its part, Art. 21 CFR protects individuals against discrimination based on any ground, including sex, race, colour, ethnic or social origin, genetic features, language, religion or belief, political or any other opinion, membership of a national minority, property, birth, disability, age or sexual orientation. Furthermore, Art. 23 CFR reinforces the prohibition of sexual discrimination in the workplace by stating that equality between men and women must be ensured in all areas, including employment, work and pay. If Arts. 21 and 23 CFR directly set out the prohibition of discrimination *inter alia* in the workplace, other provisions of the Charter indirectly contribute to the same aim. Paragraph 2 of Art. 33 shields parents from discrimination by stating that, in order to reconcile family and professional life, everyone shall have the right to protection from dismissal for a reason connected with maternity and the right to paid maternity leave and

[44] As pointed out in the Explanations by the *Praesidium*, this Article mirrors the content of Directive 89/391/EEC on the introduction of measures to encourage improvements in the safety and health of workers at work. It also draws on Art. 3 of the Social Charter and point 19 of the Community Charter on the rights of workers, and, as regards dignity at work, on Art. 26 of the revised Social Charter. Paragraph 2 is based on Directive 93/104/EC concerning certain aspects of the organisation of working time, on Art. 2 of the European Social Charter and on point 8 of the Community Charter on the rights of workers.

to parental leave following the birth or adoption of a child.[45] In addition, Arts. 15 and 16 CFR grant the right to choose an occupation and to engage in work[46] and the right to conduct a business, respectively.[47] These provisions imply that no one can be discriminated on the basis of the occupation or the business he/she freely chose to engage in.

Finally, the eradication of any form of exploitation of child labour is foreseen by Art. 32 CFR, which prohibits the employment of children altogether and prescribes appropriate levels of protection for young people at work. The provision indicates in particular the minimum age of admission to employment, which cannot be lower than the minimum school-leaving age. In addition, young people must enjoy working conditions appropriate to their age and must be protected against economic exploitation and against any occupation likely to harm their safety, health or physical, mental, moral or social development or to interfere with their education.[48]

Even if not directly reproducing the ILO core labour standards, other provisions of the Charter may equally affect the exercise of the rights and freedoms presented so far and, therefore, may have an impact on the Union's attitude towards the promotion of social rights in international trade. First of all, the exercise of the freedom of assembly and collective bargaining can be impaired should workers' right to get information and to consult within the undertaking not be guaranteed. Art. 27 CFR provides workers with such protection insofar as it prescribes that workers, or their

[45]The second paragraph of Art. 33 CFR draws on Council Directive 92/85/EEC on the introduction of measures to encourage improvements in the safety and health at work of pregnant workers and workers who have recently given birth or are breastfeeding and Directive 96/34/EC on the framework agreement on parental leave concluded by UNICE, CEEP and the ETUC. It is also based on Art. 8 (protection of maternity) of the European Social Charter and draws on Art. 27 (right of workers with family responsibilities to equal opportunities and equal treatment) of the revised Social Charter.

[46]Freedom to choose an occupation, as enshrined in Art. 15(1), is recognised in the case law of the Court of Justice (see *inter alia* Case 4/73 *Nold* [1974] ECR 491, paras 12 to 14; Case 44/79 *Hauer* [1979] ECR 3727; judgement of 8 October 1986, Case 234/85 *Keller* [1986] ECR 2897, para 8). This paragraph also draws upon Art. 1(2) of the European Social Charter, which was signed on 18 October 1961 and has been ratified by all the Member States, and on point 4 of the Community Charter of the Fundamental Social Rights of Workers of 9 December 1989.

[47]Art. 16 CFR is based on the Court of Justice's case law, which has recognised freedom to exercise an economic or commercial activity (see Case 4/73 *Nold*, n. 46 above, para 14, and Case 230/78 *SPA Eridiana and others* [1979] ECR 2749, paras 20 and 31) and freedom of contract (see *inter alia* Case 151/78 *Sukkerfabriken Nykøbing* [1979] ECR 1, para 19, and Case C-240/97 *Spain v. Commission* [1999] ECR I-6571, para 99) and Art. 4(1) and (2) TEC, which recognises free competition. The right to conduct a business is to be exercised in full compliance with Community law and national legislation. It may be subject to the limitations provided for in Art. 52(1) CFR.

[48]Art. 32 CFR is based on Directive 94/33/EC on the protection of young people at work, Art. 7 of the European Social Charter and points 20 to 23 of the Community Charter of the Fundamental Social Rights of Workers.

representatives, must be guaranteed information and consultation at the appropriate levels and under the conditions provided for by Community law and national laws.[49] Moreover, a natural corollary of the principle of non-discrimination in the workplace is the protection against unjustified dismissal, which is guaranteed by Art. 30 CFR.[50] Finally, also connected to the prohibition of discrimination is the Union's recognition of the entitlement to social security benefits and social services providing protection in cases such as maternity, illness, industrial accidents, dependency or old age, and in the case of loss of employment, as set out in Art. 34 CFR. The latter provision is complemented, at paragraph 3, by the recognition of the right to social and housing assistance with a view to ensure a decent existence for all those who lack sufficient resources.[51]

However, not all rights contained in the Charter are granted equal status. In this respect, a distinction has been proposed between provisions expressing policy clauses, ordinary rights and fundamental rights.[52] However, with regard to solidarity rights in particular, most of the rights of the worker or would-be worker are regarded as fundamental. Such is the case of the right to work, to equality, to protection for mothers, to collective bargaining and action, to healthy and safe working conditions, to limited working hours and paid holidays, as well as the case of the prohibition of child labour and the protection of young people at work.[53] Insofar as other more specific workers' rights in the Charter are concerned, they are to be considered as

[49] This Article appears in the revised European Social Charter (Art. 21) and in the Community Charter on the rights of workers (points 17 and 18). Also, there is a considerable Community *acquis* in this field: see, for instance, Directives 98/59/EC (collective redundancies), 77/187/EEC (transfers of undertakings) and 94/45/EC (European works councils).

[50] Art. 30 CFR is based on Art. 24 of the revised Social Charter. See also Directive 77/187/EEC on the safeguarding of employees' rights in the event of transfers of undertakings, and Directive 80/987/EEC on the protection of employees in the event of the insolvency of their employer.

[51] The principle set out in Art. 34(1) CFR is based on Arts. 137 and 140 of the EC Treaty and on Art. 12 of the European Social Charter and point 10 of the Community Charter on the rights of workers. The reference to social services relates to cases in which such services have been introduced to provide certain advantages but does not imply that such services must be created where they do not exist. The third paragraph draws on Arts. 30 and 31 of the revised Social Charter and point 10 of the Community Charter.

[52] A.J. Menéndez, *The rights' foundations of solidarity: Social and Economic rights in the Charter of Fundamental Rights of the European Union*, (2003) ARENA Working Papers WP 03/1, 5 ff. The difference between policy clauses, ordinary and fundamental rights lies in the issue of enforceability. In particular, Menéndez considers policy clauses those provisions of the Charter "that require public institutions to achieve a certain objective or goal, but without giving direct rise to any subjective fundamental position, [...] basically rights on which they can stand before courts".

[53] Ibid., Table 2, 9.

ordinary and not fundamental rights. The above mentioned rights to information and consultation within the undertaking, to social security benefits and to social assistance, as well as to protection in the event of unjustified dismissal are only granted status of ordinary rights.[54] This being so, it is once again apparent that fundamental workers rights as recognised within the EU perfectly coincide with, and do not go beyond, ILO prescriptions relating to core labour standards.

The provisions of the Charter presented above thus constitute the *trait d'union* between the protection of social rights within the European Union and the contribution the latter is giving to the promotion of core labour standards via more social-oriented international trade rules. Both the Commission and the Parliament had made reference to the Charter, prior to its entry into force, as one of the documents to be duly taken into account when defining the EU's position in this domain. European institutions deemed it appropriate to take the Charter into account even before it became legally binding.[55]

The question arises whether the entry into force of the Lisbon treaty and the attribution to the Charter of the same legal value of the founding treaties will change the previous situation by modifying the nature of the rights contained in the Charter from mere source of inspiration for European institutions to proper obligations under EU law. In other words, the issue to be addressed is whether binding provisions relating to workers rights will lead the EU to change its stance in relation to the promotion of core labour standards in the framework of international trade governance.

5 EU Charter Social Rights and Future Developments in EU Practice Relating to the International Promotion of Core Labour Standards: A Real Change After Lisbon?

The entry into force of the Lisbon Treaty will grant solidarity a predominant place in the system of principles characterising the EU legal order. In particular, being the success of the Charter linked in some way to that of the Lisbon Treaty, the relationship between these two instruments casts new light on the external projection of social rights guaranteed within the Union, particularly in the framework of the Common Commercial Policy.

In order to ascertain what effect workers' rights may have on the Union's attitude towards the promotion of core labour standards in international

[54] Ibid., Table 1, 8.

[55] On the impact of the Charter on the activity of the European Parliament see in this volume F. Camporesi, Chapter 14.

trade now that the Lisbon Treaty has entered into force, attention must be paid to more concrete aspects such as the scope of those rights and the function they may perform in relation to the Union's CCP.

5.1 *The Effects of the Charter Rights Beyond EU Borders*

If one is to analyse the potential effects of the recognition of the social rights included in the Charter on the EU stance in international trade negotiations, the scope of those rights must first of all be considered. The question arises whether the scope of the Charter is intended to be limited to the citizens of the Union or whether far-reaching effects can be acknowledged to the rights contained therein.

The Charter confers rights not only upon the citizens of the Union but also on citizens of third countries in so far as they are physically placed within the EU territory. This conclusion can be derived from the wording of the Preamble, where no explicit link is made between the enjoyment of rights under the Charter and the status of EU citizens. If it is true that the second paragraph of the Preamble refers to the notion of citizenship, this only highlights that the EU "places the individual at the heart of its activities". What is more, the last paragraph of the Preamble states that "The Union [...] recognises the rights, freedoms and principles set out hereafter". Once more the recognition of rights is general in nature, indicating that the drafters intended to extend the conferral of rights to persons other than EU citizens. Thus, it is the individual acting under the European jurisdiction, rather than just the European citizen, to be entitled to social rights under the Charter.

Moreover, the textual analysis of the Charter highlights that, except for rights connected to the European citizenship under Chapter V, other rights and freedoms are conferred upon "everyone" and "every worker", whereas prohibitions are imposed in relation to "no one", without any further specification as for nationality of the protected individual. This further confirms that also citizens of third countries are entitled to rights enshrined in the Charter, including social rights.

Certain provisions explicitly specify that the respective rights are also conferred upon citizens of third countries legally residing in the Union. Suffice it here to recall the freedom of choosing an occupation and the freedom of circulation within the territory of the Union. This means that all rights other than those recognised to European citizens alone or the enjoyment of which can be extended to citizens of third countries legally residing in the EU are to be considered of general applicability, and as such conferred upon every person acting within the European jurisdiction.

The applicability of the Charter to all individuals is a counterweight to the fact that, regardless of the circumstance that they are not Member States nationals, citizens of third countries are subject to the same obligations under the law of the Union and of its Member States. Referring in particular to social rights, given the increasing employment of foreigners in almost all sectors of European economy, particularly in labour intensive ones, denying the recognition of the Charter rights to nationals of third countries would undermine the stated objective of creating an even closer union among the peoples of Europe.[56]

More controversial is the case of nationals of third countries who do not live, and work, within the EU but who are nonetheless, even if only indirectly, affected by EU policy and treaty-making. The EU Common Commercial Policy is mainly enacted through the conclusion of trade agreements, both bilateral and multilateral, which involve third countries as trade partners. The terms of these agreements thus have an impact on the economy of the latter, particularly when these are developing or least developed countries. In this case, economy restructuring with a view to specialising in particular productions in order to accommodate European market demands can affect the respect of workers rights in the partner country. Thus the conclusion of a trade agreement with the European Union has an impact on social conditions of workers in that country. In the light of the new binding force of the Charter, the question is whether EU institutions are bound by the solidarity provisions contained therein while drafting the terms of an agreement under the CCP. In other words, are European institutions also supposed to protect the social rights of third country workers by negotiating commercial clauses that are respectful of core labour standards?

As previously noted, in the second paragraph of the Charter Preamble the Union is said to be "founded on the indivisible, universal values of human dignity, freedom, equality and solidarity". What is interesting here is the universal character recognised to the values that the rights of the Charter are intended to promote. One could envisage a positive answer to the aforementioned question on the basis that solidarity is conceived as a universal value and that therefore solidarity rights under the Charter are to be respected by EU institutions when exerting theirs powers, even beyond the borders of the EU. However, from a strictly legal standpoint, it is at least doubtful whether the Charter could be interpreted so as to confer rights upon citizens of third countries, even via an act of the European institutions such as a commercial agreement. The fact that such an act may indirectly affect the individual situation of workers in third countries does not automatically imply that the latter can claim the violation of their rights under the Charter.

Nonetheless, social rights in the Charter can indirectly influence the EU stance in commercial negotiations. In this context, the value of the Charter operates as a normative guideline in policy-making as well as a parameter of legality for acts adopted by the institutions.

---

[56]In this respect see Case C-22/03 *Optiver BV and Others* [2005] ECR I-1839.

5.2 *The Charter as Parameter of Legality for the EU's Commercial Policy*

Arts. 2 and 3(3) of the reformed Treaty on the European Union, inspired by the wording of the Charter's Preamble, introduce a novelty insofar as they count the principle of solidarity amongst the values common to European societies and amongst the objectives of the Union. It has been noted that the Charter will represent the natural specification and the more appropriate tool for the interpretation of Art. 2 TEU.[57]

As far as the external action of the Union is concerned, Arts. 3(5) and 21(1) TEU state that the Union's action on the international scene shall comply *inter alia* with the principle of solidarity. Solidarity thus becomes a guidelines of all aspects of the Community external relations, including the Common Commercial policy.

Moreover, the new Art. 6(1) TEU confers upon the Charter the same legal value as the founding Treaties. Therefore, with the entry into force of the Lisbon Treaty, the rights codified in the Charter acquires constitutional value within the European legal order. This implies the obligation for European institutions to respect the rights, freedoms and prohibitions contained therein. A breach of such obligations will in turn result in the annulment of the relevant acts by the EUCJ.[58]

Therefore, the Charter acts as a parameter of legality also in relation to international agreements concluded by the Union in the context of the CCP. Should a commercial agreement be found in breach of workers' rights contained in the Charter, its validity would be excluded by the Court. Given that workers' rights in the Charter essentially correspond to the ILO core labour rights, the Charter amounts to an additional tool enabling the Union to effectively contribute to the promotion of core labour standards worldwide. Nothing less, but certainly nothing more.

A critical aspect concerns the fact that it is highly unlikely that the Union will conclude commercial agreements in manifest violation of core labour standards. Therefore, attention should be paid to the indirect impact that such an agreement might have on these standards by the commercial partner. This would be for the Court to ascertain when reviewing the legitimacy of the act. However, on the one hand, it is questionable whether this falls within the competences of the Court; on the other, it is doubtful that the latter possesses the expertise to conduct such an inquiry. Such an assessment would in fact entail a very detailed economic analysis aimed at pointing the changes that the entry into force of the commercial agreement has caused in the respective economies and focusing in particular on the consequences

---

[57] L.S. Rossi, 'Il rapporto tra Trattato di Lisbona e Carta dei Diritti Fondamentali dell'UE', in G. Bronzin, F. Guariello; V. Piccon, *Le scommesse dell'Europa. Istituzioni, diritti, politiche* (Ediesse, 2009).

[58] Ibid.

for labour. Whereas the Commission disposes of the aforementioned mechanism for the Sustainability Impact Assessment to be employed before the conclusion of the agreement, the same cannot be said for the Court of Justice.

5.3 *Will the Charter be a Real Watershed?*

Apart from representing a parameter for the legitimacy of commercial agreements concluded by the Union, the Charter does not impose any obligation to internationally promote core labour standards on the European institutions. In other words, the latter are not at all bound by any of its provisions to be more assertive in this domain.

The Charter has been conceived from the very beginning not as an instrument codifying new rights and prohibitions, but rather as a catalogue that formally recognises rights de facto already in force through different sources of the Union legal order, such as international law, the constitutional traditions common to all Member States, the European Convention on Human Rights, Community and Union acts and judgements of the Court of Justice.[59]

Therefore, it can be said that the active role played so far by the European institutions from the early battles for the promotion of core labour standards in the multilateral trade framework was precisely based on the ground of fundamental rights already recognised within the Union order. This being so, one can legitimately doubt that the introduction of a binding instrument will produce a redirection in the European attitude, thus representing a watershed in the conduct of the Common Commercial Policy.

6 Final Remarks

The international community has been discussing the introduction of a social clause in multilateral agreements governing trade libersalisation for quite some time. The debate revolves around the insertion of a criterion of social conditionality in the context of multilateral trade governance, as well as around the involvement of the WTO in the enhancement of working conditions worldwide. The insertion of a social clause in multilateral trade agreements would undoubtedly promote the foundation of a social dimension of international trade. In fact, the sanctioning mechanism characterising the clause would make it far more effective than the international instruments currently in force, particularly the ILO conventions.

---

[59] Ibid.

The function of the social clause would be to refer to certain norms to apply in the workplace as parameters of social conditionality, thus creating a set of standards applicable to the benefits deriving from the liberalisation of international trade. In fact, within the international community there is an established *opinio juris* according to which certain core labour standards are of universal application, which are looked at as fundamental human rights. Therefore, it has been submitted that the social clause would be an instrument of codification of principles already in force under customary international law.

The European Union has so far given a significant contribution to the debate on how to establish a social dimension in international trade. This Chapter has indeed addressed the role of the EU Charter in this respect. The focus has been in particular on whether the provisions of the Charter impose on the EU institutions specific obligations regarding the promotion of labour standards vis-à-vis third countries.

As indicated, the EU's approach has long been based upon three main principles, namely the universality of core labour standards, the rejection of any sanction-based approaches and the support for the work of the ILO and for the co-operation between the latter and other international organisations such as the WTO. Since 1992, all agreements concluded between the EC and third countries have incorporated a human rights clause which also encompasses core labour standards (as set out in the ILO Conventions). Having regard to specific measures adopted in the framework of its trade policy, the EU promotes core labour standards by requiring conditionality unilaterally through the GSP and the GSP+. The 'punitive approach' coexists with a special regime of incentives for sustainable development and good governance. The new GSP has already had the significant result of speeding up the ratification of ILO core labour standards conventions; however, the Commission has recently underlined the need to make the instrument even more performing.

Regarding the protection of social rights within Europe, the Preamble of the Charter defines solidarity as one of the indivisible and universal values founding the European Union, together with human dignity, freedom and equality. The social rights proclaimed in the Charter can be ascribed to four macro areas corresponding to core labour standards recognised as such by the international community. These rights constitute the *trait d'union* between the protection of social rights within the European Union and the contribution the latter is giving to the promotion of core labour standards via the promotion of more social-oriented international trade rules. Even before the entry into force of the Lisbon Treaty, European institutions had already made reference to the Charter in official documents, notwithstanding the fact that it had no legal bite at that time.

It has been noted that, in any event, the Charter does not impose any *specific obligation* on the European institutions to internationally promote core labour standards. With the Lisbon Treaty in force, the Charter will certainly be granted a more concrete role. Under Art. 6(1) TEU it has acquired the status of primary Union law, thus acting as parameter of the legitimacy of acts of European institutions, including commercial agreements entered into by the Union. However, the Charter has been primarily conceived as a catalogue formally recognizing rights which are already de facto in force. It has been argued that the active role played so far by the European institutions for the promotion of core labour standards in the multilateral trade framework has precisely been based on this assumption. Therefore, it has been suggested that it is at least questionable whether the introduction a binding Charter will change the attitude of the EU, further enhancing its support for core labour rights. In other words, it is difficult to see how the Charter could 'upgrade' what is already a top priority for the EU.

The Lisbon Treaty confirms and expands the previous normative arrangements on the need to guarantee that the Union's external action is coherent. In general terms, Art. 7 TFEU states that: "The Union shall ensure consistency between its policies and activities, taking all of its objectives into account and in accordance with the principle of conferral of powers". More precisely, consistency must be ensured between the different external policies and actions taken by the Union. Art. 26 TEU entrusts this delicate task to the Council and the High Representative of the Union for Foreign Affairs and Security Policy. On the other hand, it is of the utmost importance that the action taken at the internal and external level is coherent. To that effect, Art. 21 (3) TEU specifically requires the Union to "ensure consistency between the different areas of its external action and between these and its other policies". When it comes to the coordination between internal and external aspects of EU policies, not only the Council and the High Representative, but also the Commission is called upon to ensure such consistency, whereas all these institutions act under the duty to cooperate to that effect.

Given the consistency requirement, with a binding Charter imposing a certain standard of protection within the EU legal order, it would undoubtedly become difficult to explain an uneven commitment towards fundamental rights promotion outside the Union. This would certainly pose major problems in terms of policy consistency, which – as just said – the Lisbon Treaty aims at guaranteeing.

The European Charter of Fundamental Rights After Lisbon: A "Timid" Trojan Horse in the Domain of the Common Foreign and Security Policy?

Luca Paladini

1 Preliminary Remarks

The entry into force of the Lisbon Treaty[1] and the binding nature of the Charter of Fundamental Rights (hereafter, CFR or the Charter) proclaimed therein[2] calls for a close analysis of the possible consequences on the functioning of the Common Foreign and Security Policy (hereinafter, CFSP).

The general obligation to respect fundamental rights extends to all domains falling within the EU competences so that the Charter will also apply to the CFSP, regardless of the specificities which will continue to characterize it. This will of course represent a limit to the traditional discretionary power reserved to the EU Council in this field of law. Moreover, the reform has provided for a legal remedy that individuals can activate.

The combination of these two innovations should permit a more extensive and effective protection of fundamental rights when dealing with sensitive issues such as the fight against terrorism. As will be seen, this undoubtedly represents a major turning point in the evolution of the EU legal order which will force the amendment of the much criticized practice concerning restrictive measures against individuals, one of the most common 'CFSP tools' in contrasting terrorism.

L. Paladini (✉)
Robert Schuman Centre for Advanced Studies, European University Institute, Florence, Italy
e-mail: luca.paladini@eui.eu

[1]Amongst the various commentaries on the Reform Treaty, see S. Griller and J. Ziller, *The Lisbon Treaty. EU Constitutionalism without a Constitutional Treaty?* (Springer, 2008) and M. Dougan M., 'The Treaty of Lisbon 2007: winning minds, not hearts', (2008) 45 *Common Market Law Review* 617.

[2][2007] OJ C 303/1. For an exhaustive overview of the legal doctrine on the subject-matter, see in this volume G. Di Federico, Chapter 2'.

G. Di Federico, *The EU Charter of Fundamental Rights*, Ius Gentium: Comparative Perspectives on Law and Justice 8, DOI 10.1007/978-94-007-0156-4_14,

With a view to assess the impact of a binding Charter on the legislative and executive acts adopted in this field, this Chapter will examine the relation between the Charter and the CFSP after the entry into force of the Lisbon Treaty with particular regard to measures adopted against individuals. A brief outline of the previous practice regarding restrictive measures will suffice to single out the fundamental rights criticalities in this area. Particular attention will be devoted to the case law developed by the community courts, starting from, and concluding with, the landmark *Yusuf* and *Kadi* judgements.[3] Lastly, the general duty to respect fundamental rights and the new legal remedy introduced into the CFSP will be addressed. On the one side, it will be interesting to verify the possible impact of a legally binding Charter on the ex ante control concerning the adoption of CFSP acts; on the other, attention should be paid to the ex post mechanism of judicial review provided for under Art. 275 of the Treaty on the Functioning of the European Union (TFEU). The combination of these two elements can be provocatively depicted (the question is obviously open to debate) as a Trojan horse allowing for a possible communitarization of the CFSP.

2 The New Article 6 TEU and the Binding Nature of Charter

After the amendments brought about by the Lisbon reform, Art. 6 TEU reads:

> The Union recognises the rights, freedoms and principles set out in the Charter of Fundamental Rights of the European Union of 7 December 2000, as adapted at Strasbourg, on 12 December 2007, which shall have the same legal value as the Treaties.

By expressly affirming the binding nature of Charter,[4] despite its collocation outside the treaties,[5] the provision expresses with renewed vigour the limit of the respect of fundamental rights in the EU legal system. Furthermore, it should be underlined that Art. 51 of the Charter provides that the Istitutions and Member States implementing Union law will have to respect the rights and principle enshrined therein when implementing EU law. Moreover, they will have to promote the observance of the

---

[3]See Case T-306/01 *Yusuf and Al Barakaat* [2005] ECR II-3533; Case T-315/01 *Kadi* [2005] ECR II-3649 and Joined cases C-402 and 415/05 P *Kadi and Al Barakaat* [2008] ECR I-6351.

[4]As pointed out by G. Strozzi, 'Prime considerazioni sul Trattato di Lisbona', 2008, online: www.sudineuropa.net the Charter amounts to a treaty with the same legal value as the TEU.

[5]It has been argued that compared with the collocation it had in the Constitutional Treaty, the Charter might be perceived as "less important". By contrast, some authors have suggested that being placed outside the treaties the Charter acquires more visibility to the advantage of all Europeans. See J. Ziller, *Il nuovo Trattato europeo* (Bologna, 2007), at 135; L.S. Rossi, 'I diritti fondamentali nel Trattato di Lisbona', 2007, online: www.europeanrights.eu.

Charter in accordance with their respective powers. In this regard it has been stated that "giving the Charter legally binding force would incite the EU institutions to pay 'the utmost attention to respecting these fundamental rights.'"[6] This undoubtedly reflects the EU commitment to respect the rights included in the Charter. Finally, the envisaged accession of the EU to the ECHR should be noted.[7]

This set of provisions is not completely innovative, but outlines a legal framework for the protection of fundamental rights which seems to have clearer contours and to be more effective than the previous one.

3 The CFSP After the Treaty of Lisbon (a Brief Outline)

It goes beyond the scope of this contribution to dwell on the many institutional reforms introduced by the Lisbon Treaty but it appears nonetheless necessary to frame the CFSP in the new EU legal system.

It is well known that the Reform Treaty has inherited a good deal of the results achieved in adopting what has been defined as the unlucky Constitutional Treaty,[8] although removing, in a sort of 'iconoclastic fury',[9] all provisions (vaguely) recalling the idea of a Constitution. The EU is a single organization with international legal personality;[10] its activities will be regulated by the TEU and by the TFEU; the traditional three-pillar structure has been dismantled and the EU appears as a monolith[11] (still, the issue is open to debate as some commentators argue that it stands on two columns).[12]

The CFSP maintains its specificity[13] departing from the Community method. The CFSP is regulated by the provisions of Title V TEU and it

---

[6]See House of Lords, EU Committee, Tenth Report of Session 2007–2008, *The Treaty of Lisbon: an impact assessment,* Vol. I, (London, 2007–2008), at 98.

[7]On the possible consequences of such an accession, see in this volume the contribution by G. Di Federico, n. 2 above.

[8]See A. Aust, *Modern Treaty Law and Practice* (Cambridge University Press, 2007) at 419.

[9]See U. Villani, 'La riforma di Lisbona', 2008, online: www.sudineuropa.net.

[10]This view appears to be shared, amongst others, by the House of Lords that stated: "there is just one organization, the Union" (House of Lords n. 6 above, at 19).

[11]For example, Sir Jacobs reckons that "a patchwork system (...) widely regarded as opaque, incoherent and generally unsatisfactory" (House of Lords, n. 6 above, at 19) will be removed. This opinion is shared by M. Dony, *Après la reforme de Lisbonne – Les nouveaux traités européens* (Éditions de l'Université de Bruxelles, 2008) at XIII, who insists on the disruption of the three pillar structure.

[12]Dashwood argues that: "...the result of the Reform Treaty would be to create a two-pillar structure" (House of Lords, n. 6 above, at 181).

[13]See new Art. 11 TEU. With reference to the possible "future scenarios" for the CFSP/ESDP provisions (and their implementation), see R. Whitman and A. Junicos 'The Lisbon Treaty and the Foreign, Security and Defence Policy: Reforms, Implementation and the Consequences of (non-)Ratification' (2009) *European Foreign Affairs Review* 25.

is part of the EU's external action. The objectives of the latter include the activities previously shared between the Community (external relations) and the Union (CFSP). It follows that the EU's external action should have a composite yet consistent structure, as confirmed by the new Art. 21 (2) TEU.

Notwithstanding these peculiarities, it should be underlined that the CFSP shall comply with the CFR. In fact, as previously indicated, the latter has a general scope of application and its provisions must be respected in all fields falling within EU competences.

4 The CFSP Practice on Restrictive Measures

That being said, it is possible to analyze the CFSP practice on restrictive measures and the problems related to an effective protection of fundamental rights. In this regard, the procedure followed for imposing such measures on States and individuals has originated an intense political, institutional and doctrinal debate. The concerns expressed for fundamental rights violations seemed to be comforted by the findings of the Court of First instance in the *OMPI* judgement,[14] and of the European Court of Justice (hereafter ECJ or EUCJ) in the *Kadi* appeal.[15] Independently from the clarifications which may result from the pending cases, it is suggested that the binding nature of the Charter and the future CFSP regime will prevent dangerous backslides.

The practice on restrictive measures preceeds the creation of the EU by the Maastricht Treaty; for instance, sanctions were imposed on Argentina during the Falkland-Malvinas war in 1982 and on China for the violent repressions which took place in the Tiananmen Square in 1989.[16] These sanctions are functional to the attainment of one of the main goals of the CFSP, namely maintaining peace and international security. Indeed, they have often been ordered pursuant to the United Nations Security Council (UNSC) resolutions adopting sanctions. The use of such measures is considered "an important way to maintain and restore international peace and security in accordance with the principles of the UN Charter and of our common foreign and security policy" and it is part of the "efforts to fight terrorism and the proliferation of weapons of mass destruction and as a

[14]Case T-228/02 *Organisation des Modjahedines* [2006] ECR II-4665.

[15]See n. 3 above.

[16]As to the former, see B. Conforti, *Le sanzioni CEE contro l'Argentina e la loro legittimità alla luce del diritto comunitario*, in N. Ronzitti, *La questione delle Falkland-Malvinas nel diritto internazionale* (Giuffré, 1984). The latter stem from the Declaration by the European Council of Madrid, 27 June 1989. See generally European Commission, *Sanctions or restrictive measures in force (measures adopted in the framework of the CFSP)*, online: http://ec.europa.eu/external_relations/cfsp/sanctions/measures.htm.

restrictive measure to uphold respect for human rights, democracy, the rule of law and good governance."[17] These are CFSP objectives, as confirmed by Art. 11 TEU. Moreover, the EU Council uses restrictive measures "as part of an integrated, comprehensive policy approach which should include political dialogue, incentives, conditionality and could even involve, as a last resort, the use of coercive measures in accordance with the UN Charter,"[18] and therefore as one of the EU's external action legal instruments.

Under the former treaties, the mechanism of imposing sanctions was based on the adoption of a CFSP Common Position against third States or individuals. The responsibility to implement the latter rested with the Member States.[19] Naturally, if the Common Position involved the exercise of a Community competence, namely when the measure ordered the freezing of funds, the adoption of an EC Regulation was also necessary.[20]

5 Restrictive Measures Directed to States

For the purposes of this contribution, the focus will be on measures imposed on individuals. Still, given their scope of application, some clarifications are needed with respect to the many sanctions adopted against third States.[21] Firstly, it should be noted that also individuals holding a public office can be affected by these measures. This occurs because of the overlap of their official activities with the conduct of the State (so-called smart sanctions[22]). This bond has been considered enough to justify the

---

[17] European Union Council, *Basic Principles on the Use of Restrictive Measures (Sanctions)" of 7 June 2004*, doc. 10198/1/04.

[18] Ibid.

[19] For example, the Member States – if so required by the EU act – will have to impose an embargo or provide for a visa ban against individuals. This obligation derives from the principle of loyal cooperation which is inherent to the EU legal order (see Case C-105/03 *Pupino* [2005] ECR I-5185, para 42). With particular reference to the CFSP, this principle is specifically invoked in Art. 11 TEU. See also Council of the European Union, *Update of the EU Best Practices for the effective implementation of restrictive measures*, Brussels, 24 April 2008, doc 8666/1/08.

[20] See *Guidelines on implementation and evaluation of the restrictive measures in the framework of CFSP* of December 2003 (online: http://register.consilium.eu.int/pdf/en/05/st15/st15114.en05.pdf). The version of this document dated 2 December 2005 includes a sort of *vademecum* to follow in drafting CFSP acts and EC regulations.

[21] Amongst the possible sanctions: embargo, suspension of political contacts and freezing of funds.

[22] The aim is to exercise an effective pressure on the targeted regimes while containing the economic and social repercussions that such measures can produce. See M. Garhagnati Ketvel, 'The jurisdiction of the European Court of Justice in respect of the Common Foreign and Security Policy' (2006) *International and Comparative Law Quarterly* 107.

sanctions, although the responsibility of the subject in question has not been demonstrated before an impartial tribunal established by law, which is not exactly in line with the presumption of innocence, the right to a fair trial and the right of defence.

In other cases individuals are not public servants but "associated persons". A well-known example is represented by Common Position 2000/626/CFSP ordering measures against the Federal Republic of Yugoslavia.[23] The latter affected the former President Milosevic, but also some persons associated to him, including relatives. Naturally, there are other more recent cases, such as, for instance, the measures adopted against Liberia[24] and Burma.[25] On other occasions, the "associated persons" were legal entities and persons who benefited from the government's economic policy as, for instance, in the case of Iran.[26] As to relatives – parents, brothers, wives, sons and sons-in-law – the link with the State is the relationship with a member of the governmental apparatus (even if already deceased).[27] In this regard, the *Guidelines on implementation and evaluation of the restrictive measures in the framework of EU CFSP*[28] clarify that, in principle, individuals should not be targeted because of their civil status, but on the basis of their effective responsibility.[29] Relatives can therefore be targeted in order to freeze funds that were hidden through registrations of convenience (i.e. registered in favour of relatives, but available to the members of the governmental structures) in presence of clear elements of liability.

Those responsibilities do not emerge from the respective CFSP acts.[30] Here a distinction should be drawn between lists which are drafted and updated directly by the EU and lists which are elaborated within the UNSC. The former have been subject to judicial review via the relevant EC regulations freezing funds since the *OMPI* judgement of 12 December 2006,

---

[23] Common Position 2000/696/CFSP, [2000] OJ L 287/1.

[24] Common Position 2004/487/CFSP and EC Regulation 872/2004, [2004] OJ L 162, and following modifications.

[25] Common Position 2006/318/CFSP, [2006] OJ L 116 and EC Regulation 194/2008, [2008] OJ L 66, and following modifications.

[26] Common Position 2007/140/CFSP, [2007] OJ L 61 and EC Regulation, [2007] 423/2007.

[27] As occurred, for example, with the daughter (and her husband) of the dead former Burmese Prime Minister Soe Win, n. 25 above.

[28] See *Guidelines on implementation and evaluation of the restrictive measures in the framework of CFSP*, n. 20 above.

[29] See the 2005 version of the *Guidelines on implementation and evaluation of the restrictive measures in the framework of CFSP*, n. 20 above, p. 7. The document refers only to children, but this criterion should apply also to other relatives.

[30] In the case of Burma, the Common Positions refers to the deterioration of the internal situation and the only indication concerning relatives concerns children under 18, who in principle should not be targeted.

where the CFI insisted on the need for the EU to respect fundamental rights and partially annulled the contested measures. Common Positions and the respective EC Regulations had to be well founded, i.e. refer to the concrete responsibilities of the relatives (and/or of the individuals benefiting from the governmental economic policy[31]) or at least to the existence of some documents demonstrating such responsibilities. This was even more desirable since the funds available to the individuals are not necessarily registrations of convenience. And yet no trace of such motivations appeared in the CFSP acts.

The situation was rather different when the relevant CFSP act transposed in toto the list approved by the UNSC. With reference to these cases the CFI stated that the EU measure escaped the scrutiny of the Courts. In *Minin*, it dismissed the action by virtue of "the restriction on the review of legality that the Court must carry out in respect of Community measures implementing decisions of the Security Council or of its Sanctions Committee."[32] As anticipated, though, in the *Kadi* appeal the ECJ stated that implementing UN resolutions does not exclude a judicial review of EC acts concerning fundamental rights violations.

6 Restrictive Measures Against Non-state Actors

Most of the restrictive measures against non-State actors were decided after the terroristic attacks of 11 September 2001, in the framework of the international antiterrorism strategy. The EU adopted restrictive measures against non-State actors before 2001, although less frequently and without raising the attention which characterizes the most recent ones. The first measures ordered against individuals can be found in Common Position 97/193/CFSP concerning the Mostar incidents,[33] where sanctions were imposed on persons identified as the perpetrators of violent

---

[31]See Case T-181/08 *Tay ZA*, pending. Here, an individual – Mr. Tay ZA – has claimed to annul EC Regulation 194/2008, [2008] OJ L 66/1, repealing EC Regulation 817/2006, which lists him amongst the targeted persons in the context of the sanctions against Burma without specifying the reasons for this, thereby violating his right to property, to a fair hearing and to an effective judicial protection.

[32]Case T-362/04 *Minin* [2007] ECR II-2003, para 101. Mr. Minin was listed as an associated person in the framework of Common Position 2004/487/CFSP, [2004] OJ L 162/116 concerning restrictive measures against Liberia, in particular its former President Taylor and other associated persons and entities. The CFSP act transposed into EU law the list drawn up by the Sanctions Committee created by the UNSC Resolution 1521 (2003). Amongst the sanctions there was the freezing of funds, established by EC Regulation 872/2004, [2004] OJ L 162/32. The applicant was listed (see EC Regulation 1149/2004, [2004] OJ L 222/17) because the subject had been deemed to finance the former President Taylor.

[33][1997] OJ L 81/1.

crimes.[34] In accordance with the recommendations made by the Office of the High Representative in Sarajevo, the Common Position prescribed a visa ban against them.[35] More recently, the EU has passed Common Position 2004/133/CFSP on extremists in the Former Yugoslav Republic of Macedonia (FYROM).[36]

In both instances, the (alleged) responsibilities had not been proven in the course of a fair trial before an impartial tribunal, as in the case of restrictive measures imposed on Third States (and associated persons). Similarly, the listing procedure failed to establish adequate guarantees for the addressees but with the notable difference that in the latter case the affected subjects were individuals. Moreover, in the Mostar and FYROM cases the decision to adopt the aforementioned sanctions was based on the recommendations of the High Representative, whose nature and powers have been the object of a lively doctrinal debate.[37]

Since the ECJ lacked jurisdiction over acts adopted in the second pillar, individuals were left with no effective judicial remedy. Moreover, such Common Positions did not entail the adoption of an EC regulation and no act could actually be contested before the Court. These shortcomings[38] were addressed in *Segi* and *Gestoras* where the judges acknowledged that the legal protection offered by the EU in the field of CFSP was less extensive than under the first and third pillars.[39]

---

[34]The list included three persons (the deputy Chief of the Mostar Police and two officers) deemed to be responsible for shooting some Muslims that went to the cemetery to visit the graves of their dead relatives.

[35]The International Police Task Force (UN) and the local police have carried out the necessary investigations in order to arrest and proceed against persons deemed to have committed war crimes (OHR Bulletin 37, 18 February 1997, online: http://www.ohr.int/). The IPTF handed in a report (26 March 1997), indicating three individuals "identified" as authors of the shooting against escaping persons (OHR Bulletin 38, 26 February 1997; OHR Bulletin 42, 29 March 1997).

[36][2004] OJ L 39/19 amended by Common Position 2009/116/CFSP, [2009] OJ L 40/56.

[37]L. Gradoni, 'L'Alto rappresentante per la Bosnia-Erzegovina davanti alla Corte europea dei diritti dell'uomo' (2008) 3 *Rivista di diritto internazionale* 621.

[38]Regarding measures against Macedonians, see Cases T-349/99 *Miskovic* and T-350/99 *Karic*. Here, the claimants argued that the Council lacked competence to order visa bans in the domain of CFSP. Unfortunately, the CFI did not render a judgement in these cases as the applications were dismissed after the revision Council Decision 1999/612/CFSP.

[39]The jurisdiction of the Court in the domain of CFSP is limited under Arts. 46 and 47 TEU. The ECJ was nevertheless competent to ensure that acts of the CFSP did not encroach upon the powers conferred by the EC Treaty to the Community. The first judgement on an hypothetical 'trespassing' of the CFSP in the competences of the Community was handed down on 20 May 2008. See Case C-91/05 *ECOWAS* [2008] ECR I-3651, where the Court found that the Council had infringed Art. 47 TEU by adopting a decision in the domain of the CFSP, instead of a first pillar act (since the provision fell within the development cooperation policy) and therefore annulled the contested measure (see, in particular, paras 75–78). See further C. Hillion, R.A. Wessel, 'Competence distribution

6.1 Restrictive Measures Against Non-state Actors in Fighting Terrorism and the Listing Procedures

With particular regard to restrictive measures directed to non-State actors in the context of the fight against terrorism, two CFSP acts implementing UNSC resolutions after the attacks of 9/11 are noteworthy: Common Position 2001/931/CFSP of 27 December 2001 on the application of specific measures to combat terrorism[40] and Common Position 2002/402/CFSP of 27 May 2002 concerning restrictive measures against Usama bin Laden, members of the Al-Qaida organisation and the Taliban and other individuals, groups, undertakings and entities associated with them.[41] Providing for the freezing of funds, both acts required the adoption of an EC Regulation.[42] Still, while the list attached to the former was established by the Council,[43] the list annexed to the latter had been elaborated by the Sanction Committee created in accordance with UNSC resolution 1267 (hereinafter, the "1267 Committee") and simply transposed into EU law by virtue of the Common position.[44]

The procedure followed in drafting the lists undoubtedly represents the most problematic aspect[45] and deserves further consideration. As far as Common Position 2001/931/CFSP is concerned, the list was elaborated on the basis of "precise information" or "material in the relevant file which indicates that a decision has been taken by a competent authority in respect of the persons, groups and entities concerned, irrespective

in EU external relations after ECOWAS: Clarification or continued fuzziness?' (2009) 46 *Common Market Law Rev.* 551 at 556 and L. Paladini, 'I conflitti fra i pilastri dell'Unione europea e le prospettive del Trattato di Lisbona' (2010) *Il Diritto dell'Unione Europea*, (forthcoming).

[40] [2001] OJ L 344/93. Common Position 2001/931/CFSP was adopted to implement UNSC resolution 1373 (2001) and subsequently amended by Common Position 2009/468/CFSP, [2009] OJ L 151/45. See also Common Position 2001/930/CFSP, adopted on the same day.

[41] [2001] OJ L 139/4. The Common Position was adopted to implement UNSC resolutions 1267 (1999) and 1390 (2002).

[42] See EC Regulation 2580/2001, [2001] OJ L 344/70 and EC Regulation 881/2002, [2002] OJ L 139/9, respectively.

[43] See Art. 1 of the Common Position.

[44] Art. 7 of EC Regulation 881/2002 entitled the Commission to amend the list in accordance with the indications provided by the UNSC or the '1267 Committee'. This has occurred 114 times, the last of which in 2009 (see EC Regulation 954/2009, [2009] OJ L 269/20). The 101st amendment was necessary to comply with the judgements in the Kadi and Al Barakaat appeal cases. Having confirmed the measures against Mr. Kadi, EC Regulation 1190/2008, [2008] OJ L 322/25 is the object of case T-85/09, *Kadi*, pending before the GC.

[45] See G. Armone, *Terrorismo, listing e diritti umani*, 2007, online: www.europeanrights.eu.

of whether it concerns the instigation of investigations or prosecution for a terrorist act, an attempt to perpetrate, participate in or facilitate such an act based on serious and credible evidence or clues, or condemnation for such deeds."[46] The list could include persons, groups and entities identified by the UNSC as being related to terrorism and against whom sanctions have been ordered. A periodical review is contemplated and was carried out by the EU through the adoption of other Common Positions.[47]

In 2007 the procedure was reviewed with the aim of making it more transparent.[48] Its criticalities had long been underscored and ultimately led the CFI, in the above mentioned *OMPI* judgement,[49] to state that in drafting the list of targeted individuals the EU must respect fundamental rights. Pursuant to the new procedure, the act adopting sanctions against individuals shall be motivated so that: (a) the individuals are informed of the reasons for their listing and (b) the Court will be able to carry out the judicial review requested by the applicant. Moreover, individuals will be informed, both through notification and publication in the Official Journal.

Notwithstanding these improvements, the procedure is still not able to fully guarantee the respect of fundamental rights. For example, the reference to the "perceived future intentions" as one of the elements that can justify a revision of the list appears arbitrary and difficult to reconcile with the rule of law.[50]

As to Common Position 2002/402/CFSP, the list was elaborated by the "1267 Committee" following the *Guidelines of the Committee for the conduct of its work*:[51] an intergovernmental procedure, lacking guarantees for the protection of fundamental rights. As pointed out by AG Poiares Maduro in his opinion in *Kadi*,[52] the procedure does not allow access to the information on which the decision to include the individual in the list was based. In addition, it fails to provide for judicial review of the contested

[46]For the purposes of the procedure "competent authority" shall mean a judicial authority or an equivalent competent authority.

[47]See Common Position 2007/448/CFSP, [2007] OJ L 169/69 and 2007/871/CFSP, [2007] OJ L 340/109.

[48]Online: http://www.consilium.eu.int/uedocs/cmsUpload/080715_combat%20terrorism_EN.pdf.

[49]Case T-228/02 *Organisation des Modjahedines*, n. 14 above and Case T-229/02 *PKK* [2008] ECR II-45, paras 57 ff.

[50]Pursuant to the 2007 guidelines (n. 48 above, at 4): "For the purpose of the review, the CP 931 Working Party carries out a thorough assessment as to whether the grounds for each listing are still valid. It takes into account all relevant considerations, including the person's, group's or entity's past record of involvement in terrorist acts, the current status of the group or entity and the *perceived future intentions* of the person, group or entity" (italics added).

[51]http://www.un.org/sc/committees/1267/index.shtml.

[52]Joined cases C-402 and 415/05 P, *Kadi and Al Barakaat*, n. 3 above, AG Poiares Maduro, para 51.

measures: the UNSC neither created an international tribunal ad hoc, nor indicated any jurisdictional *forum* to which listed individuals can apply.[53]

Although the UN procedure is clearly more censurable than the one related to the Common Position 2001/931/CFSP, in both cases the listing operations do not respect fundamental rights and more precisely the right of defence, the presumption of innocence, the right to a fair trial and to an effective judicial remedy. Furthermore, when funds are frozen, the effects of listing also imply the sacrifice of the right to property.

In sum, these procedures infringe Art. 6 TEU, as well as the EU *Basic Principles on the Use of Restrictive Measures (Sanctions)* and the above mentioned *Guidelines* – both emphasising the need to respect fundamental rights[54] – not to mention the rights foreseen in the Charter.

6.2 Weighing Security Against Fundamental Rights Protection in the Fight on Terrorism

The balancing of security against fundamental rights is pivotal for the respect of the rule of law. In this regard, a well known Italian constitutionalist, Roberto Bin, has argued that:

> It is commonly accepted that the fight on international terrorism represents a serious threat to constitutional rights. And yet, neither terrorism, nor its 'international' dimension, nor the practice of restricting individual freedoms for the sake of national secutity are new phenomena. On the contrary" [translation mine, LP].[55]

The fight against terrorism is marked as a priority in international and national agendas. Factors such as swiftness and effectiveness are of particular importance. In this sense, the listing procedures appear to be

[53] J. Almquist, 'A human rights critique of European judicial review: Counter-terrorism sanctions' (2008) *International and Comparative Law Quarterly* 309.

[54] The Basic Principles of 2004, n. 17 above, specify that sanctions against non-State actors will be adopted "in full respect of human rights and the rule of law". Regarding the Guidelines, n. 20 above, the document confirms that "(t)he introduction and implementation of restrictive measures must always be in accordance with international law. They must respect human rights and fundamental freedoms, in particular due process and the right to effective remedy. The measures must always be proportionate to their objective"; "As indicated above, the restrictive measures should, in particular, be drafted in light of the obligation under Art. 6(2) TEU for the EU to respect fundamental rights, as guaranteed by the European Convention on Human Rights and as they result from the constitutional traditions common to the Member States, as general principles of Community law" (5 ff.).

[55] See R. Bin, *Democrazia e Terrorismo*, 2006, online: www.forumcostituzionale.it. The original version is: "Che la sfida del terrorismo internazionale causi una seria minaccia per la tutela dei diritti costituzionali è affermazione corrente. Una prima osservazione mi sembra però indispensabile. Né il terrorismo, né la sua dimensione "internazionale", né la politica di restrizione dei diritti di libertà in nome della difesa della sicurezza dello Stato sono fenomeni nuovi, tutt'altro".

speedy and the freezing of funds seems an adequate measure to stop people from (financially) supporting terrorism. These needs are clearly expressed in the *UNSC Guidelines* where it is stated that: "It is important that the EU implement such UN restrictive measures as quickly as possible. Speed is particularly important in the case of asset freezer where funds can move quickly".

Of course, the pursuance of promptness can go to the detriment of fundamental rights. Hence, the question arises as to how to weigh the necessity to contrast terrorism against the duty to respect fundamental rights. According to the Commission, when it comes to international peace and security the Court should apply "less stringent criteria for the protection of fundamental rights".[56] This view is not shared by Advocate general Poiares Maduro who affirmed that:

> The claim that a measure is necessary for the maintenance of international peace and security cannot operate so as to silence the general principles of Community law and deprive individuals of their fundamental rights.[57]

In other words, as confirmed by the ECJ, fundamental rights cannot be disregarded in the EC legal order: if any restriction thereof proves necessary, it must be in line with the rule of law and judges are responsible for ensuring the observance of this principle.

6.3 The Case-Law

Until recently the will to contrast terrorism has prevailed over the need to protect fundamental rights, but this has changed by virtue of the latest judgments. A brief survey of the cases originating from Common Positions 2001/931/CFSP and 2002/402/CFSP (and the respective EC Regulations) should help understand the reasons for this.

In a number of cases applicants acted for the annulment of the EC Regulations implementing the Common Positions under Art. 230 TEC. Some claims were directed at obtaining the (total or partial) annulment of the Common Positions, but they were unsuccessful in light of the lack of jurisdiction of the Court in the CFSP.[58] On other occasions the applicants

[56] This was the position adopted by the Commission (and by the United Kingdom) in the Kadi appeal, n. 3 above, para 35. More precisely, as reported by Advocate general Poiares Maduro in his opinion on the case, the Commission held that: "when the risks to public security are believed to be extraordinarily high, the pressure is particularly strong to take measures that disregard individual rights, especially in respect of individuals who have little or no access to the political process".

[57] Joined cases C-402 and 415/05 P *Kadi and Al Barakaat*, n. 3 above, para 34.

[58] Cf. Case T-299/04 *Selmani* [2005] ECR II-20, and Case T-228/02 *Organisation des Modjahedines*, n. 14 above.

opted for compensation of damages suffered as a result of the listing related to Common Position 2001/931/CFSP but their requests were dismissed.[59]

The violations alleged by private parties include the infringement of the principle of legal certainty,[60] of the presumption of innocence and of the rights of defence (comprising the right to a fair hearing and the right to an effective judicial remedy) and in general of the rule of law. The entities involved have claimed the violation of the freedom of association and expression[61] as well as of the principle of equality.[62] Because the measures in question provided for the freezing of funds, the undue restriction of the right to property has been argued in all cases. Some applicants have also invoked the right to the peaceful enjoyment of their private and family life[63] and the right to dignity in order to obtain the annulment of the relevant measures.[64] Hence, it should not come as a surprise that in various instances the ECHR[65] and the Charter[66] have been quoted.

The CFI has already dealt with several cases and has yet to decide others.[67] Some appeals have already reached the Court and some are currently pending.[68] The Court has nonetheless decided on some CFI orders and

---

[59]Case C-355/04 P *Segi* [2007] ECR I-1657; Case C-354/04 P *Gestoras Pro Amnistía* [2007] ECR I-1579.

[60]Case T-253/04 *Kongra-Gel* [2008] ECR II-46.

[61]Case T-206/02 *KNK* [2005] ECR II-523 and Case C-354/04 P, *Gestoras*, n. 59 above.

[62]Case T-253/04 *Kongra-Gel*, n. 60 above.

[63]Case T-49/04 *Hassan* [2006] ECR II-52.

[64]Case T-253/02 *Ayadi* [2006] ECR II-2139.

[65]Cf. Case T-318/01 *Othman* [2009] *nyr*, with regard to the breach of Arts. 3, 8 ECHR, and Case T-47/03 *Sison* [2007] ECR II-73, with regard to the breach of Arts. 6, 7, 10, 11 ECHR and of its Protocol no. 1.

[66]Joined cases T-37 and 323/07 *El Morabit* [2009] *nyr*, making reference to both the ECHR (Art. 6) and the Charter (Arts. 47 and 48).

[67]The following cases are currently pending before the CFI/GC: Case T-135/06 *Al-Faqih*; Case 136/06 *Sanabel Relief Agency*; Case T-137/06 *Abdrabbah*; Case T-138/06 *Nasuf*; Case T-49/07 *Fahas*; Case T-76/07 *El Fatmi*; T-348/07 *Al-Aqsa*; T-409/08 *El Fatmi*; T-85/09, *Kadi* (for the annulment of the Regulation adopted after the ECJ appeals judgements in the *Kadi* and *Al Bakaraat Foundation* cases and confirming the restrictive measures). The following cases are also pending, but they concern restrictive measures against individuals 'in the wake' of sanctions against States: Case T-181/08 *Tay ZA* (Burma); Case T-121/09 *Al Shanfari* (Zimbabwe); Case T-145/09, *Bredenkamp* (Zimbabwe). In all these cases applicants have contested the infringement of their fundamental rights. In the similar and recently decided Case T-390/08 *Melli Bank* (Iran), the CFI, whilst acknowledging the Kadi appeal judgment, dismissed the action considering, *inter alia*, that "given the primary importance of maintaining international peace and security, the disadvantages caused are not inordinate in relation to the ends sought, especially because, first, those restrictions concern only part of the applicant's assets and, secondly, Arts. 9 and 10 of Regulation No 423/2007 provide for certain exceptions allowing the entities affected by fund-freezing measures to meet essential expenditure" (para 71).

[68]The following cases are currently pending before the Court of Justice: Case C-399/06 P *Hassan*; Case C-403/06 P *Ayadi*; Case C-576/08 P *OMPI*; Case C-27/09 P *France v OMPI*. The latter two cases are appeals against, respectively, the CFI judgements in the

has delivered a preliminary ruling. More recently the ECJ has decided on the *Kadi* appeal.[69] The most famous CFI decisions are those rendered in *Yusuf* and *Kadi*,[70] much criticized by legal commentators.[71] In those two judgements the CFI justified the restriction of fundamental rights arguing in favour of a sort of jurisdictional immunity of UNSC Resolutions. That position was presented in milder terms in the following *Ayadi* and *Hassan* judgements,[72] but the major break- through came with the mentioned *OMPI* judgement. This precedent, more favourable to fundamental rights protection, was later confirmed in the *Sison* and *Al-Aqsa* judgements,[73] as well as in *PKK* and *Kontra-Gel e a.*[74] and, more recently, in two other cases brought by *OMPI*.[75]

The same support for fundamental rights protection can be found in the case law of the ECJ. Firstly, in the *PKK* and *KNK* case,[76] where the Court was called upon to set aside the CFI order dismissing an action for annulment against an EC listing measure considered to be inadmissible[77]. Here the judges referred the case back to the CFI, stating that "(f)undamental rights form an integral part of the general principles of law the observance of which the Court ensures".[78] In the subsequent *Segi* and *Gestoras* judgements, the Court reaffirmed that the EU "is founded on the principle

---

cases T-256/07 and T-284/08, n. 74 below). It should also be mentioned that the House of Lords has recently submitted a preliminary reference to the ECJ (Case C-340/08, *M (FC) e a.*).

[69] Joined Cases C-402/05P and C-415/05, *Kadi and Al Barakaat*, n. 3 above.

[70] Case T-306/01 *Yusuf and Al Barakaat* and Case T-315/01, Kadi, n. 3 above.

[71] The legal literature on these judgements is extensive. Ample references can be found in L. Paladini, *Le misure restrittive adottate nell'ambito della PESC: prassi e giurisprudenza*, (2009) *Il Diritto dell'Unione europea* 365.

[72] Case T-253/02 *Ayadi*, n. 64 above and Case T-49/04 *Hassan*, n. 63 above. The CFI has confirmed the position expressed in Yusuf and Kadi but, with regard to the de-listing, added that "the Member States are bound, in accordance with Art. 6 EU, to respect the fundamental rights of the persons involved, as guaranteed by the ECHR and as they result from the constitutional traditions common to the Member States, as general principles of Community law".

[73] Case T-47/03 *Sison*, n. 65 above and Case T-327/03 *Al-Aqsa* [2007] ECR II-79. For a review of these judgements, see A. Johnston, 'Freezing terrorist assets again: walking a tightrope over thin ice?' (2008) 67 *The Cambridge Law Journal* 31.

[74] Case T-229/02 *PKK*, n. 49 above, para 69 and Case T-253/04, *Kongra-Gel*, n. 60 above, para 103.

[75] Case T-256/07 *OMPI* [2009] nyr, and Case T-284/08, *OMPI* [2009] nyr.

[76] Case C-229/05 P *PKK and KNK* [2007] ECR I-439.

[77] Case T-206/02 *KNK*, n. 61 above.

[78] Ibid., paras 76 ff. The 3 April 2008 the CFI, relying on the arguments used in *OMPI* (Case T-228/02, n. 14 above) annulled the Council Decision in so far as it concerned the applicant. The CFI has recognized (para 69) that "In the present case, as a result of the absence of any reasoning expressly appearing in the contested decision or provided immediately thereafter, the applicant was not placed in a position in which it is able to understand, clearly and unequivocally, the reasoning by which the Council considered

of the rule of law and it respects fundamental rights as general principles of Community law. It follows that the institutions are subject to review of the conformity of their acts with the treaties and the general principles of law, just like the Member States when they implement the law of the Union".[79] In those judgements the Court dismissed the actions aimed at obtaining the compensation for damages suffered as a consequence of a listing procedure,[80] but claimed the necessity of respecting fundamental rights in the EU, not only in the First Pillar.[81]

Moreover, with the *Möllendorf* judgement[82] the Court has made another step forward. In this instance, the preliminary reference presented by the Kammergericht Berlin concerned the interpretation of EC Regulation 881/2002, where the annexed list was drafted by the "1267 Committee" and was acritically transposed into the EU legal order.[83] The Court stated that when implementing EC law (including Regulation 881/2002) Member States are bound, as far as possible, to respect fundamental rights.[84]

The most recent judgement of the Court is that rendered in the *Kadi* and *Al Bakaraat Foundation* appeals.[85] In his opinion the Advocate general Poiares Maduro suggested a strong changing of course: he proposed to annull the CFI decision as well as EC Regulation 881/2002, in so far as it concerned the appellant. Being a Community based on the rule of law the EC had the obligation to provide for judicial control over implementing measures decided by the UNSC.[86] Hence the respect of fundamental rights amounted to a parameter of legality for acts imposing measures against individuals, even when the latter implement UNSC Resolutions.

The ECJ accepted the Advocate general's suggestions confirming that the EC is (*rectius*, was) a community based on the rule of law and that

---

that the conditions laid down in Art. 1(4) of Common Position 2001/931 and in Art. 2(3) of the contested regulation had been satisfied in the circumstances of the case".

[79]See Case C-355/04 P *Segi* and Case C-354/04 P *Gestoras Pro Amnistía*, n. 59 above, para 51.

[80]Listing related to Common Position 2001/931/CFSP, n. 40 above.

[81]Paras 53 ff. The Court has stated that: "The right to make a reference to the Court of Justice for a preliminary ruling must therefore exist in respect of all measures adopted by the Council, whatever their nature or form, which are intended to have legal effects in relation to third parties". Amongst the latter, the Common Positions adopted within the Third Pillar, which could be the object of an action for the annulment under Art. 35 TEU.

[82]Case C-117/06 *Möllendorf* [2007] ECR I-8361.

[83]It should be recalled that, notwithstanding the permissive approach adopted in *Ayadi* and *Hassan* (n. 63 and n. 64 above), the previous case-law had only recognized the protection of fundamental rights guaranteed under the category of *jus cogens*.

[84]Case C-117/06 *Möllendorf*, n. 82 above, para 78.

[85]Joined cases C-402 and 415/05 P *Kadi and Al* Barakaat, n. 3 above.

[86]See n. 52 above, para 31.

fundamental rights are a parameter of legality of secondary law.[87] So much so that the Court states that the EC Treaty amounts to a Constitutional Charter. The latter imposes full observance of fundamental rights and the obligations imposed by an international agreement cannot have the effect of hindering the principles thereof.[88] It seems that the ECJ set the EC legal order's boundaries with respect to international law, UNSC resolutions in particular. That sounds similar to the position of the ECJ in *Costa v. Enel*, where the autonomy of the Community vis à vis national legal orders was clearly asserted.[89]

The Court acknowledged that the rules applying to UN resolutions do not exclude a judicial review of EC acts concerning fundamental rights violations.[90]. Such a limit cannot be found in the Treaty and although derogations are provided for in certain instances[91]:

> the Community judicature must, in accordance with the powers conferred on it by the EC Treaty, ensure the review, in principle the full review, of the lawfulness of all Community acts in the light of the fundamental rights forming an integral part of the general principles of Community law, including review of Community measures which, like the contested regulation, are designed to give effect to the resolutions adopted by the Security Council under Chapter VII of the Charter of the United Nations.[92]

It is worthwhile underlining that the CFI has reacted promptly and in line with the ECJ's decision.[93]

---

[87] Ibid., paras 283 and 284. More precisely, in his opinion concerning the *Kadi* appeal, AG Poiares Maduro stressed that in the *Bosphorus* judgement the Court accepted as self-evident what AG Jacobs had felt useful to spell out, i.e. that the respect of fundamental rights is a necessary condition for the legality of Community acts, n. 49 above, para 27.

[88] Ibid., paras 281and 285.

[89] Case 6/64 *Costa v Enel* [1964] ECR 585. For further considerations on the matter see C. Eckes, 'Test Case for the resilience of the EU's constitutional foundations', (2009) 15 *European Public Law* 351, at 375 and A. Gattini, (2009) *Common Market Law Rev.* 213 at 224.

[90] Joined cases C-402 and 415/05 P, *Kadi and Al Barakaat*, n. 3 above, para 299. It should also be noted that the ECJ insists on the fact that "the review of lawfulness [...] to be ensured by the Community judicature applies to the Community act intended to give effect to the international agreement at issue, and not to the latter as such" (para 286). Moreover, with specific reference to the contested EC Regulation, the Court observes that it "is intended to give effect to a resolution adopted by the Security Council under Chapter VII of the Charter of the United Nations" concluding that: "it is not, therefore, for the Community judicature, under the exclusive jurisdiction provided for by Art. 220 EC, to review the lawfulness of such a resolution adopted by an international body, even if that review were to be limited to examination of the compatibility of that resolution with *jus cogens*" (para 287).

[91] Ibid., paras 301 and 302.

[92] Ibid., para 326.

[93] Case T-318/01 *Othman*, n. 65 above.

7 The Effects of a Binding Charter in the CFSP

It is now time to evaluate the practice on restrictive measures addressed to individuals (including persons considered associated to a State) in the light of a binding Charter.

Until the Lisbon Treaty individuals could not benefit from preventive guarantees nor could they rely on an exhaustive system of judicial remedies. In fact, while it was possible to challenge EC regulations ordering the freezing of funds, there were no remedies against the non-economic sanctions adopted in the domain of CFSP (e.g. a ban on visas). Moreover, as recognised in *OMPI*, the procedure followed to sanction individuals did not comply with the EU's fundamental rights protection standard.[94] The considered practice – which will continue to operate through decisions and regulations – would infringe the newly binding Charter (via Art. 6 TEU), and more specifically the right to an effective judicial remedy and to a fair trial, the presumption of innocence and the right of defence,[95] as well as the right to property.[96]

That being so, although even after the entry into force of the Lisbon Treaty the EUCJ has no general jurisdiction in the field of CFSP, the new version of Art. 6 TEU seems to strengthen the duty to respect fundamental rights by assigning full legal force to the Charter, by providing for the accession to the ECHR and by confirming that fundamental rights are general principles of EU law. The Charter itself offers Europeans more transparency by making fundamental rights more visible and understandable.

Furthermore, there is a break in the "Chinese wall of the CSFP injusticiability", since pursuant to Art. 275 TFEU the EUCJ can annul decisions adopting restrictive measures against individuals. Thus, in relation to the protection of fundamental rights, the legal force attributed to the Charter is believed to affect the EU action in the field of CFSP in at least two ways: on the one side, an ex ante mechanism will guarantee that decisions are adopted respecting fundamental rights; on the other, an ex post mechanism will ensure judicial review over restrictive measures against natural or legal persons.

8 The Ex Ante Mechanism . . .

As previously stated, when considering the practice of restrictive measures against individuals, an ex ante form of control already existed (by virtue

[94] In this sense, the revision of the listing procedure related to Common Position 2001/931/CFSP can be considered as a sort of self-incrimination on the part of the EU.

[95] Arts. 47 to 50 CFR.

[96] Art. 17 CFR.

of former Art. 6 TEU),[97] but did not find application in this field of law, where compliance with fundamental rights has basically been left to the self regulation (i.e. self-restraint) of the EU Council.

This mechanism is particularly important when adopting restrictive measures. Lists attached to CFSP acts will have to be drafted in accordance with the presumption of innocence (i.e. in the presence of serious evidence against the individuals) and respecting the rights of defence (e.g. by informing individuals of the inculpatory evidence at the time of or immediately after the adoption of the measures in question). Moreover, the sanctions will have to be proportionate[98] and individuals will have the right to an effective legal remedy and to a full judicial protection. Some of these guarantees have to be envisaged during the listing operations.

With reference to the listing operations carried out by the UN Sanctions Committees, the position adopted by the ECJ in the *Kadi* appeal is particularly relevant. Here it is stated that the respect of UN obligations cannot determine a limitation of fundamental rights. As previously noted, the ECJ, following in this respect the Advocate general's opinion, insisted on the fact that the EC was a community based on the rule of law. This stance could be opposed to the findings of the Court in *Segi* and *Gestoras*, where the Court made express reference to the EU legal order.[99] In other words, although with respect to EC regulations the ECJ was firm in claiming the need for a preliminary evaluation on the respect of fundamental rights, it remained unclear whether the same would hold true for CFSP acts implementing UNSC Resolutions. The Court left the Council with the difficult task of establishing a procedure complying with the judgement, but only as far as first pillar acts were concerned.[100] As to the EU listing procedure, it has been pointed out that the reference to the "perceived future intentions" to commit terroristic acts[101] jeopardises the respect of fundamental rights, and in particular the rights of defence.

---

[97] In addition, it is recognized in the EU documents (e.g. the "Basic Principles", n. 17 above) and by the case-law, most notably the *OMPI* judgement (n. 14 above).

[98] The breach of the principle of proportionality has been invoked in several cases. See e.g. Case T-229/02 *PKK and KNK*, n. 76 above; Case T-327/03 *Al-Aqsa*, n. 67 above; Case T-47/03 *Sison*, n. 65 above; Case T-253/02 *Ayadi*, n. 63 above; Case T-49/04 *Hassan*, n. 64 above; Case T-299/04 *Selmani*, n. 58 above. Amongst the pending cases before the CFI see Cases T-135/06 *Al-Faqih*, T-137/06, *Abdrabbah*, T-363/07 *Hamdi* and T-181/08 *Tay ZA*, n. 67 above.

[99] Case C-355/04 P *Segi* and Case C-354/04 P *Gestoras Pro Amnistía*, n. 59 above, para 51.

[100] Joined cases C-402 and 415/05 P, *Kadi and Al* Barakaat, n. 3 above, paras 374 ff. The Commission, empowered to amend EC Regulation 881/2002 according to Art. 7, adopted EC Regulation 1190/2008 in line with the ECJ's position, but confirming Mr. Kadi and Al Barakaat in the list of the individuals affected by restrictive measures (see n. 44 above).

[101] See Section 6.1 above.

In conclusion, Art. 6 TEU reaffirms the ex ante mechanism as an 'internal limit' to the adoption of CFSP decisions addressing restrictive measures to individuals. The Institutions – and in particular the EU Council[102] – must exercise CFSP competences accordingly. This internal limit, operative since the first proclamation of the Charter in 2000 by the three main institutions but which suffered some notable exceptions in the field of CFSP,[103] is all the more evident now that novelties introduced by the Lisbon Treaty have finally entered into force. As will be seen shortly, the latter are directed at, and allegedly capable of, enhancing the legitimacy of the EU.

9 . . . And the Ex Post Mechanism

The Treaty of Lisbon also introduces an ex post mechanism aimed at ensuring the respect of fundamental rights[104]. Art. 275 TFEU, which reflects Art. III-376 of the Constitutional Treaty[105], confirms that the EUCJ has no jurisdiction in the field of CFSP[106], but affirms that it:

> shall have jurisdiction to monitor compliance with Article 40 of the Treaty on European Union and to rule on proceedings, brought in accordance with the conditions laid down in the fourth paragraph of Article 263 of this Treaty, reviewing

---

[102] See D. Curtin, R. van Ooik, 'The sting is always in the tail: The personal scope of application of the EU Charter of Fundamental Rights' (2001) *Maastricht Journal of European and Comparative Law* 102. This was true since the first proclamation of the Charter.

[103] According to Judge Wathelet (quoted by H. Bribosia, *Perspectives des droits fondamentaux et de la citoyennete européenne*, in G. Amato and others (ed.), *Genesis and destiny of the European Constitution: Commentary on the Treaty establishing a Constitution for Europe in the light of the travaux préparatoires and future prospects* (Bruylant, 2007) at 998) the Charter was binding for the Institutions since the first proclamation on the basis of the Latin brocard *patere legem quam ipse* fecisti, being an interinstitutional agreement. In the opinion of A.J. Menéndez (*Some elements of a theory of European fundamental rights*, in E.O. Eriksen, A.J. Menéndez (eds.), *Arguing fundamental Rights* (Springer, 2006) at 161) the Charter has legal value and legal force as confirmed by the practice of the Institutions. This position is well founded although the restrictive measures adopted under the second Pillar seem to indicate that the Charter is not perceived to be compulsory in the domain of CFSP.

[104] See D. Thym, 'Charter of Fundamental Rights: Competition or consistency of human rights protection in Europe?' (2003) *The Finnish yearbook of international law* 11, who underlined how jurisdictional remedies in CFSP would have been necessary with a binding Charter.

[105] This is one of the provisions that escaped the aforementioned iconoclastic fury (see n. 9 above). In relation to the jurisdiction of the Court in the domain of CFSP, see the Discussion circle organized by the ECJ (doc. 10, Circle 1, 12 March 2003).

[106] Pursuant to Art. 275 TFEU: "The Court of Justice of the European Union shall not have jurisdiction with respect to the provisions relating to the common foreign and security policy nor with respect to acts adopted on the basis of those provisions".

> the legality of decisions providing for restrictive measures against natural or legal persons adopted by the Council on the basis of Chapter 2 of Title V of the Treaty on European Union.

It seems that the Treaty of Lisbon purports a sort of habeas corpus against the EU,[107] partially filling the well-know judicial gap in the domain of CFSP.[108] In fact, individuals can act to annul CFSP decisions imposing restrictive measures. That represents a remarkable innovation, since it will be possible to contest EU decisions adopting all kinds of santions.[109] In this regard, it should be recalled that under the former treaties individuals could only contest EC acts prescribing economic sanctions, while CFSP acts concerning non-economic sanctions escaped judicial control.

In regard to Art. 275 TFEU, a further specification is due. When that provision refers to decisions, it refers to all acts that can be adopted in the domain of CFSP. In fact, Art. 25 TEU states that in the field of CFSP *general guidelines* and *decisions* (together with the other acts necessary to enforce them) are adopted defining the actions and positions to be taken by the EU. Reference is to the former Joint Actions and Common Positions and related decisions adopted to implement them. This means that the restrictive measures will be decided adopting "decisions defining [...] positions to be taken by the Union", which in light of Art. 275 TFEU can be reviewed by the Court when they infringe rights such as the presumpion of innocence or the right of defence.[110] CFSP decisions will be declared null and void if the EUCJ finds the "infringement of the Treaties or of any rule of law relating to their application", in particular the violation of Art. 6 TEU and the "linked" Charter.[111] The latter, in fact, "may be used to challenge and ultimately

[107] See L.S. Rossi, 'I diritti fondamentali nel Trattato di Lisbona', n. 5 above.

[108] Since the first proclamation of the Charter, Curtin and van Ooik, n. 102 above, at 111, stressed the lack of judicial review over acts falling within the (former) Second and Third Pillar.

[109] The provision appeared in Art. III-376 (2) of the Constitutional Treaty. Cf. M. Garbagnati Ketvel, n. 22 above, at 116; M. Cremona, 'The Union's external action: constitutional perspectives', in Amato et al. (ed.), *Genesis and destiny of the European Constitution: commentary on the Treaty establishing a Constitution for Europe in the light of the travaux préparatoires and future prospects* (Bruylant, 2007) at 1200.

[110] For example, depriving individuals of the possibility to be informed in due time about the measures taken by the Council and therefore allowing them to contest the latter in court. Cf. Joined cases C-402 and 415/05 P, *Kadi and Al* Barakaat, n. 3 above, paras 349 ff.

[111] The same will be true for the infringement of the new Art. 39 TEU. This provision inserts a new legal basis for the protection of individuals with regard to the processing of personal data by the Member States when carrying out activities which fall in the domain of CFSP. It follows that the protection of fundamental rights will be enhanced for individuals targeted by restrictive measures. On the impact of a binding Charter on the Protection of personal data within the Area of Freedom Security and Justice, see further in this volume V. Bazzocchi, Chapter 10.

strike down EU legislation which does not comply with its provisions".[112] Thus, CFSP acts which elude the above mentioned ex ante mechanism will be caught by the ex post mechanism.

10 The Binding Charter: A Trojan Horse Within CFSP?

The Lisbon Treaty creates a system for the protection of fundamental rights in the domain of CFSP. That will be possible by virtue of the ex ante mechanism, whereby all CFSP decision will have to comply with the Charter, and of the ex post mechanism, which extends the remedy foreseen by former Art. 230 TEC to CFSP decisions ordering sanctions against individuals. These changes are remarkable (and long awaited) and will allow for a higher standard in fundamental rights protection.[113] In particular they affect the traditional exclusion of judicial review in the field of CFSP, which has been argued to derive (and uphold) the intergovernmental nature of the former Second Pillar.

The Lisbon Treaty and the resulting new framework for the respect of fundamental rights in the domain of CFSP (in particular the ex post mechanism), is permeated by elements of Community Law. This is why the title of this contribution refers to the myth of the Trojan horse, suggesting that, far from disrupting the (confirmed) specificity of the CFSP, the Lisbon Treaty and the binding Charter represent the basis for an effective legal protection in this field of law. Indeed, although it is difficult to foresee when and how it will disclose its potential added value, it is hard to imagine a regression from this situation. The new mechanisms applicable to the CFSP are bound to characterize all future developments in this area, and can hardly be seen to be a sort of mithridatism carried out against the Community method. Hence, it is suggested that the CFSP is taking its first steps towards communitarization, thereby deepening the European integration process.

---

[112] House of Lords, n. 6 above, at 97.

[113] Based on the *Segi* and *Gestoras* case law, n. 59 above, individuals could benefit from a more extensive judicial protection if they were entitled to activate a non contractual liability claim against the EU (See M. Cremona, n. 109 above, at 1204 with reference to the Constitutional Treaty).

Bibliography

Ackermann, T., 'Case-note on Omega', (2005) 42 *Common Market Law Review* 1107

Adam, R., 'La prospettata adesione delle Comunità alla Convenzione di Roma: si devono anche modificare i trattati comunitari?', (1980) *Rivista di diritto internazionale* 883

Agerbeek, F.R., 'Freedom of expression and free movement in the Brenner corridor: The Schmidberger case', (2004) 29 *European Law Review* 255

Akandji-Kombé, J.F., 'L'application de la Charte sociale européenne: La mise en oeuvre de la procédure de réclamations collectives', (2000) 11 *Droit social* 888

Albi, A., 'Ironies in human rights protection in the EU: Pre-accession conditionality and post-accession conundrums', (2009) 15 *European Law Journal* 49

Albors-Llorens, A., 'The standing of private parties to challenge community measures: Has the European court missed the boat?', (2003) 62 *Cambridge Law Journal* 72

Alemanno, A., 'Libertés fondamentales et droits fondamentaux', (2004) 4 *Revue du Droit de l'Union Européenne* 731

Alkema, E.A., 'The European Convention as a Constitution and Its Court as a Constitutional Court', in P. Mahoney, F. Matscher, H. Petzold and L. Wildhaber (eds.), *Protecting human rights: The European perspective* (Carl Heymans, 2000) 41

Allott, P., 'Fundamental rights in the EU', (1996) 3 *The Cambridge Law Journal* 409

Almquist, J., 'A human rights critique of European judicial review: Counter-terrorism sanctions' (2008) *International and Comparative Law Quarterly* 309

Alston, P., *The EU and human rights* (Oxford University Press, 1999)

Amadeo, S., 'Il Protocollo n. 30 sull'applicazione della Carta a Polonia e Regno Unito e la tutela "asimmetrica" dei diritti fondamentali: molti problemi, qualche soluzione', (2009) 14 *Il Diritto dell'Unione europea* 720

Anagnostaras, G., 'The quest for an effective remedy and the measure of judicial protection afforded to putative Community law rights', (2007) 32 *European Law Review* 727

Anzon, A., 'La Costituzione europea come problema', (2000) *Rivista di Diritto Costituzionale* 656

Armone, G., Terrorismo, listing e diritti umani, 2007, online: www.europeanrights.eu

Arnull, A., 'Case C-432/05, Unibet (London) Ltd and Unibet (Internationa l) Ltd v. Justitiekanslern', (2007) 32 *Common Market Law Review* 1763

Arnull, A., 'National courts and the validity of community acts', (1988) 14 *European Law Review* 125

Arnull, A., 'Out with the old', (2006) *European Law Review* 1

Arnull, A., 'Private applicants and the action for annulment under Art. 173 of the EC Treaty', (1995) 32 *Common Market Law Review* 7

Arnull, A., A. Dashwood, M. Dougan, M. Ross, E. Spaventa and D. Wyatt, Wyatt & Dashwood's, *European Union Law* (Sweet & Mawwell, 2006)

G. Di Federico, *The EU Charter of Fundamental Rights*, Ius Gentium: Comparative Perspectives on Law and Justice 8, DOI 10.1007/978-94-007-0156-4,

Ashiagbor, D., 'EMU and the shift in the European labor law agenda: From Social Policy to Employment Policy', (2001) 7 *European Law Journal* 311

Aust, A., *Modern treaty law and practice* (Cambridge University Press, 2007)

Avbeij, M., 'The European Court of Justice and the question of value choices' (2004) Jean Monnet Working Paper 06/04, accessible at http://www.jeanmonnetprogram.org, accessed on 2 June 2008

Azoulay, L. and F. Ronkes Agerbeek, 'Conseil Contitutionnel, Decision No. 2004-505 DC of 19 November 2004, on the Treaty establishing a Constitution for Europe', (2005) *Common Market Law Review* 871

Azzena, L., 'Prospettive della Carta dei diritti e ruolo della giurisprudenza', in F. Ferrari (ed.), *I diritti fondamentali dopo la Carta di Nizza. Il costituzionalismo dei diritti* (Giuffré, 2001) 123

Baker, E., C. Harding, 'From past imperfect to future perfect? A longitudinal study of the Third Pillar', (2009) 34 *European Law Review* 47

Balboni, M., 'Diritti dei fanciulli e commercio equo: clausola sociale o altro?', in L.S. Rossi (ed.), *Commercio internazionale sostenibile?: WTO e Unione europea* (Il Mulino, 2003) 119

Ballarino, T., 'Diritti fondamentali dell'Unione europea', in S. Cassese (ed.), *Dizionario di diritto pubblico* (Giuffré, 2006) 1892

Ballarino, T., *Costituzione e diritto internazionale privato* (CEDAM, 1974)

Ballestrero, M.V., 'Europa dei mercati e promozione dei diritti', (2007) 55 *WP CSDLE* "Massimo D'Antona" 2

Baratta, R., 'Le principali novità del Trattato di Lisbona', (2008) 13 *Il Diritto dell'Unione europea* 69

Barav, A., 'Effectiveness of judicial protection and the role of national courts', in M. Minieri, *Judicial protection of rights in the Community legal order* (Bruylant, 1997) 259

Barbera, A., 'La Carta dei diritti dell'Unione europea', (2001) *Il Diritto dell'Unione europea* 241

Barnard, C., 'EU Citizenship and the Principle of Solidarity', in E. Spaventa and M. Dougan (eds.), *Social welfare and EU law*, (Hart, 2005) 168

Baruffi, M.C., 'Sul diritto di accesso al fascicolo nei procedimenti giurisdizionali comunitari', (1999) *Diritto pubblico comparato ed europeo* 691

Battista, J., 'Is participation in the Commission's administrative procedure a necessary condition for legal standing?', (2008) *European State Aid Law Quarterly* 317

Bazzocchi, V., 'Il Mandato d'arresto europeo e le corti supreme nazionali', (2007) *Il Diritto dell'Unione europea*, 663

Bebr, G., 'The Reinforcement of the Constitutional Review of Community Acts under Article 177 EEC Treaty', (1988) 25 *Common Market Law Review* 667

Beitzke, G., *Grundgesetz und international privatrecht* (Kruger, 1961)

Benoït-Rohmer, F., *La Charte des droits fondamentaux de l'Union européenne* (2001), 19 Chronique, 1483

Benoit-Rohmer, F., 'Les droits de l'homme dans l'Union européenne: de Rome a Nice', in L.S. Rossi (ed.) *Carta dei diritti fondamentali e Costituzione dell'Unione europea* (Giuffré, 2002) 19

Benoit-Rhomer, F., *The European Parliament as a champion of European values* (European Parliament, Office for Official Publications of European Communities, 2008)

Benoït-Rohmer, F., (ed.), 'La Charte des droits fondamentaux de l'Union européennes', (2000) 12 *Revue Universelle des droits de l'Homme,* 1

Besselink, L., *A composite European Constitution* (Europa Law, 2007)

Biernat, E., 'The locus standi of private applicants under Article 230 (4) EC and the principle of judicial protection in the European Community' (2003) Harvard Jean

Monnet Working Paper no. 12/03, accessibile at http://www.jeanmonnetprogram.org/papers/03/031201.html, accessed on 5 May 2008
Bifulco, R., M. Cartabia, A. Celotto, (eds.), *L'Europa dei diritti. Commento alla Carta dei diritti fondamentali dell'Unione europea* (Il Mulino, 2001)
Bifulco, R., M. Cartabia, A. Celotto, 'Introduzione', in R. Bifulco, M. Cartabia and A. Celotto (eds.), *L'Europa dei diritti* (Il Mulino, 2001) 12
Billet, P., 'La constitutionnalisation du droit de l'homme à l'environnement. Regard critique sur le projet de loi constitutionnelle relatif à la Charte de l'environnement', (2003) *Revue juridique de l'environnement* 35
Bin, R., Democrazia e terrorismo, 2006, online: www.forumcostituzionale.it
Biondi, A., 'Free trade, a mountain road and the right to protest: European economic freedoms and fundamental individual rights', (2004) *European Human Rights Law Review* 1
Biondi, A., 'The European Court of Justice and certain national procedural limitations: Not such a tough relationship', (1999) 36 *Common Market Law Review* 1271
Bitsch, M.-T., *Histoire de la construction européenne de 1945 à nos jours* (Complexe, 1996)
Blackburn, R. and J. Polakiewicz (eds.), *Fundamental rights in Europe: The European Convention on Human Rights and its member States, 1950–2000* (Oxford University Press, 2001)
Bobek, M., 'Learning to talk: Preliminary rulings, the courts of the new Member States and the Court of Justice', (2008) 45 *Common Market Law Review* 1611
Borgetto, M. and R. Lafore, 'Article II-94', in A. Levade, L. Burgorgue-Larsen and F. Picod (eds.), *Traité établissant une Constitution pour l'Europe, Tome 2: La Charte des droits fondamentaux de l'Union* (Bruylant, 2005) 452
Borrás, S. and K. Jacobsson, 'The Open Method of Coordination and new governance patterns in the EU', (2004) 11 *Journal of European public policy* 185
Boschiero, N., 'The forthcoming European enforcement order. Towards an European law-enforcement area', (2003) 86 *Rivista di Diritto Internazionale* 688
Braiband, G., 'La Charte des droits fondamentaux', (2001) 12 *Droit Social* 69
Brandtner, B. and A. Rosas, 'Human rights and the external relations of the European Community: An analysis of doctrine and practice', (1998) 9 *European Journal of International Law* 490
Bray, R. (ed.), *Procedural law of the European Union* (Sweet & Maxwell, 2006)
Bribosia, H., 'Liberté, sécurité et justice: l'imbroglio d'un nouvel espace', (1998) *Revue du Marché de l'Union européenne* 34
Bribosia, H., *Perspectives des droits fondamentaux et de la citoyennete européenne*, in G. Amato and others (ed.), *Genesis and destiny of the European Constitution: commentary on the Treaty establishing a Constitution for Europe in the light of the travaux préparatoires and future prospects* (Bruylant, 2007)
Bronzini, G. and V. Piccone, 'Parlamento europeo, Corte di Giustizia e Corte di Strasburgo rilanciano la Carta di Nizza: un messaggio alla futura Conferenza intergovernativa?', accessible at www.europeanrights.eu, accessed on 18 September 2008
Broussy, E., F. Donnat and C. Lambert, 'L'obligation d'interpréter le droit national conformément au droit communautaire s'applique également aux décisions-cadres, (2005) *L'actualité juridique – Droit Administratif* 2336
Brown, C., 'Case C-112/00, Eugen Schmidberger, Internationale Transporte und Planzüge v. Austria', (2003) 40 *Common Market Law Review* 1499
Brown, C., J. Morijn, 'Case C-263/02 P, Commission v. Jego-Quere & Cie SA', (2004) 41 *Common Market Law Review* 1639
Brumber-Coret, P., N. Pourbaix, 'La communication interprétative de la Commission européenne relative à l'intégration des exigences environnementales dans le droit des marchés publics', (2001) 3 *Revue du droit de l'Union européenne* 739

Bulterman, M., 'Case C-540/03, Parliament v. Council, Judgment of the Grand Chamber of 27 June 2006 [2006] ECR I-5769', (2008) 45 *Common Market Law Review* 245

Bulterman, M.K. and H.R. Kranenbourg, 'What if rules on free movement and human rights collide? About laser games and human dignity: The Omega case', (2006) 31 *European Law Review* 93

Burrows, N., 'Question of Community accession to the European Convention determined', (1997) 1 *European Law Review* 58

Butt, M.E., 'Fundamental social rights in Europe', (2000) *Social Affairs Series*, SOCI 104-02/2000

Buzelay, 'Libre circulation des travailleurs en Europe et protection sociale', (2003) 470 *Revue du Marché Commun et de l'Union européenne* 452

Cannizzaro, E., 'Tutela dei diritti fondamentali nell'ambito comunitario e garanzie costituzionali secondo le Corti costituzionali italiana e tedesca', (1990) *Rivista di diritto internazionale* 372

Capotorti, F., 'Sull'eventuale adesione della Comunità alla Convenzione europea dei diritti dell'uomo', (1980) *Rivista di diritto internazionale* 5

Caravita, B., 'Costituzione, principi costituzionali e tecniche di normazione per la tutela dell'ambiente', in S. Grassi, M. Cecchetti and A. Andronio (eds.), *Ambiente e Diritto* (Olschki, 1999) 175

Caravita, B., *Diritto dell'ambiente* (Il Mulino, 2001)

Caretti, P., 'Il Tribunal constitucional e il Conseil constitutionnel sulla Costituzione per l'Europa', (2005) *Quaderni costituzionali* 419

Carlier, J.-Y., 'Case C-200/02, Kunqian Catherine Zhu, Man Lavette Chen v. Secretary of State for the Home, Department with annotation', (2005) 42 *Common Market Law Review* 1124

Carrera, S., 'What does free movement mean in theory and practice in an enlarged EU?', (2005) 11 *European Law Journal* 700

Carrera, S., F. Geyer, 'The Reform Treaty and Justice and Home Affairs: Implications for the Common Area of Freedom, Security and Justice', in E. Guild and F. Geyer, (eds.), *Security versus Justice? Police and Judicial Cooperationin the European Union* (Ashgate, 2008) 303

Carretti, P., *I diritti fondamentali. Libertà e diritti sociali* (Giappichelli, 2005)

Cartabia, M. and A. Celotto, 'La giustizia costituzionale in Italia dopo la Carta di Nizza', (2002) *Giurisprudenza Costituzionale* 4485

Cartabia, M., *Princìpi inviolabili e integrazione europea* (Giuffré, 1995)

Cartabia, M., 'I diritti fondamentali e la cittadinanza dell'Unione', in F. Bassanini and G. Tiberi (eds.), *Le nuove istituzioni europee. Commento al Trattato di Lisbona* (Il Mulino, 2008) 105

Cartabia, M., 'La Carta di Nizza, i suoi giudici e l'isolamento della Corte costituzionale italiana', in A. Pizzorusso, R. Romboli, A. Ruggeri, A. Saitta and G. Silvestri (eds.), *Riflessi della Carta europea dei diritti sulla giustizia e la giurisprudenza costituzionale: Italia e Spagna a confronto* (Giuffré, 2003) 211

Cassia, P., 'Quelles perspectives pour la recevabilité du recours en annulation des particuliers?', (2002) *Recueil Le Dalloz Jur* 2825

Celotto, A., 'Giudici nazionali e Carta di Nizza: disapplicazione o interpretazione conforme?', in G. Bronzini and V. Piccone (eds.), *La Carta e le Corti. I diritti fondamentali nella giurisprudenza europea multilivello* (Chimienti, 2007) 30

Celotto, A. and G. Pistorio, 'L'efficacia giuridica della Carta dei diritti fondamentali dell'Unione europea' (2005) *Giurisprudenza Italiana* 434

Cesoni, M.L., 'La mise en œuvre ne droit européen des dispositions internationals de lutte contre le terrorisme', (2004) *Revue Générale de Droit Public International* 475

Cheynel, B., 'Intérêt à agir et participation à la procédure', (2008) 14 *Revue Lamy de la Concurrence: droit, économie, regulation* 43
Chu, G., 'Playing at killing freedom of movement', (2006) 33 *Legal Issues of Economic Integration* 85
Cicero, 'The Republic', in N. Rudd (ed.), *The republic and the laws* (Oxford University Press, 1998) 68
Coffey, C., 'The EU Charter of Fundamental Rights: The Place of the Environment', in K. Feus (ed.), *The EU Charter on Fundamental Rights: Text and commentaries* (Federal Trust, 2000) 132
Cohen-Jonathan, G. and J.-F. Flauss, *La réforme du système de contrôle contentieux de la Convention européenne des droits de l'homme* (Bruylant, 2005)
Coldron, K. and L. Ackers, '(Ab)using European Citizenship? EU retired migrants and the exercise of healthcare rights', (2007) 14 *Maastricht Journal of European and Comparative Law* 299
Collier, U., 'EU Energy Policy in a Changing Climate', in A. Lenschow (ed.), *Environmental Policy Integration: Greening sectoral policies in Europe* (Earthscan, 2002) 175
Comoglio, L.P., 'Il "giusto processo" civile nella dimensione comparatistica', (2002) 57 *Rivista di Diritto Processuale* 702
Condinanzi, M., A. Lang, and B. Nascimbene, *Citizens of the Union and free movement of persons* (Nijhoff, 2008)
Conforti, B., *Le sanzioni CEE contro l'Argentina e la loro legittimità alla luce del diritto comunitario*, in N. Ronzitti (ed.), *La questione delle Falkland-Malvinas nel diritto internazionale* (Giuffré, 1984)
Constantinesco, V., 'La cittadinanza dell'Unione: una "vera" cittadinanza?', in L.S. Rossi (ed.), *Il progetto di Trattato-Costituzione. Verso una nuova architettura dell'Unione europea* (Giuffrè, 2004) 225
Constantinesco, V., Y. Gautier, and V. Michel (eds.), *Le Traité établissant une Constitution pour l'Europe. Analyses & commentaires* (Presses Universitaires de Strasbourg, 2005)
Conti, R., 'La Dignità Umana Dinanzi alla Corte di Giustizia', (2005) 4 *Corriere Giuridico* 488
Coppel, J. and A. O'Neill, 'The European Court of Justice: Taking rights seriously?', (1992) 29 *Common Market Law Review* 669
Corbett, R., F. Jacobs, and M. Shacklethon, *The European Parliament* (John Harper, 2007)
Corlett, D., *Stormy Weather: The challenge of climate change and displacement* (Sidney University of New South Wales Press, 2008)
Costa, J.P., 'Vers une protection jurisdictionelle des droits économiques et sociaux en Europe?', in *Les droits de l'homme au seuil du troisième millénaire: Mélanges en hommage à Pierre Lambert* (Bruylant, 2000)
Costello, C. (ed.), *Fundamental social rights: Current European legal protection and the challenge of the UE Charter of Fundamental Rights* (Irish Centre for European Law, 2001)
Cotte, O., 'Des précisions bienvenues quant aux garanties applicables lors de l'adoption de mesures de gels de fonds dans le cadre de la lutte contre le terrorisme', (2007) 22 *L'Europe des libertés: revue d'actualité juridique* 19
Coutron, L., 'L'arrêt Schul: une occasion manquée de revisiter la jurisprudence Foto-Frost?', (2007) 43 *Revue trimestrielle de droit européen* 491
Craig, C., 'The Treaty of Lisbon: process, architecture and substance', (2008) 33 *European Law Review* 137
Craig, P. and G. De Búrca, *EU law: Text, cases and materials* (Oxford University Press, 2003)

Craig, P., 'Legality, standing and substantial review in Community law', (1994) 14 *Oxford Journal of Legal Studies* 507

Craig, P., 'The Community Rights and the Charter', (2002) 1 *Revue européenne de droit public* 196

Cremona, M., 'Enlargement: A Successful Instrument of EU Foreign Policy?', in T. Tridimas and P. Nebbia (eds.), *European Union law for the twenty-first century: Rethinking the new legal order*, vol. I (Oxford University Press, 2003) 268

Cremona, M., 'EU enlargement: Solidarity and conditionality', (2005) 30 *European Law Review* 3

Cremona, M., 'The Union's external action: Constitutional perspectives', in Amato et al. (ed.), *Genesis and destiny of the European Constitution: Commentary on the Treaty establishing a Constitution for Europe in the light of the travaux préparatoires and future prospects* (Bruylant, 2007) 1032

Crosetti, A., *Diritto dell'ambiente* (Laterza, 2005)

Curti Gialdino, C., 'Schengen et le troisième pilier: le contrôle juridictionel organisé par le traité d'Amsterdam', (1998) *Revue du Marché de l'Union européenne* 105

Curtin, D. and R. Van Ooik, 'The sting is always in the tail: The personal scope of application of the EU Charter of Fundamental Rights' (2001) *Maastricht Journal of European and Comparative Law* 102

Czuczai, J., 'The EU Charter of Fundamental Rights: Is it a new accession condition for the candidate countries especially in light of the post-Nice IGC?', in T. Tridimas and P. Nebbia (eds.), *European Union law for the twenty-first century: rethinking the new legal order* vol. 1 (Hart, 2004)

Daniele, L., 'Carta dei diritti fondamentali dell'Unione europea e Trattato di Lisbona, (2008) 13 *Dir. Un. Eur.* 655

Daniele, L., 'Parlamento europeo e Corte di giustizia: Chi la dura la vince?' (1991) *Foro Italiano* 1

Dashwood. A., and A. Johnston, 'The institutions of the enlarged EU under the regime of the Constitutional Treaty', (2005) 42 *Common Market Law Review* 1481

Davies, A.C.L., 'One step forward two, steps back? The Viking and Laval Cases in the ECJ', (2008) 37 *Industrial Law Journal* 139

Davies, R.W., 'Citizenship of the Union… rights for all?', (2002) 27 *European Law Review* 121

De Amicis, G., O. Villoni, 'Mandato d'arresto europeo e legalità penale nell'interpretazione della Corte di giustizia', (2008) *Cassazione penale* 383

De Búrca, G., 'Beyond the Charter: How Enlargement has Enlarged the Human Rights Policy of the EU', (2003–04) 27 *Fordham International Law Journal* 679

De Búrca, G., 'On enlargement of the European Union: Beyond the Charter: How enlargement has enlarged the human rights policy of the European Union', (2004) 27 *Fordham International Law Journal* 696

De Schutter, O., 'The implementation of the EU Charter of Fundamental Rights through the Open Method of Coordination', Jean Monnet Working Paper 07/04, (2004) *New York School of Law*

De Schutter, O., 'Written contribution for the hearing in Paris on 11 September 2007', in Committee on Legal Affairs and human rights, Accession of the European Union/European Community to the European Convention on Human Rights, accessible at http://assembly.coe.int

De Witte, B. and G. Toggenburg, 'Human Rights and Membership of the European Union', in S. Peers and A. Ward (eds.), *The European Union Charter of Fundamental Rights* (Oxford, 2004) 73

De Witte, B., 'Direct Effect, Supremacy, and the Nature of the Legal Order', in P. Craig and G. De Búrca (eds.), *The evolution of EU law* (Oxford University Press, 1999) 177

Dell'Agli, L., 'L'accesso all'energia elettrica come diritto umano fondamentale per la dignità della persona umana', (2007) 5 *Rivista Giuridica dell'ambiente* 713

Dhondt, N., *Integration of environmental protection into other EC policies: Legal theory and practice*, (Europa Law Publishing, 2003)

Di Turi, C., 'La prassi giudiziaria relativa all'applicazione delle Carta di Nizza', (2002) *Il Diritto dell'Unione europea* 681

Di Turi, C., 'Liberalizzazione dei flussi commerciali internazionali, norme di diritto internazionale del lavoro e promozione della dignità umana' (1998) 37 *Diritto comunitario e degli scambi internazionali* 51

Di Turi, C.,'Globalizzazione dell'economia e diritti fondamentali in materia di lavoro' (2000) *Rivista di diritto internazionale* 113

Diez-Picazo, L., 'Notes sur la nouvelle Charte des droits fondamentaux de l'Union européenne', (2002) *Revue Européenne de Droit Public* 937

Dony, M., *Après la reforme de Lisbonne – Les nouveaux traités européens* (Éditions de l'Université de Bruxelles, 2008)

Dougan, M. and E. Spaventa, '"Wish You Weren't Here..." New Models of Social Solidarity in the European Union', in M. Dougan and E. Spaventa (eds.), *Social Welfare and EU Law* (Hart, 2005) 181

Dougan, M., 'The Treaty of Lisbon 2007: Winning minds, not hearts', (2008) 45 *Common Market Law Review* 617

Douglas-Scott, S., 'A tale of two Courts: Luxembourg, Strasbourg and the growing European human rights acquis', (2006) 43 *Common Market Law Review* 629

Douglas-Scott, S., 'Rule of Law in the EU-Putting the Security in the Area of Freedom Security and Justice, (2004) 29 *European Law Review* 219

Doumbe-Bille, S., 'Charte ET the droit international', (2005) *Revue juridique de l'environnement* 191

Dubouis, L., 'A propos de deux principes généraux du droit communautaire (droit au contrôle juridictionnel effectif et motivation des décisions des autorités nationales qui portent atteinte à un droit conféré par la règle communautaire)', (1988) *Revue française de droit administrative* 691

Dutheil de la Rochère, J., 'Les droits fondamentaux reconnus par la Charte et leurs applications', (2002) 1 *Revue européenne de droit public* 227

Dworkin, R., *Law's empire* (Harvard University Press, 1986)

Dworkin, R., *Taking rights seriously* (Duckworth, 1978)

Eccher, L., 'Il libro verde della Commissione europea sull'adattamento ai cambiamenti climatici', (2007) 5 *Rivista giuridica dell'ambiente* 933

Eckes, C., 'Case T-22802, Organisation des Modjahedines du peuple d'Iran v. Council and UK (OMPI)', (2007) 44 *Common Market Law Review* 1117

Eckes, C., 'Test Case for the Resilience of the EU's Constitutional Foundations International Sanctions against Individuals: A Test Case for the Resilience of the European Union's Constitutional Foundations, (2009) 15 *European Public Law* 351

Editorial, Comments., 'Two-speed European citizenship? Can the Lisbon Treaty help close the gap?'. (2008) 45 *Common Market Law Review* 1

Eeckout, P., 'The EU Charter of fundamental rights and the federal question', (2002) 29 *Common Market Law Review* 971

Eide, A., 'Future Protection of Economic and Social Rights in Europe', in A. Bloed, L. Leicht, M. Nowak, A. Rosas (eds), *Monitoring human rights in Europe: Comparing international procedures and mechanism* (Martinus Nijhoff, 1993) 187

Evju, S., 'The European Social Charter', in R. Blanpain (ed.), *The Council of Europe and the social challenges of the XXI century* (Kluwer Law, 2001) 19

Fabre, C., 'Social Rights in European Constitutions', in G. De Búrca and B. De Witte, *Social rights in Europe* (Oxford University Press, 2005) 22

Facenna, G., 'Eugen Schmidberger: Freedom of expression and assembly vs. free movement of goods', (2004) 1 *European Human Rights Law Review* 73
Faist, T., 'Social citizenship in the European Union: Nested membership', (2001) 39 *Journal of Common Market Studies* 37
Ferrari Bravo, L., 'Problemi tecnici dell'adesione delle Comunità europee alla Convenzione europea dei diritti dell'uomo', (1979) 4 *Rivista di diritto europeo* 347
Ferrari, G.F. and L. Montanari, 'I diritti nel progetto di Costituzione europea', (2003) *Diritto Pubblico Comunitario ed Europeo* 1716
Ferrari, G.F, (ed.), *I diritti fondamentali dopo la Carta di Nizza. Il costituzionalismo dei diritti* (Giuffré, 2001)
Ferrera, M., 'Towards An "Open" Social Citizenship? The New Boundaries of Welfare in the European Union', in G. De Búrca (ed.), *EU Law and the Welfare State. In Search of Solidarity* (Oxford University Press, 2005) 11
Fierro, E., *The EU's approach to human rights conditionality in practice* (Martinus Nijhoff, 2003)
Fitzmaurice, M., 'Environmental human rights before the English courts', (2006) *Annuaire international des droits de l'homme* 351
Flauss, J.F., 'La Cour Européenne des droits de l'homme est-elle une cour constitutionnelle?' (1999) 36 *Revue française de droit international* 711
Fletcher, M., 'Extending "indirect effect" to the third pillar: The significance of Pupino?', (2005) 30 *European Law Review* 862
Fleurke, F.M., 'What use for Article 95(5) EC?', (2008) 20 *Journal of Environmental Law* 267
Flynn, L., 'When national procedural autonomy meets the effectiveness of Community law, can it survive the impact?', (2008) 9 *Era Forum scripta iuris europaei,* 245
Franzina, P., 'Il coordinamento fra *lex fori* e norme uniformi nell'accertamento del titolo di giurisdizione secondo il regolamento (CE) n. 44/2001', (2004) 2 *Rivista di diritto internazionale* 384
Fridensköld, E., 'Locus standi in Article 88(2) cases: No cure for the Plaumann-blues I', (2008) *European Law Reporter* 17
Friess, S. and J. Shaw, 'Citizenship of the Union: First steps in the European Court of Justice', (1998) 4 *European Public Law* 533
Gaja, G., 'Court of justice opinion 2/94, Accession by the Community to the European Convention for the protection of human rights and fundamental freedoms given on 28 march 1996, not yet reported' (1996) 33 *Common Market Law Review* 973
Gaja, G., 'Opinion 2/94, Accession by the Community to the European Convention for the Protection of Human Rights and Fundamental Freedoms, given on 28 March 1996, not yet reported', (1996) 4 *Common Market Law Review* 973
García Ureta, A., '"Qui custodiat custodes?" Sobre las investigaciones de la Oficina Europea de Lucha contra el Fraude', (2006) 8–9 *Unión Europea Aranzadi* 13
Garhagnati Ketvel, M., 'The jurisdiction of the European Court of Justice in respect of the Common Foreign and Security Policy' (2006) *International and Comparative Law Quarterly* 107
Gebbie, G., '"Berlusconi" v. "Pupino": Conflict or Compatibility?', (2007) 1 *Journal of European Criminal Law* 31
Gennusa, M. E., 'La Dignità umana vista da Lussemburgo', (2005) *Quaderni Costituzionali* 174
Gerbet, P., *La construction de l'Europe* (Impremerie Nationale, 1983)
Gerkrath, J., *L'emergence d'un droit constitutionnel pour l'Europe* (Editions de l'Université de Bruxelles, 1997)
Gestri, M., *Abuso del diritto e frode alla legge nell'ordinamento comunitario* (Giuffrè, 2003)
Geyer, F., *A synthesis of the former EP resolutions in the field of fundamental rights* (EP publication, 2007)

Gil y Gil J.L., 'Los derechos sociales en la Carta de los derechos fundamentales de la Union Europea', (2003) 8 *Relaciones laborales: Revista Critica de Teoria y Pratica* 93

Giubboni, S., 'Free movement of persons and European solidarity', (2007) 13 *European Law Journal* 367

Goffin, L., 'De l'incompétence des juridictions nationales pour constater l'invalidité des actes d'institutions communautaires', (1990) *Cahiers de droit européen* 216 and Case 461/03 *Gaston Schul* [2005] ECR I-513

Gomez Fernandez, I., 'Una svolta nella giurisprudenza del *Tribunal Constitucional spagnolo*', (2005) *Quaderni costituzionali* 424

Gradoni, L., 'L'Alto rappresentante per la Bosnia-Erzegovina davanti alla Corte europea dei diritti dell'uomo', (2008) 3 *Rivista di diritto internazionale* 621

Granger, M., 'Standing for the judicial review of community acts potentially harmful to the environment: Some light at the end of the tunnel?', (2003) 5 *Environmental Law Review* 45

Grassi, S., 'Costituzioni e tutela dell'ambiente', in S. Scamuzzi (ed.), *Costituzioni, razionalità, ambiente*, (Bollati Boringhieri, 1994) 404

Grassi, S., 'La Carta dei diritti e la tutela dell'ambiente (art. 37)', in G. Vettori (eds.), *Carta europea e diritti dei privati* (CEDAM, 2002)

Greaves, R., '*Locus standi* under Art. 173 EEC when seeking annulment of a regulation', (1986) 11 *European Law Review* 119

Greer, S., 'Protocol 14 and the Future of the European Court of Human Rights', (2005) *Public Law* 83

Greer, S., *The European Convention on Human Rights* (Cambridge University Press, 2006)

Griller, S. and J. Ziller, *The Lisbon Treaty. EU Constitutionalism without a Constitutional Treaty?* (Springer, 2008)

Grimeaud, D., 'The integration of environmental concerns into other policies: A genuine policy development?', (2000) 9 *European Environmental Law Review* 216

Guild, E., 'Citizens, Immigrants, Terrorists and Others', in S. Peers and A. Ward (eds.), *The European Union Charter of Fundamental Rights* (Hart, 2004) 234

Gunvén, L., 'EU:s stadga om de grundläggande rättigheterna – arbetet med att ge EU en "själ"', (2001) *Europarättslig tidskrift* 13

Hailbronner, K., 'Die Unionsbürgerschaft und das Ende rationaler Jurisprudenz durch den EuGH?', (2004) 57 *Neue Juristische Wochenschrift* 2185

Hailbronner, K., 'Union Citizenship and access to public benefits', (2005) 42 *Common Market Law Review* 1254

Hamilton, A., 'The Federalist no. 84', in A. Hamilton, J. Jay and J. Madison (eds.), *The Federalist* (Everymans Library, 1992) 444

Hammje, 'Droits fondamentaux et ordre public', (1997) 86 *Revue Critique du Droit International Privé* 1

Harding, C., 'The private interest in challenging Community action', (1980) 5 *European Law Review* 345

Harlow, C., 'Towards a theory of access for the European Court of Justice', (1992) 12 *Yearbook of European Law* 213

Harpaz, G., 'Judicial review by the European Court of Justice of UN 'Smart Sanctions' against terror in the Kadi dispute', (2009) 14 *European Foreign Affairs Review* 65

Harpaz, G., 'The European Court of Justice and its relations with the European Court of Human Rights: The quest for enhanced reliance, coherence and legitimacy', (2009) 46 *Common Market Law Review* 105

Hart Ely, J., *Democracy and distrust – A theory of judicial review* (Harvard University Press, 1980)

Haumont, F., 'Le droit constitutionnel belge à la protection d'un environnement sain: état de la jurisprudence', (2005) 41 *Revue juridique de l'environnement* 41

Hectors, K., 'The Chartering of environmental protection: Exploring the boundaries of environmental protection as human right', (2008) *European Energy and Environmental Law Review* 165

Hijmans, H., A. Scirocco, Shortcoming in EU data protection in the third and second pillars, Can the Lisbon Treaty be expected to help?', (2009) 46 *Common Market Law Review* 1485

Hillion, C. and R.A. Wessel, 'Competence distribution in EU external relations after ECOWAS: Clarification or continued fuzziness?' (2009) 46 *Common Market Law Rev.* 551

Holmes, S., *Passions & constraint – On the theory of liberal democracy* (Chicago University Press, 1995)

Hoskins, M., 'Tilting the balance: Supremacy and national procedural rules', (1996) 21 *European Law Review* 365

House of Lords, Constitution Committee, 6th Report of Session 2007–08, 'European Union (Amendment) Bill and the Lisbon Treaty: Implications for the UK Constitution' (London: The Stationery Office Ltd, 2008) 35, para 136

Howse, R. and M. Mutua, 'Protecting human rights in a global economy. Challenges for the World Trade Organization' (2000), accessible at http://lic.law.ufl.edu/~hernandez/Trade/Howse.pdf, accessed on 7 August 2008

Huber, P.M., 'The unitary effect of the Community's Fundamental rights: The ERT doctrine Needs to be revised', (2008) 14 *European Public Law* 323

Ianniello-Saliceti, A., 'Cittadinanza dell'Unione', in P. De Cesari (ed.), *Persona e famiglia* (Giappichelli, 2008) 106

Iapichino, L., 'L'environnement en tant que droit individuel dans l'Union européenne' in J. Rideau (eds.), *La protection des droits fondamentaux dans l'Union européenne, Actes du Colloque de Nice,* (Bruylant, 2009)

Iliopoulou, A. and H. Toner, 'Case C-184/99, Rudy Grzelczyk v. Centre public d'aide sociale d'Ottignies-Louvain-la-Neuve, with annotation', (2002) 39 *Common Market Law Review* 616

Iliopoulou, A., 'Assurer le respect et la promotion des droits fondamentaux: un nouveau défi pour l'Union européenne', (2007) *Cahiers de droit européen* 433

Iovane, M., 'La participation de la société civile à l'élaboration et à l'application du droit international de l'environnement', (2008) 3 *Revue Général de Droit International Public* 465

Ippolito, F., 'Ricominciamo dalla Carta dei diritti', in G. Bisogni, G., Bronzini and V. Piccone (eds.), *I giudici e la Carta dei diritti dell'Unione europea* (Chimienti, 2006) 24

Ipsen, H.P. and G. Nicolaysen, 'Haager Kongress für Europarecht und Bericht über die aktuelle Entwicklung des Gemeinschaftsrechts', (1964) 17 *Neue Juristische Wochenschrift* 339

Jack, B., 'Locus standi and the European Court of Justice: A faint light on the horizon?', (2004) 6 *Environmental Law Review* 266

Jacobs, F.G., 'Citizenship of the European Union – A legal analysis', (2007) 13 *European Law Journal* 598

Jacobs, F.G., 'Effective judicial protection of individuals in the European Union, now and in the future', (2002) 2 *Il Diritto dell'Unione europea* 203

Jacobs, F.G., 'Human Rights in the European Union: The role of the Court of Justice', (2001) 26 *European Law Review* 331

Jacobs, F.G., 'Introduction', in E. Guild (ed.), *The legal framework and social consequences of free movement of persons in the European Union* (Kluwer, 1999)

Jacobs, F.G., 'The European Convention on Human Rights, the EU Charter of Fundamental Rights and the European Court of Justice. The impact of European Union accession to the European Convention on Human Rights', accessible at http://www.ecln.net/elements/conferences/book_berlin/jacobs.pdf

Jacqué, J.-P., 'Article II-105', in A. Levade, L. Burgorgue-Larsen and F. Picod (eds.), *Traité établissant une Constitution pour l'Europe,* Tome 2: *La Charte des droits fondamentaux de l'Union* (Bruylant, 2005) 575

Jacqué, J.-P., 'Charte des droits fondamentaux et droit à un recours effectif. Dialogue entre le juge et le "constituant"', (2002) 1 *Il Diritto dell'Unione europea* 1

Jacqué, J.-P., 'Communauté Européenne et Convention européenne des droits de l'homme', in *Mélanges à Boulouis* (Dalloz 1991) 325

Jacqué, J.-P., 'La Charte des Droits Fondamentaux de l'Union européenne: présentation générale', in L.S. Rossi (ed), *Carta dei diritti fondamentali e Costituzione dell'Unione Europea* (Giuffré, 2002) 55

Jacqué, J.-P., 'Les principes constitutionnels fondamentaux dans le projet de traité établissant la Constitution européenne', in L.S. Rossi (ed.), *Vers une nouvelle architecture de l'Union européenne* (Bruylant, 2004) 71

Jacqué, J.-P., 'Primauté du droit international versus protection des droits fondamentaux' (2009) *Revue trimestrielle de droit européen* 161

Jans, J. H., H. B. Vedder, *European Environmental Law,* 3rd ed. (Europa Law Publishing, 2000)

Jans, J.H., 'The effects in national legal systems of the prohibition of discrimination on grounds of age as a general principle of Community law', (2007) 3 *Legal Issues of European Integration* 53

Jegouzo, Y., 'La genèse de la Charte constitutionnelle de l'environnement', (2003) *Revue juridique de l'environnement* 23

Johnston, A., 'Freezing terrorist assets again: Walking a tightrope over thin ice?' (2008) 67 *The Cambridge Law Journal* 31

Jordan, A. (ed.), *Environmental policy in the European Union* (Earthscan, 2005)

Kakouris, C., 'Do the member States possess judicial procedural autonomy?', (1997) 34 *Common Market Law Review* 1389

Katrougalas, G.S., 'The implementation of social rights in Europe', (1996) 2 *Columbia Journal of European Law* 277

Katz, D., 'Les "critères de Copenhague"', (2000) 40 *Revue du Marché Commun et de l'Union Européenne* 483

Keller, H., A. Stone Sweet, *A Europe of rights, the impact of the ECHR on National legal systems* (Oxford University Press, 2008)

Kirsch, N., 'The open architecture of European human rights law' (2008) 71 *Modern Law Review* 183

Kiss, A.C., 'The European Charter of Fundamental Rights and Freedoms, Environment and Consumer Protection', in S. Peers and A. Ward (eds.), *The EU charter of fundamental rights* (Oxford University Press, 2004), 247

Kitver, P., 'The composite case for national parliaments in the European Union: Who profits from enhanced involvement?'. (2006) 2 *European Constitutional Law Review* 331

Kochenov, D., 'Behind the Copenhagen façade. The meaning and structure of the Copenhagen political criteria of democracy and the rule of law', (2004) 8 *European Integration On-Line Papers* 10

Koeman, N.S.J. (ed.), *Environmental law in Europe* (Kluwer, 1999)

Kokott, J., 'German constitutional jurisprudence and European integration', (1996) 2 *European Public Law* 237

Kokott, J., 'Die Freizügigkeit der Unionsbürger als neue Grundfreiheit', in P.-M. Dupuy, B. Fassbender, M.N. Shaw and K.-P. Sommermann (eds.), *Völkerrecht als*

Wertordnung – Common Values in International Law, Festschrift für/Essays in honour of Christian Tomuschat (Kehl am Rhein: N.P. Engel Verlag, 2006) 207

Kombos, C., 'Fundamental rights and fundamental freedoms: A Symbiosis on the basis of subsidiarity', (2006) 12 *European Public Law* 433

Kombos, C., 'The recent case law on *locus standi* of private applicants under Art. 230 (4) EC: A missed opportunity or a velvet revolution?', (2005) *European Integration Online Paper*, accessibile at http;//eiop.or.at/eiop/texte/2005-017a.htm

Kostakopoulou, D., 'European Union citizenship: Writing the future', (2007) 13 *European Law Journal* 635

Koukoulis-Spiliotopoulos, S., 'Towards a European Constitution: Does the Charter of Fundamental Rights "maintain in full" the *acquis communautaire*?', (2002) 1 *Revue européenne de droit public* 57

Koukoulis-Spiliotopoulos, S., 'Which Charter of Fundamental Rights was incorporated in the draft European Constitution?', (2005) 1 *Revue Européenne de Droit Public* 295

Koutrakos, P., 'Development and foreign policy: Where to draw the line between the pillars', (2008) 33 *European Law Review* 289

Krämer, L., 'Droit communautaire et état de l'environnement en Europe', (2007) 1 *Revue du droit de l'Union européenne,* 127

Krämer, L., *Casebook on EU environmental law*, 2th ed. (Hart, 2002)

Krämer, L., *EC environmental law*, 6th ed. (Sweet & Maxwell, 2007)

Krämer, L., 'Mieux légiférer et déréglementation du droit de l'environnement européen', (2007) 4 *Revue du droit de l'Union européenne,* 801

Kronenberger, V. and P. Dejmek, '*Locus standi* of individuals before community courts under Article 230 (4) EC: Illusions and disillusions after the Jégo-Quéré (T-177/01) and Unión de Pequeños Agricultores (C-50/00) judgments', (2002) 5 *European Legal Forum* 257

Kruger, C., 'Reflections concerning accession of the European Communities to the European Convention on Human Rights', (2002–2003) 21 *Penn. Int'l Law Rev* 97

Labayle, H., 'Un espace de liberté, de sécurité et de justice', (1997) *Revue trimestrielle de Droit européen* 863

Ladenburger, C., 'Fundamental Rights and Citizenship of the Union', in G. Amato, H. Bribosia and B. De Witte (eds.), *Genesis and destiny of the European constitution* (Bruylant, 2007) 318

Ladenburger, C., 'Police and Criminal Law in the Treaty of Lisbon. A new Dimension for the Community Method', (2008) 4 *European Constitutional Law Review* 21

Lannon, E., K. Inglis and T. Haenebalke, 'The Many Faces of EU Conditionality in Pan-Euro-Mediterranean Relations' in M. Marescau and E. Lennon (eds.), *The EU's enlargement and Mediterranean strategies. A comparative analysis* (Basingstoke, 2001) 110

Leary, V.A., 'The WTO and the Social Clause: Post-Singapore', (1997) 8 *European Journal of International Law* 118

Lee, M., *EU Environmental Law: challenges, change and decision-making* (Hart, 2005)

Lenaerts, K. and P. Foubert, 'Social rights in the case-law of the European Court of Justice: The impact of the Charter of Fundamental rights of the European Union on standing case-law', (2001) 28 *Legal Issues of European Integration* 267

Lenaerts, K. and E. De Smijter, 'A "Bill of Rights" for the European Union', (2001) 38 *Common Market Law Review* 275

Lenaerts, K. and E. De Smijter, 'Le Traité d'Amsterdam', (1998) *Journal des Tribunaux Droit européen* 30

Lenaerts, K. and M. Desomer, 'New models of constitution-making in Europe: The quest for legitimacy', (2002) 39 *Common Market Law Review* 1217

Lenaerts, K. and T. Heremans, 'Contours of a European social union in the case-law of the European Court of Justice', (2006) 2 *European Constitutional Law Review* 107

Lenaerts, K., 'Fundamental rights in the European Union', (2000) 25 *European Law Review* 599

Lenaerts, K., D. Arts, and I. Maselis (eds.), *Procedural law of European Union* (Sweet & Maxwell, 2006)

Lenaerts, K., P.V. Van Nuffel, and R. Bray (eds.), *Constitutional law of European Union* (Sweet & Maxwell, 2007)

Lindfelt, M., *Fundamental rights in the EU – Towards a higher law of the land?* (Abo: Abo Akademi University Press, 2007)

Locke, J., *Two treatises of government* [1689] (Cambridge University Press, 1988) 407

Lorber, P., 'Labour Law', in S. Peers and A. Wards (eds.), *The EU charter of fundamental rights* (Hart, 2004) 211

Louis, J.V., 'National parliaments and the principle of subsidiarity', in I. Pernice and E. Tanchev (eds.), *Ceci n'est pas une constitution – Constitutionalisation without a constitution?* (ECLN Conference Sofia, 2008)

Lucarelli, A., 'Articolo 37', in R. Bifulco, M. Cartabia and A. Celotto (eds.), *L'Europa dei diritti. Commento alla carta dei diritti fondamentali dell'Unione Europea* (Il Mulino, 2001) 261

Luciani, M., 'Diritti sociali e integrazione europea', (2000) 3 *Politica del Diritto* 367

Ludewig, P.G., 'A lost opportunity: No new approach to the concept of locus standi under Article 230 EC', (2002) *European Law Reporter* 259

MacDonald, K., 'A right to a healthful environment – humans and habitats: Re-thinking rights in an age of climate change', (2008) 17 *European Energy and Environmental Law Review* 213

Majone, G., 'The EC between social policy and social regulation', (1993) 31 *Journal of Common Market Studies* 153

Malmberg, J., T. Sigeman, 'Industrial actions and EU economic freedoms: The autonomous collective bargaining model curtailed by the European Court of Justice (2008) 45 *Common Market Law Review* 1115

Mancini, F. and D. Keeling, 'Democracy and the European Court of Justice', (1994) 57 *The Modern Law Review* 175

Mancini, F., 'The making of a Constitution for Europe', (1989) 26 *Common Market Law Review* 595

Manessis, A., in J. Iliopoulos-Strangas (ed.), *La protection des droits sociaux fondamentaux dans les Etates membres de l'Union européenne: étude de droit comparé* (Bruylant, 2000) 19

Manin, P., 'L'Adhésion de l'Union Européenne à la Convention de sauveguarde des droits de l'homme et des libertés fondamentales', in L.S. Rossi (ed.), *Vers une nouvelle architecture de l'Union européenne* (Bruylant, 2004) 265

Manzella, A., 'Dopo Nizza: la Carta dei diritti "proclamata"', in L.S. Rossi (ed.), *Carta dei diritti fondamentali e Costituzione dell'Unione europea*' (Giuffré, 2002) 245

Maresceau M. and E. Lannon (eds.), *The EU's enlargement and Mediterranean strategies: A comparative analysis* (London, 2001)

Maresceau, M. and E. Montaguti, 'The relations between the European Union and Central and Eastern Europe: A legal appraisal', (1995) 6 *Common Market Law Review* 1328

Maresceau, M., 'Pre-accession', in M. Cremona (ed.), *The enlargement of the European Union* (Oxford University Press, 2003) 9

Marshall, T.H., *Citizenship and social class* (Pluto Press, 1992)

Martin, D., 'Comments on *Förster* (Case C-158/07 of 18 November 2008), *Metock* (Case C-127/08 of 25 July 2008) and *Huber* (Case C-524/06 of 16 December 2008)', (2009) 11 *European Journal of Migration and Law* 100

Masson, A., C. Micheau, 'The Werner Mangold case: An example of legal militancy', (2007) 32 *European Public Law* 587

Maupain, F., 'La protection internationale des travailleurs et la libéralisation du commerce mondial: un lien ou un frein?' (1996) *Revue Générale de Droit international Publique* 45

Mayer, F.C., 'The European Constitution and the Courts', in A. Von Bogdandy and J. Bast (eds.), *Principles of European constitutional law* (Hart, 2006) 281

Menéndez, A.J., 'The sinews of peace: Rights to solidarity in the Charter of Fundamental Rights of the European Union', (2003) 16 *Ratio Juris* 379

Menéndez, A.J., 'Chartering Europe: Legal status and policy implications of the Charter of Fundamental Rights of the European Union', (2002) 3 *Journal of Common Market Studies* 471

Menéndez, A.J., *Some elements of a theory of European fundamental rights*, in E.O. Eriksen and A.J. Menéndez (eds.), *Arguing fundamental rights* (Springer, 2006) 155

Menéndez, A.J., *The rights' foundations of solidarity: Social and Economic rights in the Charter of Fundamental Rights of the European Union*, (2003) ARENA Working Papers WP 03/1

Mengozzi, P., 'La tutela dei diritti umani nella giurisprudenza comunitaria', in L. S. Rossi, *Carta dei diritti fondamentali e Costituzione dell'Unione europea* (Giuffré, 2002) 51

Mitsilegas, V., 'The third wave of Third Pillar law. Which direction for EU criminal justice?', (2009) 34 *European Law Review* 557

Moiny, Y., 'Le contrôle, par le juge européen, de certaines mesures communautaires visant à lutter contre le financement du terrorisme', (2008) 149 *Journal des tribunaux/droit européen* 137

Monaco, R., 'Les principes d'interprétation suivis par la Cour de Justice des Communautés Européennes', in *Mélanges offerts à Henri Rolin* (Pedone, 1964)

Monetti, V., 'Sentenze della Corte di Strasburgo', in G. Bisogni, G. Bronzini and V. Piccone (eds.), *I giudici e la Carta dei diritti dell'Unione europea* (Chimienti, 2006) 115

Montanari, L., 'Una decisione del Tribunale di prima istanza fra CEDU e la Carta di Nizza', (2001) *Diritto Pubblico Comunitario ed Europeo* 670

Moorman, Y., 'Integration of ILO core rights labor standards into WTO' (2001) 39 *Columbia Journal of Transnational Law* 555

Moravcsik, A., 'The origins of human rights regimes: Democratic delegation in post war Europe', (2000) 54 *International Organization* 217

Moriceau, A., 'Le traité de Lisbonne et la Charte des droit fondamentaux', (2008) 519 *Revue du Marché Commun et de l'Union Européenne* 361

Morijn, J., 'Balancing fundamental rights and common market freedoms in Union Law: Schmidberger and Omega in light of the European Constitution', (2006) 12 *European Law Journal* 15

Mortati, C., *La Costituzione in senso materiale* (Giuffrè, 1940)

Moura Ramos, M.R., 'Public policy in the framework of the Brussels Convention. Remarks on two recent decisions by the European Court of Justice', in M.R. Moura Ramos (ed.), *Estudios de derecho international privado e de derecho processual civil internacional* (Coimbra, 2002) 283

Moussis, N., 'Le traitè de Lisbonne: une Constitution sans en avoir le titre', (2008) *Revue du marché commun et de l'Union europèenne* 161

Mouthaan, S., 'The BECTU Case: A la recherche de la charte oubliée', (2001) 12 *European Current Law* xi

Muir Watt, H., 'Evidence of an emergent European legal culture: Public policy requirements of procedural fairness under the Brussels and Lugano Conventions', (2001) 36 *Texas International Law Journal* 539

Nascimbene, B., 'L'incorporazione degli Accordi di Schengen nel quadro dell'Unione europea e il futuro ruolo del Comitato parlamentare di controllo', (1999) *Rivista Italiana di Diritto Pubblico Comunitario* 738

Nascimbene, B., 'Le Protocole n. 14 à la Convention Européenne des droits de l'homme à la lumière de ses travaux préparatoires', (2006) 67 *Revue Trimestrielle de droits de l'homme* 531

Neuwahl, N., 'Article 173 Paragraph 4 EC: Past, present and possible future', (1996) 21 *European Law Review* 112

Nichol, D., 'Original intent and the European Convention on Human Rights', (2005) *Public Law* 152

Nollkaemper, A., 'Three Conceptions of the Integration Principle in international Environmental Law', in A. Lenschow, (ed.), *Environmental policy integration. Greening sectoral policies in Europe* (Earthscan, 2002)

Nowak, M., 'Human rights "conditionality" in relation to entry to, and full participation in, the EU', in P. Alston (ed.), *The EU and Human Rights* (Oxford University Press, 1999) 687

O'Keefe, D., 'Union Citizenship', in D. O'Keefe and P. Twomey (eds.), *Legal issues of the Maastricht Treaty* (Wiley, 1994) 106

O'Leary, S., 'Putting flesh on the bones of European citizenship', (1999) 24 *European Law Review* 68

O' Leary, S., 'Solidarity and citizenship rights', in G. De Bùrca (ed.), *EU Law and the Welfare State – In search of solidarity* (Hart, 2005) 39

O'Leary, S., *The evolving concept of Community citizenship. From the free movement of persons to Union citizenship* (The Hague: Kluwer, 1996) 119

Obradovic, D., 'EC rules on public participation in environmental decision-making at the European and national levels', (2007) 32 *European Law Review* 839

Oliver, P. and W.-H. Roth, 'The internal market and the four freedoms', (2004) *Common Market Law Review* 41

Oliver, P., 'Le droit communautaire et les voies de recours nationales', (1992) 3–4 *Cahiers de Droit Européen* 348

Oppenheimer, A., *The relationship between European Community law and National law: The cases* (Cambridge University Press, 1994) 410

Orlandi, M., 'Libera circolazione delle merci e deroghe giustificate da esigenze di tutela dei diritti fondamentali', *(2003) Il Diritto dell'Unione Europea* 903

Pachauri, R. K., *Acceptance speech for the Nobel Peace Prize awarded to the Intergovernmental Panel on Climate Change* (IPCC), online publication accessible at http://www.ipcc.ch/graphics/speeches/nobel-peace-prize-oslo-10-december-2007.pdf

Paciotti, E. (ed.), *Per un'Europa costituzionale* (Ediesse, 2006)

Paladini, L., 'I conflitti fra i pilastri dell'Unione europea e le prospettive del Trattato di Lisbona' (2010) *Il Diritto dell'Unione Europea*, (forthcoming)

Paladini, L., *Le misure restrittive adottate nell'ambito della PESC: prassi e giurisprudenza*, (2009) *Il Diritto dell'Unione europea* 365

Passos, R., 'Recent developments concerning the role of national parliaments in the European Union' (2008) *ERA* 25

Pawlak, P., 'Made in the USA? The Influence of the US on the EU's Data Protection Regime', accessible at http://www.ceps.be

Pechstein M. and C. Drechler, 'Die Auslegung und Fortbildung des Primärrechts', in K. Reisenhuber (eds.), *Europäische Methodenlehre. Handbuch für Ausbildung und Praxis* (Berlin, 2006) 172

Peers, S., 'Salvation outside the Church: Judicial protection in the third pillar after the Pupino and Segi judgments', (2007) 44 *Common Market Law Review* 883

Peers, S., 'The ECJ's Jurisdiction Over EC Immigration and Asylum Law: Time for a Change?, in H. Toner, E. Guild and A. Baldaccini (eds.), *EU immigration and asylum law and policy* (Hart, 2007)

Peers, S., *EU justice and home affairs law* (Oxford University Press, 2006)

Pellecchia, E. 'Il caso Omega: La dignità Umana e il delicate rapporto tra diritti fondamentali e libertà fondamentali nel diritto comunitario', (2007) 1 *Europa e Diritto Privato* 181

Pernice, I., 'Multilevel constitutionalism in the European Union', (2002) 27 *European Law Review* 511

Pernice, I., 'The Treaty of Lisbon and Fundamental Rights', in S. Griller and J. Ziller (eds.), *The Lisbon Treaty. EU Constitutionalism without a Constitutional Treaty?* (Sprinter, 2008) 235 at 252

Perulli, A., 'La promozione dei diritti sociali fondamentali nell'era della globalizzazione' (2001) 02 *Diritto delle Relazioni Industriali* 157

Pescatore, P., 'Monisme, dualisme et effet "utile" dans la jurisprudence de la Cour de Justice de la Communauté européenne', in N. Von Colneric, D. Edward, J. Puissochet and D.R. Colomer (eds.), *Une communauté de droit. Festschrift für Gil Carlos Rodríguez Iglesias* (Berlin, 2003) 329

Petersmann, E.-U., R. Howse and P. Aston, 'Trade and human rights : An Exchange', *Jean Monnet Working Papers* WP 12/2002

Pinelli, C., 'La Carta europea dei diritti e il processo di "costituzionalizzazione" del diritto europeo', in A. Pizzorusso, R. Romboli, A. Ruggeri, A. Saitta and G. Silvestri (eds.), *Riflessi della Carta europea dei diritti sulla giustizia e la giurisprudenza costituzionale: Italia e Spagna a confronto* (Giuffré, 2003) 70

Pinfell, C., 'Conditionality and enlargement in the light of EU constitutional development', (2004) 10 *European Law Journal* 354

Piris, J.C., 'L'Union européenne a-t-elle une Constitution? Lui en faut-il une? (1999) *Revue Trimestrielle de Droit Européenne* 599

Poiares Maduro, M., 'The Double Constitutional Life of the Charter of Fundamental Rights of the European Union', in T. Hervey and J. Kenner (eds.), *Economic and social rights under the EU Charter of Fundamental Rights: A legal perspective* (Hart, 2003) 281

Poiares Maduro, M., 'Contrapunctual Law: Europe's Constitutional Pluralism in Action', in N. Walker (ed.), *Sovereignty in Transition* (Oxford University Press, 2003) 526

Poiares Maduro, M., 'Interpreting European law: Judicial adjudication in a context of Constitutional pluralism', (2007) 1 *European Journal of Legal Studies* 12

Poiares Maduro, M., 'Striking the Elusive Balance Between Economic Freedom and Social Rights in the EU', in P. Alston, M. Bustelo and J. Heenan (eds.), *The EU and Human Rights* (Oxford University Press, 1999) 452

Poiares Maduro, M., G. Grasso, 'Quale Europa dopo la sentenza della Corte costituzionae tedesca sul Trattato di Lisbona', (2009) *Il Diritto dell'Unione europea* 503

Poillot Peruzzetto, S., 'L'ordre public international en droit communautaire. A propos de l'arrêt de la Cour de Justice des Communautés du 1er juin 1999 (affaire Eco Swiss China Tima Ltd)', (2000) 2 *Journal de Droit International* 299

Ponzano, P., 'Le traité de Lisbonne: l'Europe sort de sa crise institutionnelle', (2007) *Revue du droit de l'Union européenne* 569

Pozzo, B., 'L'articolo 37 e la tutela dell'ambiente come diritto fondamentale', in M.D. Panforti (ed.), *I diritti fondamentali in Europa* (Giuffrè, 2002) 171

Prieur, M., 'La Charte, l'environnement et la Constitution', (2003) *Actualité juridique. Droit administratif* 353

Principato, L., 'I diritti sociali nel quadro dei diritti fondamentali', (2001) *Giustizia Costituzionale* 873

Puissochet, J.P., 'La Cour européenne des droits de l'homme, la Cour de Justice des Communautées européennes et la protection des droits de l'homme', in P. Mahoney, F. Matscher, H. Petzold and L. Wildhaber (eds.), *Protection des droits de l'homme: la perspective européenne* (Heymanns, 2000) 1139

Ragolle F., 'Access to justice for private applicants in the Community legal order: Recent (r)evolutions', (2003) 28 *European Law Review* 90
Rasmussen, H., 'Why is Article 173 interpreted against private plaintiffs?', (1980) 5 *European Law Review* 112
Rehman, J., *International human rights law: A practical approach* (Harlow: Pearson Education, 2003) 192
Reich, N., 'The Constitutional relevance of citizenship and free movement in an enlarged Union', (2005) 11 *European Law Journal* 680
Ress, G., 'The Legal Relationship Between the European Court of Human Rights and the Court of Justice of the European Communities According to the European Convention on Human Rights', in H.-J. Blank and S. Mangiameli (eds.), *Governing Europe under a Constitution – The hard road from the European Treaties to a European Constitutional Treaty* (Springer, 2003) 279
Ricci, G., 'BECTU: An unlimited right to annual paid leave', (2001) 30 *Industrial Law Journal* 401
Rideau, J., 'Présentation des actes juridiques dans la Constitution', in E. Álvarez Conde and V. Garrido Mayol (eds.), *Comentarios a la Constitución Europea*, vol. I (Valencia: Tirant lo Blanch, 2004)
Rizzo, A., 'Il problema della tutela dei diritti fondamentali nell'Unione Europea', (2001) *Europa e diritto privato* 59
Rodotà, S., 'La Carta come atto politico e documento giuridico', in A. Manzella, P. Melograni, E. Paciotti, S. Rodotà (eds.), *Riscrivere i diritti in Europa* (Il Mulino, 2001) 73
Rodotà, S., 'Ma l'Europa già applica la nuova Carta dei diritti?', in *La Repubblica*, 3 January 2001
Rodotà, S., 'Nel silenzio della politica i giudici fanno l'Europa', in G. Bronzini, V. Piccone (eds.), *La Carta e le Corti. I diritti fondamentali nella giurisprudenza europea multilivello* (Chimienti 2007) 27
Rodriguez Iglesias, G.C., 'La protecion de los derechos fundamentales en la Union Europea', in *Scritti in onore di F. Mancini*, II (Giuffré, 1998) 831
Romboli, R., 'Carta europea dei diritti e garanzie giurisdizionali (notazioni introduttive)', in A. Pizzorusso, R. Romboli, A. Ruggeri, A. Saitta, G. Silvestri (eds.), *Riflessi della Carta europea dei diritti sulla giustizia e la giurisprudenza costituzionale: Italia e Spagna a confronto* (Giuffré, 2003) 110
Romi, R., 'La Charte de l'environnement, l'avatar constitutionnel?', (2004) *Revue du droit public et de la science politique en France et à l'étranger* 1485
Romi, R., 'Les principes du droit de l'environnement dans la 'Charte constitutionnelle':'jouer le jeu' ou mettre les principes 'hors-jeu'?', (2003) *Revue juridique de l'environnement* 46
Rossi, L.S., 'Le rapport entre Charte des droits fondamentaux et Traité de Lisbonne', online publication accessible at http://www.europeanrights.eu, accessed on 15 september 2008
Rossi, L.S. (ed.), *Carta dei diritti fondamentali e costituzione europea* (Giuffré, 2002)
Rossi, L.S., '"Costituzionalizzazione" dell'UE e dei diritti fondamentali', in L.S. Rossi (ed.), *Carta dei diritti fondamentali e Costituzione dell'Unione europea* (Giuffré, 2002) 267
Rossi, L.S., 'How fundamental is a fundamental principle? Primacy and fundamental rights after the Lisbon Treaty', *Yearbook of European Law* (Oxford University Press, 2008) 65
Rossi, L.S., 'How Fundamental are fundamental principles?', in G. Venturini, S. Bariatti (eds.), *Individual rights and international justice* – Liber Fausto Pocar (Giuffré, 2009) 801

Rossi, L.S., 'I beneficiari della libera circolazione delle persone nella giurisprudenza comunitaria'. (1994) VI *Foro italiano* 101

Rossi, L.S., 'I diritti fondamentali nel Trattato di Lisbona', 2007, accessible at http://www.europeanrights.eu, accessed on 15 September 2008

Rossi, L.S., 'Il parere 2/94 sull'adesione della Comunità europea alla Convenzione europea dei diritti dell'uomo', (1996) 1 *Il Diritto dell'Unione Europea* 839

Rossi, L.S., 'Il Rapporto tra Trattato di Lisbona e Carta dei Diritti Fondamentali dell'UE', in G. Bronzin, F. Guariello; V. Piccon, *Le Scommesse dell'Europa. Istituzioni, diritti, politiche* (Ediesse, 2009)

Rossi, L.S., 'L'integrazione differenziata nel Trattato di Lisbona', (2008) 1 *Sud in Europa* accessible at http://www.sudineuropa.net/articolo.asp?ID=317&IDNumero=31

Rossi, L.S., 'Supremazie incrociate: Trattato costituzionale europeo e Costituzioni nazionali, in L. Daniele (ed.) *La dimensione internazionale ed europea del diritto nell'esperienza della Corte Costituzionale* (ESI, 2007) 399

Rossi, L.S., 'Uguaglianza-Cittadinanza', in L.S. Rossi (ed.), *Carta dei diritti fondamentali e Costituzione dell'Unione europea* (Giuffrè, 2002)

Rossi, L.S., 'Verso la Costituzione europea?' in L.S. Rossi (ed.), *Carta dei Diritti Fondamentali e Costituzione europea* (Giuffré, 2002) 249

Rossi, L.S., 'Verso una parziale "comunitarizzazione" del terzo pilastro', (1997) *Il Diritto dell'Unione euopea* 249

Rothenberger, S., O. Govt, 'The "Orange Card": A fitting response to national parliaments' marginalisation in EU decision making?', Paper presented at the conference *Fifty Years of Interparliamentary Cooperation*, 13 June 2007, Bundesrat, Berlin

Rubenstein, K., 'Citizenship in a borderless world', in C.G. Weeramantry, A. Anghie and G. Sturgess (eds.), *Legal visions of the 21st century: Essays in honour of Judge Christopher Weeramantry* (Nijhoff, 1998) 203

Ruggeri, A., 'Tradizioni cosituzionali comuni e controlimiti, tra teoria delle fonti e teoria dell'interpretazione', in P. Falzea, A. Spadaro and L. Ventura (eds.) *La Corte costituzionale e le Corti d'Europa* (Giappichelli, 2003) 505

Ruggieri, A., 'Carta europea dei diritti e integrazione interordinamentale, dal punto di vista della giustizia e della giurisprudenza costituzionale (notazioni introduttive)', in A. Pizzorusso, R. Romboli, A. Ruggeri, A. Saitta and G. Silvestri (eds.), *Riflessi della Carta europea dei diritti sulla giustizia e la giurisprudenza costituzionale: Italia e Spagna a confronto* (Giuffré, 2003) 12

Sadursky, W., 'Charter and enlargement', (2002) 3 *European Law Journal* 340

Sadursky, W., 'The role of the EU Charter of Rights in the process of enlargement' in G. Bermann and K. Pistor (eds.), *Law and governance in an enlarged European Union* (Hart, 2004) 61

Saggio, A., 'Incidenza della giurisprudenza della Corte di Giustizia sulle norme processuali', (2001) 1 *Corriere Giuridico* 114

Sanna, S., 'Diritti fondamentali dei lavoratori: ruolo dell'OIL e dell'OMC' (2004) 78 *Diritto del lavoro* 147

Schermers, H.G. and D. F. Waeibroek, *Judicial protection in the European Union* (The Hague/London/New York, Kluwer Law International, 2001); E. Szyszczak, 'Making Europe more relevant to its citizens: Effective judicial process', (1996) 21 *European Law Review* 351

Scheuing, D.H., 'Freizügigkeit als Unionsbürgerrecht', (2003) 38 *Europarecht* 785

Schmitt Von Sydow, H., 'Liberté, démocratie, droits fondamentaux et état de droit. Analyse de l'art 7 du Traité UE', (2001) 2 *Revue du Droit de l'Union Européenne* 285

Schrauwen, A., 'European Union citizenship in the Treaty of Lisbon: Any change at all?', (2008) 15 *Maastricht Journal of European and Comparative Law* 59

Schwarze, J., 'The legal protection of the individual against regulations in European Union law', (2004) 10 *European Public Law* 285

Scott, J, (ed.), *Environmental protection: European law and governance* (Oxford University Press, 2009)

Shany, Y., *The competing jurisdictions of international courts and tribunals* (Oxford University Press, 2003)

Shaw, J., 'The Constitutional Development of Citizenship in the EU Context: With or Without the Treaty of Lisbon', in I. Pernice and E. Tanchev (eds.), *Ceci n'est pas une Constitution - Constitutionalisation without a Constitution?* (Nomos, 2008) 106

Sieberson, S.C., 'Dividing lines between the European Union and its Member States. The impact of the Treaty of Lisbon' (Asser Press, 2008) 95

Simon, D., 'Non-recevabilité de l'action contre une décision de recours en justice', (2006) 303 *Europe* 10

Siroën, J.-M., 'Organisation mondiale du commerce, clause sociale et développement' (1997) 98 *Mondes en Developpement* 29

Skouris, V., 'La protezione dei diritti fondamentali nell'Unione europea nella prospettiva dell'adozione di una Costituzione europea', in L.S. Rossi, (ed.), *Il progetto di Trattato-Costituzione. Verso una nuova architettura dell'Unione europea* (Giuffré 2004) 249

Skouris, V., 'Fundamental rights and fundamental freedoms: The challenge of striking a delicate balance', (2006) *European Business Law Review* 227

Smets, H., 'L'environnement dans les Constitutions des quinze et de la Suisse, (2003) *Revue juridique de l'environnement* 139

Smisman, S., 'Reflexive law in support of directly deliberative polyarchy: Reflexive-deliberative polyarchy as normative frame of the OMC', in O. De Schutter and S. Deakin (eds.), *Social rights and market forces: Is the open method of coordination of employment and social policies the future of social Europe?* (Bruylant, 2005)

Smismans, S., 'The Open Method of Coordination and Fundamental Social Rights', in G. De Bùrca and B. De Witte (eds.), *Social rights in Europe* (Oxford University Press 2005) 237

Smith, K.E., 'The evolution and application of EU membership conditionality', in M. Cremona (ed.), *The enlargement of the European Union* (Oxford University Press, 2003) 109

Snell, J., 'And Then There Were Two: Products and Citizens in Community Law', in T. Tridimas and P. Nebbia (eds.), *European Union law for the twenty-first century. Rethinking the new legal order*, vol. 2: *Internal market and free movement policies* (Hart, 2004) 69

Soler, E. and I. Lecha, 'Debating Turkey's Accession: National and Ideological Cleavages in the European Parliament', in M.E. Barbé Izuel and A. Herranz (eds.), *The role of parliaments in European foreign policy: Debating on accountability and legitimacy* (IUEE 2005) 55

Sotis, C., 'Il Trattato di Lisbona e le competenze penali dell'Unione europea', (2009) *La Magistratura* 27

Spadaro, A. 'Verso la Costituzione europea. il problema delle garanzie giurisdizionali dei diritti', in A. Pizzorusso, R. Romboli, A. Ruggeri, A. Saitta and G. Silvestri (eds.), *Riflessi della Carta europea dei diritti sulla giustizia e la giurisprudenza costituzionale: Italia e Spagna a confronto* (Giuffré, 2003) 147

Spaventa, E., 'Opening Pandora's Box: Some reflections on the constitutional effects of the decision in Pupino', (2007) 3 *European Constitutional Law Review* 5

Spaventa, E., 'Seeing the woods despite the trees? On the scope of EU citizenship and its constitutional effects', (2008) 45 *Common Market Law Review* 13

Spencer, J.R., 'Child witnesses and the European Union', (2005) 64 *The Cambridge Law Journal* 569

Sperduti, G., 'Le rattachement des Communautés Européenne à la Convention de Rome sur la sauvegarde des droits de l'homme et des libertés fondamentales', (1980) 2 *Revue du Marché Commun* 170

Stern, N., *The Economics of climate change. The Stern Review* (Cambridge University Press, 2006)

Strozzi, G., 'Prime considerazioni sul Trattato di Lisbona', 2008, online: www.sudineuropa.net, accessed on 8 January 2009

Syrpis, P., 'The Treaty of Lisbon: Much ado... but about what?', (2008) 37 *Industrial Law Journal* 232

Taschner, H.C., 'Free Movement of Students, Retired Persons and Other European Citizens. A Difficult Legislative Process', in H.G. Schermers, C. Flinterman, A.E. Kellermann, J.C. Van Haersolte and G.W.A. Van der Meent (eds.), *Free movement of persons in Europe. Legal problems and experiences* (Nijhoff, 1993) 431

Temple Lang, J., 'Actions for declarations that Community regulations are invalid: The duties of national courts under Article 10 EC', (2003) 28 *European Law Review* 102

Tesauro, G., 'I Diritti fondamentali nella giurisprudenza della Corte di Giustizia', (1992) *Rivista Internazionale dei Diritti dell'uomo* 426

Thym, D. , 'Charter of Fundamental Rights: Competition or consistency of human rights protection in Europe?' (2003) *The Finnish yearbook of international law* 11

Tillotson J. and N. Foster, *Text, cases and materials on European Union law* (Cavendish, 2003)

Tizzano, A. and S. Fortunato, 'La tutela dei diritti', in A. Tizzano (ed.), *Il diritto privato dell'Unione Europea*, XXVI, II, 1271, in M. Bessone (directed by), *Trattato di diritto privato* (Torino, 2000)

Tizzano, A., 'Durata "ragionevole" dei processi comunitari e problemi di convivenza a Lussemburgo', (1999) *Il Diritto dell'Unione Europea* 174

Tizzano, A., 'L'azione dell'Unione Europea per la promozione e protezione dei diritti umani', (1999) 1 *Il Diritto dell'Unione europea* 149

Tizzano, A., 'La protection des droits fondamentaux en Europe: la Cour de justice et les juridictions constitutionnelles nationales', (2006) 1 *Revue du Droit de l'Union Européenne* 9

Tizzano, A., 'Qualche riflessione sul contributo della Corte di Giustizia allo sviluppo del sistema comunitario' (2009) 14 *Dir. Un. Eur.* 141

Toggenburg, G.N., 'The role of the new EU Fundamental Rights Agency: Debating the "sex of angels" or improving Europe's human rights performance?' (2008) 3 *European Law Review* 384

Tomuschat, C., 'Case C-85/96, María Martínez Sala v Freistaat Bayern, with annotation', (2000) 37 *Common Market Law Review* 453

Tomushat, C., 'Common values and the place of the Charter in Europe', (2002) 1 *Revue européenne de droit public*, 159

Toner, H., 'Case C-185/95 P, Baustahlgewebe GmbH v. Commission', (1999) 36 *Common Market Law Review* 1345

Trifonidou, A., 'Reverse discrimination in purely internal situations: An incongruity in a citizens' Europe, (2008) 35 *Legal Isuues of Economic Integration* 43

Trubek, D.M. and L.G. Trubek, 'Hard and soft law in the construction of Social Europe: The role of the open method of coordination', (2005) 3 *European Law Journal* 343

Usher, J., 'Direct and individual concern. An effective remedy or a conventional solution', (2003) 28 *European Law Review* 575

Van der Mei, A.P., 'Residence and the evolving notion of EU citizenship', (2003) 5 *European Journal of Migration and Law* 431

Van der Mei, A.P., 'Union ctizenship and the "de-nationalisation" of the territorial welfare state', (2005) 7 *European Journal of Migration and Law* 207

Van der Mei, A.P., *Free movement of persons within the European Community. Cross-border access to public benefits* (Hart, 2003) 147

Van Peijpe, T., 'Collective labour law after Viking, Laval, Ruffert and Commission v Luxembourg', (2009) 25 *International Journal of Comparative Law* 81
Van Raepenbusch, S., 'La réforme institutionnelle du Traité de Lisbonne: l'émergence juridique de l'Union européenne', (2008) 43 *Cahiers de Droit Européen* 578
Vandamme, T., 'Prochain Arrêt: La Belgique! Explaining Recent Preliminary References of the Belgian Constitutional Court', (2008) 4 *European Constitutional Law Review* 127
Varju, M., 'Case C-131/03, Reynolds tobacco and others v. Commission', (2007) 44 *Common Market Law Review* 1101
Verdier, L., 'Vers une constitutionnalisation du droit de l'environnement: prolégomènes sur la Charte de l'environnement', (2003) *Bulletin du droit de l'environnement industriel* 4
Verhoeven, A., 'How democratic need European Union members be? Some thoughts after Amsterdam', (1998) 1 *European Law Review* 217
Villani, U., 'La riforma di Lisbona', 2008, online: www.sudineuropa.net
Von Bogdandy, A., P. Cruz Villalón and P.M. Huber (eds.), *Handbuch ius publicum Europaeum*, vols. I–II (Müller, 2007)
Von Bogdandy, A., 'The European Union as a human rights organisation? Human rights and the core of the European Union', (2007) 4 *Common Market Law Review* 1307
Von Bogdandy, A., J. Von Bernstorff, 'The EU Fundamental Rights Agency within the European and International Human Rights Architecture: The Legal Framework and Some Unsettled Issues in a New Field of Administrative Law, (2009) 46 *Common Market Law Review* 1035
Von der Groeben, H., *The European Community. The formative years. The struggle to establish the Common Market and the Political Union* (The European Perspective Series, Commission of the EC, 1987)
Wachsmann, P., 'L'avis 2/94 de la Cour de la justice relatif à l'adhésion de la Communauté européenne à la Convention de sauvegarde des droit de l'homme et des libertés fondamentales', (1996) 2 *Revue trimestrielle de droit européen* 467
Wachsmann, P., 'Les droits de l'homme', (1997) *Revue trimestrielle de Droit européen* 890
Wasmeier, M., 'The integration of environmental protection as a general rule for interpreting community law', (2001) 38 *Common Market Law Review* 159
Wathelet, M., 'La Charte des droits fondamentaux: un bon pas dans une course qui reste longue', (2000) 5–6 *Cahiers de Droit Européen* 584
Weatherill, S., *The EU Charter of Fundamental Rights: Politics, Law and Policy* (Oxford, 2004)
Weidenfeld, W. and W. Wessels, 'The role of the new EU Fundamental Rights Agency: Debating of the 'sex of angels' or improving Europe's human rights performance? (2008) 33 *European Law Review* 385
Weiler, J.H.H. and N.J.S. Lockhart, 'Taking rights seriously: The European Court of Justice and its fundamental rights jurisprudence', (1995) 32 *Common Market Law Review* 51
Weiler, J.H.H., *The Constitution of Europe: "Do the new clothes have an emperor?" And other essays on European integration* (Cambridge University Press, 1999)
Weyembergh, A., P. De Hert and P. Paepe, 'L'effectivité du troisième pilier de l'Union européenne et l'exigence de l'interprétation conforme: la Cour de justice pose ses jalons (note sous l'arrêt Pupino, du 16 juin 2005, de la Cour de justice des Communautés européennes)', (2007) 18 *Revue trimestrielle des droits de l'homme* 269
Weyembergh, A. and V. Santamaria, 'Lutte contre le torrorisme et droits fondamentaux dans le cadre du trosième pilier. La décision-cadre du 13 juin 2002 relative à la lutte

contre le terrorisme et le principe de la légalité', in J. Rideau, (ed.), *Les droits fondamentaux dans l'Union européenne. Dans le village de la Constitution européenne* (Bruylant, 2009) 200
Whitman, R. and A. Junicos 'The Lisbon Treaty and the Foreign, Security and Defence Policy: Reforms, implementation and the consequences of (non)ratification' (2009) *European Foreign Affairs Review* 25
Wildhaber, L., 'A Constitutional future for the European Court of Human Rights' (2000) 23 *Human Rights Law Journal* 161
Williams, A., 'Enlargement of the Union and human rights conditionality: A policy of distinction?', (2000) 25 *European Law Review* 601
Williams, A., 'Respecting Fundamental Rights in the New Union: A Review', in C. Barnard, *The fundamentals of EU law revisited: Assessing the impact of the constitutional debate* (Oxford University Press, 2007) 71
Williams, A., *EU human rights policies. A study in irony* (Oxford University Press, 2004)
Wouters, J., 'The EU charter of fundamental rights: Some reflections on its external dimension', (2001) 1 *Maastricht Journal of European and Comparative Law* 3
Zagrebelsky, G., *Diritti e Costituzione nell'Unione europea* (Laterza, 2003)
Ziller, J., 'Solange III (or the Bundesverfassungsgericht's Europefriendliness). On the decision of the German Federal Constitutional Court over the ratification of the Treaty of Lisbon', (2009) *Rivista Italiana di Diritto Pubblico Comunitario,* 973
Ziller, J. (ed.), *Il nuovo Trattato europeo* (Il Mulino, 2007)
Ziller, J., *Les nouveaux traites européens: Lisbonne et après* (LGDJ, 2008)
Zivy, F., 'Le prolongement excessif de la phase d'instruction peut permettre une violation des droits de la défense', (2006) 4 *Revue des droits de la concurrence* 115

Table of Cases

European Court of Human Rights

Appl. No 2122/64, *Wemhoff v. Germany*, (1968) A7
Appl. No 1936/6327, *Neumeister v. Austria*, (1968) A8
Appl. No 4451/70, *Golder v. The United Kingdom*, (1984) A18
Appl. No 7525/76, *Dudgeon v. UK*, (1981) 4 EHRR 149
Appl. Nos 7604/76, 7719/76, 7781/77 and 7913/77, *Foti v. Italy*, (1982) Series A, vol. 56
Appl. Nos 7819/77 and 7878/77, *Campbell-Fell v. The United Kingdom*, (1984) A80
Appl. No 9310/81, *Powell and Rayner*, (1990) Series A no. 172
Appl. No 9616/81, *Erkner-Hofauer v. Austria*, (1987) A124-D
Appl. No 11804/85, *Manzoni v. Italy*, (1991) A 195-B
Appl. No 12005/86, *Borgers v. Belgium*, (1991) A214-B
Appl. Nos 12325/86 and 14992/89, *Kemmache v. France*, (1991) A-218
Appl. No 13023/87, *Salesi v. Italy*, (1993) Series A, vol. 257-E
Appl. No 13258/87, *M & Co v. FDR*, (1990) 64 *DR* 138
Appl. No 14234/88 and 14235/88, *Open Door and Dublin Well v. Ireland*, (1992) Series A No 246
Appl. No 14556/89 *Papamichalopoulos v. Greece*, (1995), A/330B
Appl. No 14967/89, *Guerra and others v. Italy*, (1998) RD 1998-I
Appl. No 15318/89, *Loizidou v. Turkey*, (1995) Series A No 25
Appl. No 16798/90, *López Ostra v. Spain*, (1994) Series A no. 303-C
Appl. No 17862/91, *Cantoni v. France*, (19969 Reports 1996-V ECHR
Appl. No 18357/91, *Hornsby v. Greece*, (1997) 24 EHRR 250
Appl. No 19075/91, *Vermeulen v. Belgium*, (1996) Reports 1996-I
Appl. No 20323/92, *Pafitis v. Greece*, (1999) 27 ECHRR 566
Appl. No 43/1994/490/572, *Saunders v. United Kingdom*, (1997) 23 EHHR 313
Appl. No 24833/94, *Matthews v. United Kingdom*, (1999) Reports 1999-I
Appl. No 26083/94, *Waite and Kennedy v. Germany*, (1999) Reports 1999-I
Appl. No 27824/95, *Posti & Rahko v. Finland*, (2002) Reports 2002-VII
Appl. No 28541/95, *Pellegrin v. France*, (2001) 31 EHRR 651
Appl. No 28934/95, *Beer and Regan v. Germany*, (1999) unreported
Appl. No 28957/95, *Goodwin v. The United Kingdom*, (2002) 35 EHRR
Appl. No 30240/96, *D. v. The United Kingdom*, (1997) Reports 1997-III
Appl. No 31631/96, *Procaccini v. Italy*, (2000) unreported
Appl. No 34256/96, *Di Mauro v. Italy*, (1999) Reports 1999-V
Appl. No 34503/97, *Demir and Baykara v. Turkey*, (2008) unreported
Appl. No 34503/97, *Demir and Baykara v. Turkey*, (2008) unreported

Appl. Nos 35673/97, 35674/97, 36082/97 and 37579/97, *Schweighhofer and Others v. Austria*, (2001) unreported
Appl. No 36022/97, *Hatton and Others v. the United Kingdom*, (2001) unreported
Appl. No 36022/97, *Hatton and Others v. the United Kingdom*, (2003) Report 2003-VIII
Appl. No 37971/97, *Ste Colas Est and others v. France*, (2002) 39 EHRR 17
Appl. No 38212/97, *F.E. v. France*, (1998) Reports 1998-VIII
Appl. No 39594/98, *Kress v. France*, (2001) Reports 2001-VI
Appl. No 40892/98, *Poirrez v. France*, (2003) Reports 2003-X
Appl. No 44647/98, *Peck v. UK*, (2003) EHRR I
Appl. No 45036/98, *Bosphorus v. Ireland*, (2005) Reports 2005-VI
Appl. No 48939/99, *Öneryildiz v. Turkey*, (2004) Reports 2004-XII
Appl. No 51717/99, *Guerin v. 15 Member States of the EU*, (2000) unreported
Appl. Nos 52562/99 and 52620/99, *Sørensen v. Denmark and Rasmussen v. Denmark*, (2006) Reports 2006-I
Appl. No 53924/00, *Vo. v. France*, (2004) Reports 2004-VIII
Appl. No 54810/00, *Jalloh v. Germany*, (2006) Reports IX
Appl. No 58675/00, *Martinie v. France*, (2006) Reports 2006-VI
Appl. No 59909/00, *Giacomelli v. Italy*, (2006) unreported
Appl. No 62023/00, *Emesa Sugar v. the Netherlands*, (2005) unreported
Appl. Nos 71412/01 and 78166/01, *Behrami and Saramati v. France*, (2007) unreported
Appl. No 73049/01, *Anheuser-Busch inc. v. Portugal*, (2007) unreported
Appl. No 6422/02, *Ségi et al. v. 15 Member States*, (2002) Ser. A, 56
Appl. No 28738/02, *Le Blenchennec v. France*, (2006) unreported
Appl. No 36391/02, *Salduz v. Turkey*, (2009) unreported
Appl. No 10249/03, *Scoppola v. Italy*, (2009) unreported
Appl. No 13229/03, *Saadi v. The United Kingdom*, (2008) unreported
Appl. No 14939/03, *Zolotukhin v. Russia*, (2009), unreported
Appl. No 18603/03, *André and Others v. France*, (2008) unreported
Appl. No 7925/04, *Pishchalnikov v. Russia*, (2009) unreported
Appl. No 13645/05, *Cooperatieve Producentenorganisatie van de Nederlandse Kokkelvissarij v. The Netherlands*, (2009) unreported
Appl. No 17056/06, *Miccalef v. Malta,* (2009) unreported
Appl. No 55759/07, *Maresti v. Croatia,* (2009) unreported
Appl. Nos 17173/07 and 17180/07, *Sevinger and Eman v. The Netherlands*, (2007) unreported

Court of Justice of the European Union

Case 25/62 *Plaumann* [1963] ECR 95
Case 26/62 *Van Gend & Loos* [1963] ECR 1
Case 75/63 *Unger* [1964] ECR 177
Case 6/64 *Costa v. Enel* [1964] ECR 585
Case 40/64 *Sgarlata* [1965] ECR 279
Case 34/67 *Lück* [1968] ECR 245
Case 29/69 *Stauder* [1969] ECR 419
Case 11/70 *Internationale Handelsgesellschaft* [1970] ECR 1125
Case 4/73 *Nold* [1974] ECR 491
Case 67/74 *Bonsignore* [1975] ECR 297
Case 36/75 *Rutili* [1975] ECR 1219
Case 33/76 *REWE* [1976] ECR 1989
Case 30/77 *Bouchereau* [1977] ECR 1999
Case 151/78 *Sukkerfabriken Nykøbing* [1979] ECR 1

Case 230/78 *SPA Eridiana and others* [1979] ECR 2749
Case C-44/79 *Hauer* [1979] ECR 3727
Case 136/79 *National Panasonic* [1980] ECR 2033
Case 53/81 *Levin* [1982] ECR 1035
Joined Cases 50-58/82 *Administrateur des Affaires Maritimes, Bayonne and Procureur de la République* [1982] ECR 3949
Case 77/83 *Cilfit* [1984] ECR 1257
Case 294/83 *Parti écologiste "Les Verts"* [1986] ECR 1339
Joined Cases 60 and 61/84 *Cinéthèque* [1985] ECR 2605
Case 222/84 *Johnston* [1986] ECR 1651
Case 66/85 *Lawrie-Blum* [1986] ECR 2121
Case 139/85 *Kempf* [1986] ECR 1741
Case 154/85 *Commission v. Italy* [1987] ECR 2717
Case 234/85 *Keller* [1986] ECR 2897
Case 314/85 *Foto-Frost* [1987] ECR 4199
Case 222/86 *Unectef* [1987] ECR 4097
Joined cases 46/87 and 227/88 *Hoechst AG* [1989] ECR 2859
Case 85/87 *Dow Benelux NV* [1989] ECR 3137
Case 187/87 *Land de Sarre* [1988] ECR 5013
Case C-5/88 *Wachauf* [1989] ECR 2609
Case C-106/89 *Marleasing* [1990] ECR I-4135
Joined Cases C-143/88 and C 92/89 *Zuckerfabrik* [1991] ECR I-415
Case C-213/89 *Factortame* [1990] ECR I-2433
Case C-260/89 *ERT* [1991] ECR I-2925
Case C-292/89 *Antonissen* [1991] ECR I-745
Case C-357/89 *Raulin* [1992] ECR I-1027
Case C-62/90 *Commission v. Germany* [1992] ECR I-2575
Case C-159/90 *Grogan* [1991] ECR I-468
Case C- 239/90 *SCP Boscher, Studer et Fromentin* [1991] ECR I-2023
Opinion 1/91 [1991] ECR I-6079
Case C-97/91 *Borelli* [1992] ECR I-6313
Case C-168/91 *Konstantinidis* [1993] ECR I-1191
Case C-91/92 *Faccini Dori* [1994] ECR I-3325
Case C-334/92 *Wagner Miret* [1993] ECR I-6911
Case C-465/93 *Atlanta* [1995] ECR I-3761
Opinion 2/94 [1996] ECR I-1759
Case C-13/94 *P. v. S.* [1996] ECR I-2143
Case C-84/94 *UK v. Council* [1996] ECR I- 5755
Case C-237/94 *O'Flynn* [1996] ECR I-2617
Joined Cases C-4/95 and C-5/95 *Stöber and Pereira* [1997] ECR I-511
Case C-70/95 *Sodemare* [1997] ECR I-3395
Case C-120/95 *Decker* [1998] ECR I-1831
Case C-185/95 P *Baustahlgewebe* [1998], ECR I-8417
Case C-265/95 *Commission v. France* [1997] ECR I-6959
Case C-299/95 *Kremzow* [1997] ECR I-2629
Case C-368/95 *Familiapress* [1997] ECR I-3689
Case C-54/96 *Dorsch Consult* [1997] ECR I-4961
Case C-85/96 *Martínez Sala* [1998] ECR I-2691
Case C-158/96 *Kohll* [1998] ECR I-1931
Case C-249/96 *Grant* [1998] ECR I-621
Case C-274/96 *Bickel and Franz* [1998] ECR I-7637
Joined Cases C-279, 280 and 281/96 *Ansaldo* [1998] ECR I-5025
Case C-348/96 *Calfa* [1999] ECR I-11

Case C-111/97 *Evobus* [1998] ECR I-5411
Case C-126/97 Eco Swiss China [1999] ECR I-3092
Case C-185/97 Coote [1998] ECR I-5199
Case C-240/97 *Spain v. Commission* [1999] ECR I-6571
Case 292/97 Karlsson [2000] ECR I-2737
Case C-17/98 Emesa Sugar [2000] ECR I-665
Case C-49/98 Fi*nalarte Sociedade de Construção Civil Lda* [2001] ECR I-7831
Case C-207/98 *Mahalburg* [2000] ECR I-549
Case C-223/98 *Adidas* [1999] ECR I-7081
Case C-224/98 *D'Hoop* [2002] ECR I-6191
Case C-285/98 *Kreil* [2000] ECR I-69
Case C-367/98 *Commission v. Portugal* [2002] ECR I-4731
Case C-379/98 *PreussenElektra AG* [2001] ECR I-2099
Case C-173/99 *The Queen v. BECTU* [2001] ECR I-4881
Case C-184/99 *Grzelczyk* [2001] ECR I-6193
Case C-194/99 P *Thyssen Stahl AG* [2003] ECR I-10821
Case C-199/99 P *Corus UK Ltd* [2003] ECR I-11177
Case C-238/99 P *Limburgse Vinyl Maatschappij NV* [2002] ECR I-8375
Case C-274/99 P *Connolly* [2001] ECR I-1611
Case C-385/99 *Müller-Fauré* [2003] ECR I-4509
Case C-413/99 *Baumbast* [2002] ECR I-7091
Case C-459/99 *MRAX* [2002] ECR I-6591
Case C-483/99 *Commission v. France* [2002] ECR I-4781
Case C-503/99 *Commission v. Belgium* [2002] ECR I-4809
Joined cases C-20/00 e C-64/00 *Booker Aquacultur Ltd and Hydro Seafood GSP Ltd* [2003] ECR I-7411
Case C-39/00P *SARL* [2000] ECR I-11201
Case C-50/00 P *Union de Pequenos Agricultores* [2002] ECR I-6677
Case C-60/00 *Carpenter* [2002] ECR I-6279
Case C-94/00 *Roquette Freres* [2002] ECR I-9011
Case http://eur-lex.europa.eu/Notice.do?val=264237:cs&lang=en&list=277818:cs,264237:cs,&pos=2&page=1&nbl=2&pgs=10&hwords=C-112/00 *Schmidberger* [2003] ECR I-5659
Case C-440/00 *Kühne & Nagel* [2004] ECR I-787
Case C-463/00 *Commission v. Spain* [2003] ECR I-4581
Case C-13/01 *Safalero Srl* [2003] ECR I-8679
Case C-98/01 *Commission v. United Kingdom* [2003] ECR I-4641
Case C-109/01 *Akrich* [2003] ECR I-9607
Joined Cases C-397 to 403/01 *Pfeiffer* [2004] ECR I-8835
Joined Cases C-482/01 and C-493/01 *Orfanopoulos* [2004] ECR I-5257
Case C-36/02 *Omega* [2004] ECR I-9609
Case C-39/02 *Mærsk Olie & Gas A/S v. Firma M. de Haan en W. de Boer* [2004] ECR I-9657
Case C-71/02 *Karner* [2004] ECR I-3025
Case C-87/02 *Commission v. Italy* [2004] ECR I-05975
Case C-127/02 *Landelijke Vereniging tot Behoud van de Waddenzee and Others* [2004] ECR I-7405
Case C-138/02 *Collins* [2004] ECR I-2703
Case C-148/02 *García Avello* [2003] ECR I-11613
Case C-167/02 P *Rothley et a. v. EP* [2004] ECR I-3149
Case C-200/02 *Chen* [2004] ECR I-9925
Case C-224/02 *Pusa* [2004] ECR I-5763
Case C-263/02 P *Commission v. Jégo-Quéré* [2004] ECR I-3425

Case C-277/02 *EU-Wood-Trading GmbH* [2004] ECR I-11957
Case C-281/02 *Owusu* [2005] ECR I-1383
Case C-287/02 *Spain v. Commission* [2005] ECR I-5093
Case C-441/02 *Commission v. Germany* [2004] ECR I-3449
Case C-442/02 *Caixa-Bank France* [2004] ECR I-8961
Case C-456/02 *Trojani* [2004] ECR I-7573
Case C-22/03 *Optiver BV and Others* [2005] ECR I-1839
Case C-105/03 *Pupino* [2005] ECR I-5185
Case C-131/03 P *Reynolds Tobacco* [2006] ECR I-7795
Case C-147/03 *Commission v. Austria* [2005] ECR I-5969
Case C-176/03 *Commission v. Council* [2005] ECR I-7879
Case C-209/03 *Bidar* [2005] ECR I-2119
Case C-210/03 *Swedish Match* [2004] ECR I-11893
Case C-320/03 *Commission v. Austria* [2005] ECR I-09871
Case C-347/03 *Friuli Venezia* [2005] ECR I-378
Case C-443/03 *Leffler* [2005] ECR I-961
Case C-461/03 *Gaston Shul* [2005] ECR I-10513
Case C-503/03 Commission v. Spain [2006] ECR I-1097
Case C-540/03 *Parliament v. Council* [2006] ECR I- 5769
Case C-547/03P Asian Institute of Technology [2005] ECR I-845
Case C-96/04 Standes*amt Stadt Niebüll* [2006] ECR I-3561
Case C-105/04P *CEF BV and CEF Holdings Ltd v. Nederlandse Federatieve Vereniging and Technische Unie BV* [2006] ECR I-8725
Case C-144/04 *Mangold* [2005] ECR I-9981
Case C-145/04 *Spain v. UK* [2006] ECR I- 7917
Case C-301/04 P *SGL Carbon* [2006] ECR I-5915
Joined cases C-317/04 and C-318/04 *Parliament v. Council and Commission* [2006] ECR I-4721
Case C-328/04 *Vajnai* [2005] ECR I-8577
Case C-354/04 P *Gestoras Pro Amnistía* [2007] ECR I-1579
Case C-355/04 P *Segi* [2007] ECR I-1657
Case C-403/04 P *Sumitomo* [2007] ECR I-729
Case C-406/04 *De Cuyper* [2006] ECR I-6947
Case C-474/04 *Pergan Hifsstoffe* [2007] ECR I-4225
Case C-520/04 *Turpeinen* [2006] ECR I-10685
Case C-521/04 P (R) *Hans-Martin Tillack* [2005] ECR I-3103
Case C-523/04 *Commission v. The Netherlands* [2006] ECR I-3267
Case C-91/05 *ECOWAS* [2008] ECR I-3651
Case C-229/05P *PKK and KNK* [2007] ECR I-439
Case C-260/05 P *Sniace SA* [2007] ECR I-10005
Case C-266/05 P *Sison* [2007] ECR I-1233
Case C-303/05 *Advocaten voor de Wereld* [2007] ECR I-3633
Case C-305/05 *Ordre des barreaux francophone et germanophone and Others* [2007] ECR I-5305
Case C-341/05, *Laval* [2007] ECR I-11767
Case C-380/05 *Centro Europa 7* [2008] ECR I-349
Case C-438/05 *Viking* [2007] ECR I-10779
Joined cases C-402 and 415/05 P *Kadi and Al Barakaat* [2008] ECR I-6351
Case C-432/05 *Unibet* [2007] ECR I-2271
Joined cases C-439/05 P and C-454/05 P *Land Oberosterreich and Austria* [2007] ECR I-7141
Case C-441/05 *Roquette Frères* [2007] ECR I-1993
Case C-444/05 *Stamatelaki* [2007] ECR I-3185

Case C-467/05 *Giovanni Dell'Orto* [2007] ECR I-5557
Joined Cases C-11 and 12/06 *Morgan and Bucher* [2007] ECR I-9161
Case C-117/06 *Möllendorf* [2007] ECR I-8361
Case C-212/06 *Government of the French Community and Walloon Government v. Flemish Government* [2008] ECR I-1683
Case C-244/06 *Dynamic Medien* [2008] ECR I-505
Case C-246/06 *Velasco Navarro* [2008] ECR I-105
Case C-275/06 *Promusicae* [2008] ECR I- 271
Case C-286/06 *Commission v. Spain* [2008] ECR I-8025
Case C-301/06 *Ireland v. Parliament and Council* [2009] ECR I-593
Case C-346/06 *Rüffert* [2008] ECR I-1989
Case C-398/06 *Commission v. Netherlands* [2008] OJ C 128/10, [2008] ECR I-56 (summary publication)
Case C-499/06 *Nerkowska* [2008] ECR I-3993
Case C-450/06 *Varec* [2008] ECR I-581
Case C-158/07 *Förster* [2008] nyr
Case C-188/07 *Commune de Mesquer* [2008] ECR I-4501
Case C-228/07 *Petersen* [2008] ECR I-6989
Joined Cases C-22 and 23/08 *Vatsouras and Koupatantze* [2009] nyr
Case C-308/07 P *Koldo Gorostiaga Atxalandabaso* [2009] ECR I-1059
Case C-361/07 *Polier* [2008] ECR I-6
Case C-314/08 *Filipiak* [2009] nyr

General Court of the European Union

Case T-585/93 *Greenpeace* [1995] ECR II-2205
Case T-105/95 *WWF* [1997] ECR II-313
Case T-112/98 *Mannersmannröhrer-Werke* [2001] ECR II-729
Case T-54/99 *max.mobil Telekommunikation* [2002] ECR II-313
Case T-67/00 *JFE Engineering Corp.* [2004] ECR II-2501
Case T-223/00 *Kyowa Hakko Kogyo* [2003] ECR II-2553
Case T-224/00 *ADM Company and ADM Ltd* [2003] ECR II-2597
Joined cases T-377/00, T-379/00, T-380/00, T-260/01 and T-272/01 *Philip Morris* [2003] ECR II-1
Case T-77/01 *Diputación Foral de Alava e.a.* [2002] ECR I-81
Case T-177/01 *Jégo-Quéré* [2002] ECR II-2365
Case T-198/01R *Technische Glaswerke Ilmenau* [2002] ECR II-2153
Case T-210/01 *General Electric Company* [2005] ECR II-5575
Case T-236/01 *Tokai Carbon* [2004] ECR II-1181
Case T-306/01 *Yusuf and Al Barakaat* [2005] ECR II-3533
Case T-315/01 *Kadi* [2005] ECR II-3649
Case T-318/01 *Othman* [2009] nyr
Joined Cases T-377, 379, 380, 260, and 272/01 *Philip Morris* [2003] ECR II-1
Case T-206/02 *KNK* [2005] ECR II-523
Case T-211/02 *Tideland Signal Ltd* [2002] ECR II-3781
Case T-228/02 *Organisation des Modjahedines* [2006] ECR II-4665
Case T-229/02 *PKK* [2008] ECR II-45
Case T-242/02 *The Sunrider Corp. v. OHIM* [2005] ECR II-2793
Case T-253/02 *Ayadi* [2006] ECR II-2139
Case T-259/02 *Raiffeisen Zentralbank* [2006] ECR II-5961
Case T-2/03 *Verein für Konsumenteninformation* [2005] ECR II-1121
Case T-11/03 *Afari* [2004] ECR II-267

Case T-47/03 *Sison* [2007] ECR II-73
Case T-71/03 *Tokai Carbon* [2005] ECR II-10
Case T-309/03 *Camos Grau* [2006] ECR II-1173
Case T-327/03 *Al-Aqsa* [2007] ECR II-79
Case T-346/03 *Krikorian* [2003] ECR II-6037
Case T-351/03 *Schneider Electric SA* [2007] ECR II-2237
Joined Cases T-391/03 and T-70/04 *Y. Franchet and D. Byk* [2006] ECR II-2023
Case T-49/04 *Hassan* [2006] ECR II-52
Case T-193/04 *Tillack* [2006] ECR II-3995
Case T-194/04 *The Bavarian Lager* [2007] ECR II-4523
Case T-253/04 *Kongra-Gel* [2008] ECR II-46
Case T-299/04 *Selmani* [2005] ECR II-20
Case C-317/04 *Parliament v. Council* [2006] ECR I-4721
Case T-439/04 *Eurohypo AG* [2006] ECR II-1269
Joined cases T-37 and 323/07 *El Morabit* [2009] nyr
Case T-256/07 *OMPI* [2008] ECR II-3019
Case T-284/08 *OMPI* [2008] ECR II-3487

National Constitutional Courts

Belgian Constitutional Court, Cour d'Arbitrage belge, judgment 13 July 2005, No 124/2005
Belgian Constitutional Court, Judgment 23 January 2008, No 10/2008
Belgian Constitutional Court, Judgment 12 February 2009, No 17/2009
Belgian Constitutional Court, Judgment 19 March 2009, No 58/2009
Cypriot Constitutional Court, judgment 7 November 2005, No 294/2005
French Constitutional Council, Decision 19 November 2004, No 2004-505 DC
French Constitutional Council, Decision 20 December 2007, No 2007-560 DC
German Constitutional Court, judgment 29 May 1974, No BvR 52/71
German Constitutional Court, judgment 22 October 1986, No 2 BvR 197/83
German Constitutional Court, judgment 12 October 1993, No 2 BvR 2134/92
German Constitutional Court, judgment 7 June 2000, No 2 BvR 1/97 (Banenmarktordnung)
German Constitutional Court, *Bundesverfassungsgericht*, judgment 18 July 2005, 2 BvR 2236/04
German Constitutional Court, judgment 30 June 2009, No BvR 2 BvE 2/08 2 BvE 5/08 -2 BvR 1010/08 -2 BvR 1022/08 –2 BvR 1259/08 – 2 BvR 182/09
Italian Constitutional Court, Judgment 24 April 2002, No 135/2002
Italian Constitutional Court, Judgment 24 October 2002, No 445/2002
Italian Constitutional Court, Judgment 23 October 2006, No 393/2006
Italian Constitutional Court, Judgment 8 November 2006, No 394/2006
Italian Constitutional Court, Order 5 March 2007, No 93
Italian Constitutional Court, Judgment 15 December 2008, No 438/2008
Italian Constitutional Court, Judgment 15 December 2008, No 438/2008
Italian Constitutional Court, Judgment 11 March 2009, No 86
Polish Constitutional Court, *Trybunal Konstytucyjny*, judgment 27 April 2005, No P 1/05
Portuguese Constitutional Court, Judgment 9 July 2009, No 359/2009
Spanish Constitutional Court, Judgment 13 December 2004, DCT 1/2004
Spanish Constitutional Court, Judgment 30 November 2000, No 292
Spanish Constitutional Court, Judgment 13 February 2006, No 41
Spanish Constitutional Court, Judgment 22 December 2008, No 176

Index

Lightning Source UK Ltd.
Milton Keynes UK
20 December 2010

164571UK00005B/47/P